RESEARCH METHODS FOR BUSINESS

JOSEPH HAIR
ARTHUR MONEY
MIKE PAGE
PHILLIP SAMOUEL

BICENTENNIAL
1807
WILEY
2007
BICENTENNIAL

John Wiley & Sons, Ltd

This edition published 2007 by John Wiley & Sons Ltd, The Atrium, Southern Gate, Chichester, West Sussex PO19 8SQ, England
This edition © 2007 John Wiley & Sons Ltd

Telephone: (+44) 1243 779777

Authorised adaptation of the first edition by Joseph F. Hair, Barry Babin, Arthur H. Money & Phillip Samouel, Essentials of Business Research Methods (ISBN 0 471 42925 2), published by John Wiley & Sons, Inc. Copyright © in the United States of America by Leyh Publishing, LLC.

US Edition © 2003 Leyh Publishing, LLC
The US edition was published by John Wiley & Sons, Inc. under exclusive licence from Leyh Publishing, LLC.

Email (for orders and customer service enquiries): cs-books@wiley.co.uk
Visit our Home Page on www.wiley.com

Other Wiley Editorial Offices

John Wiley & Sons Inc., 111 River Street, Hoboken, NJ 07030, USA

Jossey-Bass, 989 Market Street, San Francisco, CA 94103-1741, USA

Wiley-VCH Verlag GmbH, Boschstr. 12, D-69469 Weinheim, Germany

John Wiley & Sons Australia Ltd, 42 McDougall Street, Milton, Queensland 4064, Australia

John Wiley & Sons (Asia) Pte Ltd, 2 Clementi Loop #02-01, Jin Xing Distripark, Singapore 129809

John Wiley & Sons Canada Ltd, 6045 Freemont Blvd, Mississauga, ONT, L5R 4J3, Canada

Wiley also publishes its books in a variety of electronic formats. Some content that appears in print may not be available in electronic books.

Library of Congress Cataloging-in-Publication Data

Research methods for business / Joseph Hair ... [et al.].
   p. com.
  European adaptation of the US textbook: Essentials of Business Research Methods, 2003.
  Includes bibliographical references and index.
  ISBN-13: 978-0-470-03404-0 (pbk. : alk. paper)
  ISBN-10: 0-470-03404-1 (pbk. : alk. paper)
  1. Business – Research.   I. Hair, Joseph F.   II. Essentials of Business Research Methods.
  HD30.4.R475 2007
  650.072 – dc22

                   2006023993

British Library Cataloguing in Publication Data

A catalogue record for this book is available from the British Library

ISBN-13: 978-0-470-03404-0
ISBN-10: 0-470-03404-1

Typeset in 10/11 Bembo by Laserwords Private Limited, Chennai, India
Printed and bound in Great Britain by Scotprint, Haddington, East Lothian
This book is printed on acid-free paper responsibly manufactured from sustainable forestry
in which at least two trees are planted for each one used for paper production.

RESEARCH METHODS FOR BUSINESS

BRIEF CONTENTS

CONTENTS

PREFACE

Business research in a knowledge-based, global economy presents many challenges for managers. Businesses are challenged to be more decisive and offer higher quality products and services and they must do so with fewer people at lower costs. This means modern business managers must make more decisions in a shorter period of time, and those decisions must be better. Fortunately, the tools and technologies available to business professionals have expanded dramatically. Computing power, storage capacity and software expertise no longer represent significant barriers to processing information. The speed and memory of PCs has been doubling every 18 months while prices drop. Windows-based and other user-friendly interfaces have brought sophisticated data analysis software packages into the "click-and-point" era, greatly reducing the need for specialized computer skills to access electronic data processing capability. Now, even "unsophisticated" users can analyse large quantities of complex data with relative ease. The knowledge that emerges from application of these new tools and technologies contributes to better decision making.

Research turns information into knowledge. Better business knowledge is essential to improved decision making. This book is about making better decisions by using knowledge that only research can create. The book places minimal emphasis on statistical theory and makes maximum effort to provide basic skills that cover a wide range of potential business research applications. By using the concepts and principles presented in this book, the reader will be better able to cope with the fast-paced decision-making environment that is business today and tomorrow.

MANAGERS NEED BUSINESS RESEARCH SKILLS

The amount of information available for decision making has exploded in recent years, and will continue to do so in the future. Until recently, much information just disappeared. It either was not collected, or was discarded, often because there was no cost-effective way of keeping it. Today this information is collected and stored in data warehouses and it is available to be "mined" for improved decision making. Sometimes, the information can be analysed and understood with simple analytical tools. Other times, turning it into business intelligence requires more complex approaches. In this book, we cover the simple as well as some of the more complex tools in an easy to understand manner. Without knowledge of these business research tools, managers and entrepreneurs simply cannot benefit from the intelligence emerging from this expanded database of information.

Most business research texts are quite long and take an encyclopaedic approach. This book covers the important topics in a concise manner and focuses on the essentials of business research for managers. It includes coverage of the increasing role of knowledge management as well as how to conduct information-gathering activities more effectively in a rapidly changing business environment. The fundamentals of business research, such as research design, use of qualitative and quantitative data, sampling and questionnaire design, are presented in a highly readable format. Illustrations are used in conjunction with many practical examples to highlight significant points.

A "research in action" feature provides applied examples of actual research problems and current issues. Some research in action examples summarize actual research studies. Others describe Web sites that help researchers analyse qualitative data, locate secondary data sources, or design better survey questionnaires. Case studies involving applications of research approaches also are included as well as instructions on how to use statistical software to analyse data. With more than 100 "Research in Action" boxes, the text material is truly brought to life! In addition to the Research in Action examples, we have Internet applications/questions at the end of all chapters that provide interactive exercises for the students as well as discussion questions that pose analytical issues beyond just repeating topics covered in the chapters. Finally, each chapter has an ethical dilemma case to stimulate thinking on and understanding of ethics topics.

The book is based on the need for managers to make better decisions. Thus, research is couched within the greater decision-making context. Managers must make decisions increasingly based on almost unlimited information in data warehouses, so we provide more coverage of data-analysis techniques in this book than do other texts. We recognize that most managers and business students will not be data analysts but an understanding of data analysis techniques will help them to better utilize the increasing amounts of information they will be expected to apply in decision making. Our straightforward, hands-on approach makes the book particularly successful with advanced undergraduates in all business disciplines and graduate business students, both in traditional and executive programmes. The book also will serve as an effective reference guide for advanced users including basic researchers and beginning doctoral students.

Changes in the business environment have created opportunities as well as uncertainty, and they make the role of business research even more important in improving decision making. For example information technology has made more accurate financial forecasting possible, has improved employee productivity, and enables more information to be collected and stored at a reasonable price. Knowledge is power but managers must convert the increasing amount of information into knowledge before they can use this power. Businesses that are best able to harness this power will be the ones who are successful in the long run. Hence, a main focus of the text is the collection, evaluation, understanding and use of information from the manager's perspective.

EXCELLENT PEDAGOGY

Our pedagogy has been developed from many years of conducting and teaching business research. To bring the concepts to life and make the text more interesting, we focus on a single case throughout the book. Phil Samouel is a restaurant entrepreneur in London. His Greek restaurant competes with Gino's Italian Ristorante. Phil hires a business research consultant to help him and the case study is used to illustrate the principles of business research throughout the text. The consultant has recommended two surveys—one of customers and the other of Phil's employees. Both questionnaires are included in the text and two databases from the results of the surveys are used to demonstrate the data-analysis techniques. A sample report of the surveys' initial findings is available on our Web site at www.wileyeurope.com/college/hair.

Exercises at the end of the chapter provide an opportunity for students to examine the findings of the two surveys further and to use them in preparing a more comprehensive report on the restaurant case study. Electronic copies of the questionnaires and data bases are available on our Web site.

The Samouel's restaurant continuing case provides a running example saving the reader time in gaining familiarity with different cases from chapter to chapter. We refer to the case when we discuss research design alternatives as well as when we evaluate different sampling approaches. The thinking behind the employee questionnaire is provided in the measurement and scaling chapter and the rationale for the customer survey questionnaire is reviewed in the questionnaire design chapter. In all of the data-analysis chapters we use the case study data to illustrate SPSS, Excel and various statistical techniques. A copy of the research proposal given to Phil Samouel is provided in Chapter 2 and a summary of the research report is on our Web site at www.wileyeurope.com/college/hair. The focus on a single case study throughout the text enables the reader to more easily understand the benefits and pitfalls of using research to improve business decision making.

Coverage of quantitative data analysis is more extensive and much easier to understand than other texts. Specific step-by-step instructions are included on the Web site on how to use SPSS and Excel to execute data analysis for all statistical techniques. This enables instructors to spend much less time teaching students how to use the software the first time. It also saves time later by providing a handy reference for students when they forget how to use the software, which they often do. For instructors that want to cover more advanced statistical techniques (multivariate) our book is the only one that includes this topic. Thus, the approach of our book is much more balanced between qualitative and quantitative than are other books.

ORGANIZATION OF THE BOOK

The text and all major supplements are organized around the learning objectives shown at the beginning of the chapters. Instead of a single summary of the chapter, there are summaries by each learning objective. This organizational approach makes the book very readable for students and easy to teach for instructors. In short, it delivers value for both students and teachers.

The organization of the book follows the logic of the business research process. It is organized into five parts. Part I introduces the reader to business research, the trends that are emerging, the research process, and the role of ethics. Part II provides an overview of how to begin the business research process, from defining the problem to research design. Part III covers data collection, including sampling, measurement and questionnaire design. In Part IV we examine data analysis and interpretation for both qualitative and quantitative research. We end the book with Part V on writing reports and presenting research findings.

COMPREHENSIVE INSTRUCTOR AND STUDENT RESOURCES

The text has an extensive set of resources for instructors and students. For instructors, there is a test bank providing a wide variety of questions on all the major concepts in the book. The instructor's manual includes lecture outlines, answers to end-of-chapter questions, and teaching notes for the exercises. Each chapter has 20 to 30 PowerPoint slides to summarize and illustrate the key concepts. Two datasets for the restaurant case in both SPSS and Excel format are provided for instructors to use in teaching quantitative analysis, and students to use in learning. Additional end-of-chapter assignments give the user an opportunity to experience a wide range of analytical applications using the datasets. This eliminates the need for instructors and/or students to hunt for data demonstrating business research concepts and techniques. We make it available to the user in our teaching supplements.

The text Web site (www.wileyeurope.com/college/hair) includes a wide array of supplementary materials for instructors use to facilitate their teaching. In addition to electronic copies of all instructors' teaching support materials, the book has copies of sample questionnaires used in research projects, answers to frequently asked questions on business research provided by the text's authors, and copies of the datasets. In short, we believe it is one of the most comprehensive Web sites of any business research text.

ACKNOWLEDGEMENTS

We would like to thank the reviewers for their valuable comments on earlier drafts of the book. Their useful suggestions helped to make the book much better. We give our thanks and appreciation to Judith Thomas, Teresa Smallbone, Paul Williams. Ralf Müller and Nirundon Tapachai.

There are many people to thank. First, we thank our families and colleagues for encouraging us to write the book, and then for their support and comments throughout the completion of the book. Second, from Wiley, Deborah Egleton, Sarah Booth, Anneli Anderson, Matt Duncan, Emma Cooper and Mark Styles provided many helpful editorial and design suggestions. We also are grateful for Dianne Bevelander's reviews of early drafts and her many direct contributions as well as Ella Boniuk for her support in finding appropriate examples and datasets. Finally we owe a debt of gratitude to our past students who inspired us to write this book. Their questions and comments helped us to know what and how to cover the many important topics. We also thank those special teachers who inspired us to a lifelong mission of learning and sharing knowledge. Moreover, we hope that future students by using this book will enjoy a much easier pathway to learning business research and data analysis than was typical for us.

Joe Hair, Kennesaw State University, USA
Arthur Money, Henley Management College, UK
Phillip Samouel, Kingston Business School, UK
Mike Page, RSM, The Netherlands

PART I
INTRODUCTION

Chapter 1
Business Research for the 21st Century

CHAPTER 1
BUSINESS RESEARCH FOR THE 21ST CENTURY

CONTENTS

LEARNING OUTCOMES

- Provide an orientation to modern-day business research.
- Define business research and the people who use it.
- Discuss recent business trends and how they affect business research.
- Examine research-related technologies.
- Introduce the continuing case used throughout the text.

INTRODUCTION

Research is a discerning pursuit of the truth. Those who do research are looking for answers. In our everyday lives, we all play the role of researcher. A trip to the cinema is rarely undertaken without some period of consideration. During this process, prospective cinema goers first determine what type of film would best fill their present desire. They may form a preliminary opinion of several films based on previous knowledge of the actors and producers involved. "Is *The Mystery of the Blue Dog Café* worth seeing?" Media sources, previews and input from personal acquaintances often provide information to answer this question. Thereafter, if you are confident about your conclusion, a decision is made. This simple illustration contains the basic elements of business research. Good decision making depends upon accurately predicting whether you will enjoy the film The Mystery of the Blue Dog Café.

Although formal research training is relatively new to the business world, business research is perhaps as old as commerce itself. International commerce expanded rapidly with the rise of Phoenician traders during the Early Classical period, about 500 BC.[1] Investors in trading expeditions soon realized it was too risky to simply load ships with surplus goods and sail from port to port until a buyer was found. So, they began to gather information about how goods might be altered to appeal to specific markets. With this information, merchants made strategic decisions involving product differentiation and market segmentation. Merchants discovered the existence of price and quality segments. Wine from the countries of Thaos and Chios was highly sought after by some markets. Thasian and Chiot wine sold for as much as one drachma per litre compared to 1/4 a drachma per litre for other wines. Wine makers from southern Italy performed research while peddling their own goods on the seas. Thus, they too attempted to capitalize on this new intelligence. While they were unable to match the quality of Thasian or Chiot wines, they appealed to these markets by making imitations of higher quality wines. Consequently, research may have led to the first product "knock-offs".[2]

Research also proved a key to success in selling crockery (dinnerware or china). The Corinthians lost out to the Athenians in serving the early Etruscan market for crockery. The Athenians produced a style known as Tyrrhenian. Tyrrenian crockery more closely matched Etruscan "taste". It was "cheap and gaudy...and often carried mock inscriptions, presumably to impress Etruscans who would not have been able to read".[3] Perhaps they were the pink flamingos of the day. There seems to be little doubt, therefore, that the products were produced with a specific market in mind based upon information gathered from that market.

Increasing literacy, the industrial revolution, continued advances in transportation, the advent of various forms of computing, and the general expansion of commerce worldwide have changed the way research is done. Frederick Taylor used early motion picture technology to film workers and demonstrated how they could improve their productivity. Similarly, General Electric was among the first companies to use consumer research to design new products.

Today, there are literally thousands of companies whose primary activity involves providing research services that help businesses answer key strategic, tactical and operational questions. Research has become much more formalized and technical. But its purpose remains much the same as enquiries undertaken by the Phoenician merchants. How do I find the answers to improve my performance and make life better for customers, employees and owners? Business research is designed to answer these questions.

BUSINESS RESEARCH DEFINED

Business research includes several interrelated components. The most important are described in the sections that follow.

A TRUTH-SEEKING FUNCTION

We began with a simple definition of science as a truth-seeking function. **Science** seeks to explain the world that really is. "Real-world" or physical scientists seek the truth about the world's physical realities. Chemists deal with chemical phenomena, biologists with biological phenomena, and so forth. Social scientists, such as psychologists and sociologists, seek to describe the realities of individual human behaviour and the interactions of humans within a society. **Business researchers** generally fall more in line with social scientists because in reality business is about people.

Like the scientists described above, business researchers pursue the "truth" about business phenomena. The essence of business is people serving people through participation in a value-creating process with exchange at its core. This includes all the support systems necessary to facilitate the process. **Business research** seeks to predict and explain phenomena that taken together comprise the ever-changing business environment. Thus, business research is a truth-seeking function that gathers, analyses, interprets and reports information so that business decision makers become more effective.

ELEMENTS OF BUSINESS RESEARCH

The scope of business research is broad and the types of phenomena that business researchers study are expanding rapidly. Time and motion studies are relatively infrequent today, although they were essential in the development of scientific business management. Instead, we may study employee productivity as a function of a communication channel's bandwidth or how purchasing patterns have changed because of the Internet. Thus, business research is truly dynamic in that researchers are constantly studying new issues with new tools. Below is a list of key elements of business research that help provide a clearer picture of what is involved.

1. Business research is broad. It involves the study of a range of phenomena related to:
   a. Studying people including employees, customers, supervisors, managers and policy makers.
   b. Understanding systems or groups of people including strategic business units, offices, labour in factories, management groups, boards of directors, managing directors, market segments, cultures, subcultures, corporate cultures, communities, companies and industries.
   c. Examining the interaction of people with systems including accounting or audit systems, legal systems, management practices, compensation systems, manufacturing systems, production processes and financial systems.

2. Business research can be formal. Researchers may undertake systematic and sometimes exhaustive projects aimed at answering very specific questions. As an illustration, Toyota was interested in knowing the effects of "one-price" retailing where car prices are not subject to negotiation on car purchases. They tested the idea in several countries. Customers in Montreal for example, generally preferred the one-price system by about two to one.[4] But

the effect of one-price retailing may extend beyond customers. Toyota could also research the effect this would have on their dealer network and employees. Thus, this single issue results in a fairly comprehensive study. This is a good example of a one-shot research project. One-shot research projects are performed to address a single issue at a specific point in time.

3. Business research can be informal. Restaurant owners and/or managers often spend a portion of each night circulating through the dining room. They will stop at each table and ask: "Is everything all-right?" The information they receive in return helps identify patterns that will improve decision making and enhance the restaurant experience for their customers. While this sort of research is easy for small entrepreneurial ventures, it's more of a challenge for larger firms. New technologies are creating ways, however, where informal feedback can be input electronically so that regularities can be identified, perhaps through data mining or some expert system, and the appropriate actions can be taken. Informal research is often ongoing. This means it is performed constantly and not directed toward any specific issue.

4. Good research is **replicable**. A goal of scientific research is to be as objective as possible. That is, scientists are more or less play-by-play announcers who describe events as they observe them. When research is objective, it is generally replicable, meaning that another researcher could produce the same results using the identical procedures employed by the original researcher. Coca Cola's research into a better tasting product was motivated in part by the Pepsi Challenge. The Pepsi Challenge was a promotion in which consumers were intercepted in a supermarket, allowed to taste two unidentified colas, and given a six-pack of the one they preferred. Pepsi routinely televised these on live television. More people chose Pepsi in the Pepsi Challenge. Coca Cola, questioning the authenticity of this research, conducted their own taste challenges, but kept them out of the public eye. Coca Cola's research confirmed the Pepsi Challenge results. When consumers didn't know what they were drinking, they preferred the taste of Pepsi. Thus, the Pepsi Challenge research was replicable.

5. Good research should provide more benefit than it costs. Ultimately, this is of primary importance in determining if the research was any good. Management shouldn't commission a €100,000 research project to make a €25,000 decision. Many decisions are made with little or no research because they do not involve a lot of risk. At other times, research is done in a perfunctory manner in an effort to limit the cost relative to the potential benefits of the decision.

Business research is scientific inquiry. But the terminology of business research differs depending upon what motivates a particular study. **Applied business research** is motivated by an attempt to solve a particular problem faced by a particular organization. For example, Coke may want to know why Pepsi is gaining market share in Paris. **Basic business research** is motivated by a desire to better understand some business related phenomena as it applies to all of an industry or all of business in general. For example, why are people drinking more bottled water and less cola? Applied business research helps decision makers make specific decisions bound by time and an organization. Basic research helps develop theory that attempts to describe and predict business events, so that all business decision makers can benefit. Exhibit 1-1 below compares applied and basic business research.

Applied Research Issues	Basic Research Issues
What is the effect of digital audio and photo managing on Samsung's DVD market share?	How does technological turbulence affect business performance?
How will stocking wines from a new French vineyard in Languedoc Roussillon affect profitability of Waitrose retail outlets in the UK	What factors relate to consumer perceptions of a wine's overall quality?
How would imposing reduced working hours rather than downsizing affect employee moral at Volkswagen AG?	Is employee morale more related to reductions in the working weeks across the employee base or to staff retrenchment within the German economy?
Can using prospective employee psychological profiles reduce turnover at Erasmus University Medical Campus?	Does job stress affect the job performance and satisfaction of male and female service providers equally?

Sources: *Business Wire* (2002), "Samsung selects Planetweb's digital entertainment software to power new line of interactive DVD players", (7 January), accessed September 2006; `http://www.frenchentree.com/languedoc-herault-gard/`, and `www.financedirectoreurope.com/pdfs/humanresources/developmenttraining/19,019volkswagen.pdf`, accessed April 2006.

EXHIBIT 1-1

Examples of Applied and Basic Business Research

WHAT DOES BUSINESS RESEARCH STUDY?

The boundaries of business research today are virtually limitless. Business research is intended to result in better decision making. Business decisions often involve all aspects of business. Therefore, it should be no surprise that business research involves all aspects and all functions of business.

Marketing managers often are interested in the behaviour of the firm, brand image, customer satisfaction, brand and product positioning, among other things. Most consumers can recall times when they have responded to some type of customer satisfaction study. This information is vital in strategic decisions. Which strategic orientation should the firm take? Should it diversify or stay entrenched as a specialist within a niche market? Business researchers contribute significantly to these decisions as exemplified in the Global EFFIE Awards that honour effective and creative marketing campaigns that have been proven in multiple markets worldwide.

For manufacturing firms, efficient and effective production processes are essential if customers are to realize product quality and satisfaction. Business research is often tasked with identifying processes that create the optimal amount of product and/or service quality. Further, since employees are ultimately responsible for quality production, a great deal of research is directed at understanding employee behaviour by focusing on important variables including job satisfaction, employee performance and employee turnover (resigning intentions). In the UK, research indicates firms incur £3,933 per year in additional costs for every employee leaving their job.[5] Similarly, US firms estimate average turnover costs at $10,000 or more for each employee that leaves.[6] Thus, turnover receives a great deal of attention from researchers and decision makers.

Strategic and tactical decisions often involve capital investment. With the exception of UK-based Tesco, online grocers have not enjoyed the early success many experts predicted. Many may have underestimated the capital intensity required in such a venture. One of the keys to their eventual survival is selecting the best way to obtain this capital.[7] Business research on financing alternatives could help answer this question. Exhibit 1-2 illustrates some of the business research implications that might be involved in an entrepreneurial venture in the online grocery industry.

Accounting rules also present a need for research. Different accounting procedures bring with them different financial implications. It is clear that both Grant Thornton International and Deloitte Touche Tohmatsu should have more closely examined the accounting procedures used at Parmalat, the Italian-based multinational company.[8] So, decisions must be researched for potential tax implications as well as their impact on product and strategic business unit (SBU) financial performance.

Industries change, but the research process itself remains much the same. Research continues to be an investigation searching for truthful explanations and accurate predictions. The tools researchers use, however, have and will continue to change. **Information-only businesses** are those that exchange information or information-related services such as distribution and storage for some type of fee. As information-only products become an ever-increasing part of the economy, it will be interesting to see what new tools, if any, may be needed. Information-only businesses are a major portion of e-commerce. They include relatively small companies that, for example, might provide details of products like third-party mortgage and life insurance for small owner managed businesses. But they also include large companies such as Yahoo and Google as well as specialized firms such as Kieskeurig (www.kieskeurig.nl), which provides price information on thousands of products at the click of a mouse.

Several aspects of information-only businesses present a challenge for business researchers. For example, how will researchers identify important "attributes" of information-only products? "Stickiness" is a term that has been used to describe an important attribute of information products. **Stickiness** is how much it costs to transfer a given unit of information to an information seeker.[9] Does this cost affect the end-user, or only channel members? Further, what is the best way to determine the price of information-only products since the cost to transfer information-only products is practically zero? Should price, therefore, be determined by a buyer's willingness to pay instead of being based on cost.[10] This clearly has implications for the way pricing studies are conducted. With information-only products greater emphasis is placed on protecting the intellectual property rights. This means researchers must help to define the boundaries of infringement to provide legal protection for information-only companies.

What types of businesses benefit from research? All types of businesses can benefit from research. Large and small businesses can answer key questions about markets and about their own internal work environments.[11] Many low-technology firms use research. For example, hotels and restaurants frequently collect information on satisfaction and lodging and dining out patterns to enable them to better serve their customers. The new, ever-growing class of highly skilled, highly educated

Decision Involved	Research Topic	Implications
What type of capital resources should be used?	Identify the financial and risk implications associated with the various options.	Online grocers are highly capital intensive. The result is cash starvation during the early months of operation.
What markets should we serve?	Identify the potential profitability of potential markets.	Online grocers must identify markets with high volume potential relative to a small service area
What product assortments should be emphasized?	Identify the shopping value associated with product acquisition of various types.	Online grocers must determine the products for which customers believe physical product interaction is a value added process.
What type of personnel should be involved in operations?	What is the impact of outsourcing on perceived service quality?	Online grocers may find it more cost effective to outsource certain operational components including product delivery.
How should customers be attracted?	What is the potential response rate from the different options for inducing trial?	Customer acquisition costs are extremely high for online retailers. Therefore, successful online grocers will likely enjoy relative efficiency in enticing customers.

EXHIBIT 1-2

Business Research Applications for a Start-Up Venture in Online Grocery Sales

entrepreneurs also understand the key to success is being able identify new ways to provide customers with enduring and more satisfying bundles of benefits.[12] Clearly, research has played a key role in technological development as it addresses various aspects related to the adoption of new technologies.

Business research is no longer confined to for-profit businesses. Nonprofit institutions have also found research useful in addressing questions related to the core client segment they serve. As an example, the Information Centre about Asylum and Refugees in the UK (ICAR) conducts ongoing research on refugees and asylum seekers' needs and experiences to help organizations working with these marginalized groups to refine their service delivery and develop more targeted services. Thus, far from being exclusive to a small set of large companies, all types of businesses can benefit from research. See the Research in Action box to learn more about how voluntary sector organizations working within the UK refugee sector utilize research activities to support them in achieving their strategic objectives.

RESEARCH IN ACTION   RESEARCH IN SUPPORT OF REFUGEES

Increasingly, voluntary sector organizations and NGOs (nongovernmental organizations) are conducting rigorous research to inform practice and stimulate discourse. Although, the tradition of "evidence-based" practice may be considered more prevalent in statutory service provision, it is becoming increasingly common with voluntary sector service providers such as those working with marginalized communities.

NGOs conduct research depending on their primary aims and responsibilities, their client group and the issues they are concerned with. Some of this research may have a general focus and attempt to collect a wide range of information about a particular group whilst other research may be more targeted. As illustration, research into broad factors affecting the welfare of refugees and asylum seekers in the UK may address a wide range of issues from health to education and employment. A more targeted research agenda may examine the education or health challenges facing the children of Somali refugees within the UK.

The Information Centre for Asylum and Refugees in the UK uses knowledge gained through research to inform the development of services and influence working practices, as the basis for seeking funds, to investigate instances of best practice and how they might help organizations working in the field, to monitor policy changes and assist with strategic planning. Importantly ICAR also uses research to inform advocacy and campaigning by raising awareness of particular issues amongst the public, the media and policy makers.

Additional examples of voluntary sector and NGO groups within the UK that conduct research related to refugees and asylum seekers include; (1) the North of England Refugee Service (NERS); (2) Asylum Aid; (3) Scottish Refugee Council; (4) the Medical Foundation for the Care of Victims of Torture; (5) the Somali Education and Cultural Community Association (SECCA); and (6) the Ethiopian Community Centre in the UK (ECCUK).

Together with ICAR, OXFAM and others, the above organizations involve themselves in a wide range of multifaceted research issues that all have an impact on refugee communities in the local and national context. These include housing, children, poverty, health, employment, community cohesion and so forth.

Source: http://www.icar.org.uk/, accessed April 2006. ∎

TRENDS IMPACTING BUSINESS RESEARCH

Recent business trends have affected business research in many ways. They have helped shape the types of research performed, the way research is conducted and the phenomena that are studied, as well as the importance of research in business decision making. Among the more important trends impacting business research are expanding market freedom, internationalization, relationship marketing, and particularly the information revolution.

EXPANDING MARKET FREEDOM

Since the removal of the Berlin Wall in November 1989, free markets have emerged in many formerly closed markets. Prior to this many managers in the former Soviet Union were not motivated to develop or acquire research capabilities because consumers represented a captive audience except for the black market.[13] There was little job mobility so there was little incentive to study the internal, organizational workings of the firm. Little advantage could be gained through the added intelligence that research could bring.

As free and competitive markets emerged, companies became motivated to answer questions about the types of products and services customers wanted. One result has been a greater emphasis on product quality requiring input from both customers and employees. The Volga, perhaps the best-known Russian automobile, has a long and infamous history as a symbol of the poor product quality that epitomized Soviet industry. More recently, Gorkovsky Avtomobilny Zavod (GAZ), the Russian manufacturer of the Volga, has used research input to expand its product line and market share. GAZ assessed market trends, then entered the mini-van market with the Gazelle and has penetrated markets in Iraq, Hungary and even the US![14]

Russian managers also must learn to deal with free labour markets. Job satisfaction in Russia remains low. In fact, many skilled Russian workers have been attracted to the West by better working conditions.[15] Since Russian labour markets traditionally have been understudied,[16] business research may provide gains to managers that are even greater than those resulting from similar studies in developed economies. As firms benefit from improved decision making, research becomes an essential part of effective decision making.

INTERNATIONAL RESEARCH

Business research today is truly an international endeavour. Firms around the globe now perform business research to improve their decision making. This research influences decisions often involving unfamiliar cultures. For example, foreign acquisition decisions can be made with much more certainty when the competitive and economic market structures are known. Similar to the Volga, Skoda was the Communist nationalized automotive producer from the Czech Republic. Skoda also had an infamous reputation for quality. After its initial introduction to the UK market in 2000, 98 % of British consumers rated it as a "low-quality, low-end product". Since Volkswagen acquired Skoda, however, business research has been used to improve product quality and design promotional campaigns that use humour to counter the negative image. By careful consumer profiling, Skoda targets consumers who are highly rational in their decision making rather than emotional. The result has been a dramatically increased response to direct marketing appeals and sales increases exceeding 20 %.[17]

Internationalization means business research also must take an international focus.[18] Difficult managerial decisions involving consumers and employees in a foreign culture are made even more difficult by an array of communication barriers, both verbal and nonverbal. These decisions require research regarding cultural differences, including the ability to translate meaning from one language into the same meaning in another language.

The Internet means many businesses now consider the world their market. But to do so, the company's Web site must be available in multiple languages. In such cases, translational equivalence becomes essential. **Translational equivalence** means text can be translated from one language to another, then back to the original language with no distortion in meaning. See Exhibit 1-3 for examples of translational inequivalence.

Description of Situation	Intended Meaning (Product Name/Slogan)	Interpreted Meaning
English name of a US product and its German interpretation.	Clairol mist stick	Piece of manure
English name of a US product and its Spanish interpretation.	Matador (AMC auto)	Killer auto
Japanese interpretation of English name.	Guess jeans	Vulgar/low-class/ugly jeans
German interpretation of English name.	Puffs Tissue	Whorehouse tissue
German interpretation of product term.	Credit card	Guilt card
Japanese interpreter's translation from Japanese into English to be sold in China	Anti-freeze	Hot piss spray
Japanese interpreter's translation from Japanese into English to be sold in China	Ready to eat pancakes	Strawberry crap dessert

Sources: Semon, T. T. (2001), "Cutting Corners in Language Risky Business", *Marketing News*, 35 (April 23), 9. Cohen, A. (1998), "What You Didn't Learn in Marketing 101", *Sales and Marketing Management*, 150 (February), 22–25. Steinmetz, G. (1997), "Germans Finally Open Their Wallets to Credit Cards But Aren't Hooked Yet", *The Wall Street Journal*, (April 6), A14. Reese, S. (1998), "Culture Shock", *Marketing Tools*, 5 (May), 44–49.

EXHIBIT 1-3

Research Could Prevent Errors Like These

Beyond mere translational equivalence,[19] researchers must investigate Internet usage patterns as well as the technical details of browsers and computers. Different languages are accompanied by different alphabets. Many computer system configurations are unable to properly translate these characters. Without the proper hardware and software, for instance, a Russian Web page can easily end up looking like Chinese!

Issues such as these are sure to arise as businesses cross international boundaries. Research designed to understand the cultural dimensions of doing business is more cost effective than a mistake that creates an undesirable or ambiguous meaning.

RELATIONSHIP MARKETING

Business has entered the relationship marketing era. **Relationship marketing** emphasizes long-term interactions between a business and its stakeholders. It seeks to identify mutually beneficial exchanges where both the firm and the stakeholder maximize value. The emergence of relationship marketing is changing research in terms of whom and what is studied.

A principal component of relationship marketing is the realization a firm cannot be everything to everybody. That is, the firms have to recognize that not every customer, not every employee and not every shareholder provide a good match for a long-term relationship. Frederick Rheichheld encourages firms to be "picky" and choose relationship partners carefully.[20] Otherwise, limited resources will be spent on unprofitable customers.

Successful companies have loyal customers, loyal employees and loyal stakeholders.[21] Relationship marketing has placed an increased emphasis on the study of loyalty-related factors. Employee loyalty issues such as turnover and organizational commitment have been studied often because of their relationship to firm performance.[22] Turnover represents the average tenure of an employee and suggests a replacement rate needed to maintain production. Organizational commitment is the degree to which an employee identifies with the goals and values of a firm.[23] When employees are highly committed they exhibit high loyalty. Knowledge of turnover and commitment factors increases the likelihood of organizational success.

Researchers now extend the idea of loyalty to customer and shareholder populations. New concepts such as customer share and customer churn are increasingly studied. **Customer share is** the proportion of resources a customer spends with one firm in a given competitor set.[24] For example, a customer that goes to McDonald's five out of ten times when eating fast-food would have a customer share of about 50%. **Customer churn** is the annual turnover rate of customers. Wireless phone companies are using research to reduce customer churn because it averages about 30% annually and is very costly. Businesses also are researching **customer commitment** – the degree to which customers identify with the values of a firm. They have learned that like loyal employees, customers are willing to sacrifice to maintain valuable relationships.[25] None of these areas was researched as recently as 20 years ago.

Similarly, companies have placed greater emphasis on relationships with employees. The dramatic increase in dual-income families has placed greater stress on employees as their free time becomes more constricted. Thus, employers have to pay attention to life outside of the workplace in an effort to maintain a cohesive workplace. Research such as this has led to a number of innovative programmes designed to help employees deal with routine aspects of everyday life. Childcare support is far from the least of the innovative workplace characteristics stemming from this work.

INFORMATION REVOLUTION

The information age has facilitated many research processes. Technological advances in computing and electronic storage have dramatically increased research efficiency. This has happened in a very short period of time. For example, most individuals reading this book were born before the widespread diffusion of desktop personal computers. Likewise, most readers of this book have never heard of a "card reader". A card reader enabled an analyst to feed data into a computer using elongated cardboard index cards. By punching patterns of holes in the card, different values could be represented. Thus, it wasn't unusual for a researcher to carry around stacks of literally thousands of cards. One stack contained the data while the other contained the computer program that would hopefully analyse the data, assuming no errors in the pattern of holes existed. The researcher typically would place the cards in a card reader and then go for an extended lunch. It might take hours for the mainframe computer to process the program. Upon returning from lunch, the analyst would fetch a printout that either contained results or more commonly for first-time runs, an error message.

Cards had to be guarded with great care. A dropped stack of cards caused more than a few broken hearts for researchers. Now, the data contained in the thousands of cards can be stored on a single USB stick. Moreover, the data is likely to be placed into a file in "real-time" programs that analyse it in a manner never before seen by the researcher who simply "points and clicks" and relies on the computer to run even the most advanced statistical programs in a fraction of a second.

Just as certainly as the card reader is now obsolete, more new technologies will emerge that will make our current methods of data input, storage and analysis obsolete. The following are several information technology developments having a great impact on business decision making and research:

Electronic communication. Email and technologies such as video conferencing and Skype are examples of electronic communication methods. These methods and others have replaced the telephone and traditional "snail-mail" for many types of business communications, including many matters directly related to research. Questionnaires are now routinely administered through email directly or by providing access to a hosted Web site. Chapter 8 contains a more complete description of the technological advances in data collection. Electronic communication is also impacting the developments discussed below.

Networking. Networking refers technically to systems of computers that are connected to each other through various servers. The Internet connects your computer to nearly every other computer in the world. From a business perspective, networking allows greater communication and data transfer between interested parties. In some cases, networking allows for "real time" (instantaneous) information transfer from markets to the analyst. The European Container Terminal (ECT) provides an example of real-time information transfer in that it provides a 24-hour container tracking system for its clients. Firms use intranets as well. These are Internet-like networks that link computers internally within a single organization. For example, a researcher who needs sales and profit data for the last 20 quarters can tap into a company's financial records directly and retrieve the desired information. No paperwork is necessary and no delay occurs while waiting for the accounting department to process the request!

A company can expand its intranet network so that suppliers and vendors also have access to the network. This capability allows for automated purchase systems and increased manufacturing flexibility. Intranet technology has been advantageous to Heineken in reducing its procurement costs, inventories and shortening its cycle times by introducing an "extranet" or private network connecting the company's central database to its customers, suppliers and salespeople.[26]

Data warehouses. Company information is now stored and cataloged in an electronic format in **data warehouses**. Twenty years ago, data may have been stored on computer cards or magnetic tape, but generally it would have been accessed through paper reports generated by a computer program. Today, these electronic data warehouses replace other more costly approaches to storing data. For example, the cost of storing one megabyte of information in 1992 was about £10 but today it is only £0,001. Electronic data warehousing clearly has changed the way analysts and decision makers do their jobs.

Some research tasks have been made infinitely easier through the availability of off-the-shelf data. **Off-the-shelf** data are readily available information compiled and sold by content provision companies. For example, an analyst researching several different locations for a new branch office within the UK or France can access all the needed statistical data without every leaving the office. United Kingdom census data are catalogued electronically and accessible in numerous formats through the Web site of the Office for National Statistics.[27] The French census data are similarly provided through its National Institute for Statistics and Economic Studies.[28] Previously, the researcher would have had to go to a national or government agency library, find the correct volumes, then find the correct tables, then manually transfer the numbers into some usable format. A laborious process that may have taken days or weeks is now reduced to hours. Likewise, retail site location research projects that would have taken weeks previously are now nearly automated through the use of **geographic information systems** (GIS). These systems can create, within a few minutes, numerous maps that overlay information from census data inventories on top of satellite photo imagery. For example, it may identify the location of households with income profiles between €75,000 and €125,000 and two teenage children at home.

Numerous industry statistics are now available electronically. In the past, for example, global wholesalers and retailers anxiously awaited national monthly or quarterly reports giving trade turnover statistics that they then needed to integrate. Now these are readily available in various convenient downloadable formats. As an example, the European Commission provides free downloadable information at both a national and aggregated level via its Eurostat statistics portal http://epp.eurostat.cec.eu.int/portal/.

Organizational learning. Motivated by the low cost of electronically storing information and a desire to better understand multiple relationships, many organizations have developed formal systems aimed at recording all important events in a database. The resulting database is an electronic representation of organizational memory. Some input into these systems is automated. Information from routine financial and market reports, for instance, is fed automatically into a database. Other information, such as a list of effective employee motivational tools, must be input through a special report. The result is an internal data warehouse. Organizational learning can be defined as the internalization of both external and internal information to be used as an input to decision making. Within a few short years, organizational learning has taken on a central role in the selection of business strategies aimed at improving firm performance.[29]

One relatively new organizational learning tool is data mining. **Data mining** electronically mines data warehouses for information that identifies ways to improve organizational performance. Data mining is not performed with a pick or a shovel. Rather, the analyst's tool is an **algorithm** (a lists of steps that are computer commands) that automatically analyses potential relationships between events stored in the electronic warehouse.

Data mining represents "knowledge discovery in databases" or **KDD**.[30] The KDD process involves the following steps:

1. Establishing access to relevant data.

2. Selecting the set of events (data) to be analysed.

3. Cleaning these data so they are understood by the algorithm.

4. Developing and using rules for selecting interesting relationships.

5. Developing a report of relationships that may affect firm performance.

Data mining began with the early advent of significant computing power in the 1960s. Researchers developed **Automatic interaction detection** (AID) software that considered possible relationships between all pairs of quantified data within a data set.[31] During the 1960s, a mainframe computer took literally hours to analyse all potential relationships between a dozen or so variables. For example, a data set with 24 variables requires 16,777,216 (2^{24}) computations. Today, sophisticated data mining tools use more powerful statistical procedures. Tools like data mining enable variables to be analysed more than two at a time and in greater number. If we analysed 24 variables in all possible three-way comparisons, 282,429,536,481 computations are required. We won't even attempt to demonstrate what would be required with more variables and more combinations! But, modern computing power enables even these types of analyses to be performed with a personal or laptop computer in seconds. Thus, researchers have much greater power to find information that will improve business performance.

An interesting, perhaps disturbing, example of data mining is its use by regional and national taxation departments around the world. Taxation authorities are somewhat renowned for using the technique to identify patterns in income taxation returns that may signal a high potential for unreported (and therefore untaxed) income. Attention is then focused on identified individuals and companies. Similarly, companies can use data mining research to identify profitable customers, more effective employees and attractive investments, among other things. More recently, researchers are combining data mining with traditional research tools, including survey research, to further improve the value of database technology in decision making.[32]

The Research in Action illustrates how Pfizer is successfully using data mining of its past clinical trials.

RESEARCH IN ACTION — LEARNING FROM THE PAST

Pfizer is increasing its efforts to get more from its past clinical trial data. The company has moved away from the tradition of filing clinical trials once a drug has been submitted for approval. Whether or not the drug is approved for a particular application, Pfizer now adds the clinical test results to an active database that is available for continued data mining by its scientists and statisticians.

According to Mani Lakshminarayanan, a director and statistical scientist at Pfizer, the company is seeking to extract as much out of its past clinical trials as possible. Exploratory analysis of past clinical trial data helps identify specific or unknown patterns potentially of relevance for future studies.

''Secondary data'' from past clinical studies are used by Pfizer for numerous reasons that include, but are not limited to: (1) helping design new studies by providing additional information on sample size and target population; (2) supporting bridging studies when the company has approval in one national jurisdiction and wishes to apply for a licence in another; (3) supporting its capacity to undertake confirmatory and extension studies some time during the patent life of the drug to explore further opportunities; and (4) undertaking finer segmentation and look for correlated effects in targeted ethnic or age specific populations.

Examining hidden patterns in clinical data can also minimize risks associated with a particular drug. Data mining techniques can be used to interrogate multiple studies for drug interaction or safety issues that may impact a particular genetically defined group.

Source: `http://www.bio-itworld.com/newsitems/2006/february/02-23-06-news-pfizer`. Reproduced with permission. Original article written by Salvatore Salamone.■

Satellite technology. Business research even extends beyond the Earth. Many companies are gathering and analysing information obtained from global positioning satellite (GPS) devices. These allow real-time tracking of movement. For example, delivery companies can equip trucks with a GPS system. Every move the truck makes is monitored by a signal sent from a GPS device on the truck, back to a satellite, and then back to a company computer. Researchers can then analyse these patterns to increase the efficiency of the delivery system.[33] Similarly, rent-a-car companies are placing GPS devices on their cars. With this, customers enjoy the benefits of electronic directions. In return the companies now know exactly how rent-a-car customers use their cars. This may enable better services and pricing alternatives. Some research firms have hired people to wear a pocket size GPS while shopping. This enables the researchers to examine shopping centre and shop traffic patterns precisely. Information like this can be very useful in answering questions about how much rent a potential retail location could fetch.

The Research in Action box discusses GPS applications further.

RESEARCH IN ACTION GLOBAL BIG BROTHER SYSTEM?

Are there ethical dimensions to location tracking as a research tool? The exceedingly extensive mobile telephone system coverage in Europe has resulted in the development of a number of products that allow companies to use GPS and mobile telephone technology to track vehicles and report their location down to street level.

The extent of mobile telephone coverage throughout Europe facilitates systems being able to combine GPS technology with general packet radio service (GPRS) and achieve real-time tracking because vehicles can be kept connected to the Internet continuously. This enables fleet managers to monitor driver behaviour on the road and to establish whether a driver digresses along his/her route for purposes unrelated to business.

Insurance companies also are using GPS/GPRS technology for research purposes so that they can consider greater degrees of stratification in insurance policy pricing. As a specific illustration, Progressive Insurance offers drastically reduced rates for some customers and increased rates for others based upon driving performance as monitored by GPS systems. Drive less and you pay less. Drive within the speed limit and you pay less. Some consumer advocates argue that this level of monitoring is a violation of an individuals' right to privacy.

Sources: Cardwell, A. (2001), "Building a Better Speed Trap", Smartbusiness.com, 14 (December/January 2002), 28. Carnahan, I. (2000), "Insurance by the Minute", Forbes, 166 (12/11), 86, and http://www.environmental-studies.de/ GPS/gps.html, accessed March 2006. ■

The information age has transformed modern economies. Researchers are expected and are able to be more productive than they were a generation ago. Likewise, decision makers have more relevant information available to use as input to strategic and tactical decision making. Exhibit 1-4 summarizes several implications of the information age and business research.

Interestingly, some individuals are asking whether or not technology has advanced further than we desire and our ability to take advantage of it. How many people really need 2.5 Gigahertz of processing speed? This may be partly to blame for the technology industry's performance slump in recent years?[34] Exhibit 1-5 lets you test your technology IQ and see how you are adapting to the technology explosion.

THE MANAGER–RESEARCHER RELATIONSHIP

Effective decision making requires that both managers (decision makers) and researchers perform their respective roles responsibly and ethically. Ethics in the manager–researcher relationship means both parties treat the other honestly and fairly. In addition, the researcher should realize that a breech in professional ethics harms the entire research industry. Conflict between the decision maker and the researcher (even when they are one in the same person) is inevitable. The decision maker wants to spend minimal money, utilize minimal human resources, and wants the answer immediately and error free. The researcher realizes that implementing research designs can be expensive, involves substantial time and labour resources, can be time consuming and is never error free. Somewhere in between, there needs to be a reasonable compromise.

WHO PERFORMS BUSINESS RESEARCH?

The business researcher becomes formally involved in the decision-making process once a decision maker, who may be either an entrepreneur or a manager, recognizes a need for new information. The researcher's role is to fill this need. Decision makers use researchers who are either employed by the same firm or part of an external consulting agency. Researchers not employed within a firm are considered **outside research** consultants. Research decisions involve varying degrees of complexity and internal complications. Consequently, from time to time even firms that have in-house research departments may outsource a research project. The following describes several situations that make hiring an outside research consultant advantageous over doing the research "in-house".

Matter matters less	Company value is increasingly found in intangible or "soft" assets. In the new economy, knowledge is the key to success. Information-only products account for a significant portion of the economy. Therefore, researchers are required to process more and produce better information and intelligence.
Distance matters less	Many employees can perform their work from remote locations beyond the traditional workplace. Customers can shop from anywhere, including an airplane, their office, and believe it or not, their car! Researchers can conduct Delphi interviews (a type of expert opinion polling) with top executives from every continent in the world simultaneously.
Time matters more	Given the new world of 24-hour-a-day instantaneous connections, the pressure to react quickly has increased enormously. Business customers are demanding reduced cycle times. Cycle time is the amount of time consumed between the point when an order is placed with a supplying company and the time when the benefits are realized. Thus, those companies that can reduce response time will benefit greatly. Researchers must continuously trade off the demand for quick results with the desire for meaningful results.
Customization matters more	Research, including database technologies, makes it easier for companies to customize products. This is especially true for information-only products. Therefore, the need for companies to have a better and deeper understanding of their customers means more than ever.
People matter more	Convenient worldwide communication has continued to shift the power away from the top of the organizational chart. Purchasers can compare prices for products among hundreds of competing sellers with the click of a mouse. Employees can offer their skills to hundreds of potential employers in a similar manner. Traders have similar access to worldwide investment opportunities. Therefore, businesses that treat customers, employees and shareholders with true empathy and respect will maintain a unique and sustainable point of differentiation. Again, this increases the need for research into the processes by which these stakeholders receive value from their relationships. High tech solutions should also be "high touch", meaning the human element is most important.

EXHIBIT 1-4

How the Information Age is Affecting Researchers and Decision Makers

Can you match the acronyms and terms on the left with the descriptions on the right? All of these may have a significant impact on business research processes.

Acronym	Definition	Implication
1. PUSH	a. Allows real-time voice, video and data transfer by continuously reallocating unused bandwidth.	Improved and faster electronic communication.
2. SMART	b. Monitors software usage among all computers on network.	Usage patterns can be tracked and product improvements can be made with increased efficiency.
3. ATM	c. A technology which automatically delivers customized information to a person via a browser interface.	Researchers have greater access to more relevant information in less time.
4. ASP	d. A document transfer and preparation system which allows the user to focus on the logical structure of a message rather than the format codes.	More efficient information processing.
5. LATEX	e. A technology in which a microprocessor resides on a personalized card (the size of a credit card). Information can be exchanged with computer interfaces by reading the card.	Researchers can track behaviour more closely and accurately enabling decision makers to better customize solutions.
6. Crypto Rage	f. The anger associated with computer hackers' attempts to breech computer security and/or infect systems with computer viruses (not a New Age rock group).	System security should be a high priority.
7. PATROL	g. Secure, remote hosting of complex database software that enables more companies affordable access to sophisticated tracking and information gathering.	Better access to information for researchers and decision makers in a wider variety of firms.

Answers: 1-c, 2-e, 3-a (Asynchronous Transfer Mode), 4-g (Application Service Provider), 5-d (Lamport, Tex), 6-f, 7-b, and www.technology.com/encyclopedia, accessed February 2006.

EXHIBIT 1-5

Test Your Technology IQ

1. An outside research consultant may have special expertise or capabilities within a specific area of research. For example, a German firm wishing to begin operations and marketing in the UK might hire an English research firm to investigate potential locations, employee behaviours and market receptivity. Similarly, would you like to find out about some aspect of the business environment in Japan? International Business Research and Access Japan are two companies that provide specialized Japanese business research. The research firm may even be able to do the project quicker and/or cheaper when it has the corresponding degree of specialized skills and technology.

2. An outside research firm can conduct and interpret research more objectively. The outside firm is not influenced by the corporate culture or worldview. Therefore, when a decision is likely to evoke intense emotions among different factions of the company, an outside firm may be a good idea. Otherwise, the in-house researcher must present results that will anger somebody whom the researcher may have to continue to work with in the future. In some cases, the researcher may present research that suggests some manager's brainchild project is a bad idea. This is necessary despite the fact the manager may have invested many months in developing the project. The outside consultant can present the results and then return to the safety of a different company.

3. The outside firm may provide fresh insight into a problem, and new approaches, particularly when employees within the firm have been unsuccessful in studying the problem previously.

Likewise, there are reasons why internal (in-house) researchers may be advantageous.

1. Generally, **in-house researchers** can provide information more quickly than an outside agency. One reason is that since they are part of the same corporate culture they require far less time to gain an understanding of the decision issue. They already possess a great deal of the knowledge that an outside researcher would have to acquire through interviews.

2. Other employees can more easily collaborate with in-house researchers. A member of a consulting team may be viewed as an outsider and thus a threat. In contrast, many employees with whom the researcher needs to collaborate may know him or her quite well. Thus, there is a certain amount of trust in the relationship that is difficult for an outside agency to duplicate.

3. The in-house researchers can often do the research for less money. External consultants can be very expensive. Consultants may charge hourly rates in excess of €150 for research work. The one exception to this is when the research requires a specialized skill or access, which a consulting firm may already possess, and which would be expensive to obtain otherwise.

4. In-house researchers may be better able to follow up on a research project. One project often spawns the need for others. If a small follow-up study is needed, the in-house firm can begin the work right away. The outside consulting agent can also do the follow up study, but at the very least, a new contract may have to be written and agreed upon.

When we discuss the ethical obligations of researchers and decision makers further in Chapter 3, our comments generally pertain to both in-house researchers and outside consultants.

RESEARCH IN ACTION   CONDUCTING GLOBAL RESEARCH

Among the biggest challenges in conducting business research internationally is which data collection technique to use. Traditionally, telephone surveys have been effective regardless of where they are administered, but Internet surveys are becoming popular in more developed countries. Many business researchers believe in-person interviews are best for the South American and Asian markets. Since business contacts in South America are much more social in nature, conventional wisdom says the research method you use should be too. In-person interviews are viewed as more social than an impersonal telephone call. For Asian markets, in-person interviews are often suggested because they allow the researcher to show proper respect for respondents.

In designing questionnaires for global markets, the introduction and purpose of the survey should be described more fully than in the US. Respondents outside the US often are more inquisitive and require a higher degree of formality than do Americans. For example, a survey that requires 15 minutes to complete in the US may take up to 40 minutes in Germany because German respondents like to talk more and the language is less concise than English. The longer response time adds to the cost of the research.

The major stumbling block of most international research is translation. Keep in mind that if you are researching five different markets/languages, the questionnaire must state exactly the same question in the same place for each of those markets. Otherwise, you could tabulate the different sets of responses and end up with little useful information.

Can you think of some other problems that might be encountered in international marketing research? Are there countries where conducting business research is more important than in others? Any countries where research is not needed?

Source: C. Samuel Craig and Susan P. Douglas, *International Marketing Research*, John Wiley & Sons, Inc., London, 3rd edition, 2005, and Chris Van Derveer, ''Demystifying International Industrial Marketing Research'', Quirk's Marketing Research Review, April 1996, pp. 28, 35. ■

CONTINUING CASE STUDY – SAMOUEL'S AND GINO'S RESTAURANTS

To help illustrate business research principles and concepts in this text, we have prepared a case study that will be used throughout all the chapters in the book. The case study is about two restaurants in London that are competitors. One of the restaurants is Samouel's Greek Cuisine. The other restaurant is Gino's Ristorante, a southern Italian restaurant located about a few streets away. Both restaurants cater to an upmarket crowd for lunch and dinner. We refer to the case study as we discuss the various research topics and specific exercises are placed at the end of every chapter. For example, Phil Samouel hired a research company to conduct interviews with both his customers and Gino's customers. Results of the surveys will help him prepare a business plan. In Chapter 2 we provide a copy of a research proposal given to Phil so he could decide if the value of the research project justified its cost. When we discuss sampling in Chapter 7 we evaluate different sampling approaches and point out why the research company recommended exit interviews. Similarly, copies of the questionnaires used to collect primary data are shown in Chapters 9 and 10 to illustrate measurement and questionnaire design principles. In all the data analysis chapters we use the case study data to illustrate statistical software and the various statistical techniques for analysing data. Finally, a summary of the research report provided to Phil Samouel is included in Chapter 15. The focus on a single case study of a typical business research problem will enable you to understand more easily the benefits and pitfalls of using research to improve business decisionmaking.

CONTINUING CASE   SAMOUEL'S GREEK CUISINE

Samouel's Greek Cuisine restaurant is located in London. Phillip Samouel, owner of the restaurant, is a successful manager and businessman. He came to London about 15 years ago and has owned several other businesses but is relatively new to the restaurant industry. He and his brother opened the restaurant about four years ago. The décor and menu are similar to a restaurant they remember when they were growing up in Greece. The concept of the restaurant was to prepare traditional dishes with the freshest ingredients, an informal and festive atmosphere and to have a friendly and knowledgeable service staff. To make the initial decision about opening the restaurant, Phil and his brother talked with several friends but did not conduct a formal feasibility study. Also, they chose the location based on the fact that a restaurant had previously been in operation there and the cost of renovations would be much less than if they selected a location that had been another type of business.

About two streets from Samouel's location is an Italian restaurant owned and managed by Gino. Gino's Italian Ristorante has been open at its current location for about 10 years and has a southern Italian menu. Gino and his family emigrated from Sicily and started the restaurant. His mother runs the kitchen using family recipes gathered over the years and makes sure the food is properly prepared.

When Phil and his family were starting the restaurant, their background research suggested that many restaurants collect information on the characteristics of their customers, such as those listed below:

- Age.
- Income.
- Where customers live and where they work.

- Ethnic background.

- Gender.

- How often they eat out for lunch and for dinner.

- How much they typically spend when they eat out.

- Kinds of food they eat most often when dining out.

- The kind of atmosphere that is most appealing.

They have been so busy since starting the restaurant that there has been no time to collect any of these data.

Last week, when Phil Samouel was passing Gino's, he noticed a crowd of customers waiting to be seated. He believes Gino's is his major competitor because both restaurants cater to the 'upmarket' crowd for lunch and dinner. This started him thinking about the competitive positioning of his restaurant relative to Gino's. Phil's opinion is that Gino's has the advantage of being located in a higher traffic area with greater visibility, and that the length of time Gino has been in business has resulted in a larger, more loyal customer base. In addition, Phil and his brother believe that Gino's is able to charge higher prices without sacrificing business. Phil's informal research has shown that the entrees at Gino's are all about £14–15 whereas his entrees are about £10–11. Satisfied customers may be willing to reward the restaurant by paying higher prices and are likely to be more frequent patrons.

1. Is a research project needed? If yes, what kind of project?

2. What areas should the research focus on? ▪

SUMMARY

■ **Provide an orientation to modern-day business research**

Business people have been doing research for several millennia. It's as old as international trade itself. Relatively speaking, the formal study of business research is young. The need for business research increases as firms face more opportunity, in the form of increased trade, or more potential competition. These conditions create an environment in which a business stands a chance of benefiting from its decisions.

■ **Define business research and the people who use it**

Business researchers, like researchers in general, go about trying to find the truth about business-related things. Business research is a truth-seeking function responsible for gathering, analysing, interpreting and reporting information so that business decision makers become more effective. There are few limits to what a business researcher might be asked to study. The work could involve any business discipline and it could affect tactical and/or strategic business decisions. All organizations, profit and nonprofit, big or small, which manage employees, study systems or market to customers are potential users of business research.

■ **Discuss recent business trends and how they affect business research**
Several trends are affecting business research. These include relationship marketing, which has brought new concepts and a greater need to integrate research studies across multiple stakeholder groups; the internationalization of business, which requires researchers to study previously unfamiliar cultures; and the information revolution, which provides researchers easier access to greater volumes of data. These trends are increasing the importance of business research.

■ **Examine research-related technologies**
Technologies were also discussed in this chapter. Data warehousing provides the researcher with off-the-shelf data saving weeks of time and avoiding expensive data collection in many situations. Researchers' ability to network via the Internet and intranets has allowed information to be shared more readily. These tools have made the researcher more productive.

■ **Introduce the continuing case used throughout the text**
The book has a case study that is used in all chapters of the book to help you apply the concepts to a realistic situation. The case is Samouel's Greek Restaurant and how the owner, Phil Samouel, can improve his business. His direct competitor is Gino's Italian Ristorante. Gino is more successful for a variety of reasons and your task is to help Phil Samouel identify his problems and develop solutions to improve his operations. In order to do that, you will need to evaluate both primary and secondary data as sources of information to understand the situation. You will also have to comment on research designs, sampling and questionnaires, as well as use statistical software to analyse data and develop appropriate strategies. ■

Ethical Dilemma

NRG, an online music retailer, places a cookie on its customers' computers in order to identify customers whenever they log onto the company Web site. The cookie allows NRG to maintain a database of information about their customers including name, address, email address, purchase history and credit-card information. The technology even allows NRG to track their customers' movement to other Web sites. NRG analyses this information internally to make product, inventory and promotional decisions.

After a favourable article about NRG runs in a leading business publication, the marketing director of another company that is interested in targeting its customer base contacts NRG. Instead of paying a business research firm to help it identify the online shopping habits of its target audience, the company wants to know if NRG would be willing to sell its information.

What do you think NRG should do? If you would like more background information to help you answer this question, refer to Chapter 3 in this book, which covers business ethics.

REVIEW QUESTIONS

1. How was research related to business strategy in the Early Classical period over 2,500 years ago?

2. What is business research?

3. List and briefly describe trends affecting business research.

4. What is data mining? How is it related to a data warehouse?

5. Should a business do its research in-house or contract with an outside agency?

DISCUSSION AND APPLICATION ACTIVITIES

1. How do think the emergence of the computer since 1945 has affected the field of business research?

2. Explain how a company like NH Hotels (http://www.nh-hotels.com/listapaises/en/europe.html) might be able to use data mining.

3. Suppose you wished to start an entrepreneurial venture involving the manufacture of portable fax machines in Turkey for export to the UK. List at least five areas in which business research may provide information that will allow for better decision making as you begin this venture.

4. Suppose a company wished to do a research project that tested whether or not a level of management could be removed from the entire organization without any serious negative consequences. Should this project be conducted by in-house researchers or by outside consultants?

INTERNET EXERCISES   WWW

1. Use the Web search engines Google and Yahoo. Search using the key words "business research". Prepare a brief report telling what you found and how it differed on the different search engines.

2. The Roper Centre at the University of Connecticut has one of the largest collections of public opinion data in the world. Their Web site, located at www.ropercenter.uconn.edu has an online magazine and the results of many surveys. Identify two articles or studies related to this chapter and prepare a report on what you learned.

3. The European Commission monitors the evolution of public opinion within member states and publishes its findings online through its Eurobarometer surveys located at

http://europa.eu.int/comm/public_opinion/. Identify an article from the site and discuss the nature and depth of its analysis within the context of this chapter.

4. Go to www.autonomy.com. Surf the Web site and prepare a report on the types of business research support available on that site.

NOTES

1. Nevett, T. R. and Nevett, L. (1994). "The Origins of Marketing: Evidence from Classical and Early Hellenistic Greece (500-30 BC)", *Research in Marketing*, 6, 3–12.
2. Grace, V. R. (1961). *Amphoras and the Ancient Wine Trade*. Princeton, NJ, American School of Classical Studies at Athens.
3. Nevett and Nevett (1994). p. 9.
4. Gibbens, R. (2002), "Toyota Extends One-Price Retailing: Montreal now, Vancouver and Toronto to Follow", *National Post*, (January 22), FP3.
5. Roberts, Z. (2001). "UK Businesses Sustain their Highest Labour Turnover Costs", *People Management*, 7 (11 October), 11.
6. *CFO* (1998). "Please Don't Go", 14 (May), 23.
7. Sacirbey, O. (2000). "On-Line Grocers Restock Capital", *IPO Reporter*, 24 (29 May), 10.
8. *Business Week* online, 12 January 2004.
9. Von Hippel, E. (1998). "Economics of Product Development by Users: the Impact of 'Sticky' Local Information", *Management Science,* 44(5), 629–44.
10. Nezleck, G. S. and Hidding, G. J. (2001). "An Investigation into the Differences in the Business Practices of Information Industries", *Human Systems Management*, 20(2), 71–82.
11. Lingard, H. (2001). "The Effect of First Aid Training on Objective Safety Behaviour in Australian Small Business Construction Firms", *Construction Management and Economics*, 19 (October), 611–19.
12. Sahlman, W. A. (1999). "The New Economy is Stronger than you Think!" *Harvard Business Review*, 77 (November/December), 99–107.
13. Papmehl, A. (2001). "Russia has Emerged as an Enticing Business Market", *CMA Management*, 75 (November), 50–1.
14. *Eastern Economist Daily* (2000). "Russia Begins Selling Cars in the US", (12 October), Global News Wire. *MTI Econews* (2000), "GAZ to Open Office in Hungary", (30 March), MTI Hungarian News Agency.
15. Glantz, W. (2001). "Gorbachev Touts Russian Workers", *The Washington Times*, (25 April), B8.
16. Griffin, M., Babin, B. J. and Modianos, D. (2000). "Shopping Values of Russian Consumers: The Impact of Habituation in a Developing Economy", *The Journal of Retailing*, 76 (Spring), 20–53.
17. James, D. (2002). "Skoda is Taken from Trash to Treasure", *Marketing News*, 36 (18 February), 4–5.
18. Hall, E. (1999). "Broadening the View of Corporate Diversification: an International Perspective", *International Journal of Organizational Analysis*, 7 (January), 25–54.
19. Singh, J. (1995). "Measurement Issues in Cross-National Research", *Journal of International Business*, 26(3), 597–619. Steenkamp, Jan-Benedict E. M. and Hans Baumgartner (1998), "Assessing Measurement Invariance in Cross-National Research", *Journal of Consumer Research*, 25 (June), 78–90.
20. Reichheld, F. F. (2001). "Lead for Loyalty", *Harvard Business Review*, 79 (July/August), 76–84.
21. Ibid.
22. Mathieu, J. E. and Zajac, D. M. (1990). "A Review and Meta-Analysis of the Antecedents, and Consequences of Organizational Commitment", *Psychological Bulletin*, 108 (September), 171–95.
23. Reichers, A. E. (1985). "A Review and Reconceptualization of Organizational Commitment", *Academy of Management Review*, 10(3), 465–75.

24. Babin, B. J. and Attaway, J. P. (2000). "Atmospheric Affect as a Tool for Creating Value and Gaining Share of Customer", *Journal of Business Research*, 49 (August), 91–101.

25. Gilliland, D. I. and Bello, D. C. (2002). "Two Sides to Attitudinal Commitment: The Effect of Calculative and Loyalty Commitment on Enforcement Mechanisms in Distribution Channels", *Journal of the Academy of Marketing Science*, 30 (Winter), 24–43.

26. Duvall, M. (1998). "Winery Juices Up Database Link", *Inter@ctive Week*, 5 (22 November), 43.

27. www.statistics.gov.uk, accessed June 2006.

28. www.insee.fr/en/home/, accessed June 2006.

29. Hooley, G., Greenley, G., Fahy, J. and Cadogan, J. (2001). "Market-focused Resources, Competitive Positioning and Firm Performance", *Journal of Marketing Management*, 17, 503–20. Menon, A., Bharadwaj, S. G., Adidam P. T. and Edison, S. W. (1999). "Antecedents and Consequences of Marketing Strategy Making: A Model and Test", *Journal of Marketing*, 63 (April), 18–40. Minor, A. S., Bassoff, P. and Moorman, C. (2001). "Organizational Improvisation and Learning: A Field Study", *Administrative Science Quarterly*, 46 (June), 304–37.

30. Rigdon, Edward (1997). "Data Mining Gains New Respectability", *Marketing News*, 6 (6 January), 8.

31. O'Brien, T. E. and Durfee, P. E. (1994). "Classification Tree Software", *Marketing Research*, 6 (Summer), 36–40.

32. Morgan, M. S. (2000). "Research Boosts Database's Power", Marketing News, 9 (8 October), 16.

33. *Security for Buyers of Products, Systems and Services* (1998). "Customer Tracking Pays Off", 35 (August), 79.

34. Informationweek.com, "Intel's Got The Speed; Do Customers Need It?" www.informationweek.com, accessed 20 February 2002.

PART II
BEGINNING THE RESEARCH PROCESS

CHAPTER 2
OVERVIEW OF THE RESEARCH PROCESS

CONTENTS

- **Introduction**
- **The Business Research Process**
- **Theory and Business Research**
- **The Scientific Method and Business Research**
- **Research Proposals**
- **Summary**

LEARNING OUTCOMES

- Describe the phases of the business research process.
- Understand theory and how it is used in business research.
- Explain how the scientific method improves business research.
- Contrast the rigour of science with the pragmatics of business.
- Understand the role and importance of research proposals.

INTRODUCTION

Business students often struggle with starting a research project because they do not know how things like questionnaires and data analyses eventually produce results, or how to use survey findings to develop meaningful conclusions. But experienced researchers have the benefit of prior knowledge of the research issues as well as the tools available to do the job. This chapter tries to answer the question: "Where do I start?" We begin with an overview of the basic business research process.

THE BUSINESS RESEARCH PROCESS

The **business research process** provides a roadmap with directions for conducting a business research project. Generally, three phases are involved. They are the formulation, execution and analytical phases. Each is summarized in Exhibit 2-1. It should be noted that there are several steps for each of the three phases. But business research studies are not as orderly and sequenced as it may appear from this diagram. Studies sometimes skip steps because they are not necessary for a particular research design, and the steps are not always followed in the sequence identified. Indeed, it is quite common to move through the process, encounter some kind of obstacle, and have to go back to an earlier step and modify the initial research plan. The process represents a roadmap to use as a guide

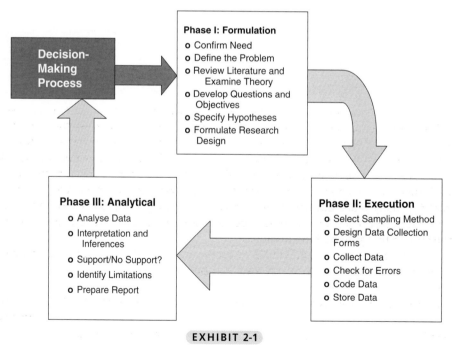

EXHIBIT 2-1

The Basic Business Research Process

to understanding where to start, what must be considered and agreed upon as you move forward, and where you can expect to be when the research is complete.

PHASE I: FORMULATION

The **formulation** phase involves defining the substance and process of the research. This phase is very much like writing a recipe. The substance of the research provides the ingredients that will eventually produce the desired result. A step-by-step set of instructions is provided with any recipe, and this is the process by which the separate ingredients are made into something meaningful. With business research a similar process is followed.

The first task in the formulation phase is to confirm the need for the research. Business research is needed when managers must make decisions but do not have enough information to do so. Determining if enough information is available is based on whether additional information can be collected quick enough to help, at a price within the firm's budget, and if it will substantially reduce the risk associated with making a decision based on the current information. If the answer is "yes" to all three questions, then business research is needed.

The second task is to define the problem. This is perhaps the most important task because an incorrectly defined problem will mean the research is of no value whatsoever. A problem is any situation where a gap exists between the actual and the desired state. But a problem does not necessarily mean that something is seriously wrong. Instead, it could be an opportunity to improve an existing situation. Thus, problem definitions can include both existing problems in the current situation as well as the opportunity to pursue a more favourable situation in the future. You will learn about defining the research problem in Chapter 4.

RESEARCH IN ACTION

HOW SHOULD TESCO DEFINE ITS PROBLEM?

Tesco, the UK's dominant supermarket chain, has decided to use its highly successful intelligence-driven retailing system as a way to move into the very competitive US food market. It will be positioning itself head-to-head against retail powerhouses Wal-Mart Stores and Costco Wholesale Corporation. With over half of its retail operations outside the UK Tesco has decided to set up shop on the West Coast of the US with a convenience store format. The company's chief executive says "We have been watching the US market for many years, but never thought we had the right approach and format for the American consumer. We could have gone in before, but our new format is tailored to the US and brings something original."

As Tesco enters the US market for groceries, how would you define its research problem as it attempts to develop the best strategy?

Source: "British Invasion: The Tesco Test", `http://customer.corante.com`, "Wal-Mart, Kroger, Safeway better watch out. The British are coming!", CNN Money, `http://money.cnn.com/2006/02/24/news/companies/tesco_us/`, and "The Virtual Grocer", `http://www.time.com/time/europe/magazine`, accessed April 2006. ■

Problems are identified and defined in a logical manner. Based on observation the manager/researcher senses that changes are occurring, or that some new behaviours, attitudes, feelings, communication patterns, etc., are surfacing. The manager typically does not understand exactly what is happening, but can definitely sense that things are not as favourable as they should be or could be. When the problem is recognized the manager undertakes preliminary data collection. Informal interviews, both unstructured and structured, are often used to get an idea or "feel" for what is happening.

The nature of the problem is confirmed when the third task of the formulation phase is undertaken – examination of the literature and relevant theory. The literature review is a comprehensive examination of the published and unpublished work from secondary data sources in the areas related to the problem. Literature reviews are used to learn what others have found out in previous research on similar problems, to avoid mistakes they may have made, and to identify any trends that are emerging. If your business problem is low morale among employees, clearly you would want to determine what factors have caused low morale in other businesses, particularly those in your industry. Finally, if relevant theories are available they can be used to specify hypotheses to be tested. Reviewing the literature is covered in Chapter 4.

Some examples of problems that can be examined with business research include:

- "How do price and quality rate in customers' evaluation of products?"
- "Is the effect of participative budgeting on performance moderated by control systems?"
- "Does better automation lead to greater asset investment per dollar of output?"
- "Has the new packaging affected the sales of the product?"
- "To what extent does the organizational structure and type of information system account for the variance in the effectiveness of managerial decision making?"
- "Will global expansion result in an improvement in the firm's image and value?"
- "What are the effects of downsizing on long-run growth?"
- "What are the components of quality of life?" and
- "What factors should be considered in creating a data warehouse for your firm?"

As you can see, business problems impact all aspects of a firm's operations.

The fourth task in the formulation phase is to specify research questions and objectives. This involves redefining the initial business problem in scientific terms. For example, assume that French Connection, the branded fashion clothing chain (www.fcuk.com), is concerned about its overall image among retail customers in the UK market. As initially defined, the research problem is: "Do marketing strategies need to be changed to improve customer satisfaction?" But after further examination and a review of published research, the following questions are posed:

- What is the awareness level of French Connection in the London area compared to other major competitors?
- What factors are important in selecting a retail store that offers fashionable, high quality products at affordable prices?
- What is the current image of French Connection in the London market?
- Who are its major competitors and what is their image?

- What is the demographic profile of French Connection customers compared to major competitors?

Translating the problem into specific questions enables managers and researchers to specify research objectives, hypotheses to be tested, information needs, and ultimately to determine the appropriate research design.

Obtaining information to answer specific research questions may involve collecting data for a specific research problem. But before collecting new data the researcher should determine if data have previously been gathered by someone else for some purpose other than the research at hand. This type of data is referred to as secondary data. Government agencies, commercial research firms, universities, trade groups and others collect and report tremendous amounts of information every year. Some of the information is free and some must be purchased. The Internet has emerged as a means of easily locating secondary data from anywhere in the world. We discuss the role and importance of secondary data in Chapter 5.

The final task of the formulation phase is research design. To complete this task, the researcher considers what information is needed to satisfy the research objectives, the type of data collection approach, sampling, when the research findings are needed, the budget and so forth. The three types of research designs are exploratory, descriptive and causal. They are discussed in Chapter 6.

PHASE II: EXECUTION

After formulating the research, the **execution** phase begins. Here the researcher actively gathers information from the appropriate sources. The information is then checked for errors, coded and then stored in a way that allows it to be analysed quickly and conveniently.

Before collecting data, the researcher must first decide on the sampling design. The sampling design process involves answering the following questions:

- Should a sample or a census be used?
- If a sample, then which sampling method is best? and
- How large a sample is necessary?

In answering these questions, the researcher must always consider ways to minimize error that might occur due to the sampling process. Sampling is covered in Chapter 7.

Data collection is an important task in the research process. Indeed, it often is among the most costly components of the research process. The type of data collection approach that is suitable depends upon the questions being asked. Data collection involves either observation or surveys. Sometimes interviewers are involved, at other times they are not. For example, interviewers are not involved when respondents complete a survey questionnaire at home by themselves or when a computer is used to record data on click-thru sequences on a Web site. Information on behaviours, attitudes, beliefs, lifestyles, expectations, perceptions and similar characteristics is collected in this phase. Once collected, the data are analysed and become the basis for improved decision making. Chapter 8 identifies the various approaches to collecting data, both qualitative and quantitative, and summarizes the advantages and disadvantages of each.

To collect data properly, researchers must have valid and reliable data collection forms. These forms are used to ask and record information gathered in business research. The forms must include the right questions in the correct sequence to ensure the research findings are valid and reliable. To ensure data collection forms collect reliable and valid data they are always pre-tested. Measurement and scaling is covered in Chapter 9 and questionnaire design in Chapter 10.

There are many opportunities for errors to occur in data collection. These errors are called nonsampling errors because they arise from sources other than the sampling process. Once data are collected the first step is to check them for errors. There may be missing data or responses that suggest the person who completed the questionnaire either did not understand it or was not properly following instructions. Other errors may be the result of inadequate interviewer training. Errors can never be totally eliminated but good researchers anticipate potential problems and design controls to minimize them.

Along with checking for errors and inconsistencies, researchers doing quantitative research must code the data and create the data file. With quantitative studies the answers to many of the questions are often precoded. That is, there are structured responses and the respondent simply ticks a 1, 2, 3 or some other number (or letter) associated with a particular response. In contrast, with qualitative studies the researcher examines the data during collection as well as after they are collected looking for commonalities or patterns. In some instances, the researcher prepares a written description of these patterns. In other instances, the researcher actually codes the answers to qualitative questions and uses software to summarize the findings.

Data preparation for qualitative research is discussed in Chapter 11, and it is covered for quantitative research in Chapter 12.

PHASE III: ANALYTICAL

The third phase is **analytical**. In this phase, the data are analysed. If the research involves hypothesized relationships, they are tested and either supported or not supported, based upon comparing the actual study outcome with the outcome predicted in the formulation phase. Results are examined to provide answers to the key research questions. A report is prepared to communicate the results to the appropriate audiences. The decision maker can then take actions based upon better knowledge of the situation.

The first task in the analytical phase is to select and apply a method to analyse the data. The method of analysis depends upon whether you have conducted a qualitative or quantitative study. With qualitative studies, the process involves identifying categories or themes for your data, assigning findings to the appropriate category, specifying relationships and in some instances testing hypotheses. These tasks are discussed in Chapter 11. In contrast, quantitative studies generally tabulate and report the data in diagrams and charts. For example, your study may find that males consume more Guinness beer and females prefer white wine. On other occasions, the data are examined to identify relationships and test hypotheses. For example, you may apply a statistical tool and learn that older workers are more concerned about being made redundant by their company than are younger workers. You will learn data analysis for quantitative studies in Chapters 13 and 14. To make your learning of data analysis easier, we will use the information provided with your book for the continuing case on Samouel's Greek Restaurant.

The last task in the business research process is preparing the report. The report is an important component of the research process because it communicates the results of your research project. The research report summarizes the findings for all the questions posed in the project. It also briefly states the limitations so individuals who use the findings will understand how much they can rely on the study to help them make decisions. Chapter 15 tells you how to prepare an effective report. It also provides suggestions on making effective presentations of the research findings.

THEORY AND BUSINESS RESEARCH

Theory is a set of systematically related statements, including some law-like generalizations that can be tested empirically.[1] A specific theory is a proposed explanation for some event. Sometimes theories have been confirmed by past research. At other times they are proposed theories with either limited or no validation. **Law-like generalizations** are expectations of what will happen under specified circumstances that allow predictions of reality.

Competition is an example of a theory in business strategy. The theory of competition predicts that firms within an industry that are able to differentiate themselves over time gain a competitive advantage. A key law-like generalization of the theory of competition is that differentiation is a competitive advantage that enables firms to charge higher prices.[2] Basic business research still tests this generalization empirically and for the most part the notion is supported. Management strategy at Harrod's Department Store has led to a commitment to a relatively highly trained workforce. This point of difference makes customers more willing to pay a higher price than they might elsewhere. Therefore, we evaluate theories based on how well they predict outcomes.

Researchers develop theory based on the accumulated body of previous research. Thus, a researcher will search out previously reported studies that involve similar phenomena. Applied business researchers also rely on the history of a particular company to help develop a set of expectations in a given research situation. Without theory, the formulation stage becomes more difficult because business researchers cannot set boundaries on the study situation.

The Fuel for Research   Theories provide key inputs into the research process. Business theories explain and predict business phenomena. Decision makers want to know the likelihood these explanations and predictions are accurate. Thus, theory helps shape the research questions and specific predictions are expressed in hypotheses. Research projects then validate or invalidate these predictions.

A problem arises because theories are often incomplete. Consider for example a theory of the relationship between advertising and sales. Given the key nature of this relationship to business success, and the variety of research questions that might be influenced by this theory, a great deal of research investigates this topic.

What do you think is the relationship between advertising and sales? Does advertising cause sales? There may be a good reason to expect it to do so. Thus, a theoretical explanation can be developed, as the following example shows.

- Increased advertising means more people will know about a business. Knowledge precedes desire and therefore advertising will eventually increase sales.

To this day, however, the advertising-sales relationship is an unsettled issue despite many, many studies of this topic. Some research counters the logic of the previous example claiming that sales cause advertising:

- The theory is that before any firm can advertise it needs resources. The resources are derived from sales. Therefore, firms that sell more can advertise more.

Since advertising is a critical business variable, many researchers attempt to develop a theory explaining how sales and advertising are interrelated. Like most theories, this one contains gaps in knowledge. For example, uncertainty over whether sales cause advertising or advertising causes sales. Such gaps motivate further research.

Normative business decision rules often are theory based. A **normative decision rule** explains what someone should do when faced with a situation described by a theory. The Continuing Case box describes how Phil Samouel, owner of Samouel's Greek Cuisine, makes a business decision based on a theory-based generalization.

CONTINUING CASE   DO LOWER PRICES RESULT IN HIGHER SALES?

Phil Samouel has been conducting some informal research about Gino's Italian Ristorante. By standing across the street on several days and observing Gino's customer levels during the middle of the day, he has learned that Gino's Ristorante does more lunch business than he does. To better understand why Gino's lunch business is bigger, he goes to the restaurant with some friends and they eat lunch. While there he discovers Gino has a separate lunch menu and the prices are much lower than the dinner prices. Samouel then does some background research on restaurant operations and finds support for the generalization that lower lunch prices lead to higher lunch-time volume. As a result, Samouel decides to follow the normative rule that a restaurant's lunch prices should be lower than dinner prices. He will now prepare a separate lunch menu with lower prices in an effort to improve his business.

Are there other generalizations about restaurant operations you can think of that Phil should examine to improve his business?

Behavioural learning theory provides managers with normative decision rules about issues dealing with the amount and timing of employee compensation. However, behavioural learning theory contains many gaps. For example, it isn't always clear why behavioural patterns result from a conditioning effect. Has the employee gained new knowledge as the result of "training", and does he/she use this knowledge to rationally perform the desired behaviour? Or, are the changes more instinctively based, like the conditioned responses observed among animals? For example, circus animals can be "trained" to do a lot of things if a food reward is associated with the desired response. Employees can be trained too, but they generally do not react as a circus animal does to a reward, such as food. Do employees use some type of higher (cognitive) learning? If so, employees can be reasoned with cognitively, placing a greater emphasis on process training. If not, employee behaviour would best be controlled by rewarding desired outcomes and providing disincentives (punishment) for undesirable outcomes. Researchers are motivated to close these gaps and to provide managers with better normative decision rules. Thus, theory provides fuel for research.

The Practicality of Theory   It has been said that: "nothing is more practical than a good theory".[3] However, an opposing view is often voiced by business people – "Your explanation is too theoretical, give us something we can use!'' Obviously, there are differences of opinion on the benefits of theory. Let's look at the role theory plays in the decision making and research process.

People who take their car in to a mechanic often describe symptoms of some problem by trying to duplicate the sound the car is producing. When the car owner doesn't give a sound, the mechanic may ask: ''What does it sound like?'' Why is everyone so concerned with the sound? It's because sound enables the mechanic to develop a ''theory'' about the car. The mechanic does this by integrating the new information about the sound with previous automotive knowledge. Using this theory, the number of parts that must be checked can be narrowed down to a manageable number. Without some type of theory, the mechanic might as well begin checking parts in alphabetical order.

This analogy illustrates one of the key roles of theory. It points us in a direction that hopefully is more likely to produce valuable results quickly. This is important to Phase I of the research process because most of the research steps will follow naturally from the theory. In particular, theory is extremely valuable because it suggests what the researcher needs to measure to provide useful results.

A great deal of research is aimed at developing descriptive theories of business, the marketplace and customer practices. **Descriptive theory** is just that – theory that describes the way things are. The theory of perfect competition in economics simply describes the effects that firms will experience when operating in an intensely competitive environment. At a micro level, a learning organization develops a better theory of itself. Specifically, learning (accumulated knowledge) is put to use acquiring resources that enable the organization to outperform others.[4] At a macro level, the overall quality of business practices within a nation is often tied directly to the quality of basic research produced there. Indeed, some say the UK's difficulties in effectively managing its railway and phone systems are a result of an inability to develop research-based theory.[5] See the Research in Action box to learn how theory is impacting the Internet.

RESEARCH IN ACTION

GOOGLE: HOW MATHEMATICAL THEORY CAN BE USEFUL?

Michel Laroche is a professor at Concordia University in Montreal, Canada. His students have been heard to say "I don't see the use of these math courses". Many might think there is nothing less practical than pure mathematical theory? But new search technologies have taken advantage of mathematical theories. Google (www.google.com) is perhaps the most effective commercial search tool available to business. The secret to Google's effectiveness lies in an esoteric branch of mathematics known as graph theory. Graph theory defines the location of points in space mathematically. For example, graph theory seeks to explain edges, which are connections between multiple points. Using this theory, Tom Leighton and Daniel Lewin, students at Stanford University, developed software that defines electronic searches in terms of mathematical edges. Thus, they drew the analogy of edges to connections between hyperlinks (the active text in a Web page that connects you to a new Web location) to invent a more efficient way of searching. Perhaps you will be thankful for theory the next time "Google" helps you to find important information.

Theory seeks to explain and predict. Researchers' goals are much the same. Theory and practice are inseparable because businesses hope to use theory to do a better job of explaining and predicting. **Rational decision making** is based upon explanation and prediction. Ultimately, good decisions are based on explanations and predictions that have high truth content. In other words, the theory including its explanations and predictions are valid.

Decisions can be made without the benefit of theory and research. But when this happens they are either wild guesses or decisions based upon pure intuition. Exhibit 2-2 contrasts the difference between theory-based and intuition-based decisions. Since businesses normally have a great deal at stake in their decision making, which is the best way to proceed?

Theory-Based Decision Rules	Intuition-Based Decision Rules
Generally, stand (do not take another card) on more than 17	Always sit on an end seat at the blackjack table
Draw (ask for another card) when the dealer is showing a face card	Tuesdays are the best days to play blackjack
The decision to stand (not take another card) or draw depends on the cards that have been seen so far	Wear a green shirt whenever playing cards

EXHIBIT 2-2

Contrasting Theory and Intuition-Based Decisions: An Illustration Based on a Theory of Playing the Card Game 21 or Blackjack

Perhaps you've heard people try to explain their reasons for investing in certain stocks or their theory of the stock market. Did the theory encourage you to follow their advice? Exhibit 2-2 shows some of the benefits of using reality-based theory. Which set of decisions is likely to describe ways of winning more often? The intuition-based rules can be tested just as the theory-based rules also can be tested. But the theory-based rules generally offer superior explanations. The explanations are derived from basic probabilities or expected values given that the game is played with a finite number of cards with equal numbers of each particular card value. In contrast, intuition-based decision rules generally do not have as compelling a rationale. An exception to this is that some managers develop judgement or intuitions based on their experiences that are sound and relatively sophisticated. Thus, whilst intuition does play a role in decision making, business people prefer to know why a certain course of action should be taken and how likely is it to bring success. Theory helps provide answers to these why questions in the form of explanation and prediction.

THE SCIENTIFIC METHOD AND BUSINESS RESEARCH

Most students first study the scientific method in lessons at school. Students are usually able to associate the scientific method with testing a hypothesis through the use of experimentation. The scientific method used by business researchers is really no different than the one learned in school.

Science is what is known about some definable subject. It tries to describe reality truthfully. The **scientific method** is the method researchers use to gain this knowledge. So, it is much the same as the basic business research process shown earlier. The business research process seeks to describe the realities of business actions and interactions truthfully.

Exhibit 2-3 describes the scientific method. The top portion includes observation, discovery and developing hypotheses. These three stages together describe the process of scientific discovery. There is no right way to discover ideas. Ideas can come from intuition, hunches, deductive or inductive reasoning. Once some order can be made of the observations, the ideas can be stated as a discovery. A review of previously conducted research on similar topics is often helpful in moving from pure observation toward some working discovery or idea. The researcher then begins a preliminary investigation to try to translate the discovery into a testable hypothesis or set of hypotheses.

A **research question** poses an issue of interest to the researcher and is related to the specific decision faced by the company. A **hypothesis** is a formal statement of some unproven supposition that tentatively explains certain facts or phenomena. A hypothesis often describes some systematic (nonrandom) events that can be tested using data. Exhibit 2–4 provides some examples of potential

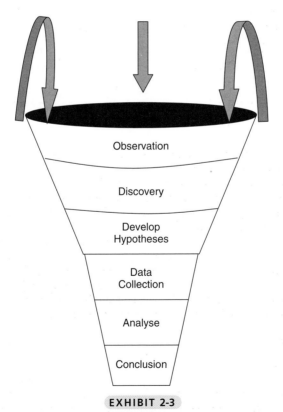

EXHIBIT 2-3

The Scientific Method Contributes to Business Decision Making Through Research

business hypotheses. Generally, a hypothesis restates a research question in more specific terms. For example, a research question may imply the existence of some relationship, but the hypothesis typically goes further by stating the direction of the relationship.

Research Question	A Corresponding Hypothesis
Are company share prices affected by unexpected capital investment announcements?	Share price performance is positively and instantaneously impacted by unexpected capital investment announcements.
Does advertising influence sales?	Advertising is positively related to sales.
Is sales territory size related to customer service ratings?	Sales territory size is negatively related to customer service ratings.
Do flexible schedules create increased labour efficiency?	Business units using flex-time have lower unit labour costs than do those using standard schedule procedures.
Does package colour affect product quality ratings?	Consumers rate products with blue packages as higher in quality than products in orange packages.
Are equity risk premiums related to company size?	Equity investors require larger returns from smaller companies to justify investing funds.
Is region related to beverage consumption?	People living in countries near the equator drink more beer per capita than do people from the countries further from the equator.
Is an employee's gender related to job satisfaction?	Female employees report higher job satisfaction than do male employees with the same job.

EXHIBIT 2-4

Research Questions Lead To Hypotheses

Research questions, hypotheses and theory are all interrelated, as shown in Exhibit 2–5. Theory provides knowledge that helps make sense out of the decision-making situation. Current events and business problems are compared with existing knowledge. Then research questions are developed with the help of theory which often identifies things that are related to each other. Further knowledge may result in stating more specific research questions and formal hypotheses. The hypotheses can then be tested by collecting data and analysing the results. The results are expected to provide answers to the hypothesized relationships and to reinforce or modify existing theory.

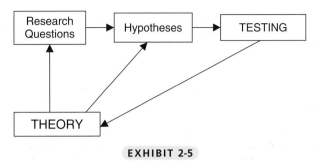

EXHIBIT 2-5

The Flow of Knowledge Between Key Research Tasks

The ability to translate research questions and hypotheses into words represents significant progress. This is illustrated in the example discussed in the Research in Action box on "dress-down Fridays".

RESEARCH IN ACTION

DOES WEARING CASUAL CLOTHING IMPROVE WORKER PERFORMANCE?

In recent years "dress-down Friday" has become commonplace in business. This means that company dress codes are relaxed on Friday. Suits and ties are replaced with jeans and casual shirts. This decision was based upon the theory that more relaxed workers are better workers. The idea can be expressed as a research question by adding additional knowledge: "Is employee dress related to job performance?" Still more specificity allows the following hypothesis to be written: "Employees in casual clothing will show higher job performance than employees in business clothing." This could be tested by comparing performance between two dress groups. Ten years of studies of this type have not supported this hypothesis. In fact, business people are deciding that for many jobs, performance is actually harmed by casual dress. As a result, estimates indicate the number of firms offering dress-down Fridays has dropped in recent years.[6] The finding that performance is lower when employees dress casually will cause a re-examination of the original theory. Perhaps relaxed workers are not always better!

RIGOUR OF SCIENCE

Beyond hypothesis development, the scientific method moves on to the testing phase (the narrow part of Exhibit 2–3) where data are collected. Relevant data represent facts about hypothesized variables. This data is then examined to determine if the findings either "support" or "do not support" the hypotheses. If the findings match the pattern described in the hypothesis, then the hypothesis is supported. Thus, a conclusion can be drawn that hopefully will allow for more informed decision making.

In the discovery phase of the scientific method there are virtually no guidelines and thus no right or wrong ways to develop ideas or inferences. But testing is quite different. Indeed, it is the rigour of testing that distinguishes the scientific method. Testing is the way to get to the conclusion, and the conclusion allows an expansion of knowledge and more informed decision making. Testing is highly critical and analytical.

Ultimately, "good" science uses the scientific method and can be characterized by the following:

1. It is empirical – meaning that it is compared against reality.

2. It is replicable or objective – meaning that the researcher's opinion is independent of the results. Other researchers conducting the study would obtain the same results.

3. It is analytical – meaning that it follows the scientific method in breaking down and describing empirical facts.

4. It is theory driven – meaning that it relies on the previous body of knowledge.

5. It is logical – meaning that conclusions are drawn from the results based on logic.

6. It is rigorous – meaning that every effort is made to minimize error.

PRAGMATICS OF BUSINESS

The rigour of science often is traded off against the pragmatics of business. Business people usually cannot get an answer too quickly. Thus, there is give and take between the desires of the business person and the desires of the researcher. For example, while the researcher may wish to use a sample representative of an entire population, this may take longer and cost more than the decision maker will spend. Researchers almost always sacrifice some rigour for expediency. While this may introduce error, as long as the decision maker is informed of this, and the results are qualified based on these shortcuts, the researcher should proceed with the project. Good research also follows the principle of **parsimony**. This means that a simpler solution is better than a complex solution. Parsimonious research means applying the simplest approach that will address the research questions satisfactorily.

RESEARCH PROPOSALS

Before conducting a research project, the business researcher must clearly understand the problem to be investigated. Once the problem is defined, a plan of action is developed to investigate and make recommendations on how to solve the problem. A **research proposal** is a formal document summarizing what the problem is, how it will be investigated, how much it will cost, and how long the research will take to complete. If accepted, it typically represents a contract between the researcher and the client (the one requesting the research be conducted).

The research proposal plays a critical role in any research project. It identifies and defines the problem to be investigated, it outlines the approach and methods the researcher will use, it specifies the deliverables from the project (what the client will actually get from the project), and it includes a budget and timeframe for completion. A formal written proposal is the result of interactions between the client and the researcher through which the client's concerns (problems) are translated into research problems, and a proposed approach to solve the problem(s) is agreed upon.

Researchers benefit from preparing written proposals. The first benefit is that proposal preparation clarifies that the problem to be investigated is the one the client requested. Business research helps managers improve their decisions. If the problem as defined in the research proposal does not facilitate improved decision making, then the problem must be redefined or the research should not be undertaken. Once the proposal is accepted, it provides a direction and a plan for the researcher. By following the plan, the researcher can assess progress on completion of the project and make adjustments as needed. Finally, the written proposal documents the agreement between the researcher and the client and minimizes the possibility of later misunderstandings. Clients know what information they will receive and researchers know what information they must provide.

Clients also benefit from a written research proposal. First, when clients review the proposal they can verify the researcher truly understands the problem to be investigated. If changes are needed, they can be made before the project is begun. Once the project is underway, the client can use the proposal as a means of ensuring the project's deliverables are what they expected, and that the project is executed as promised. Finally, a written proposal enables the client to evaluate the quality and value of a proposed project. If several proposals have been solicited, the client can compare the scope, methods and proposed budget. This helps to ensure that high-quality research that provides value for its cost will be delivered as expected. Exhibit 2–6 provides an example of a research proposal that was submitted to a healthcare organization as part of the strategic planning process.

I. Introduction and Objectives

Wilhelmina Women's Cancer Clinic (WWCC) was established in 1992 to provide care and information for women who are battling with gynaecological cancers, including breast cancer. The Clinic helps women enhance their quality of life by helping them select the right choice of treatments and support during their recovery stages.

Since its inception, WWCC has been focused on providing top medical care and support to cancer patients. Over the last few years the management of the Clinic has recognized the growing international trend towards greater holistic treatment and support for people suffering from life-threatening and terminal conditions. Management believes that WWCC needs to adopt this approach for its cancer patients for both business and ethical reasons. From a business perspective, changed medical legislation within the Netherlands permits residents to supplement state-based health insurance with additional insurance for extra care. This is likely to result in increased insurance being available for broader care that will make medical clinics equipped to provide this to preferred suppliers in what is already an internationally renowned health system. From an ethical standpoint, it is apparent that the care of cancer sufferers extends considerably beyond treatment of the physical condition.

As a result, the management team of the centre is interested in exploring the possibilities of establishing a Women's Wellness Centre that could provide a number of extra services to the Clinic's patients. In order to make informed decisions on the optimal format of such a Centre, the following research objectives have been articulated:

EXHIBIT 2-6

Research Proposal for Establishing a Women's Wellness Centre Within the Wilhelmina Women's Cancer Clinic

1. Establish the general scope and nature of existing wellness centres, and the extent that they are already supporting women with life-threatening diseases.

2. Determine the scope for services clustered into the broad categories of mental wellness, physical wellness and family wellness. Thereafter:
   i. Identify the most desired services within each of these clusters.
   ii. Establish the base requirements and preferred location for such services. This includes elements related to privacy versus group support for wellness initiatives, family involvement and participation in wellness treatment regimes, and the preference for home versus centre care.

3. Identify sources of initial and continuation funding for the Centre. What, if any, aspects of wellness treatment might fall under the standard state funding system? What aspects are currently covered within the private insurance supplements to the state system and how might this evolve? To what extent might sufferers and their families be willing to pay for wellness services that fall outside the insurance system? What seed capital (investment) might be needed to establish the Centre?

II. Scope of Project and Timeline

We recommend focusing and implementing the research project in four stages, beginning in July 2007, and finishing in November 2007 with a final presentation of results to the management team during their end-of-the year meeting. Below is an overview of the key research activities and expected timeframes.

1. *Internal Analysis with Management Team*: Our basic goal in the initial stages of the project will be to identify the current vision and expectations of the management team for the Wellness Centre of the Wilhelmina Women's Cancer Clinic and set the general framework for the research project. Major tasks include, but are not limited to: identify and review any research activities conducted so far; define the current vision of the management team for the Wellness Clinic and the exact needs and scope of the research project; request and obtain internal data to supplement secondary sources so that the exact needs and scope of the research project can be confirmed; identify key internal stakeholders to work with the research team and set feedback meeting dates and preliminary agendas. This should be completed by the end of July.

2. *Comparative analysis of what is offered in the market*: The main goal here is to develop an extensive understanding of the existing wellness centre market within the Netherlands, and more specifically within Rotterdam. This investigation must include a review of what these centres offer by way of service for individuals with life-threatening illness. This will provide the foundation for identifying the critical objectives and specialized services of the planned centre. Major tasks here include: a comprehensive analysis of the services offered by wellness centres; their structures, target clients and overall performance; current expectations of the growth potential of the wellness sector and any trends toward market segmentation and specialization.

EXHIBIT 2-6

(continued)

3. *Field Research into the demand for services to cancer sufferers*: The major purpose of this stage of the research is to identify and specify the current needs of cancer patients for specialized wellness services. This stage will focus on conducting focus groups and/or personal interviews with medical specialists, carers and the Centre's patients, as well as surveying the cancer patients of various hospitals within the Netherlands, and affected family members. This stage of the research should be completed by the end of September.

4. *Identify key strategic factors to be considered by WWCC in establishing a wellness centre*: Consolidate the comparative analysis and field research into an appropriate SWOT (strengths, weaknesses, opportunities and threats) analysis for a specialized wellness centre offered to women suffering from the ravages of cancer. Use this to help define the critical success factors for a wellness clinic in both the short and medium term. These activities should be completed by the end of October and undertaken in consultation with the identified internal stakeholders.

5. *Assessment of funding options of the proposed wellness clinic*: Although the above four components of the project need to be undertaken sequentially, funding issues will be investigated continually through the project's duration. Financial elements that will be investigated include: the scope and value of state funding for various aspects of the services anticipated as part of the Centre; insurance cover available through private premium "top-up" clauses contained in typical employment packages and costs of various elements of the wellness package that are unlikely to be included with insurance schemes (state or private).

The process we propose includes regular meetings with three or four of the key stakeholders identified in the first phase of the research. Additionally, we expect to conduct approximately five focus groups and 60 individual interviews with a cross-section of medical professionals, carers, patients and affected family members. The focus groups (general practitioner, cancer specialists, carers, patients and families) should be completed during July and into early August so that appropriate field questionnaires can be created for the various clusters of interviews through September. Two-to-three weeks will be spent consolidating the materials and finalizing the SWOT analysis prior to final identification of the critical success factors (from the service perspective). Once these are combined with the funding options, the viability of establishing the Centre can be determined and presented for management consideration in early December.

III. Consulting Team and Proposed Budget

Assuming the project can be authorized by the end of June, we are prepared to commit a very strong consulting team to Wilhelmina Women's Cancer Clinic and we are holding open our schedules accordingly. Johan Damman, Principal Investigator, will lead this engagement and participate in all aspects of the work. He has consulted for many years to the health sector within the Netherlands and broader Benelux and he is therefore

EXHIBIT 2-6

(*continued*)

well versed in the legislative environment within which Medical Clinic must operate in the country. Nico van Bemmel, a manager in our strategy services group, will coordinate the day-to-day activities. He has broad experience with projects and issues of the type proposed. Jana Vink will provide primary research support. She has a strong healthcare background and will be the key person in developing and analysing the focus group and interview data. Resumes for all three of these individuals are attached.

Our professional fee for conducting this project as proposed is estimated to be €87,500. This estimate is based on the levels of participation identified below:

Johan Damman	100 hours @ €200/hour	€20,000
Nico van Bemmel	150 hours @ €150/hour	€22,500
Jana Vink	200 hours @ €150/hour	€30,000
Focus group costs	5 groups @ €1,500/group	€7,500
Interview costs	60 interviews @ €125/interview	€7,500

Direct out-of-pocket expenses including travel and lodging, secretarial support, overnight delivery, long-distance telephone and secretarial support are charged at cost in addition to above fees. Based on our past experience with the Netherlands health sector, this is a substantial quote. Two perspectives may be helpful in assessing this proposal. Firstly, the recent changes in legislation related to the provision of state-funded care requires increased analysis and increased diligence in surveying key stakeholders given their likely lack of knowledge about the impact of changes. Secondly, wellness management as a concept within the Netherlands is relatively new and drawing informed inferences about its likely growth present more of a challenge than is the case for more standard market scale and scope investigations. Consequently, we suggest more focus groups and interviews than might be usually employed and we have assigned a team with more experienced and qualified members than we have assigned to projects of this nature in the past.

This team, quote and timetable are good through to the end of July 2007, after which time our changing availability may dictate revisions. Please accept this as a working draft, subject to additional discussion to ensure the scope of the project is in line with your needs.

EXHIBIT 2-6

(*continued*)

STRUCTURE OF A RESEARCH PROPOSAL

Research proposals can take a variety of forms. Some proposals are quite long and detailed. For example, public-domain proposals for governmental projects typically are the most detailed. Others are of moderate length, such as the one for Women's Wellness Centre shown in Exhibit 2–6. Finally, some are very short, perhaps as short as one page, such as the one shown in Exhibit 2–7. No matter what the length or level of detail, virtually all proposals should include the following:

Whitehall Research
38 Pelham Street
South Kensington
London
United Kingdom

Engagement Memo

To: Suzanne Wagner, Senior Manager
          Covent Specialty Chemicals
From: Nigel Piercy, Principal Investigator
          Whitehall Research
Re: Project Contract/Engagement, Business-to-Business Survey
Date: 26 February 2007

Project Deliverables:

- Telephone interviews based on list provided by client (N = 50)

- Complete approximately 25 to 30 interviews (about 55–60 %)

- Make ten call-backs to customer list over a three-week period

- Questionnaire same as previous survey

- Begin project first week in March; survey programming and data collection will take about four weeks; report preparation will take approximately two weeks; total project time about six to eight weeks

- Open-ended questions to be taped and transcribed; client will be provided with copy, but respondent identity will be kept confidential

- PowerPoint presentation report provided to client

- Principal investigator available for consultation regarding project

- Budget

- Cost of Project = £8,000
  - £4,000 due to initiate project
  - £4,000 due upon submission of report

- One-day site visit to discuss findings (optional)
  - £1,000 plus travel expenses

Accepted as proposed above: _____ _____
                               Suzanne Wagner   Date

EXHIBIT 2-7

Proposal to Initiate a Business-to-Business Survey

- Project title.
- Background information – specifies events leading up to request for the proposal to be prepared and submitted.
- Problem statement and research objectives.
- Research strategy and methods – data to be collected, how it will be collected and analysed. This summarizes steps that will be taken to achieve the research objectives.
- Nature of the final report to be submitted – specifies type and nature of report.
- Schedule and budget.
- Qualifications of project consultants and research firm.

The structure of the proposal is dictated by the nature of the research project being proposed. Fundamentally, the proposal should have enough information to ensure that the proposed project will solve the problem, and the results will help clients to improve their decisions.

Most business research proposals are moderate in their length and level of detail. Exhibit 2–8 shows the research proposal that was submitted to Phil Samouel to help him improve his restaurant operations.

CONTINUING CASE   **RESEARCH PROPOSAL FOR SAMOUEL'S GREEK CUISINE RESTAURANT**

Statement of Problem

Phil Samouel, owner of Samouel's Greek Cuisine restaurant, believes his revenues and profits are not as high as they could be. He wants to find out how to attract more new customers, keep his current customers and convince customers to spend more when they come and to come back more often. He also wants to ensure he is operating his restaurant as effectively and efficiently as possible.

Phil is a successful manager and businessman, but he is fairly new to the restaurant business. He, therefore, has decided the best way to improve his business is to hire a restaurant consultant. Through a contact at his advertising agency, Phil identified a business research firm called AdMark International. He contacted them and asked for them to conduct a preliminary assessment of his restaurant operations and prepare a research proposal for him to review. The proposal is expected to include proposed projects, deliverables from the projects such as recommended strategies and action plans, as well as a schedule and budget. The outcome of this preliminary assessment is summarized below.

Research Questions

After discussions with Phil Samouel and several of his employees, the account manager from the research firm concluded that the primary questions facing Samouel's restaurant are:

- Are employees being managed to maximize their productivity as well as commitment to the success of the restaurant?
- What are the best approaches to attract new customers, and to keep and grow existing customers?

Research Approach

To answer these questions, two separate but related research projects are recommended. The first project will evaluate current employees to determine their productivity, job satisfaction and commitment. To do so, a survey of employees that has been used by a wide variety of organizations will be administered and tabulated. The second project will involve a survey of customers of Samouel's and his major competitor, Gino's Italian Ristorante.

Employee Assessment Project

The employee assessment project can be broken down into three researchable questions. They are:

1. How do employees feel about the work environment at Samouel's?

2. How committed are the employees to helping make the restaurant a success?

3. Do different groups of employees have different feelings about working at Samouel's?

The first research question concerns the work environment at Samouel's. Specific aspects of the work environment to be examined include: compensation, supervision, coworkers and overall satisfaction with the work at Samouel's. Phil Samouel believes he has good employees, but knows there is always room for improvement. Moreover, he has never specifically asked his employees how they feel about working at his restaurant, and he has hired a lot of new young workers in the past year (26 new workers between the ages of 18–34), many of whom are part time.

The second employee research question focuses on how committed the employees are to ensuring the success of Samouel's restaurant. From observing employees and listening to their comments, Phil believes the age and the length of time employees have worked at the restaurant may be related to commitment to the organization. Phil's consultant says that he has read some articles in trade publications suggesting this might be typical.

The third employee research question focuses on whether there are any differences among the employees regarding how they feel about working at Samouel's. Phil's observations of employees suggest this is true and his consultant says his informal discussions with employees would support this.

Customer Assessment Project

The customer assessment project can be broken down into three researchable questions. They are:

1. What is the level of satisfaction of Samouel's customers relative to the customers of its primary competitor, Gino's?

2. Do customers rate Gino's more favourably than they do Samouel's.

3. What factors contribute to restaurant customer satisfaction?

The first research question concerns the competitive positioning of Samouel's relative to Gino's. Phil Samouel's opinion is that Gino's has the advantage of being located in a more established residential area and that its longer history has resulted in a larger, more loyal customer base. In addition, Mr Samouel believes that Gino's is able to charge higher prices without sacrificing business. Since satisfied customers may be willing to reward the restaurant by paying higher prices, it is important to examine these issues.

The second research question addresses whether customers evaluate Samouel's and Gino's differently. Customers will be asked to rate the two restaurants on 12 attributes. The question, then, is do the ratings of the two restaurants differ significantly in ways that might influence satisfaction and loyalty? If the perceptions differ on critical selection variables then action plans can be developed to overcome and problems.

The third research question asks which factors determine customer satisfaction. Mr Samouel has expressed belief that satisfaction is determined mostly by food quality and the service of his employees. This belief is supported by a search of existing basic research reported in trade and academic journals. It has been documented that customers evaluate service industries in general based on two classes of attributes. Core attributes represent those that most directly provide the primary benefit sought by most customers. In the case of a restaurant, food-related attributes would qualify as a core attribute. Relational attributes represent those that are less tangible and deal with human-human and human-environment interactions. Customer perceptions of the environment and employees fall into this category for restaurants.

Several articles in restaurant trade publications reported this breakdown. They discussed the important of food quality, including the freshness and variety, and restaurant cleanliness as two key factors shaping customer's service quality perceptions (for example, see Klara, 1999; and Stern and Stern, 2000). Thus, when customer perceptions of food, employees and atmosphere improve, their satisfaction with the restaurant also should improve. The results of this survey will be very important in assessing Samuel's restaurant to identify strategies for improvement.

Methodology

Samples

Data must be collected to examine the issues posed above. Exit interviews as customers depart Gino's Italian Ristorante and Samouel's Greek Cuisine are proposed because this will be a good way to identify and interview Gino's customers. Interviews will be conducted between 12.00 and 2.00 pm and 7.00 to 10.00 pm, Monday to Saturday, for a period of ten days. Interviews during these hours will enable comparisons between lunch and dinner customers. They will be approached randomly and asked two screening questions. One, did they just dine in the restaurant? Two, have they completed the questionnaire before? A yes for the first question and a no for the second will prompt a request to participate in the survey. If customers agree, they will be provided with a clipboard containing the study questionnaire, a comfortable place to complete it and $5 for their participation. The goal will be to obtain at least 100 interviews with customers of each restaurant. An employee survey will also be conducted. An attempt will be made to interview as many employees as possible but not fewer than 60.

Measures

Measures for the study will be developed following interviews with Phillip Samouel and his management team, as well as from consulting previous industry research. The employee survey will have been previously validated and its reliability assessed. The survey will include questions about the working conditions, compensation, coworkers, supervision, commitment to the organization, likelihood to search for another job and classification variables such as age and gender. The customer survey will include perceptions of the food, atmosphere, prices, employees and so forth. Classification questions such as age and gender as well as relationship variables like satisfaction and future patronage will also be included.

Data Analysis Approach

After the data are collected, they will be analysed and summarized in an easy-to-understand format. The statistical software SPSS will be used to ensure the relevant issues are examined in a comprehensive and cost effective manner. Both simple as well as advanced statistical techniques will be used where appropriate. Usage of the statistical techniques will be according to commonly accepted research assumptions and practices.

Schedule and Budget

Schedule

The three projects are quite extensive. The initial operational assessment will take approximately two weeks. But it will not be in final form until information is collected and analysed for relevance from the employee and customer surveys. The employee survey will take approximately 30 days to complete. This will entail obtaining interviews from as many employees as possible, but no fewer than 50 % of the workforce at the restaurant, and representation from all management employees. The customer survey will take the longest time. To design the questionnaire, collect data, analyse and interpret the findings, will take approximately eight weeks. Preliminary findings of the other projects and updates will be given every two weeks. The final report, including recommendations, will be available ten weeks after the contract has been signed, and the initial payment has been received.

Budget

The total cost for the two projects is shown below:

• Employee Survey	£5,000
• Customer Survey	15,000
Total Cost	**£20,000**

Terms: 50 % will be due to initiate the project, and the balance is to be paid when the final report is submitted.

Qualifications

Consultants assigned to this project have a combined 35 years of experience in the restaurant industry. The principal investigator has completed projects with over 400 clients in the past 14 years. Biographical sketches of the research team assigned to this project are attached for your review.

Is theory useful in business research?

Phil Samouel has been discussing the restaurant with his brother. While the restaurant is successful, they have concluded there is room for improvement. By observing the dining area, Phil has noticed that there are often open tables. This led them to consider issues like how many tables are in the dining area and the number of customers, particularly at peak serving hours during lunch and dinner. They also spent some time with the head chef and learned that some entrees are selling quite well, but that the specials for the dinner meal are seldom as popular as anticipated. Moreover, the desserts are specially prepared Greek dishes from the old country, but are not selling very well.

Last week Phil was reading the *Financial Times*. It had a story on the large number of new restaurants that had opened in London in recent years. The story said there were so many new restaurants that many potential customers were not aware of a lot of them. Phil did some research on the Internet to learn more about how individuals find out about new restaurants and found the "Hierarchy of Effects" theory described below:

Hierarchy of Effects Model	
Hierarchy Stage	**Description**
• *Unawareness*	*Not aware of your company, brand, etc.*
• *Awareness*	*Aware of your brand.*
• *Knowledge*	*Know something about your brand.*
• *Liking*	*Have a positive feeling about your brand.*
• *Intention*	*Intend to buy your brand next.*
• *Purchase*	*Actually purchase your brand.*
• *Repurchase/Loyalty*	*Purchase your brand regularly.*

1. Could this theory be useful to Phil and his family in trying to increase the number of customers?

2. Could this theory help them to understand why some of the menu items are not selling well?

3. Are there some other theories you can think of that would be useful in improving the restaurant's operations?

4. Should qualitative, quantitative, or both kinds of research be conducted?

References

Klara, R. (1999), "Fast and Fancy," *Restaurant Business*, 98 (6/1), 19–21.

Stern, J. and Stern, M. (2000), "Familiarity Usually Breeds Regular Restaurant Customers," *Nation's Restaurant News*, 34 (11/20), 24–26.

SUMMARY

■ **Describe the phases of the business research process**

This chapter introduces the basic research process. Three phases are involved. Phase I translates the overall research issues into research questions and hypotheses. Theory plays a key role in translating information about some business situation into a researchable idea. Theory, business practices and intuition enable the research questions to be translated into hypotheses. A research design is then selected to test the hypotheses. Phase II, the Execution phase, is concerned with the activities that collect data, ensure the data are valid and reliable, and prepare them for analysis. Phase III, the Analytical phase, is where the data are analysed and interpreted relative to the hypotheses. Hypotheses are either supported or not supported based upon these results. Reports must be written and often presented to communicate research results.

■ Understand theory and how it is used in business research

The first half of the basic research business process is oriented toward discovery. There are few if any rules about discovery. The primary objective is to develop some ideas worthy of testing. Testing is the second half of the research process. There is only one way to test ideas. The idea must be compared with reality or expectations. This is known as empirical testing.

Theory is a set of systematically related statements that can be tested empirically. A specific theory is a proposed explanation for some event. Sometimes theories have been confirmed by past research. At other times theories are proposed with either limited or no validation.

Theories provide key inputs into the research process. Business theories explain and predict business phenomena. Decision makers want to know the likelihood that these explanations and predictions are accurate. Thus, theory helps shape the research questions and specific predictions are expressed in hypotheses. Research projects then validate or invalidate these predictions.

■ Explain how the scientific method improves business research

In many ways, the basic business research process follows the same methodology as the scientific method. The process starts by considering all relevant input. This input is combined with current knowledge to produce research questions or hypotheses. These are then tested in an analytical way. It is important to note that no recommendation is provided for the most acceptable way to discover ideas. However, ideas can only be supported or found false through testing. The scientific method provides a process for discovering and testing ideas.

■ Contrast the rigour of science with the pragmatics of business

The rigour of testing is what distinguishes the scientific method from business. Testing is highly critical and analytical. Testing is the way to develop conclusions, and conclusions enable us to expand knowledge and make more informed decisions. The rigour of science often is traded off against the pragmatics of business. Business people usually cannot get an answer too quickly. Researchers almost always sacrifice some rigour for expediency. While this may introduce error, as long as the decision maker is informed of this, and the results are qualified based on these shortcuts, the researcher should proceed with the project.

■ Understand the role and importance of research proposals

Before conducting a research project, business researchers must understand the problem to be investigated. Once the problem is defined, a plan of action is developed to investigate and make recommendations on how to solve the problem. A research proposal is a formal document summarizing what the problem is, how it will be investigated, how much it will cost and how long the research will take to complete. If accepted, it typically represents a contract between the researcher and the client. The research proposal plays a critical role in any research project by identifying and defining the problem to be investigated, the approach and methods the researcher will use, the deliverables from the project, and includes a budget and timeframe for completion. A formal written proposal is the result of interactions between the client and the researcher through which the client's problems are translated into research problems, and a proposed approach to solve the problem(s) is agreed upon.

Ethical Dilemma

Jean-Charles Chebat is an account manager for Burgoyne Research, Ltd. He tells customers that the firm recommends they begin by conducting a survey to benchmark customer perceptions before conducting any experiments to determine how customers would react to any new business decisions. Jean-Charles' assistant is aware that Burgoyne already has the information about public perceptions of a client from a recent survey conducted on behalf of this client's major competitor. Therefore, he feels Burgoyne should present the results of the other survey as secondary research to save the client money. When he mentions his concern to Jean-Charles, Jean-Charles says it is not unethical to conduct a new survey even if they know the probable results. Instead, he believes it would be more unethical to disclose the results of work conducted on behalf of another client.

Who do you agree with?

REVIEW QUESTIONS

1. What are the three phases of the basic business research process? Briefly explain each.
2. What role(s) does theory play in the basic business research process?
3. What is the scientific method and how is it used in business research?
4. What are the characteristics of good science?
5. Why is the preparation of a written research proposal important?

DISCUSSION AND APPLICATION ACTIVITIES

1. Suppose you work for a major consumer goods company. One of the products that you represent is salad dressing. A competitor is beginning a test market involving a new spicy ranch flavour. Their salespeople are going from store to store placing it on the shelves. Your boss asks you to go to these stores and buy all the salad dressing. Why might he or she ask you to do this? What would be your reaction? Consider the ethical implications of this behaviour.
2. What are normative decision rules? Are they theory? How can they be used by business researchers?
3. Why is theory important in the design of business research studies?

INTERNET EXERCISES   www

1. Use a Web-based search engine, such as Google or Yahoo, to find the following information:
   i The number of people employed in automobile manufacturing in the US, the UK, Germany and Japan.
   ii Basic demographic profiles for the following countries: Italy, France, Spain and the UK.

2. Visit this Web site: www.advisorteam.com/. Follow the first-time user instructions to take the Keirsey Temperament Sorter II. Which personality type do you belong to? Discuss the different types in class. What types of jobs would you recommend to someone with your personality type? What types of jobs would you not recommend to someone with your personality type?

NOTES

1. Hunt, S. (1983). *Marketing Theory: The Philosophy of Marketing Science*. Homewood, IL, Irwin.
2. Chamberlin, E. H. (1939). *The Theory of Monopolistic Competition*. Cambridge, MA, Harvard University Press.
3. Lewin, C. (1948). *Resolving Conflicts and Field Theory in Social Science*. New York, Harper & Row.
4. Dickson, Peter R. (1992). "Toward a General Theory of Competitive Rationality", *Journal of Marketing*, 56 (January), 69–83. Hunt, S. D. and Morgan, R. M. (1996), "The Resource-Advantage Theory of Competition: Dynamis, Path Dependencies, and Evolutionary Dimensions", *Journal of Marketing*, 60 (October), 107–14. Hunt, S. D. and Morgan, R. M. (1997), "Resource-Advantage Theory: A Snake Swallowing Its Tail or a General Theory of Competition", *Journal of Marketing*, 61 (October), 74–83.
5. Caulkin, S. (2002). "Management: A Mess in Theory, A Mess in Practice", *Observer*, (13 January), 9.
6. Remington, L. (2002). "Arizona Firms Return to More Conservative Dress", *Tribune*, Mesa, Arizona (8 February).

CHAPTER 3
ETHICS IN BUSINESS RESEARCH

CONTENTS

LEARNING OUTCOMES

- Define business ethics and discuss its relevance to research.
- Understand the ethical obligations of business researchers.
- Understand the ethical obligations of business decision makers.
- Understand the ethical obligations of business research participants.
- Describe the potential consequences of unethical actions.
- Appreciate the challenges of gaining access to respondents.

INTRODUCTION

Business ethics is a growing field. Events such as the Ahold, Enron, Parmalat and WorldCom scandals attracted attention toward abuses of power and authority in the business world and created a demand for more ''ethical'' business people. This, in turn, has created a greater emphasis on the formal study of business ethics. In this chapter we define what business ethics is and explain its importance to business and society. We then explain ethics from three different perspectives – business researchers, business decision makers and participants in business research. We conclude the chapter with a discussion of gaining access to participants and convincing them to participate in research studies. The ethical issues of gaining cooperation and participation for respondents are discussed as well.

BUSINESS ETHICS DEFINED

Trust is an overriding issue in business ethics. If all parties involved in exchange could truly trust one another fully, there would be no need for any oversight of the exchange process. Where trust is lacking, some codified standards need to be enforced. At a simple level, there are professional codes of ethics that govern behaviour. For example, two principal aims of the British Market Research Association (BMRA) are to increase professionalism and promote confidence in market research. In part, this is achieved by requiring that all members ensure the execution, data collection and data processing responsibilities are met through following appropriate procedures and methods.

Stronger replacements for trust include rules, laws and regulations. Most of us would like to believe that employers can be trusted to take adequate measures to ensure employee's safety. However, the number and severity of worker injuries around the world questions this trust and results in the imposition of laws through numerous legislative processes. National and supra-national bodies such as the European Agency for Safety and Health at Work have been established to determine and monitor standards of occupational safety and health (OSH). Although OSH legislation results in inspections that are sometimes seen as a nuisance, they also help protect workers and reduce costs resulting from industrial injuries, compensation claims and the like. Estimates within the European Union are that a work-related accident occurs every five seconds and that one worker dies every two hours, so costs can be significant.

Business ethics, as a field of study, addresses the application of moral principles and/or ethical standards to human actions within the exchange process. Moral principles imply responsibility. Thus, the judgement of right or wrong ethical business actions involves an evaluation of actions against the responsibilities that accompany a business position. Like other business people, business researchers have social, market, legal and ethical responsibilities.[1] **Social responsibilities** involve a concern for the way actions affect society or groups of people including employees, customers and the community. **Market responsibility** means a concern for making sure that products are produced that consumers actually need and that the prices charged for these products are fair. Business researchers and business decision makers are concerned with all these responsibilities in the performance of their jobs. Consider the relevance of business ethics to university students based on the behaviour reported in the Research in Action section.

RESEARCH IN ACTION

ARE THE "BRIGHTEST AND THE BEST" THE MOST ETHICAL?

How ethical are university business students? Several international studies of ethical ideologies of business students have been conducted. Some have been country specific while others have undertaken cross-cultural comparisons. Numerous studies find that managers place more importance on ethical issues than students do. Experienced business people report lower tolerance of unethical behaviour than business students. Additionally, male students report higher tolerance of unethical behaviour than female students. Evidence has also been presented to show that taking ethics courses seems not to affect respondents' ethical results. Business schools and universities need to find new ways of making students more aware of the consequences of unethical behaviour so that they become less "relativistic" in their perception of right and wrong. More disconcertingly for business schools, a recent cross-cultural study finds that the time spent studying business does not seem to have had any positive impact on the ethical awareness of students and, in some samples, studying business appears to have had a negative impact on perceiving ethical problems.

How do the ethical standards of university students impact business research?

What can be done to improve the ethical awareness of students?

Sources: Axinn, C. N., Blair, M. E., Heorhiadi, A. and Thach, S. V. (2004). "Comparing Ethical Ideologies Across Cultures", *Journal of Business Ethics*, 54, 103–19. Ahmed, M. M., Chung, K. Y. and Eichenseher, J. W. (2003). "Business Students' Perception of Ethics and Moral Judgment: A Cross-Cultural Study", *Journal of Business Ethics*, 43, 89–102. Cole, B. C. and Smith, D. L. (1995). "Effects of Ethics Instruction on the Ethical Perceptions of College Business Students", *Journal of Education for Business*, 70 (July/August), 351–57. Varherr, P. H. Petrick, J. A., Quinn, J. F. and Brady, T. J. (1995). "The Impact of Gender and Major on Ethical Perceptions of Business Students: Management Implications for the Accounting Profession", *Journal of Academy of Business Administration*, 1 (Spring), 46–50. Singhapakdi, A. and Vitell, S. J. (1994). "Ethical Ideologies of Future Marketeers: The Relative Influences of Machiavellianism and Gender", *Journal of Marketing Education*, Spring, 34–42. ■

RELEVANCE OF BUSINESS ETHICS

Business ethics is relevant to business researchers because ethical issues occur through many phases of the research process. Ethical dilemmas are situations when a person is faced with courses of action that have differing ethical implications. For example, a business researcher may be placed in a situation in which two major competitors have both asked for similar research projects. Several dilemmas occur. For example, the researcher could take both jobs and use proprietary information to help make recommendations for each company. Alternatively, the researcher could use research paid for by one client as a basis for the recommendations of another.

Ethical dilemmas arise from questions of fairness/justice, potential conflicts of interest, responsibility issues, power discrepancies and honesty issues. All of these can occur in business research situations. Such dilemmas require sound ethical judgements. Ethical judgements ultimately involve an assessment of the fairness and justness of some course of action. Note that an ethical judgement is sometimes distinct from a contractual or legal obligation.[2]

Exhibit 3-1 helps demonstrate how various organizational, professional and individual elements provide pressures and conflicts that produce ethical dilemmas. However, organizational, professional and individual elements also provide check-points that counter motivations toward unethical actions. In the end, these three groups of elements help balance business decision making.

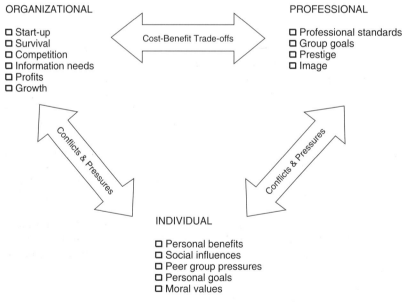

Adapted from: Rolph Anderson, (1991). *Professional Personal Selling*, Englewood Cliffs, NJ, Prentice Hall, 71. Reproduced by permission of Rolph Anderson.

EXHIBIT 3-1

Ethical Balance between Individual, Professional and Organizational Values

This balance can be illustrated with a research example. An organization may be motivated to take advantage of a data collection opportunity. Perhaps this would involve collecting information in a way that violated the rights of research respondents, such as disclosing personal information (discussed later in this chapter). Or perhaps, they might ask a researcher to provide contact information from research respondents to be used as sales prospects. While a strict interpretation of the organizational motivation of profit may suggest these actions could be carried out, neither would be ethical from a research perspective. Researchers are guided by a professional code of conduct which should stop them from willingly participating in unethical and misrepresentative data collection. Further, individual moral values often come into play and help motivate a more ethical decision. A researcher's own personal value system may prohibit participation in unethical action.

ETHICAL OBLIGATIONS OF THE RESEARCHER

Business researchers are faced with ethical considerations and possible ethical dilemmas throughout a research project. They involve researchers' dealings with management, respondents and their own professional integrity. Here we focus on the ethical considerations between the person requesting the research (the manager or decision maker) and the person doing the research, before, during and after the project.

BEFORE THE RESEARCH PROJECT

The period just prior to the initiation of a research project is perhaps the most critical point in the entire research process. During this time, the researcher must interview key decision makers to gain a working knowledge of the situation. The researcher acquires an understanding of the project objectives during these interviews. The key here is to translate a decision issue into a researchable proposition. Once a study is envisioned, researchers need to honestly assess their capabilities, and if they lack the skills or resources to carry out the project, they should decline it. Also, if researchers are unable to reach a consensus on the primary research questions, they should probe more or not accept the job.

Researchers must communicate exactly what the research will be able to do. This typically is referred to as project deliverables. In other words, they must be certain the project will be able to address the research questions. The deliverables are listed in the research proposal for the client to review and approve. The research project should begin only when the researcher and the research client are in agreement on the deliverables.

Decision makers and researchers both should realize that sometimes the best decision is not to do any research at all. The following questions can be useful in addressing this key issue. If several of these questions lack answers, perhaps the research should be postponed. Before beginning a research project, the decision maker should ask:

- What information do I need that is now unavailable?

- How could I use that information?

- What will it cost to get this information and how long will it take?

- Does the potential benefit exceed the cost?

- Do my competitors have the information? If so, how is this affecting their performance?
- What aspects of my current business situation do I not understand?

RESEARCH IN ACTION

POINTS TO PONDER WHEN CONSIDERING WHETHER TO DO RESEARCH

Researchers are sometimes faced with potentially conflicting interests. For example, suppose a researcher is retained by the UK retailer, Tesco Stores, to complete an exhaustive study of online shoppers' beliefs and sensitivities to various Web site characteristics. The project is very expensive and time consuming, but enables Tesco to more effectively penetrate electronic retailing segments through an improved electronic interface. After completing the study, the researcher is approached by Sainsburys for a research project that would help them better design their Web site for online consumers. Bear in mind that Tesco has paid the bill for this research and according to generally accepted research industry standards they ''own'' any data collected. The researcher is presented with several choices: (1) accept the job and use the data collected for Tesco Stores to help make recommendations based on ''experience''; (2) accept the job, and prepare a new report using the Tesco data; (3) accept the job and conduct a new study addressing the same research questions as in the Tesco study using the same methodology; (4) decline the job.

Only the last choice completely avoids a conflict of interest. One and two are clearly unfair as the researcher would essentially be ''stealing'' information purchased by Tesco Stores to sell to Sainsburys at maximum benefit to the researcher. Option three presents a possibility. However, should either client find out about the other study, the researcher's credibility may be harmed. ■

DURING AND AFTER THE RESEARCH

The Relationship between Researcher and Decision Maker

The researcher has a moral obligation to have a thorough working knowledge of the analytical and statistical tools necessary to complete the project. Researchers should not apply a technique unless they can do so competently and confidently. Researchers are sometimes tempted to apply a more complex tool than is needed in an effort to seem more sophisticated or perhaps even to increase the perceived worth of the research. But only the right tool should be used. This is usually the simplest tool that will provide the necessary results.

The researcher is responsible for interpreting the results honestly and fully. Researchers may have an opinion about the research questions being examined, or they may have a good idea of the research outcome that management desires. But if the results disagree with a key decision maker's desires the researcher faces a dilemma. In the late 1980s, R. J. Reynolds (RJR) invested over 300 million US dollars into Premier Cigarettes, an innovative "smokeless" tobacco.[3] At the time, F. Ross Johnson was RJR's CEO. He was a tough, aggressive, no-nonsense leader who was very enthusiastic about Premier.[4] The initial concept test results were generally positive. Consumers, both smokers and nonsmokers alike, were favourable toward the concept of a smokeless cigarette. Thus, RJR researchers enthusiastically presented these results. Further tests, using actual Premier cigarettes produced in small quantities, provided some good and some bad results. Among the discoveries was that a Premier cigarette emitted a very familiar but very undesirable odour when lit with a match. Couple this with the fact that one's taste is tied closely to smell, and the recipe is disastrous for any product consumed by mouth. Researchers presented these smell and taste results with less enthusiasm than they did the fact that nonsmokers were favourable toward the idea of Premier Cigarettes. In the end, Premier Cigarettes were introduced to the market despite these results. The point of this story is that the researcher is obligated to present the results fully and faithfully, even if the decision maker may not want to hear the results.

The researcher generally presents results both through a formal written report and a presentation. The presentation may be formal or informal. Chapter 15 discusses both the report and presentation in more detail. In presenting the findings, the researcher has an obligation to present any limitations of the research. By acknowledging and fully communicating any limitations, the decision maker has a more complete understanding of how much the results should affect the ultimate decision.

Researcher Obligations to Participants

Researchers should serve as advocates for research participants. Without their participation, the researcher might well be without a job. The researcher should show respect to participants at all times. For example, the researcher should describe the nature and extent of participation required. If a survey requires knowledge about computer basics, the researcher should make this clear in the opening instructions. It is also essential that the researcher provide a fair estimate of the amount of time that will be required to complete the research task.

Researcher Participant Relationship – Ethics and Technology

Many technological breakthroughs like those discussed in Chapter 1 benefit researchers tremendously. This benefit does not come without a cost. These new technologies also introduce new ethical dilemmas.

Technology increases the possibility that a research participant's privacy might be violated. Much of the information collected and stored in data warehouses is done so with the promise that it will not be shared with others beyond those individuals directly involved with the research. Researchers have a duty to safeguard the privacy of this information. Personal data should not be shared with outside agencies in any form in which it could be traced back to an individual respondent. Research participant lists should not be sold to other companies to be mined for potential customers. Likewise, considerable employee and/or corporate financial data are equally sensitive. The appropriate safeguards such as electronic firewalls should be in place to prohibit unauthorized access to this information. Additionally, technology improves the researchers' ability to monitor a research participant's behaviour. The researcher must exercise caution with respect to using such monitoring for purposes that would reach beyond the scope of the specific research project.

"CLICK & TELL?" PUBLIC OUTRAGE AT POTENTIAL INFORMATION PRODUCTS

Information has emerged as the hottest commodity on the Web. The more detailed it is, the more valuable it is to firms targeting a specific audience. These data can be cross-referenced with information from other businesses such as credit bureaus, retail stores and insurers. The information bundle can then be sold. DoubleClick, the largest advertisement placement firm on the Internet, found itself in the midst of a privacy controversy. It planned to link Internet users' personal information to an offline direct marketing database without consumers' permission. Although the same type of data has been collected by individual businesses for decades, DoubleClick drew public criticism from every privacy organization, and it became the target of several privacy violation lawsuits.

Knowing your customers is, of course, key in any business. But as a business researcher, you must also remember that consumer uneasiness about how gathered information is managed and sold is at an all-time high. According to one poll, 59 % of online household heads "strongly distrust companies' ability or intention to keep personal information confidential, regardless of the policies the companies have in place". Therefore businesses need to be extremely cautious when predicting how consumers will react to potential invasions of privacy.

To avoid the privacy issues, online and off, businesses need to respect customers' private information. And before trying to collect data needed to target consumers, companies should first establish trust. DoubleClick learned this the hard way. Not only did the company suspend its efforts to link online and offline databases: it created a chief privacy officer position to monitor internal and external privacy and to help develop an industry-wide privacy standard.

Sources: Elizabeth Crane, "Double Trouble", Ziff Davis Smart Business for the New Economy, October 2000, p. 62, http://www.doubleclick.com/us/, and "DoubleClick able to settle privacy suits", http://news.com.com/2100-1023-919895.html, accessed June 2006. ∎

Researcher-Participant Relationship – Ethical Dimensions of Experimental Designs

Researchers have an obligation to treat any participants in a research project ethically. The following ethical issues are always important but they become especially relevant during research studies:

- Coercing participation.
- Potential physical or psychological harm.
- Privacy.
- Informing subjects of the nature of the research.

Coercion   Subjects should not be forced to participate in a research study. Researchers often provide a modest incentive for participation. Should a potential subject choose not to participate, he/she would forego the incentive. Generally, this is relatively inconsequential. The small incentives involve money, merchandise, time off in lieu, or a few points of credit depending upon the type of person and research involved. Volunteer participants in the famous "Pepsi Challenge" received a free six-pack of the beverage they thought tasted the best. Researchers may feel obligated to find an appropriate compensation for the volunteer's time and effort. As in many areas of ethics, the line between incentive and coercion is not always clear. The incentive should never be of the type that a subject's current well being would be significantly damaged by choosing not to participate. For example, docking an employee's wages for not participating in some experiment is something beyond a mere incentive. Undue social pressure could represent coercion as well. Likewise, if a professor threatened to withhold a student's grade at the end of a term due to refusal to participate in an experiment the student would rightly feel coerced into participation.

In research studies, it may be impractical to gain 'permission' from participants. Practically every reader of this book has been a test market participant within the past few months without even knowing it. For example, test market participants are all consumers who enter into a shop where a new product test is being conducted. If you visit a supermarket, you have been subjected to a test market. In most of these cases, the experiment has such a trivial effect on any participant that there is very little possibility that someone's current well being has been harmed. In such cases, the obligation to ask permission is not needed.

Freedom from Harm   Research study participants have a general right to be protected from undue physical or psychological harm. Subjects stand the potential to be harmed even in business research studies. It might be rather obvious that potential harm may occur if a researcher studied job performance using three levels of nicotine or some other drug.

Unfortunately, the potential harm isn't always that clear. For example, you might be surprised to learn that business researchers often study odours! A researcher may wish to perform an odour study that related scents/smells to employee alertness. This may be useful for understanding whether or not certain physical job environments should be impregnated with the scents artificially. A research study could be conducted by changing the scent in a room in which a task will be accomplished. Is there potential for harm? Perhaps! It's possible that a subject may have a severe allergic reaction to one of the scents. So, before conducting such an experiment, the researcher should question subjects about potential allergies in a way that does not alert them to the study's purpose. The reason the questioning should be done carefully is because if you first ask people about allergies to various scents (like flowers, peanuts, etc.), then they encounter the scent, they are very likely to guess the study's objectives. The result is a problem that could invalidate any results.

It might also be possible to devise a study where a participant is put under undue stress. For example, if a researcher was asked to study the effect of stress on job performance, the researcher may allow participants to take different amounts of time to complete a task, and then observe if performance differs based on the amount of time taken. Another design may involve changing the punishment for a poor performance. Poor performance could be punished by informing subjects that the 15 % lowest performers in the task would: (1) have to work weekends for extra training; (2) have their pay cut; or (3) be fired. Even if the study could benefit the company a lot, do any of these levels exceed the threshold of acceptable stress?

Sometimes the harm isn't physical at all. For example, a researcher may wish to study the effect of confidence on ability to choose successful stocks. A research participant might be given a strategy to use in choosing stocks and then the performance outcome is alternated. That is, for the same strategy either the performance is always high or always low. For one group, the strategy would always work because the researcher would determine the outcome. For the other group, the strategy would never work. Is the subject harmed?

Once again, there isn't always a clear line between the ethical and unethical. But, here are two questions that can serve as a useful guide:

Is it impossible to restore the subject to his/her original condition?

Has the subject been exposed to unreasonable stress or risk without his/her knowledge?

If the answer to either of these questions is yes, the researcher should not proceed with the design. In the case of the fake stock market exercise, if the subject can be returned to his/her normal state before the study is finished, then no ethical breach has occurred. If the participants leave the study with a false impression of their ability to play the stock market (in either direction), however, then they have been harmed.

Privacy   Research participants have a right to privacy. Any research results should be used only for the intended purpose. Individual responses should be held in strict confidence unless some other prior agreement is arranged. When possible, participants should be able to remain anonymous. Not only is this the more ethical approach, but it also protects the research from bias due to any socially desirable response patterns that might emerge.

Under no circumstances should a research project be used as a cover for some other purpose. On occasion, dishonest sellers may recruit 'research' participants via the telephone, email or in person. Participation in the project is only a ploy used to try and sell something at the end of the project or to add the participant to a prospect list. This practice is unethical from both a business and a research viewpoint. Research efforts should be clearly distinguished from direct marketing or selling and vice versa. Researchers should never act as sales agents in any capacity. If the client wishes to add a sales appeal, the researcher should refuse to do the project.

Similarly, "push polls" are sometimes used in political campaigns. **Push polls** are short phone calls used to spread negative and often false information about a candidate or issue under the guise of a poll. The interview is usually less than one minute and does contain some opinion questions. However, the entire effort is designed to produce a known outcome through the information provided and the manner in which the questions are asked. Selling under the guise of research and push polling clearly represent blatant and avoidable dishonesty.

Disclosure   Researchers conducting most kinds of survey research have no reason to hide the research purpose. Thus, the instructions will generally provide a statement of the research's purpose. This statement should be as specific as necessary to enable the respondent to understand it. Some surveys, however, may present quite a different picture than standard survey research.

Some research studies involve deception by their very nature. Often, the researcher cannot disclose information about the purpose of the study. For example, in the hypothetical stock market experiment discussed previously, if the researcher revealed ahead of time that the study would be providing false outcomes from hypothetical stock purchases there would be little point in conducting the study. In other words, complete disclosure would influence the results.

Many of you have probably heard of a placebo. A **placebo** is a false treatment. In a medical experiment testing a drug's effectiveness on, for example, weight loss, the drug might be administered intravenously in one of three ways: high dosage, low dosage and no dosage (the placebo, which is often saline). All participants, even the placebo group, get an injection. Quite often, the placebo group also will show some effect. In fact, research subjects (patients) being treated for depression with a placebo sometimes show improvement equal to or better than that experienced by subjects treated by the leading prescription anti-depressants. However, participants clearly cannot be told that they are in a placebo condition because then they would realize they were not actually receiving the experimental drug. As can be seen, the psychological effects can be strong and could confound any effect shown by the true treatment.

RESEARCH IN ACTION

ELECTRIC SHOCK AND THE "RIGGED TRIAL"

Imagine you are watching a research subject taking part in an experiment examining the effect of punishment on learning. You observe a job "trainee" receiving specific instructions on how to perform a relatively simple job. Afterwards, the subject begins to perform the task. Each time the subject makes a mistake, a research assistant presses a button which gives the subject an electric shock, which you are told increases slightly each time, but which remains at a level that is safe, although perhaps uncomfortable. The trainee's job improvement initially improves. However, after about a dozen shocks, the trainee is obviously disturbed and greatly fears the possibility of another shock. His/her hand is trembling noticeably. Learning appears to be regressing not progressing. Are there ethical implications with this research?

Now, suppose the researcher left the room and came to you, the observer, and offered you a chance to take the trainee's place. You are told that the previous person has become ineffective and a replacement is needed for the experiment to proceed. Would you help?

Or, suppose you were told that the researcher assistant had to leave the room and asks you to become "the teacher". Would you cooperate and shock the trainee for incorrect responses? Would these changes affect the ethics of the experiment?

Finally, suppose you are told that the experiment is over and that in reality, the trainee was only pretending to experience pain. In actuality, no shocks were administered. Indeed, the key dependent variable was your behaviour. For example, did you agree to take the place of one of the participants? Or, how long did it take before you expressed concern for the poor trainee? How does this change the ethics of the experiment?

For a more detailed description of this type of methodology, see Baron (1977), Human Aggression. ∎

Thus, it may be impossible to fully inform potential research subjects prior to or during an actual research study. They should be provided with a general description of the study's events and provided with enough information so they can make an informed decision about participation. But participants should be given a full explanation of the research study once their participation is complete. This allows participants to be restored to their original condition.

Debriefing   Debriefing takes place after an experimental session is complete and involves revealing the true purpose of the experiment, the sponsor of the experiment and generally a question and answer session. Not only are all questions answered, but the researcher normally uses this as an opportunity to assess demand characteristics. Thus, debriefing is not only an ethical thing to do, but it is very practical as well. Finally, subjects should be offered a summary of results should they so desire.

Human Resource Review Committee   Research organizations sometimes form a human resources (sometimes known as human subjects) review committee to review all research designs using human participants. The committee should check research procedures to make sure all participants are treated ethically. Research universities routinely perform such reviews prior to providing support for university sponsored research.

Countries around the world often require that a thorough human resource review be undertaken when seeking government grant money. This particularly applies to organizations such as the European Union. Interested readers may wish to review the standards for ethics in research produced by the European Commission.[5] As illustration, the US federal government acted to withhold money from John Hopkins University researchers based on what was perceived as a poorly contrived human resource review. This action was motivated by the death of a research subject participating voluntarily in university sponsored research. The death resulted when a subject was given a medication that was not approved for use in humans. It caused a fatal toxic reaction in the victim's lungs. A government review ruled that even a cursory investigation of the drug would have revealed that it was a) not approved and b) potentially dangerous.[6]

Although business research is often much safer than medical research, businesses should nonetheless have a high degree of concern for the welfare of participants. Companies in general, and research firms in particular, should consider the benefits of a human resource review committee in favourably balancing ethical dilemmas. Given recent corporate scandals, perhaps the role should be expanded beyond that of research participants to consider the ethical consequences of business decisions on customers and employees.

ETHICAL OBLIGATIONS OF THE DECISION MAKER

Ethics typically is not a one-way street, and the researcher/decision maker relationship is no exception. The decision maker has several important ethical obligations that if breached diminish the quality and usefulness of the entire decision making process.

BEFORE THE RESEARCH

The decision maker should participate fully and openly with the researcher. It is absolutely essential that the decision maker and researcher come to a consensus on the research objectives. Generally, when both parties agree on the research questions involved, consensus is reached. Consensus on research questions becomes a key part of the research proposal, as do the research objectives. If consensus cannot be reached, the research proposal should not be approved. Furthermore, if a researcher is denied access to some piece of information that is crucial in performing the research, the researcher's obligation is reduced.

The decision maker ultimately sets the time frame and budget for the project. But researchers generally make initial requests for time and money and the two meet somewhere in the middle. However, the researcher should communicate and the decision maker should accept the fact that limitations may reduce the quality of the research project correspondingly.

Additionally, the decision maker has an obligation to develop an understanding of the researcher and the research project. This understanding doesn't require that decision makers become researchers, but it does mean they should know enough about research to ask intelligent questions. If not, the decision maker should include someone else in the discussion who understands the nature of research projects.

DURING AND AFTER THE RESEARCH

The decision maker has an obligation to give genuine consideration to the research results. That is, the research shouldn't be commissioned simply to be able to show that it was done. If decision makers have already truly made up their mind on the key issue prior to the research project, they should not request that the project be done. The researcher is placed in an awkward position when the results conflict with the decision maker's desires. It also is a waste of the researcher's time and the company's money.

Furthermore, there is an issue that is especially of interest to any potential researchers. The decision maker has an obligation to pay the researcher fully and on time. If the researcher successfully completes the project described in the research proposal, they should be paid regardless of the results. For instance, a property developer once requested a study of the traffic patterns and market potential for several different potential residential development sites. He agreed upon a proposal with a researcher who conducted the study and presented the results. However, the results did not indicate that the land had the value that the developer envisioned. The developer became quite upset and ended up paying the researcher only half of the agreed upon price and only after some months had passed. Likewise, an in-house researcher should not face repercussions if the results of a project are well thought out, but undesirable. Exhibit 3-2 summarizes some of the ethical dimensions of business research.

ETHICAL OBLIGATIONS OF THE RESEARCH PARTICIPANTS

Participants in research also have obligations. Although it is difficult to control participation, the researcher should be aware of issues of wilful and faithful participation as well as the need for participants to respond honestly and respect research privacy when asked to do so prior to their participation.

WILFUL PARTICIPATION

Researcher participants should decline the opportunity to participate if they have any doubt about whether they possess sufficient motivation to go through with the study. Most studies do not require a great deal of effort. After agreeing to participate, a respondent/subject should cooperate fully. This

Researcher	Decision Maker
■ Maintain scientific rigour	■ Educate oneself (be able to understand researcher)
■ Confidentiality (avoid involvement in research with a competitor)	■ Establish budget
■ Search for truth (do not try to confirm desires)	■ Give due consideration to the results of the research
■ Arrive at a consensus "reason" for the research	■ Arrive at a consensus "reason" for the research
■ Admit research limitations including those resulting from budget and time constraints	■ Have realistic expectations
■ Present results understandably	■ Pay on time

EXHIBIT 3-2

Ethical Dimensions of the Business Researcher – Decision-Maker Relationship

also means that participants should answer any screening questions honestly. Screening questions are preliminary questions that qualify participants as valid sample members. For example, a researcher studying aspects of retail employment may wish to develop a sample of people with recent retail experience. A participant may be tempted to admit to some experience if he/she believes there is a desirable incentive for participation. This type of behaviour will lead to response error since the participant lacks the necessary qualifications.

FAITHFUL PARTICIPATION

Participants should follow the research instructions to the best of their ability. On occasion, a participant may grow weary and begin responding without being fully attentive. Occasionally a response form may contain unusual numbers of "neutral" or "back and forth" (or ping-pong pattern) responses. If mindless responses are more random, they may be difficult to detect and create more response error. The researcher is better off with no response than with a nonsense response.

The participant should pay attention and follow instructions. These instructions may contain important information pertaining to the appropriate sequence of items or the perspective that the respondent should take. Sometimes, the sequence is contingent upon a previous response. Also, the researcher may ask the respondent to respond with something other than his/her own view. In ethics research, a researcher may ask a sales manager participating in research how a typical salesperson would respond in a given ethical dilemma. Again, the failure to follow instructions could create error that could harm the results.

HONESTY

It goes without saying that a participant should be honest. On occasion however, a respondent may have some ulterior motive. A participant may try to respond in a fashion that will produce a desirable outcome. For instance, an employer might commission an opinion survey asking unit managers whether or not small units should be closed. A manager might be torn between giving his/her honest responses about the viability of these units and a response that will help ensure that his/her job is not threatened. Participants should refuse to take part in research if they are hesitant to answer questions honestly.

PRIVACY

Researchers may sometimes request that a participant not discuss details of procedures with anyone else for a specified time. There could be many reasons for such a request. The researcher may have legitimate concerns about corporate espionage. If savvy competitors know what a company is studying, they may be able to make an educated guess about its strategy or tactics. In experiments, the researcher may not want an earlier subject to contaminate later subjects. A subject that reveals too much may increase the demand characteristics since the subjects may be able to guess what factors are being manipulated. Therefore, experimental instructions or debriefing may often include a statement requesting those who have completed the task not to inform others about the details of the study.

IMPLICATIONS OF UNETHICAL ACTIONS

It is very easy for students of business to be lulled into a false sense of security that is derived from a belief that the ethical implications from business decisions are less serious than those associated with other disciplines such as medicine or engineering. However, this view is misguided. Businesses provide value. They provide value for customers, shareholders, employees and for society at large. A breach of responsibility by one party can very seriously affect the value equation in a way that harms others.

A breakdown in responsibility during the research process usually means that business decisions will be based on untrustworthy information. For example, a company president who commissions research investigating implications associated with three strategic acquisitions might request research simply to appease the Board of Directors. That is, the company chief executive officer (CEO) may already know which strategy will be implemented based on a strong personal preference. The actual research may strongly suggest that the second strategy has the most positive effect on key business outcomes and thereby conflict with the CEO who has a preference for the third strategy. Worse yet, the CEO could ask the researcher to present results in a way that make his/her choice, namely the third strategy, seem most attractive. By enacting the strategy nonetheless, the CEO increases the likelihood that strategic decisions will not lead to the best outcome.

Such actions could be bad for customers, employees, shareholders and for society more broadly. The implications for customers might mean obtaining a less than most desirable product. This could have dire consequences in the case of potentially hazardous or health-related products. Employees may end up working in conditions that are not as good as they might be had the research been followed. For shareholders, a lower long-term return might result. So, customers may be harmed, particularly for products with direct health and safety implications. Shareholders may find their portfolios become stagnant or decline. Employees may face long periods with no pay raises or even suspension from their regular job duties.

The impacts on each or all of the above three stakeholders may also have a "ripple effect" that has an unnecessary and negative impact on broader society. Business decision makers should be ever mindful that the lives of families of employees, customers, shareholders and communities are affected significantly by the quality of the decisions made. Likewise, since researchers provide input into these decisions, they share in this responsibility. Thus, ethics should be taken very seriously. Unethical decisions usually cause harm to at least one of the parties involved in business exchange, as described in the Research in Action box below.

RESEARCH IN ACTION

ESTABLISHING INTERNATIONAL RESEARCH STANDARDS

Today, successful business research depends upon public confidence that it is carried out honestly and objectively, and that it respects the impact it may have on respondents. This confidence is best achieved by the adherence of researchers to appropriate professional codes of practice.

The International Chamber of Commerce and ESOMAR recognized this as early as 1977 when they combined forces to publish a single international code of practice. Significant revisions have followed in response to the changing nature of business research methods and to the significant increases in international activities of many practitioners. This resulted in a new document being published in 1994 that sets out basic ethical and business principles governing business and social research practice. The code addresses research aspects that relate to the general public as well as to the business community specifically in its 29 clauses, and it specifically stresses the need for professionals to follow both the letter and spirit of the document.

Log on to the Web site shown below. Are the provisions of this document sufficient to meet today's needs for business researchers?

Source: ICC/ESOMAR (2005), "International Code of Marketing and Social Research Practice", www.esomar.org, accessed February 2006. ∎

Ethics in decision making does not always mean the company chief executive officer should act consistently with the research. However, it does mean that the researcher should only undertake research that will provide information considered in the decision-making process. Other issues may sometimes be more persuasive than the research, and these issues may include experience and intuition.

Researchers should also be mindful of protecting their own integrity, the moral image of their company and the image of their discipline. Recently, public perceptions of questionable behaviours committed by auditors overseeing the financial reporting of Enron, Inc. have seriously damaged the reputation of the individual auditors, their employer, Arthur Anderson, Inc. and the accounting industry overall.[7] Similarly, accusations were made against auditors Price Waterhouse when the Bank of Credit and Commerce International (BCCI) collapsed and against Deloitte & Touche following the Barings bankruptcy. Thus, unethical actions of a small number of researchers can severely damage the industry overall.

One simple guide for business researchers and researchers generally, when considering ethical issues, is to always act as though your actions will be public. This guideline is based on the assumption that your superiors, family and friends will all know what you have done. This emphasizes the role played by one's conscience in shaping moral behaviour.

An **ethics checklist** can also be useful. This is a list of questions that can be useful in guiding decision making. Researchers and decision makers may consider the following questions useful in ensuring an ethical decision-making climate:

- Will the actions taken harm this institution?
- Will the actions taken harm individuals, including coworkers, clients, research participants or customers?
- Will the information involved be misused by others?
- Will the actions taken harm my discipline, company or industry?
- Will the actions taken do harm to the personal integrity of researchers and/or decision makers?
- Will the actions taken harm society at large?

ACCESS TO RESPONDENTS: STRATEGIES AND TACTICS

The purpose of collecting data is to answer research questions. Therefore the key to successful business research is to obtain relevant data to address the questions. Without data business research cannot develop solutions.

Access to data sources is critical, whether one is conducting secondary or primary research, or both. When the research design is selected, attention must be given to strategies and tactics for gaining access to respondents so the data can actually be collected from the data sources identified. By following appropriate strategies and tactics, reliable and valid data can be obtained to address the research questions. Finally, the issue of research ethics, discussed earlier in this chapter, cannot be overlooked.

ISSUES IN OBTAINING ACCESS

Business research is dependent on the cooperation of individuals and the willingness of the organization to participate in providing data pertinent to the research. Thus, it is incumbent upon the researcher to ensure that the research design for data collection minimizes obstacles that may hinder access.

Developing a strategy for access should be both pragmatic and systematic. To achieve this requirement some considerations are listed below:

1. The nature of the research question and research paradigm adopted.

2. The source(s) from which data are required.

3. Gaining access to the source.

4. A plan for collecting data.

The impact of the research question and research paradigm on obtaining access to respondents is illustrated through the two examples described in Exhibit 3-3

Example #1

The research question was concerned with strategic orientation, executive values and organizational performance in the UK. The objective was to obtain cooperation of knowledgeable individuals who were managers/executives of large organizations.

Issues to be considered:

- Is the research concerned with a single organization or a cross-section of organizations?
- Is the research within a single industrial sector or across sectors?
- Which data are already available and which need to be collected?
- Will the views of the CEO suffice, or is input needed from other executives.
- Will the data be collected by means of face-to-face interviews, computer-assisted interviews, telephone, postal or Internet-delivered questionnaires.
- Timing of data collection may be very important.
- Number of participants required, length of time to complete the interview, and number of times participants must be interviewed can all impact access.

Example #2

The research question was concerned with business-to-business relationships and the relational norms or supportive norms that help with the trading exchange. Responses were needed from both trading partners, for example both the supplier and the buyer.

Issues to be considered:

- Identifying the bilateral relationship – franchisor and franchisee; OEM and manufac- turers; banks and corporate client; brewers and public houses etc.
- Identifying key respondents – from both trading partners.
- Obtaining views of both sides of a business relationship.

EXHIBIT 3-3

Issues Associated with Obtaining Access to Respondents

The following illustrates how some of the issues can be resolved in developing a strategy for access to respondents in Example #1 in Exhibit 3-3.

- If the study requires the views of the CEO or Managing Director, as in this situation, access to such individuals is difficult. Intermediaries may facilitate an introduction, but it can still be a challenge. Therefore, identifying "gatekeepers" may be a critical component of your access strategy. Developing a relationship with the gatekeeper can be helpful in obtaining their support to encourage and remind the respondent to cooperate. But if this is not possible, then consider shipping the questionnaire via overnight delivery. When this is done the gatekeeper will place it on the respondent's desk in a prominent location and the respondent will believe it is truly important to respond.

- Sometimes researchers find it difficult to contact organizations directly. On such occasions the researchers may use intermediaries such as trade associations, the Institute of Directors, management research companies, management consultants, or university research centres.

The following illustrates how some of the issues can be resolved in developing a strategy for access to respondents in Example #2 in Exhibit 3-3.

- Access to both sides of the bilateral exchange may be achieved by firstly identifying the principal trading partner. This individual can in turn identify and provide an introduction to the main account holders in the bilateral exchange. Ethical considerations become paramount here. For example, confidentiality of information provided rests with the researcher.

- Timing considerations may be important. In the case of the brewer-public house exchange, access to the publican is very difficult during trading hours. Thus, if a face-to-face or telephone survey is used to gather the data, then the best time is outside trading hours, e.g. before opening 11.00 a.m. or after closing at 11.00 p.m. In both cases this is rather inconvenient for both the respondent and researcher. Thus, although the brewers may have given permission the publican may be unwilling to cooperate.

The best plan for access to data collection may not materialize due to unforeseen circumstances. In the case of the brewery and public house study, commitment was given to cooperate in the research by a consortium of brewers who approved access to their tied public houses. Change in government policy just prior to commencement of data collection, however, resulted in the Brewer consortium reneging on the undertaking. Therefore, alternative backup or contingency strategies should be anticipated in the initial planning stages. In this case the Yellow Pages provided a listing of potential public houses and after considerable time and effort the study was completed.

BARRIERS TO ACCESS

There are some generic obstacles to accessing key sources for data. These include:

- The opportunity of direct access to key informants.
- The research questions have little appeal.
- The sensitive nature of the research questions.
- The credibility and perceived value of the research.

- The confidence in the researcher's ability to articulate in a clear manner the purpose and sponsorship of the research.

- The overall impression formed of the researcher, including physical appearance, trustworthiness, not intrusive and non-threatening etc.

These obstacles need to be anticipated and planned for in any operational approach for gaining entry to an individual or organization. A key consideration in developing the plan is to factor in ample time. For example, the extent of time required is dependent on the level of access required. It is likely there will be several interactions before the relevant informant has been identified and the individual or organization has agreed to participate by providing data. Gaining access may therefore take 2–3 months or longer, so start this process early.

The operational plan must incorporate tactics to assist in gaining access. Tactics for gaining access are dependent upon the approach taken, which can be direct or indirect. The approach used will have a significant impact on the willingness of individuals or organizations to participate.

A direct approach could be mailing a questionnaire accompanied by a cover letter, or through a direct telephone call or email. An indirect approach involves the use of intermediaries to arrange an introduction, or even to help with the data collection.

To encourage access and participation, a letter or presentation could address the following issues:

- The purpose of the research.

- The nature of the access desired.

- The usefulness of the findings.

- The manner in which sensitivity and confidentiality are dealt with.

- The credentials and affiliation of the researcher.

- The benefits to individual or organization, which could be in the form of a report of the results or even assistance with an in-house project or some other inducement.

Throughout the process of gaining access a researcher needs to adhere to the highest ethical standards. This extends to delivering on the promises made, particularly with regard to privacy and minimization of negative reactions by respondents to research topics.

Different methods of data collection involve different approaches to contacting potential respondents. If the method of data collection is a self-completion postal questionnaire, overnight delivery or similar technique, then a properly developed covering letter is very important. Exhibit 3-4 provides a good example of a covering letter that has enjoyed success in previous studies conducted by the authors. For telephone or Internet studies, and some types of personal interviews, a covering letter is sent to potential respondents before the questionnaire is sent.

It is impossible to develop a standardized appeal or covering letter that will be effective with all types of survey situations. There are, however, guidelines that provide direction in communicating with potential respondents, whether through a covering letter, a telephone contact, a personal interview, or a request for cooperation in an Internet-based survey. Exhibit 3-5 lists the factors and a general description of how to use them to obtain higher respondent cooperation.

Henley Management College
Henley-on-Thames, Oxfordshire, UK

1 May 2007

Name
Address of Individual
City, Country, etc.

Hello,

You are one of a select group of people who, within the past two years, purchased a Weber outdoor barbecue.

My name is Dr Arthur Money and I am a Business Professor at Henley Management College, UK. I have been retained by Floyds Group, Ltd to collect information that will help you and other customers be served better.

I am writing to ask for your help with this study. Please know that:

- We are not trying to sell you anything. We just want your opinions.
- Your answers will be reported in combination with others and **will not** be associated with your name, address, or other personal identifying information.
- We **do not** sell personal information or opinions to third parties.

The survey is easy to complete and will take about 15 minutes of your time. Please have the person who was most involved with the purchase of your new Weber outdoor barbecue complete the survey and return it in the reply paid envelope.

As a token of our appreciation, when we receive your completed questionnaire we will notify your local B&Q dealer to credit your account with **£50.00** towards your next purchase of barbecue accessory products.

In addition, to solicit early participation, each response postmarked by **15 December** will be entered into a drawing whereby two (2) customers will be awarded a **£1,000 coupon** towards your next purchase of outdoor barbecue and furniture products.

We appreciate the invaluable role you are playing in this study and thank you for your time and input. If you have any questions, please call me at +44 (0) 1491 418989.

Sincerely,

Arthur Money, PhD

EXHIBIT 3-4

Sample Covering Letter to Gain Participant Cooperation

Factors	Description
Personalization	Email or written contacts with respondents should be addressed to the specific respondent and be on either the research firm's stationery or that of a well-known and respected organization. Personally signed communications from the individual conducting the research also are helpful.
Identify the organization doing the study	Identify the name of the research firm or university conducting the study. The actual sponsor of the study may be disguised or revealed, depending on its potential impact on the study's findings.
Establish credibility	Different appeals work with different audiences. If the researcher is a professor with a prestigious university this can be a positive attribute and showing their name and title in the communication can be helpful. A well-known organization affiliated with the study can also help.
Clearly identify study's importance and purpose	Describe the general nature of the research and emphasize its importance to the respondent. Explain how the respondent was chosen and stress the importance of their input in the study's success.
Anonymity and confidentiality	Provide assurance that the respondent's name or identifying information will not be revealed or shared with any other groups.
Time frame for completing the study	Indicate how long the study will last and when the questionnaire is due. Do not say "Can we have a few moments of your time to…" as it is easy to say "No" to such a request.
Reinforce importance of respondent's participation	Where appropriate, communicate the importance of the respondent's participation in the study. Clearly explain and emphasize who is to complete the questionnaire and why.
Time requirements and compensation	Tell respondent the approximate time required to complete the questionnaire and point out incentives.
Completion date and where and how to return the questionnaire or get answers to questions	Provide clear and complete instructions for returning the completed questionnaire and who to contact if questions arise.
Advance thank you for willingness to participate	Thank the respondent for his or her cooperation.

Source: Adapted from Hair, J. F., Bush, R. and Ortinau, D. (2006). *Marketing Research*. New York, McGraw-Hill, Inc., 3rd edition. Reproduced with permission of McGraw-Hill, Companies. All rights reserved.

EXHIBIT 3-5

Guidelines for Obtaining Respondent Cooperation

CONTINUING CASE   SAMOUEL'S GREEK CUISINE

The account manager from the research firm recommended two separate but related research projects to provide information to Phil Samouel on what could be done to improve the restaurant. Recall from the proposal outlined in Chapter 2 that the objective of the first project is to evaluate current employees to determine their productivity, job satisfaction, and commitment to the restaurant. Topics to obtain information on included: compensation, supervision, coworkers, loyalty, understanding of their job responsibilities, and likelihood to search for another job in the next year. The second project involves collecting information from customers of Samouel's restaurant and his major competitor, Gino's Italian Ristorante. Possible topics to collect information on included: prices, food quality, employees, satisfaction and so forth.

1. Are there any ethical considerations that need to be explored with the employee survey?

2. What about the customer survey?

3. If yes, what are the considerations and how should they be dealt with?

4. Should Phil develop a code of ethics for his restaurant? What about an ethics checklist?

SUMMARY

■ **Define business ethics and discuss it's relevance to research**

Business ethics is defined as the application of moral principles and/or ethical standards to human actions within the exchange process. The ethical dimensions of the relationships between researcher and decision maker and between researcher and participant were discussed. All have important duties before, during and after the research. Above all, researchers and decision makers should behave as professionals. Being professional means working with the knowledge that your actions affect other people's lives. Therefore, research should be done with great care and as much precision as the time and economic budget allow. Above all, effective communication is a key to minimizing conflict between researchers and decision makers.

■ **Understand the ethical obligations of business researchers**

Business researchers have several important ethical obligations. They should strive to communicate effectively and develop a consensus reason for the research among all the key actors involved.

Researchers should also use the right tool for the job, which means avoiding overly complex research tools. Researchers should decline a job for which they lack expertise. They should also take great care to treat research participants fairly. The chapter discusses key aspects of this and includes a list of useful questions concerning the fair treatment of research participants. Human resource committees can provide useful reviews that ensure the research addresses each question in an ethical way. Researchers should strive to communicate simply and clearly. Reports and presentations should be prepared with the level of sophistication of the audience in mind. Finally, researchers should clearly communicate all research limitations.

■ **Understand the ethical obligations of business decision makers**

Decision makers also have important ethical obligations. These involve the treatment of researchers, other employees, consumers and the public in general. Decision makers should also work to establish a consensus reason for doing research. They should not order research without the intention of seriously considering it when making decisions. Decision makers cannot hold the researcher responsible in any way for results that may be considered undesirable.

■ **Understand the ethical obligations of business research participants**

Research participants can also negatively influence business decision making. Unethical participant actions can lead to response error, which in turn, could lead to poor decision making. Research participants should participate wilfully or decline the opportunity to participate. This means they should follow the research instructions faithfully and give the task the level of involvement required. Participants should provide honest responses and not seek to respond in a manner that seeks to bias the results and thereby affect any eventual decisions. Also, participants should respect the confidentiality of the research project if requested by the researcher.

■ **Describe the potential consequences of unethical actions**

Finally, researchers and decision makers should be mindful of the direct and indirect effects of unethical actions. The quality of decision making is affected by the integrity of the research. If decisions are made that serve to do something other than accomplish socially legitimate business goals, someone is likely to be harmed. Those potentially harmed include: employees, consumers, society, the institution and the discipline or industry.

■ **Appreciate the challenges of gaining access to respondents**

Access to data sources is critical whether one is conducting secondary or primary research, or both. When the research design is selected, attention must be given to strategies and tactics for gaining access to respondents so the data can actually be collected from the data sources identified. Business research is dependent on the cooperation of individuals and the willingness of the organization to participate in providing data pertinent to the research. Thus, it is incumbent upon the researcher to ensure that the research design for data collection minimizes obstacles that may hinder access. Developing a strategy for access should be both pragmatic and systematic. To achieve this requirement some considerations include: the nature of the research questions and research paradigm adopted, the source(s) from which data is required, gaining access to the source and cooperation, and having a plan for collecting the data.

Ethical Dilemma

Mr Ralf Sanders owns a data imaging firm with over 100 employees in the main office. Ralf commissions a study of the organizational culture within his company. The researcher suggests that employees may not respond accurately to a structured questionnaire because of the sensitivity of some of the topics. Instead, he suggests recording the conversations of employees in the company lunchroom using hidden microphones. The resulting conversations could be analysed using content analysis software. This would reveal key themes around which organizational culture may be structured. Should Mr Sanders agree to this approach for collecting information? Why or why not? If not, what changes can be made to the proposed research design to make it more ethically acceptable?

REVIEW QUESTIONS

1. Define business ethics.

2. What things take the place of trust in the exchange process?

3. What is an ethical dilemma? List at least three ways one can occur in the business decision-making process.

4. What are four important considerations that should be given to research participants?

5. What is a human resource review committee? What benefits does it provide?

6. What does it mean for a decision maker to give "due consideration" to business research results?

DISCUSSION AND APPLICATION ACTIVITIES

1. Several recent studies raise questions about student integrity, such as discussed in the Research in Action box entitled "Are the brightest and the best the most ethical". Do you believe there is a relationship between the ethical behaviour exhibited by a university student and the ethical behaviour he/she will exhibit in the business world? Prepare a one-page position statement that either agrees or disagrees with the statement that "unethical university students will make unethical business people".

2. How might the balancing act depicted in Exhibit 3-1 help ensure that human resources are not treated unfairly even if there are a few employees of questionable moral character involved in decision making?

3. Find information on a current event that questions the ethics of some business. Could researchers have played a role in preventing this event?

4. What steps do you believe business researchers should take to ensure that research participants fulfil their ethical obligations in the research process?

INTERNET EXERCISES   W W W

1. Go to http://europa.eu.int/comm/research/science-society/home_en.cfm. This Web site presents the European Commission perspective on research including a European Charter for Researchers and perspectives on ethics in research. What elements of the European Commission's perspectives on ethics in research do you consider most pertinent to broadly-based business research?

2. Go to http://www.qrca.org/default.asp. Comment on codes of ethics and practices of the Qualitative Research Consultants Association. How closely do you feel the perspectives presented for this association conform to the ideas presented in the chapter? What other points, if any, does the association emphasize that you believe add value to your understanding of ethics in business research? In which of the aspects they present do you feel training can be employed to improve the quality of decision making? Which areas do you feel are harder to develop through training interventions and must be controlled by legal means?

NOTES

1. Ferrell, O.C. and Fraedrich, J. (1997). *Business Ethics*. Boston, MA, Houghton Mifflin.
2. Robin, D. P., Reidenbach, E. R. and Babin, B. J. (1997). "Ethical Judgments", *Psychological Review*.
3. McNath, R. M. (2002). "Smokeless Isn't Smoking", *American Demographics*, 18 (October), 60.
4. Saporito, B. (1988). "The Tough Cookie at RJR Nabisco", *Fortune*, 118(2), 32–41.
5. Evers, K. (2004). "Standards for Ethics in Research", *Codes of Conduct*. Luxembourg, Office for Official Publications of the European Communities.
6. Begley, S., Donna, F. and Rogers, A. (2001). "Dying for Science", *Newsweek*, 138(7/30), 36.
7. Brown, K. and Jonathon, W. (2002). "When Enron Auditors Were on a Tear", *Wall Street Journal*, 239 (3/21), C1.

CHAPTER 4
DEFINING THE RESEARCH PROBLEM AND REVIEWING THE LITERATURE

CONTENTS

LEARNING OUTCOMES

- Identify the characteristics of a quality research topic.
- Describe how to convert research ideas to research questions.
- Understand what a literature review is and how it helps your research.
- Identify the major sources for a literature search.
- Explain how to plan and write a literature review.
- Confirm research questions with the literature review.

INTRODUCTION

To a significant extent, success in any research endeavour begins with a clear definition of the research problem. While this may seem obvious, defining the research problem is often the most difficult part of the research process to execute properly. Researchers should avoid adopting a laissez-faire approach at this early stage because a poorly defined problem results in lack of direction and purpose that may only become apparent after considerable time, effort and money have been spent pursuing nonproductive avenues elsewhere in the scope of work. For example, a poorly defined research problem can be the major cause of an incorrectly structured field study that does not deliver the data required.

Once research problems are initially identified, researchers undertake background research to refine further the definition of the problem and to ensure that past work has been considered in clarifying the scope of the proposed research project. The background research, often referred to as a literature review, provides the basis for converting research problems to research questions and objectives. In this chapter we first discuss selecting good research problems. Then we cover converting research ideas to questions and objectives. Next we explain how to plan and conduct background research (literature review), and we end with an overview of how to write a literature review.

CHARACTERISTICS OF A QUALITY RESEARCH TOPIC

When undertaking commissioned research, the research brief often represents the primary means used by the sponsor to communicate his or her initial perception of the research problems or questions. The **research brief** is an overview of the sponsor's (company or individual) initial perceptions of the problem or opportunity and may be written or presented orally. The proposal prepared in response by the researcher provides his or her diagnosis and understanding of the problem previously summarized by the sponsor. Dialogue between the two parties (researcher and sponsor) prior to finally signing off on the research is obviously vital in ensuring that a common understanding exists. Focusing this dialogue on the problem definition rather than too quickly turning to methodology may be the best way of achieving the clarity and accuracy of purpose necessary for a successful outcome.

Whether or not the research is commissioned by a third party, defining the research problem can be remarkably time-consuming and needs to be specified in both general and specific terms. What is the broad nature of the problem that needs to be addressed by the research activities? What are the specific components of the problem that need to be examined? Experienced researchers iterate through these questions many times to achieve the clarity of purpose considered necessary for success. They recognize that time devoted to problem definition prevents misunderstanding and avoids errors. It also produces better research questions and objectives, better research design and, ultimately, better execution.

Research topics are identified and examined by businesses to understand problems and/or opportunities better, and to develop the best solutions. Similarly, research topics are identified and pursued for academic purposes when students are in research master or doctoral level programmes. Whether developed for academic or business purposes, good research topics exhibit numerous characteristics in common. These are presented in Exhibit 4-1 and discussed in some depth below.

- The research is developed from a sound theoretical base.

- The research is of interest to both the sponsor and the researcher.

- The research problem is well defined and the research questions and objectives that flow from it are specific and possible to address through a rigorous research design.

- Resource requirements in terms of time, finance and data access are well understood early in the research process.

- The research is expected to make a contribution to knowledge independently of the orientation of the findings. This characteristic is particularly important for academic theses and dissertations.

EXHIBIT 4-1

Characteristics of a Quality Research Topic

First amongst these is that the topic should be developed from a sound theoretical base. Topics that are informed by theory have a clearer overall purpose, method and expected outcome. This ensures that well-informed and rigorous decisions flow from the research. Theory places the research topic within the context of a broader field of business and enables both the sponsor and the researcher to benefit from prior work in the field, enhance the quality of the research project, and limit the resources needed to achieve the research objectives.

Theoretical underpinnings of research projects are particularly important when the research is undertaken as part of an academic thesis or dissertation. Not only is scanning the literature a necessary step in ensuring that the topic meets the requirements of the examiners, but it also helps confirm your interest in the broader field of study. Although a lot has been written about the importance of selecting a research topic that can sustain your interest for the entire duration of the project, an underlying objective of your thesis (or dissertation) must be to help confirm your career choice and improve your employability in the field you have selected. Your thesis is an important part of this process.

The second characteristic relates to the importance of the topic to the research sponsor. Greater commitment by the sponsor increases his or her engagement from an early stage and reduces the potential for conflict as the process continues. This is obviously important when carrying out research for commercial purposes. The sponsor plays a role not only by specifying the objectives of the research and approving the scope, commitment and understanding, but ensures that the inevitable unknowns that arise during the research process can be discussed in an honest and open fashion. This increases the likelihood that the researcher will be able to make decisions deemed necessary in a mutually supportive environment.

While academic research topics may not have an obvious external sponsor, the research supervisor can be viewed in this light. The supervisor guides the research and provides support when problems arise. He or she also understands the requirements for success with regard to the theoretical background, the primary data requirements and the depth of analysis required. For instance, some degrees may require that the thesis investigate a "real business problem" and gather new primary data, while others find a less applied approach acceptable with little or no primary data collection required. Obviously, the greater the supervisor's interest in the topic, the more he or she will commit to the process and the greater will be the time and energy provided. No matter how passionate you may feel about a thesis topic, success is significantly enhanced if your supervisor shares this passion.

The third element of the research topic relates to how the problem is defined, the quality of the research questions, and the way the objectives of the research have been articulated. Defining the problem requires that the sponsor focus on the decisions that need to be made once the research is completed. This ensures the research design addresses gaps in the knowledge base necessary to make these decisions and, as such, helps in developing questions and setting objectives. **Quality research topics** are those that address gaps in existing knowledge that currently inhibit informed decision making. Consequently, well stated research questions focus on the organization and/or personal objectives of the research sponsor.

Once questions have been established and full agreement exists between the sponsor and the researcher, the questions need to be converted into explicit research objectives. Ultimately, the research design is built around achieving specific research objectives and, not surprisingly, quality research projects that deliver on their promise and have explicit, focused and well-articulated objectives.

Objective setting represents a significant challenge for researchers undertaking research activities on behalf of others. It is common for research sponsors to find it difficult to set clear objectives for the research. Sponsors with limited research experience tend to state their desires in general terms and it is up to the researcher to convert these desires into objectives that are of operational importance and that make the scope of the research more explicit.

The fourth characteristic of research topics concerns the resource requirements necessary to achieve the desired outcome. These resources include knowledge, time, finance and access to needed data. No matter how worthy the initial problem is of research, little will be achieved if the researcher lacks the ability to investigate the topic properly. Researchers who are skilled in quantitative research using closed-ended and well structured questionnaires often do not have the skills or temperament to undertake qualitative research based upon focus group research and in-depth interviews. Before accepting a research commission, researchers need to examine honestly their existing skill sets and their capacity to develop the knowledge and approaches necessary.

While the importance of this may be obvious for commercial research, students undertaking research projects should reflect carefully upon their own capacities when selecting their topics. The time and financial resources necessary to complete research projects vary widely. Some topics may lend themselves to a much higher proportion of desk research while others might require extensive travel to interview key stakeholders. A rigorous assessment of the time and finances required to complete a research project should be made as early as possible in the research process. For commissioned research this is necessitated by the need to quote a research budget. But students must also reflect on these points to reduce the possibility that they cannot meet deadlines set by the university or college, or that the scope of the topic needs to be scaled down because of unexpected cost over-runs and time required.

Data accessibility also should never be taken for granted. Early in the research process researchers need to confirm they can gain access to the required data as promises made and assumptions about secondary data availability may not be justified. As an example, accounting data for micro-businesses is generally far more difficult to access than may seem apparent from the taxation obligations these organizations have in common with their larger and Stock Exchange-listed counterparts. Recall that we discussed data accessibility earlier in Chapter 3.

Finally, an important characteristic of a research topic particularly relevant for academic purposes is that it should produce a valuable outcome independent of the orientation of the findings. In other words, research projects that form part of the requirements for a degree or qualification should be worth submitting whether or not the research questions are confirmed. This capacity greatly reduces the probability that months of effort must be discarded because the final outcome of the research does not make the necessary scholarly contribution to knowledge. It is important that students anticipate possible outcomes and the research value under various scenarios before spending too much effort pursuing the research topic.

The Research in Action box poses the question of whether the particular situation is a quality research topic as well as whether research will be useful in a particular situation.

RESEARCH IN ACTION

WHAT KIND OF RESEARCH IS NECESSARY?

One Stop is a convenience store business with over 500 neighbourhood shops throughout England and Wales, employing over 6,000 staff. Until recently, the retailer outsourced its financial management system for the management of general operations and financial accounting, back ups, recoveries, disaster recovery, hardware maintenance of the Unix operating system and its Oracle database. With the contract up for renewal, One Stop decided to look at alternative solutions for its financial management system and the possibility of bringing its financial business processes in-house.

Do you consider this a quality research topic? Could research be useful in deciding about outsourcing financial management functions, or bringing them in-house?

Source: http://www.hoovers.com accessed June 2006. ∎

CONVERTING RESEARCH IDEAS TO RESEARCH QUESTIONS AND OBJECTIVES

Research ideas may be generated by the researcher or provided by the sponsor in the form of a business problem around which an informed decision needs to be made. When the researcher rather than sponsor is expected to come up with the idea as part of an examination or performance requirement, a variety of approaches can be adopted to generate the initial idea and refine it into a research problem worthy of investigation. When the idea is provided by somebody else, such as the sponsor in commissioned research projects, the researcher still must refine the idea by transforming it into explicit questions and objectives.

Research ideas that do not flow immediately from a business problem that requires investigation may often be clarified by questioning senior researchers, executives and decision makers about problems they face, by examining published research in fields of interest, or by examining past research projects that may suggest areas worthy of subsequent investigation.

Discussions with individuals who are either experienced researchers or individuals who frequently use research to inform their own decision making can provide an interesting insight and suggest opportunities for further research. Experienced researchers are well aware of the fact that most research projects, no matter how successfully implemented, can be an interesting source of new questions. Research conducted to test one or more specific hypotheses can lead researchers to reflect upon new hypotheses and questions. Similarly, commissioned research designed to support a specific management decision results in action by the decision maker that can lead to further decision requirements and other research opportunities. Dialogue with experienced researchers and decision makers offers considerable opportunity to develop research ideas that are grounded in prior empirical work and therefore have a high probability of being based on appropriate research processes.

Published literature is a further source of research ideas. Textbooks and academic and professional articles are interesting sources of research ideas. Academic articles are probably the best source of "new thinking" and research ideas generated from them are likely to be topical and of value because they will naturally reflect current research trends. Professional articles may offer less explicit insight into research ideas, but they definitely increase the probability that ideas are of practical significance and that they are considered important by the business community.

Although textbooks may seem an obvious source of ideas for individuals new to research, they should be used with some caution if their publication date has long passed. Most textbooks used by students and executives contain research ideas that have already been published elsewhere and are somewhat outdated as sources of new ideas. Business and community reports occupy a position somewhat between articles and textbooks. Their content is usually considerably fresher than that contained in textbooks but they generally occupy a space closer to applied or professional articles than they do to peer reviewed academic articles.

The capacity to extract vast numbers of articles at the click of a computer mouse means the need for focus prior to beginning a literature scan to establish a worthwhile research objective has become increasingly important. Personal motivation and excitement about a particular field of study should inform the initial focus when scanning the literature.

A final external source of research ideas is past empirical research of both a professional and academic nature. The nature of research is that it raises new questions at the same time as it answers others. Areas for further research are often mentioned quite explicitly in the conclusions of most academic research papers and, if not explicitly, often implicitly in research that has been commissioned for professional or business purposes.

Once a suitable research idea has been identified, the researcher needs to narrow down the topic to produce research questions that can be answered through the application of appropriate research techniques as well as clear, succinct objective statements. Initial discussions, literature searches and reviews of past research can help develop great research ideas but research success requires that these broad ideas be further refined and developed.

Before attempting to refine the idea, researches should convince themselves that the topic is of personal interest. This is particularly important when the underlying objective of the research is to obtain a qualification. Feeling passionate about an initial research idea is important, but insufficient until the researcher has a better grasp of the likely avenue the research can take, as the idea is transformed into a set of specific questions to be answered. Research ideas generated by employers of post-experience students or by organizations that offer student placements are often far broader than desirable for a research topic. This can be fortunate because it provides the opportunity to scale back an idea provided by someone else into a topic of specific interest to the student. For example, a prospective employer might suggest that you investigate how to increase organizational commitment and thereby enhance service quality amongst front line staff of the organization. Such a topic is unlikely to be achievable as a single piece of research but does contain elements that might have considerable appeal to you and are of sufficient scope to meet your study requirements. These might include: (1) an investigation into the level of organizational commitment amongst employees;[1,2] (2) an investigation into the antecedents of service quality proposed by prior researchers and how they manifest themselves in the company,[3,4] or; (3) measuring the various dimensions of service quality and the service quality gaps.[5,6] Each of these ideas is likely to be sufficient for an in-company research project and each could be considered a necessary first step to addressing the overall topic originating from the prospective employer.

Exploratory work undertaken while developing the idea should be extended through more robust questioning and an examination of the literature. A preliminary study might even be considered to help in this regard. The study may be restricted to further desk research or it may involve some initial field work. Whatever the approach, the work must be done comprehensively enough to address the areas mentioned in Exhibit 4-1 as being important for a quality research topic.

While it can be debated as to whether research questions precede or follow from research objectives, both are crucial components that help focus the research idea and produce the specificity necessary for the project plan. The *Concise Oxford English Dictionary* (eleventh edition) suggests that the word "objective" has two interpretations as a noun. The first is "a goal or aim" while the second is "the lens in a telescope or microscope nearest to the object observed". Both interpretations can be usefully considered when seeking to convert initial ideas into research questions and objectives. Each objective needs to state explicitly what the goal or aim of the research, or a particular element of it, is. As such the researcher needs to reflect on the desired outcome very closely when stating objectives. He or she needs to project to the desired end-point of the research. Objective statements can also be viewed as the starting point of rigorous research in that they demonstrate the potential legitimacy of the research project in far stronger terms than a statement of the research idea can. Experienced researchers can assess the feasibility of a stated research objective precisely because of its specificity. This is far more difficult to do when presented with a more general statement of an idea.

Research questions can range from a broad interest statement such as "How do corporate incentive systems work?" to "What is the relationship between executive stock options and corporate performance?" Clearly, the first of these questions does not meet the requirements of specificity. It provides no focus to a research topic examining incentive systems and it is of no help in developing research objectives or a research agenda to explore the relationship between incentive systems and corporate performance. The second question does achieve this goal and it is therefore appropriate as a research question.

Developing appropriate research questions is not easy because they need to occupy the space between what is considered too easy and probably not worthy of research in the first place and what is considered too complex to guide the research design and execution plan. Easy questions tend to be those that require descriptive answers such as "What is the average term of employment of staff?" and "What are the sick leave statistics for the company?" While both questions may be relevant to an investigation into organizational commitment, they are insufficient for the task, in that all they require is a descriptive answer or bar chart. A more appropriate set of research questions would be: "To what extent does organizational commitment correlate with incidents of sick leave?" and "Does length of service influence this relationship in any way?"

Developing research questions and objectives can be made easier by continually referring back to your background research. Keep in mind that research questions ultimately inform the exact plan of execution. The questions you ask when undertaking field work, the data you compile from secondary sources and the method of analysis you intend to follow are all extensively informed by the questions you have set. We discuss preparing your literature review and converting research questions to research objectives in more detail later in this chapter.

RESEARCH IN ACTION   **CASH, CREDIT CARD OR DEBIT CARD?**

Developed countries have used some form of money for more than 3,000 years. But with new technology customers are increasingly migrating to digital money payment systems. Cheque usage has fallen to its lowest level ever in many European countries and even credit cards are being used less. Moreover, online billing, Internet banking and other forms of digital transactions are replacing traditional payment methods. In Japan, "proximity payment" methods such as PDAs (personal digital assistants) and mobile phones are often waved in front of a reader at fastfood restaurants, vending machines, petrol stations, cinemas and shops, and similar purchasing situations. Indeed, trading shares and betting at the horse races are becoming commonplace digital transactions.

Customers are quickly and easily embracing the digital payment systems, particularly younger people. But the spread of digital transactions is slow because merchants and retailers must adopt the system, which requires the purchase of expensive new technology.

What is the research problem? How would you conduct a literature review to learn more about obstacles slowing the adoption of digital payment systems? What key words would you try in your search?

Source: "Time runs short for cash as electronic money grows", *The Business*, www.thebusinessonline.com, 30 April 2006, p. 8, http://www.virtualschool.edu and http://www.digitalmoneyforum.com/, accessed June 2006. ∎

THE ROLE OF THEORY IN RESEARCH

The importance of theory when undertaking research cannot be overstated because it provides the essential foundation upon which quality research is built. This applies whether the research is being undertaken as part of an academic thesis or for a commercial client. It is quite likely that most readers of this textbook have heard someone comment: "Oh, that is far too theoretical and it has no relevance to the real world!" This is usually the statement of an individual who does not fully understand what theory is, or the statement of an individual trying to justify a weak argument or personal bias through using anecdotal observation.

Theory can be viewed as a conceptual model based on foundational statements that are presumed to be true. A theory postulates a relationship between two or more variables under certain environmental conditions. In other words theory provides the informed framework for analysis by suggesting relationships or causalities that may be worthy of investigation and that have the potential for generalization to a larger population. Researchers must avoid the trap of considering theory as somehow the opposite end of a continuum from practice and recognize the truth in the often-quoted adage that "there is nothing as practical as a good theory". Equally, practitioners need to realize that their decisions are often based upon some internalized theory that they are just incapable of making conscious. As Keynes stated as long ago as 1953, "practical men, who believe themselves to be quite exempt from any intellectual influences are usually the slaves of some defunct economist."

Developing a research project with a sound theoretical footing offers numerous benefits. Firstly, reviewing theory helps you refine your measurement constructs, particularly when you need to measure complex variables like commitment, loyalty and quality. Secondly, theory provides justification for relationships you wish to investigate and it suggests causality that helps orient a research project. For instance, an experimental design that seeks to examine the strength of the relationship between two variables of interest may be far more robustly constructed if theory suggests which variable is causal. Equally, theory may suggest that there is a third variable in the relationship. Leaving the third variable unmeasured might greatly reduce the potential of the research to confirm the relationship between the two variables initially of interest.

As long as the purpose of the research extends beyond pure intelligence gathering,[7] as is usually the case, it involves some form of theoretical reflection. Research seeking to demonstrate cause-effect relationships, such as "if x then y", presume some underlying theoretical relationship between the cause, or independent variable, and the effect, or dependent variable. Providing conceptual definitions for the variables of interest may be considered part of the theoretical construction and a vital first step in developing operational definitions of the variables that are amenable to measurement and observation in practice. This can be done directly or through the use of appropriate indicators. As an example, while an operational definition of performance can be established when investigating the causal relationship between incentive systems (independent variables) and performance (dependent variable), performance needs to be measured using indicators such as revenues, profits and share price appreciation.

Just as theory is necessary to inform the overall research topic, it also provides structure and the rationale for converting research questions into hypotheses or statements that can be tested with empirical data and found to be probably true or probably false. In this sense, theory may be viewed as explaining the why of a research plan while hypotheses provide the means to answer the questions that arise from the why.

RESEARCH IN ACTION — CRAIGSLIST: COMPETITION FOR NEWSPAPER CLASSIFIEDS?

Craig Newmark set up a list of local Web listings in his garage in San Francisco in 1995. Since then his business model has spawned offshoots in 175 cities across 35 countries and has generated traffic that matches Amazon – a staggering 2.5 billion page views per month. This development has left newspaper executives reeling, and saying "The List is not bad news; it's terrible news". By taking away classified advertising, the business model cuts at the heart of newspaper profitability. CraigsList is doing about 6,000 pages a month in London and that's without consciously trying to work the market. In the UK, where the press enjoys about 40 % of all advertising spend, the vulnerability to this new advertising phenomenon is substantial.

The model of free advertising competes so fundamentally with how most newspapers have structured their businesses that it's hard to see a clear path for the two to coexist. The basic problem: these ads are free and newspaper ads are expensive. These ads are available 24/7 and can be updated and tweaked with all the beauty of digital publishing; newspapers can never be. These ads reach people around the corner and around the world; print is still anchored in one place. And these ads are in the medium that a whole new generation calls home. Newspapers that simply take the defensive strategy of putting their ads online are not even scratching the surface of what this is about. In a nutshell, CraigsList is the collision of the new economy and traditional business models.

If you were a newspaper executive, what kind of research would you undertake to prepare yourself for this kind of competition? How would you define the business problem? How might theory be useful in researching this topic?

Sources: Craig's blog at `www.cnewmark.com`, `www.craigslist.org` and `http://london.craigslist.org`, accessed June 2006. ∎

PREPARING A LITERATURE REVIEW

Business students may wonder why it is necessary to undertake a **literature review**. This is often because they do not understand what a literature review is and how it can help them in their research. A literature review prevents researchers from duplicating previous research. It may also answer research questions and therefore eliminate the need for a particular research project. Whatever the situation, the literature review typically has two broad objectives. Firstly, it helps to develop and expand your research ideas. Secondly, although you may have some knowledge of your research topic, the literature review ensures you are familiar with recent developments and have a complete understanding of the relevant topics.

The literature review follows the clarification of the problem/opportunity in the formal research process. You may well have previously researched the topic. But that research typically would have involved searching briefly for publications or reports that help you to better understand the research problem. It may also have consisted of informal interviews with colleagues or coworkers who may have similar research interests. No matter which approach you relied upon, previous efforts to gather information were probably less formal and not as well organized.

Literature reviews are often divided into two stages. The first stage reviews the literature to identify existing themes, trends and relationships between variables. The end result of this initial effort is to generate ideas related to your topic that have not been researched in the past, or have not been examined using the same methods you propose to use. For example, there may be previous research that examines your ideas or theory using qualitative approaches, but none based on quantitative, empirical research.

The second stage of your literature review is much more extensive. It focuses on identifying and describing past theoretical research that is related. Theories are then included in your work if they are directly related. If they are not closely related and therefore not included, you probably will need to explain how and why. But in the final analysis you must complete a literature review that examines and comments on what has already been researched.

The literature review helps you to develop an understanding of the relevant previous research. If your research interest is examining why employees are quitting your organization, you would first look at the findings of other research into the loss of employees. In most cases, there will be quite a bit of previous work related to your area of interest. If this is not the case, then you are probably researching a topic that has emerged from recent changes in the business environment. For example, research on how the Internet is impacting organizational policies and plans is limited. But if relevant research is limited, then you must attempt to adapt previous research approaches to your new and innovative topic. For example, if you chose to study factors that influence the adoption of information technologies facilitating electronic records capture and storage in the medical field, research would be limited. On the other hand, there is a lot of previous research on the adoption of innovations in general. Thus, you could examine this general area to determine what is applicable to your research.

Some of the previous research may be directly related to your research. If you are examining how employees accept and adopt change in the workplace, or the concepts of trust or loyalty, there will be many directly related previous studies. But there will be other work that is less directly related. For example, there are fewer studies of "shared values" in an organization or the "climate for acceptance" yet these factors may influence whether change in an organization is readily accepted. Thus, these areas must be examined to determine how they might relate to your research.

Review of previous research related to your topic should identify variables that are used to measure concepts, such as job satisfaction, corporate reputation, organizational performance, motivation and so forth. It should also suggest how these variables are related to each other. As you conduct your literature review, however, you will often find that the same variables are defined differently by different researchers. Moreover, the literature may reveal different views on how the variables are related. Thus, a necessary outcome of the literature review is to resolve the dilemmas encountered when research variables are defined differently and relationships between variables are inconsistently reported.

If your research does not closely match previous work, you may be concerned because you think there is nothing of value to build upon. But it can also be encouraging in that it may answer another frequent question: "What can I do that is unique and will make a contribution?" If you are finding it difficult to find related previous research, you are probably looking at it from too narrow a perspective. For example, if you are looking for information on "adoption of new software to increase productivity in not-for-profit organizations", you will find literature on the adoption process and productivity, but may find none on the adoption process for new software or the adoption process in a not-for-profit setting. When confronted with a situation like this, you must look for ways to adapt previous research to your context. For example, find previous research on the adoption process for software or similar new processes in a for-profit setting and adapt it to fit your context.

The literature review has purposes other than to understand previous work in the area. It may help to refine existing research questions and/or objectives or to develop new ones. In other instances you may identify problems and/or issues that have been overlooked in previous research. Previous researchers may have suggested areas for future research so you may identify areas for research suggested by past work. Of course, you should at least be able to identify current trends and opinions published in scholarly and trade journals as well as newspapers and industry reports that will provide insights into the research questions and objectives you may not have otherwise considered.

The literature review is one of the first steps in your research project. But even though it begins early in the process, it often continues till the end. For example, assume you are researching the relationship between job satisfaction, organizational commitment and turnover. Early in the process, you may be searching for information about how supervision and compensation influence job satisfaction. Later, you may read an article or discuss your research with someone and decide that attitudes towards coworkers should also be examined. Thus, you then will have to expand the scope of your research to include coworkers and their possible influence on job satisfaction.

An important question that will eventually have to be answered is "When do you have enough literature to stop searching?" The answer to that question is not easy. You must at least include all of the most recent studies (those published in the last ten years) as well as the most important literature on the topic historically. There may also be somewhat less important work that needs to be included because it is viewed as an emerging field or was conducted by someone who is supervising your research. One strategy is to look at the references cited in recent research as well as important articles and be sure to include those that are cited most often. The answer given most often is you need to make sure you include literature on all relevant issues. But since the definition of "relevant" often changes in the course of your research you need to be prepared to re-open your literature search if necessary.

A consideration that is also important is the balance between applied/business and scholarly sources. To distinguish between the two types, consider the following. Scholarly sources are written in a more formal and rigorous style and have many citations from the most prestigious journals. In contrast, applied or business sources are written in a much less formal style and typically have only a few references. Moreover, scholarly sources are always subject to peer review while business publications generally are reviewed only by the publication's editor. Business publications include sources such as *Business Week*, *Forbes*, the *Financial Times* and *Wall Street Journal Europe*. On the other hand, the *British Journal of Management*, *Economic Business Review*, *Corporate Reputation Review*, the *Journal of Marketing Management*, the *Asia Pacific Journal of Management* and the *European Journal of Operational Research* are considered scholarly sources and their content generally emphasizes theory as much or more than practice. Reliance on business publications is useful because their stories tend to cover the most recent developments. In contrast, scholarly journals often take several years for studies to be published so they do not report the most recent developments. Ultimately the balance depends upon the audience for your research. For a predominantly academic audience the emphasis is on scholarly publications. In contrast, for a business audience applied sources are more often cited.

An important point to remember in conducting your literature review is that you will need to examine publications across a wide range of fields. Depending on your specific topic, you should first consider looking at the literature in all major business disciplines, including management, marketing, information technology, finance, accounting and economics. Unlike some other fields of study, however, in business you will also need to examine the literature from social science disciplines in general, such as psychology, sociology, agriculture, geography and so forth. These disciplines often conduct similar research or have previously developed theories or concepts that can be adapted to business situations.

How do you actually conduct a literature review? Exhibit 4-2 lists the typical steps to follow in doing a literature review.

CONTRIBUTIONS OF THE LITERATURE REVIEW

Most research reports have a section that provides an overview of the literature related to your research topic. Only very applied reports that are limited in scope will not include a literature

1. Clarify research questions and objectives.

2. Locate and evaluate sources of information.

3. Start collecting the literature.

4. Review and make a record of the information.

5. Start writing the initial literature review.

6. Identify gaps in the literature.

7. Examine your research questions and objectives again.

8. Collect additional literature to fill gaps.

9. Prepare final literature review.

EXHIBIT 4-2

Steps to Conduct a Literature Review

review. The reason for including a literature review is that it helps your research in many ways. Specifically, the literature review helps define the research problem and clarify your research questions, provides a background of the major issues, suggests potential hypotheses and identifies research methods and data analysis and interpretation approaches used by other researchers on similar projects.

DEFINING THE RESEARCH PROBLEM

Recall that defining the research problem is an important first step in the research project. If you focus on the symptoms and not the problem your project will be a waste of time. One way to ensure you focus on the problem and not the symptoms is to conduct preliminary interviews with knowledgeable people. Another way is to look through books, scholarly literature and business publications to identify similar situations. Scholarly literature published in academic journals will be heavily based on defining and testing business theories. In contrast, popular business publications are typically much more applied and more recent, and do not have academic research to support them. For example, wireless technology whether through mobile phones, Internet access, or tracking inventory and employees through RFID (Radio Frequency Identification Devices), is creating new workplace issues. The field is so new, however, that it is being reported in business publications but has not been addressed in scholarly publications. Thus, scholarly publications may suggest appropriate research methods, but business publications will be better sources for identifying issues and problems to study.

BACKGROUND INFORMATION

The literature can be helpful in providing background information for your research project in several ways. Among the most important is that previously published literature can be used to justify your particular research problem as deserving further study. If the problem is a new and cutting-edge topic the business literature may be the best source of information. But if the problem is an extension or new application of an established problem, then academic as well as business literature should be helpful.

A background study also helps you to summarize all the major aspects of a problem. The relevant literature is identified and described to demonstrate you have a full understanding of past research and how it relates to your project. The background can be quite lengthy depending upon what is considered relevant. An early strategy is to examine and collect information on almost any topic that may be related. But as the process continues you must decide what the most important issues are and what can be left out. Using this approach the end result is a summary of the theories, arguments and findings from both the business and scholarly literature. It is often helpful to identify the gaps in previous research that may suggest directions for your own work. The end result is a document that identifies what has and has not been done on the subject and where your research fits into this body of knowledge.

Students required to complete a master's dissertation or doctoral thesis frequently want to know what they can do that is unique. Experienced researchers and tutors knowledgeable about a particular field can help here. As an initial guide, we suggest the approach shown in Exhibit 4-3.

From the point of view of a masters or doctoral student it is important to follow well established procedures and thus be able to claim the research has been rigorous and made a contribution to intellectual capital. If research approaches are used that are not well recognized the risk of an examiner rejecting them is considerable. It is useful to think of the risk profile of a research degree as having two dimensions. The first dimension is the novelty of the research method and the second dimension is the degree to which the field of study is established. As can be seen from Exhibit 4-3, if a new methodology is used in a new field of study the risk of the research not being accepted is high. But if an old methodology is applied to a well researched field of study there is the possibility that the researcher will not be able to argue that he or she has actually added something new to the body of theoretical knowledge. The safer areas for the research student are when they either apply a new methodology in an established field of study, or an established methodology in a new field of study.

Settling on a research approach is an important part of the research degree process. Thus, the supervisor needs to take a lot of time to explain the decision criteria for selecting a topic. Indeed, the process of selecting a topic may have to be explained several times. The issues often are so complex

	New Method	Old Method
New Field	High risk of criticism and possibly failure	Should produce a satisfactory result
Old Field of Study	Should produce a satisfactory result	May be of little value and not worthy of a degree

EXHIBIT 4-3

Risk Profile of a Research Topic
Source: Adapted from D. Remenyi, and A. Money, *Research Supervision for Supervisors and Their Students*, Academic Conferences Limited, 2004. Reproduced by permission.

that it takes time for the full implications of different strategic choices to be fully absorbed. Students who ignore the advice of their supervisors in selecting a topic do so at a high risk.

RESEARCH QUESTIONS AND HYPOTHESES

The literature review also helps to refine your research questions and develop hypotheses. Possible relationships are identified and those that are unlikely are rejected. Moreover, factors that influence relationships should be identified. For example, you may find that younger workers are more likely to change jobs more often, or that older workers find it more difficult to adapt to innovations in the workplace. You may also find that gender is associated with the frequency of changing jobs or the willingness to accept change. By using the literature to identify and suggest relationships, you can create hypotheses to be tested in your study. We discuss developing research hypotheses in Chapter 6.

METHODOLOGIES

The literature can be very helpful in identifying methodologies used by previous researchers to study a problem. There is no need to reinvent what has proven useful in the past. Questionnaires, measurement scales, statistical techniques and research designs from other studies should be examined to see if they might be useful. If they produced valid findings before, they probably can be used in another study. Statistical methods and research designs often require few changes, but questionnaires and scales usually must be updated and revised to meet the needs of a new study. For example, a study that used a perceived self-efficacy scale as part of a study of decision making in an industrial plant would have to be adapted for use in a healthcare setting. In other situations, there may not be a previously published scale. For example, there are many scales measuring observed supervisor leadership behaviour but the authors are not aware of a scale measuring expectations of supervisor leadership behaviour.

Scales that require only small revisions often can be adapted based on the input of knowledgeable experts. Scales that must be extensively revised should always be pretested. Where there is no existing scale an entirely new scale must be developed. New scale development is described in Chapter 9 of this book.

Whether using a qualitative or quantitative approach, researchers almost always can learn from the data-analysis approaches used in previous research. With a qualitative approach, the literature review may help you decide when and how to use computerized software and which packages are best. If you are doing quantitative research, other studies can suggest the appropriate statistical technique, or whether to use summated scales or factor scores to represent constructs. Using the literature to learn about possible methodologies and to support a particular research method is therefore an important step in designing your research.

INTERPRETATION

When reviewing the literature you should also look at how other researchers are interpreting their findings. What levels of significance are accepted? Which relationships are positive and which are negative? How are decisions made regarding acceptance or rejection of hypotheses? What sources are other researchers citing to support their interpretations? When the findings of your research are consistent with other studies you can use this to support your interpretation. If your findings are not consistent with previous studies, then you must explain why. Previous research may identify reasons for your findings being different, such as using a different sample or difficulty with a particular published scale. Your task as a researcher, therefore, is to use the literature to design and execute research in a way that increases the likelihood you will obtain accurate results.

SOURCES OF LITERATURE

There are many different sources of literature. Until recently much of the literature was difficult to locate. But developments in information technology have made locating sources much easier. Virtually all libraries have online computerized systems to locate published work on almost any topic of interest. Some of the information is more limited, such as bibliographic citations or abstracts only. But increasingly there are databases which provide the complete text of an article that can be printed out.

Newspapers, published articles, conference proceedings, textbooks, syndicated studies and government documents, as well as many other sources, are all now available online in databases. Information technology has facilitated the copying, storage, updating and display of many documents. Most scholarly journals in management, marketing, accounting and other functional areas of business are available online from their date of origin. For example, the *Journal of Marketing* is available at a library near one of the authors from its inception in July 1936. Similarly, many newspapers and other publications are available dating from the early 1900s. For most researchers, locating relevant work begins by turning on the computer and going online.

BOOKS

New researchers usually begin their literature search by reviewing books. For most topics, there are many books from which to choose. Textbooks in particular provide an overview of most recent and relevant research, and cite the most important articles in journals. The material is organized by topic and easy to read so books are a good source to begin developing an overview of your research. But researchers never rely entirely on books because the information is typically several years old.

JOURNALS AND CONFERENCE PROCEEDINGS

Until recently, most scholarly journals were available only in hard copy. Today, most universities have electronic catalogues that enable users to find relevant research using the appropriate search terms and key words. For example, ABI/Inform enables users to search using key words or authors names. The result is abstracts,. pdf files, and sometimes the full text of an article. Unfortunately, too often, required journals are not available through a user's library. Also, even if the journals are available, generally the most recent articles (6 to 12 months) are not included. Thus, while journals are an important source of literature, it is often a challenge to get access to the material.

Professional and trade journals, as well as practitioner publications, should also be examined for relevant articles. These journals are published by professional associations, such as the British Computer Society, the Chartered Institute of Accountants in England and Wales (ICAEW), European Society of Marketing Research (ESOMAR http://www.esomar.org/), European Association for Business in Society, HR Focus, Asian Private Equity Review, and the Chartered Institute of Management Accountants (CIMA). They generally contain more applied articles on topics of interest to their members as well as news items, notices of new products and services, and on occasion summaries of research published in other sources. These articles can seldom be used by themselves, but often point researchers in new directions because of the "thought" pieces they include by prominent individuals in the field.

Professional associations typically sponsor annual meetings. These meetings often publish proceedings of the papers presented. Examples of conferences that publish proceedings include British Academy of Management, Corporate Reputation Institute Conference, European Conference on Information Systems, Academy of Marketing, EFMD (European Foundation for Management Development), CEEMAN (Central and East European Management Association) and the European Conference on Knowledge Management. The quality of research published from these proceedings is generally not as good as journals, but is more recent and often includes new directions in research topics.

GOVERNMENT AND INDUSTRY

Government and industry reports can be very helpful for some research topics. This is particularly true in accounting, finance, economics, sociology and demography. More developed countries publish much statistical information and often have catalogues of their materials. The Department of Trade and Industry (DTI) is an example of a UK government agency that publishes many research reports. For Europe and some other areas finding government and industry reports can be challenging because the studies are often published in the country's native language. This creates problems not simply in reading the reports, but in first finding them. In addition to government and industry reports, some international organizations publish reports. These include, but are not limited to, the United Nations, the International Monetary Fund, European Central Bank, European Commission/Council of Europe, the Association of African Universities, the Association of South East Asian Nations (ASEAN) and the World Bank. Generally these types of reports require some payment, but in some cases summaries are available. Reports like this are increasingly available from Internet databases and other similar sources.

THESES AND DISSERTATIONS

Universities that have graduate programmes with research degrees keep copies of MPhil dissertations and doctoral theses in their libraries. Masters theses generally are not indexed and therefore difficult to locate. Doctoral theses are listed in the British Library Public Catalogue, the Index to Theses, and the British National Bibliography (BNB). References to dissertations are often found in Internet searches. If the dissertation research is not readily available, which it generally is not, we recommend sending an email directly to the author. We have found that researchers generally respond favourably to such enquiries, often sending electronic copies of summaries of their research.

ELECTRONIC DATABASES

Another source of information for financial, economic, marketing and other statistics are online directories and databases. These databases cover a wide range of topics across many disciplines. Examples include the Wall Street Journal Index, Business Periodicals Index (BPI), Datastream, Fame, Bloomberg, Reuters, ABI/Inform Global, INFOTRAC and so forth. These and other databases can be accessed anywhere you can connect to the Internet. If you do not know the source, Google, Yahoo or another search engine can help locate them. Additional material on electronic databases is given in Chapter 5 on secondary sources.

INTERNET SEARCHES

The Internet, and particularly search engines like Google, has had a significant impact on literature searches. These tools search Web sites looking for key words and phrases that match what the user inserts. Thus, the key to success here is using the correct words and phrases. Indeed, more often than not the user is faced with "information overload" because of the difficulty of determining the best key words and the overwhelming amount of information available on the Internet. Additional guidelines on conducting Internet searches are provided in Chapter 5 on secondary sources.

PLANNING THE LITERATURE SEARCH

The literature search process is tedious and time consuming, often taking much longer than originally planned. Planning the literature search is important therefore, because it helps you locate relevant literature and not waste time pursuing useless documents. Exhibit 4-4 contains guidelines for planning your literature search.

The objective of a literature review is to summarize the major issues related to your research. In most cases you will discuss what different authors have reported, what their methodology was and how their findings are similar as well as different. For research findings that are similar you may well point out why. Where the findings are different, you should suggest reasons for this as well. In all cases you should indicate how their findings influenced your own research.

The literature review describes and provides a critical analysis of the prior research that has been conducted on your topic. The topics included in the literature review are based on your research questions and objectives. For example, if your research is looking at factors that cause employees to search for a new job then your literature review would examine work environment factors such as compensation, supervision, teamwork, communications, and so forth. Your literature review will summarize what you found out about the questions posed by your research. The issues not answered, often called gaps, will be identified and your research will focus on one of the gaps in past research.

- Define the scope of your subject area, for example, leadership, conflict management, customer satisfaction, and so on.

- Identify which disciplines must be examined, for example, marketing, psychology, management, and so on.

- Identify the context of your research, for example, business-to-business or consumer.

- Decide on what geographic area will be studied, for example, Europe, Asia, and so on.

- What time period will be examined, for example, at minimum the most recent ten years, but probably a quick review of at least 20 years.

- Identify the languages relevant research is likely to be published in and which ones you will be able to either read yourself or have translated.

- Beyond books and scholarly journals, identify which other sources will be examined, such as conference proceedings, industry publications, and so on.

EXHIBIT 4-4

Guidelines for Planning Your Literature Search

The format and length of the literature review will vary depending on the type of research project. Commercial and consulting projects will have a limited literature review covering only the essential information. Projects seeking funding support, such as European Union grants, will have a much more extensive literature review. Educational research such as master's dissertations, and particularly doctoral theses, will have the most extensive literature reviews. Shorter reviews often are limited to a few pages. Longer reviews will be at least a chapter and sometimes more.

You should start your literature review by reflecting on your research objectives. Review each research objective and identify the topics that are the same and those that differ across objectives. For example, if your research questions involve examining factors related to job satisfaction and loyalty, then there are at least four topics to be included in your literature review. The four topics are: (1) what is job satisfaction and how is it defined; (2) what is loyalty and how is it defined; (3) what factors are related to job satisfaction and how are they defined; and (4) what factors are related to loyalty and how are they defined? Of course, there may well be some overlap in topics, particularly with the factors related to job satisfaction and loyalty.

Once you have identified the topics to be covered, you should start generating search terms or key words. This is particularly true since today most literature reviews rely on a computer search engine to identify related research. If you have the correct search terms, you will find the appropriate literature. If your search terms do not include all of your topics, then you will not find the literature you need to fully understand the background of your topic.

Identification of search terms and key words often begins with the most recent articles published in the literature. Review articles and meta-analyses of a particular topic are generally the most helpful. They will not only identify key words, but will also reference other similar articles to be reviewed. Another excellent source is theses and dissertations in the libraries of research universities. Handbooks, encyclopaedias, dictionaries and thesauruses are useful as well. Fortunately, most of these are available in electronic versions today. Brainstorming with fellow students or colleagues as well as with scholars in your field of study once you have a good idea of your topic can generate many search terms. Finally, do not overlook the power of email. In the past, researchers were limited to contacting individuals close to them or over the phone, but today one should never hesitate to contact scholars from overseas who are publishing in your area for ideas. The main guideline here is to be prepared well enough to ask intelligent questions. Do not just send general enquiries such as "What key words would you use to find out about job satisfaction?"

WRITING A LITERATURE REVIEW

Writing the literature review is a difficult task, particularly for inexperienced researchers. Conflicting findings should be reported but you must comment on and explain the differences. For example, if the research focuses on the concept of motivation among employees then it would be important to discuss how motivation is defined in each study and whether the same or a similar scale was used to measure motivation. Motivation could easily be defined differently for employees in different job settings and if so this must be pointed out. A good literature review demonstrates the researcher has an excellent understanding of previous research and how it is related. Citing an extensive list of references is not good enough, and could be risky. An examiner might question you about a particular one and be upset if you were unable to comment on it.

Researchers must clearly interpret previous research and show the linkages between studies. Exhibit 4-5 provides guidelines to give you direction in preparing your literature review.

- The literature review should start from a broad perspective and move to a narrow one that focuses on your specific topic. This often is referred to as the "funnel" approach.

- The literature in your review should be closely related to your research objectives and questions.

- The literature should cite the major experts in the field in which you are working.

- The literature should cite the most recent publications that are considered important contributions.

- The literature review should identify the gaps in existing research, how your research is related, and what its contribution will be.

- If there are publications that suggest a different viewpoint than your own they should be cited and you should indicate how your research is different.

- In evaluating the contributions of other researchers you should be objective and reasonable in commenting on their work. If in doubt, ask other knowledgeable individuals less involved in your work to evaluate your comments.

- The literature review should include a comprehensive conceptual model showing all relevant constructs/variables and their proposed relationships.

EXHIBIT 4-5

Guidelines for Preparing a Literature Review

Most researchers will have access to a library. This is important because libraries provide access to the literature. Firstly, libraries contain the books that have been written on your topic. But often even more important, libraries pay annual subscription fees to get access for their users to applied and scholarly publications, as well as government documents and some industry reports.

Start your literature review by looking at your library's catalogue to determine which publications it has and what it may be able to obtain over the Internet. Another source is interlibrary loan, but in most cases this service must be paid for and users should make sure items ordered this way are relevant. A good rule of thumb is that books, well-known journals and government publications not otherwise available are generally worth the expense associated with interlibrary loans.

As you collect your literature, you should begin evaluating it. Indeed, during the process of locating information you will be examining what you have collected to determine if it justifies further effort. Some articles will be discarded immediately while others will be set aside. The authors of your text have found that dividing the literature into three categories is useful. The first category is definitely a useful category, the second is useful at least in a limited way, and the third is possibly useful but set aside till later because you will have to further evaluate its relevance. Suggestions regarding what to include in a literature review are given in Exhibit 4-6.

During the literature review you will download articles from the Internet, photocopy pages from books and reports, and make copies of articles. While you are completing the process of collecting information, it is important to prepare notes. Your notes will summarize the contribution of each

- Is the reference more than ten years old? If yes, make sure a more recent publication has not replaced the earlier reference.

- Is the source reliable, or potentially biased? If the source is potentially biased, be very careful about relying on it in your work.

- Has the reference been cited in other reliable and useful sources?

- Beyond the theory, is the methodology useful as a guide to your approach?

- Can the topics reported in the research be used to organize your report?

- Which conclusions can be built upon and need to be cited?

- If the findings are different from your research, how do you deal with it? It is not a good idea to simply not report contradictory studies since others, such as research supervisors, will often be familiar with these studies.

EXHIBIT 4-6

Deciding What to Include in a Literature Review

publication to your research as well as the complete bibliographic information. This will make it easier to properly reference sources cited in your research. Database software is available to help you do this so be sure to check it out. The process of preparing notes will help you organize your thinking and make you more efficient when you are actually writing down your ideas.

When is your literature search completed? In reality, it is not complete until you stop researching a particular field. You should continue to search and review until you finish your research. If you do this you will not overlook a recently published significant research study. You must at least review all the major literature closely related to your topic. For topics that have been extensively researched for many years, it is generally easier to focus only on the most relevant research. But for new and emerging topics, you will necessarily have to extend your review to somewhat related fields. A good rule of thumb for when this process is nearing completion is that you will begin seeing citations already in your list of references.

RESEARCH IN ACTION

INCREASING THE PRODUCTIVITY OF THE EUROPEAN WORKER

In the US human relations development approaches base performance improvement on psychological aspects. Human resource management in the US is rooted in psychology and focuses on the improvement of individual worker motivation and needs. As a result, human relations approaches emphasize the analysis of individual employee needs, reward systems and job enrichment as a means of improving individual worker performance. But in Europe, the management of people in organizations has evolved from a sociological perspective that focuses on the social system, the economic and political context, and the nature of the relationships among government, unions and management. Thus, a primary concern in many European countries is who has the power to decide which issues. This means industrial democracy comes under the domain of workers and industrial policy is associated with government policy. For example, there are laws that determine how worker organizations are represented on German company boards, the authority of quality of work–life councils in Sweden, and the influence of labour codes in France, Spain and Latin American countries. The employment relationship between employee and employer, both legally and psychologically, varies from country to country. While law dictates what is regulated and to what degree, the social paradigm establishes mutual expectations between workers and companies.

What are some challenges you would encounter conducting a literature review focusing on improving productivity among European workers?

Sources: Hofstede, G., Bond, M. and Luk, C. (1993). ''Individual Perceptions of Organizational Cultures: A Methodology'', *Organization Studies*, 14(4), 483; Fisher, C. (1989). ''Current and Recurrent Challenges in HRM'', *Journal of Management*, 15, 157–80 and Schneider, S. and Barsoux, J.-L. (1997). *Managing Across Cultures*. London, Prentice Hall. ■

CONFIRM RESEARCH QUESTIONS WITH THE LITERATURE REVIEW

The literature review should lead to a redefinition of the research problem or opportunity in scientific terms. That is, the literature review enables you to develop research questions that focus on the real problem issues and not the symptoms. Issues are not the same as symptoms. **Issues** are the things that if altered will close the gap between the actual and desired states. Like a medical doctor, the business professional will create a much better long-term outcome if the real issue is treated, not just symptoms. **Symptoms** are signals that some change may be needed to avoid further problems or take advantage of some opportunity. A runny nose and a sore throat are symptoms that could indicate some type of viral or bacterial infection. Likewise, decreased employee productivity could be symptomatic of some organizational management problem or of some problem with the physical workplace environment. These two issues would produce research questions involving entirely different variables. In either case, simply treating the symptom itself may make the problem worse.

Research questions are often phrased in a what, when, where, who and why format. Questions that result from this approach can be specific or very broad. But specific research questions are more useful in writing actionable research questions that include managerial variables. **Research questions** rephrase research issues into a form that is researchable. In other words, the variables are described in a way that provides helpful information to business decision makers. Examples of symptoms, issues and research questions are shown in Exhibit 4-7. Clarifying research issues and

Symptom	Potential Issues	Research Questions
Low customer service ratings	Sales rep territories are too large? Training is inadequate?	What factors influence customer service ratings?
Stock-outs are higher than last year	Shelf space increases have lowered retail inventories?	What is the relationship between shelf space and retail sales?
Sales are lower than expected	Forecasting techniques are inadequate?	What variables are the best predictors of sales?
Churn-rate is highest in the market	Wireless coverage is poor? Prices are too high? Service provider employees are unfriendly?	What factors are related to churn rate?
Labour costs are higher than the competition's	Employee sick days are too high? Productivity is low?	Do flexible schedules create increased labor efficiency (lower labour costs)?

EXHIBIT 4-7

Examples of Symptoms, Issues and Research Questions

questions is important because they play a prominent role not only in the research design but in the research outcome.

Group efforts generally result in the most effective research questions. The researcher is responsible for posing the initial questions based on the literature review. But after that involving experts or other knowledgeable people can often be helpful in revising or expanding questions. These other individuals typically participate in brainstorming sessions but increasingly researchers are relying on email as a means of soliciting input.

After the research questions are developed research objectives must be formulated. The process of converting research questions to objectives is illustrated in Exhibit 4-8.

Theory was defined in Chapter 2 as a set of systematically related statements or a proposed explanation for some event that can be tested empirically. We noted that some theories have been confirmed by past research while others have either limited or no validation. Whether your theory has been confirmed or is a new proposition, it should be used to develop research questions and objectives. For example, Exhibit 4-9 displays a marketing theory called the "hierarchy of effects". The theory proposes to explain how individuals become customers as a series of stages, from lack of awareness to awareness, knowledge and so on. We could use this theory to develop research questions, objectives and ultimately hypotheses. For example, a potential question is "In which stage

Research Questions	Research Objectives
What can be done to improve employee morale?	To identify factors that influence employee morale.
When has employee training been effective?	To describe the situations and criteria when employee training has been effective.
Where should we sell our products?	To determine in which geographic areas (countries or regions) our products are most likely to sell.
Who should we consider outsourcing our manufacturing to, and for which products?	To determine the criteria that should be used in selecting countries and companies to consider outsourcing of manufacturing.
Why is employee productivity low?	To identify which conditions are related to productivity and how those conditions are influencing your firm's productivity.

EXHIBIT 4-8

Converting Research Questions to Objectives

Hierarchy Stage	Description
1. Unawareness	Not aware of your brand, etc.
2. Awareness	Aware of your brand.
3. Knowledge	Know something about your brand.
4. Liking	Have a positive feeling about your brand.
5. Intention	Intend to buy your brand next.
6. Purchase	Actually purchase your brand.
7. Repurchase/Loyalty	Purchase your brand regularly.

EXHIBIT 4-9

Theory of Hierarchy of Effects

of the hierarchy is the 50+ market segment?'' This question could then lead to the research objective: ``To describe what the 50+ market segment knows about our company and products/services.'' Finally, a hypothesis to test might be: ``The 50+ market segment is not buying our products because they are not familiar with their features and benefits.''

From the research questions and objectives a preliminary idea of the types of data necessary to complete the research project is also formulated. This process involves answering a series of questions such as: "Are data available in the firm's data warehouse that can solve the problem or clarify the opportunity?" "Can other secondary data be obtained either from trade associations, government documents, or similar sources?" and "What are the budget and time constraints for the project?" At this point, it is common to make adjustments in the initial research objectives because of time and budget constraints. Ultimately, the researcher and the manager must decide if the value of the information is greater than the cost of obtaining it and whether the data can be obtained quickly enough to be useful. If the answer is yes, the research questions are translated into research objectives and the research design is selected.

CONTINUING CASE   SAMOUEL'S GREEK CUISINE

Developing Research Questions and Objectives

Phil Samouel has concluded that the problems needing to be investigated for his restaurant should involve research on both customers and employees. To obtain a better understanding of each of these issues he logged on to the Yahoo.com and Google.com search engines. He also spent some time at the local library. From this review of the literature, he identified some "Best Practices" guidelines on how restaurants should be run. Below is a summary what he found:

- If you do not have enough customers, first examine the quality of your food, the items on your menu and the service.

- Your service staff must fit the image and character of your restaurant. How your employees act and behave is extremely important. They must be well groomed, knowledgeable, polite and speak clearly and confidently.

- Your menu items must represent good value for the money.

- Service must be efficient, timely, polished and cordial.

- Cleanliness in and around your restaurant has a strong impact on the success of your business.

- Follow the marketing premise of "under promise and over deliver", always finding ways to please your customers.

- Empower your employees to make decisions to keep your customers happy. For almost all customer complaints, and hopefully there will be few, train your employees on what to do to resolve the situation instead of coming to the manager.

- Create a pleasant dining atmosphere, including furniture and fixtures, decor, lighting, music and temperature.

- Find out if your restaurant appeals to women. For family outings or special occasions, women make the decision on where to dine about 75 % of the time.

  With this information, Phil and his brother need to specify the research questions to be examined.

1. What research questions should be examined in the employee research?

2. What research questions should be examined in the customer research?

3. Should Phil continue his literature search? If yes, for what additional topics should he seek to find information?

SUMMARY

■ **Identify the characteristics of a quality research topic**
The characteristics of a quality research topic include: the research is developed off a sound theoretical base, the research is of interest to both the sponsor and the researcher, the research problem is well defined and the research questions and objectives that flow from it are specific and possible to address through a rigorous research design, resource requirements in terms of time, finance and data access are well understood early in the research process, and the research is expected to make a contribution to knowledge independently of the orientation of the findings.

■ **Describe how to convert research ideas into research questions**
Research ideas may be generated by the researcher or provided by the sponsor in the form of a business problem around which an informed decision needs to be made. Research ideas that do not flow immediately from a business problem that requires investigation often may be clarified by questioning senior researchers, executives and decision makers about problems they face, by examining published research in fields of interest, or by examining past research projects that may suggest areas worthy of subsequent investigation. Once a suitable research idea has been identified, the researcher needs to narrow down the topic to produce research questions that can be answered through the application of appropriate research techniques as well as clear, succinct objective statements. Initial discussions, literature searches and reviews of past research can help develop great research ideas but research success requires that these broad ideas be further refined and developed into good research questions and specific objectives.

■ **Understand what a literature review is and how it helps your research**
The literature review follows the clarification of the problem/opportunity in the formal research process. You have probably previously researched the topic. But that research typically would have involved searching briefly for publications or reports that help you to understand the research problem better.

It may also have consisted of informal interviews with colleagues or coworkers who may have similar research interests. No matter which approach you relied upon, previous efforts to gather information were probably less formal and less well organized. The literature review helps you to develop an understanding of the relevant previous research. Some previous research may be directly related to your own research. But other work will be less directly related. You use a literature review to demonstrate your knowledge of relevant research and how your research makes a unique contribution to the field.

■ **Identify the major sources for a literature search**

There are many different sources of literature. Until recently much of the literature was difficult to locate. But developments in information technology have made locating sources much easier. Virtually all libraries have online computerized systems to locate published work on almost any topic of interest. Some of the information is more limited, such as bibliographic citations or abstracts only. But increasingly there are databases which provide the complete text of an article that can be printed out. Newspapers, published articles, conference proceedings, textbooks, syndicated studies and government documents, as well as many other sources, are all now available online in databases.

■ **Explain how to plan and write a literature review**

The literature search process is tedious and time consuming, often taking much longer than originally planned. Planning the literature search is important therefore, because it helps you locate relevant literature and not waste time pursuing useless documents. The objective of a literature review is to summarize the major issues related to your research. In most cases you will discuss what different authors have reported, what their methodology was and how their findings are similar as well as different. For research findings that are similar you will need to point out why. Where the findings are different, you should suggest reasons for this as well. In all cases you should indicate how their findings influenced your own research.

Writing the literature review is a difficult task, particularly for inexperienced researchers. Conflicting findings should be reported, but you must comment on and explain the differences. For example, if the research focuses on the concept of motivation among employees then it would be important to discuss how motivation is defined in each study and whether the same or a similar scale was used to measure motivation. Motivation could easily be defined differently for employees in different job settings and if so this must be pointed out. A good literature review demonstrates the researcher has an excellent understanding of previous work and how it is related. Citing an extensive list of references is not good enough, and could be risky. Researchers must clearly interpret previous research and show the linkages between studies.

■ **Confirm research questions with the literature review**

The literature review should lead to a redefinition of the research problem or opportunity in scientific terms. That is, the research questions must focus on the real problem issues and not the symptoms. Research questions often are phrased in a what, when, where, who and why format. Questions that result from this approach can be specific or broad. But specific research questions are more useful in writing actionable research questions that include managerial variables – ones that provide helpful information to business decision makers. By clarifying the issues, your research questions will lead to more accurate objectives. ■

Ethical Dilemma

The managing director for a chain of retail clothing outlets has observed that the number of employees choosing to resign is very high, particularly in certain branches. She wants to identify ways to reduce the loss of employees. One possibility involves improving the compensation plan. The managing director does not believe she has enough information on what compensation options are possible and what might be more desirable to employees. Carmen Roberts, Head of Personnel, is asked to research compensation options and recommend the best alternative at the next management meeting. Carmen is asked to survey other retailers about the compensation packages they offer their employees and to interview employees about what they want. Because of pressure to fill several unexpected employee openings that same month, Carmen only has time to check with their major competitor and contact three small retailers about their benefits packages. In addition, the only employee input she has gathered comes from the group of employees who eat lunch with her regularly. When the time for the meeting arrives, Carmen indicates that she has carried out the requested research herself. Based upon the results, she recommends that the firm adopt a plan similar to the one used by their major competitor. She presents only this idea and recommends approval. The next day an employee who has been offered a job by another firm shows Carmen the compensation package she was offered. It seems much more desirable and perhaps more economical than the package Carmen recommended. What should Carmen do now? Where did Carmen go wrong?

REVIEW QUESTIONS

1. What are the characteristics of a quality research topic?

2. What is a literature review and why is it important to the research process?

3. What are the major sources of business literature?

4. What are the steps in planning a literature review?

5. Describe the differences in research questions and objectives?

DISCUSSION AND APPLICATION ACTIVITIES

1. You are having difficulty in deciding whether your research topic will make a unique contribution to intellectual capital. Suggest an approach to help you determine if your topic is sufficiently unique.

2. You are trying to begin your literature search on the "adoption of new technology" in business organizations. What are some issues you need to resolve before actually starting to collect and review the literature?

INTERNET EXERCISES   WWW

1. Go to this Web site: `http://www.utoronto.ca/writing/litrev.html`. It provides tips on how to conduct a literature review. If you are doing a research project how might these guidelines help you to do a better literature review?

2. The Language Centre at the Asian Institute of Technology in Thailand provides information on their Web site on how to write a literature review. The web address is: `http://www.languages.ait.ac.th/EL21LIT.HTM`. Using this Web site, prepare a report on how to write a good literature review.

3. Go to the following Web site: `http://www.umich.edu/~ncpi/52/LitReview.html`. It discusses the relationship between literature reviews and a conceptual framework. Prepare a report on how effective the authors were in demonstrating the link between literature and conceptual frameworks. How could their approach be applicable in business research?

NOTES

1. Brown, B. B. (2003). "Employees' Organisational Commitment and Their Perception of Supervisors' Relations-Oriented and Task-Oriented Leadership Behaviours." Doctoral Dissertation, Virginia Polytechnic Institute and State University.
2. Lok, P. and Crawford, J. (1999). "The Relationship between Commitment and Organisational Culture, Subculture, Leadership Style and Job Satisfaction in Organisational Change and Development", *Leadership and Organisation Development Journal*, 20(7), 365–74.
3. Allen, N. J. and Meyer, J. P. (1990). "The Measurement and Antecedents of Affective, Continuance and Normative Commitment to the Organisation", *Journal of Occupational Psychology*, 63, 1–18.
4. Pitt, L. F., Foreman, S. K. and Bromfield, D. (1995). "Organisational Commitment and Service Delivery: Evidence from an Industrial Setting in the UK", *International Journal of Human Resource Management*, 6(1), 369–89.
5. Philip, G. and Hazlett, S. A. (1995). "The Measurement of Service Quality: A New P-C-P Attributes Model", *International Journal of Quality and Reliability Management*, 14(3), 260–86.
6. Zeithaml, V., Berry, L. and Parasuraman A. (1996). "The behavioral consequences of service quality". *Journal of Marketing*, 60(2), 31.
7. Phillips, E. M. and Pugh D. S. (2000). "How to get a PhD?" 3rd edition. Buckingham, Maidenhead: Open University Press.

PART III
RESEARCH DESIGN, SAMPLING AND DATA COLLECTION

CHAPTER 5
SECONDARY DATA

CONTENTS

LEARNING OUTCOMES

- Define the nature and scope of secondary data.
- Discuss the advantages and disadvantages of using secondary data.
- Describe the various sources of secondary data.
- Evaluate the validity, reliability and potential bias of secondary data sources.
- Appreciate ethical issues that may be associated with secondary data.

INTRODUCTION

The natural inclination of researchers seeking to answer business questions is to gather new data on the topic or objective at hand. While this approach may seem appropriate, researchers should give some thought to whether data may already exist to answer the research question. Searching for existing data may save time, effort and expense in spite of the fact that the data may not have been originally collected with the current research question in mind. In other words, these data may be efficient, valid and useful sources of both quantitative and qualitative information.

The high cost of collecting data makes it important that researchers check to see if data already collected by others are available. This should be done whether the project lends itself to quantitative and qualitative approaches. This chapter first defines secondary data. Next we outline sources and types of secondary data as well as the advantages and disadvantages. We end with comments on the quality of secondary data.

SECONDARY DATA DEFINED

Data used for research that was not gathered directly and purposefully for the project under consideration are termed **secondary data.** As this chapter will show, such data can, and do, play an important role in answering many research questions. However, the fact that the original purpose for collecting them does not relate to the study under consideration means that the researcher needs to devote considerably more thought to questions of validity and reliability.

Sources of secondary data include the researcher's company as well as various external agencies such as data collection companies, municipal or central governmental agencies, nongovernment organizations (NGOs) and trade or consumer associations. Whatever the source, the data may be provided in either raw or summarized form, they may be free of charge or only available for a one-off or some form of licence fee, and they may be provided in either "printed" or "digital" form.

Most of us have been called upon at some point to provide data on ourselves by one or more of the above agencies. Sometimes the purpose for which the data are collected is narrow and explained to us at the time it is collected. An example of this would be when you are stopped in a supermarket and asked to sample and comment on a particular product. At other times the purpose of data collection is broader and it is less clear how the data will be used. The data provided by households during national census studies is a good illustration of the type of collection where people probably do not know how or where the data will be used.

The difference between primary and secondary data is not always clear. To illustrate this, a researcher may decide to add more data to that initially collected for a report or research paper that has already been published. Whether the new data, which extend the original study, are considered secondary data is open to debate. The answer is based on the extent to which the scope of the revised report expands the original study.

SOURCES AND TYPES OF SECONDARY DATA

Business research uses various forms of secondary data for both descriptive and explanatory purposes. These data are used to support studies designed for extrapolation to general populations and for specific case study analyses where the ability to generalize plays a lesser role in the research design.

Traditionally, economists have been the leading users of secondary data within the broad field of business research. Statistics gathered by stock markets, bond markets, national governments and international agencies such as the International Monetary Fund (IMF) and World Bank are extensively used by econometricians to investigate relationships between policy choice and economic performance. In recent years however, secondary data have also become popular for research studies ranging from education and healthcare through to corporate governance, ethics and social responsibility. From a demand side, this popularity has also been driven by an expanded interest in large comparative studies undertaken nationally and internationally. From a supply side, technology has greatly enhanced the capacity of data providers to leverage their databases for commercial purposes and this has increased the nature and extent of the data they provide.

Data obtained from secondary sources may be either qualitative or quantitative. For instance, only qualitative interpretation may be possible from a secondary source that includes summary comments or graphical presentation of the underlying raw data. Although the original data may have met all the requirements for quantitative analysis, they may have been compiled by the researcher in a manner that makes them amenable only to qualitative analysis as a secondary source. Conversely, a research organization that provides the raw data used in the original study or compiled tabular summaries of that data, may be providing secondary data that lends itself to further quantitative analyses. For example, data on population and income statistics by country might be used to develop a trend analysis.

A useful way to categorize secondary data is by source, format and type, as shown in Exhibit 5-1. While secondary data are generally considered to be data that are obtained from third-party or

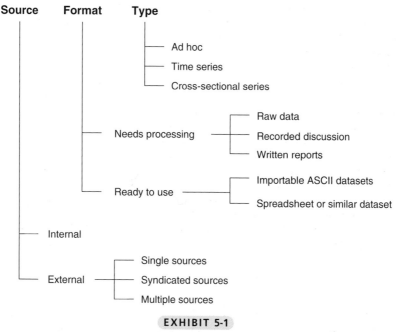

EXHIBIT 5-1

Secondary Data and their Sources

external sources, they can also come from within a company. When they come from within the company they are considered an **internal source**. When they are obtained outside the company secondary data are considered to be from an **external source**. External sources include organizations or individuals that are the primary gathers of the data and syndicated service organizations that act as brokers and consolidators of data initially gathered by others. Sometimes you can obtain data from a single external source. At other times you will need to use multiple external sources to compile the data needed for your research. This occurs when there is no single provider who has all the data needed and is willing to sell it to third parties.

External providers of secondary data also include local, regional and national governments, industry and professional associations, supra-national organizations such as the European Union, nongovernmental organizations, and commercial enterprises that are either direct distributors of data or that gather data and sell the information to others. Investment broking firms are a good example of commercial organizations that generate data for their own purposes but also sell or distribute them to their clients.

Secondary data provided by nonbusiness entities include census and other macroeconomic and social statistics published by various government agencies as well as reports developed by NGOs as part of their service mission and to substantiate lobbying activities they may be engaged in. Increasingly, these publications are electronic in nature and obtainable as CDs, DVDs or as downloadable files from the Internet.

Whatever the source, secondary data may not be available in a format that is immediately useful. For example, written reports, recorded discussions and meeting notes are illustrations of secondary sources that require considerable analysis to convert them to a convenient format for further processing. Sometimes even raw data may be stored in a way that requires re-entry into an electronic database for analysis. This requirement is not restricted to external sources. Even internal secondary data may be stored in a format that requires effort to get it into an appropriate form for analysis. Examples here include certain customer characteristics that are not fully integrated into a company's CRM system but are gathered from customers at the start of the business relationship and kept on file, such as brands previously purchased or lifestyle information. Generally, however, internally sourced secondary data are part of a company's standard management information structure and services. As such, the data can be extracted in a format that is relatively easy to integrate with newly acquired primary data gathered specifically for the research project being undertaken.

Increasingly, individual and syndicated sources are making their data available electronically via the Internet, through proprietary online services, or off-line via CD, DVD or USB memory sticks. Whatever the method, the data is usually in a convenient format that includes popular text, spreadsheet and database files.

Finally, secondary data can be classified by type. They can be sourced from single ad hoc investigations undertaken for a specific purpose with no initial intention to expand the research over time or across market segments. Alternatively, they may come from a source, or sources, that repeatedly collect data as part of longitudinal studies or to compare findings across different markets. For example, the European Union and its constituent governments produce large quantities of secondary data that are relevant to business researchers. These data and statistical reports are readily accessible from the central statistical offices of the national governments and from the Statistical Office of the European Community. Some of the data are gathered according to a regular schedule and presented as time series in raw or indexed form. Other data are collected to compare market, social or environmental conditions across member countries. Finally, data also are collected for specialized one off reports.

Examples of longitudinal data include gross domestic product, interest rates, inflation statistics and employment data. Given that these data are also collected for individual member states, they also represent cross-sectional secondary data. An example of a one off report is the discussion document titled *Furthering the Bologna Process* that was submitted to the Ministers of Education of the signatory countries at their Prague meeting in May 2001. The impact of higher education on developing a suitable labour force to meet the needs of the European knowledge economy makes this report and the response it received an important source of secondary data for a human resource department study on employee acquisition and retention. See the Research in Action box for an example of secondary data gathered for trend assessment purposes.

RESEARCH IN ACTION / EMPLOYMENT TRENDS IN GERMANY

The economic cost of the reunification of Germany on 3 October 1990 has sparked considerable debate over the years. Vast amounts have been written about the relative advantages and disadvantages of reunification to citizens of both the previous German Democratic Republic (GDR) and Federal Republic of Germany (FRG). Arguments have also been presented suggesting that the performance of the European Union and the changing position of Germany on certain key issues are due to the estimated €1.5 trillion it has spent on reunification activities. Labour migration within Germany has also occurred following the privatization of previous GDR state enterprise and the consequent "deindustrialization" of the region.

As part of an economics paper, a university student decides to investigate trends in employment and pay for Germany as a whole, as well as across the two previously defined countries. Secondary data sourced from the German Federal Statistical Office show a growth in the number of unemployed between 1991 and 2004. Over this 13-year period, unemployment numbers have increased by 68.4 % for Germany as a whole, by 74.2 % within the FRG (excluding West Berlin) and by 59.1 % within the GDR (including Berlin). These percentages suggest that unemployment has grown faster in the previous West Germany (FRG). However, as the graph on the next page illustrates, the employable population has declined by 19.3 % in the previous GDR and increased by 14.9 % in the previous FRG. Overall, the growth in employable population has been 5 % over the 13-year interval. Consequently, migration patterns from the east to west explain the apparent growth in unemployment in the west of the reunified Germany. Average unemployment as a percentage of economically active people over the 13 years has been 10.7 % for the country as a whole, 8.8 % for the previous West German (FDR) and 17.1 % for the previous East Germany (GDR).

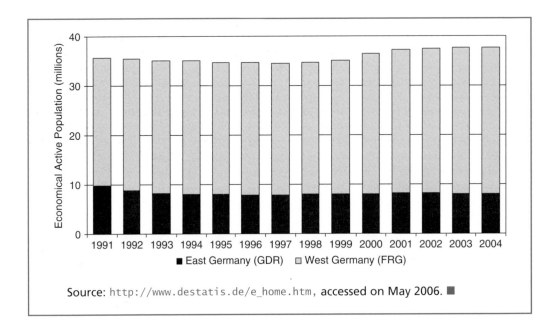

Source: http://www.destatis.de/e_home.htm, accessed on May 2006. ∎

LOCATING SECONDARY DATA

The list of potential sources of secondary data is virtually endless. Generally, the researcher begins by examining internal sources. Data previously collected by the organization itself include primary data from prior studies and routine record inventories. Useful data from the sales domain include sales staff itineraries, sales invoices, customer complaint records, product returns and prior customer surveys. Within the financial realm, company financial reports and records provide information on assets acquisition, cash flows, research and development, marketing expenditure and financial performance. Minutes of meetings throughout an organization as well as strategic planning documents and the like are also key internal sources of secondary data. Finally, research into motivation and commitment of staff members may be developed from secondary data on pay, employee coaching and evaluation reports and training investment.

Once internal sources have been exhausted, researchers may turn to external secondary data sources. There are countless volumes of secondary data available from both profit and nonprofit organizations. Fortunately, these data are increasingly accessible and searchable through electronic means. Many of us find "googling" a daily activity and we appreciate that the key to a successful computer search is inputting useful key words. The wrong choice of keywords leads to either too restrictive a list of identified items or, worse still, a list that is so long as to be fundamentally useless.

Most libraries have access to several search engines that can identify relevant research articles and/or data. Individuals and private companies can also subscribe to an online database vendor for a fee. These "specialist" search engines typically provide access to abstracts or full text articles from trade periodicals, academic journals and general business magazines. Some of them also provide access to specialized statistical data.

Although electronic searches now dominate the landscape, some historical material of interest may be available only in library archives. You should not presume that all interesting and valid sources of external secondary data will be accessible via electronic search. In addition, be aware of the fact that electronic sources and the data provided are subject to change. Companies, government agencies and nonprofit organizations may change their Internet addresses (URLs) and Web page content. Downloadable files may also be updated periodically as statistics are revised by the initial provider. As an example, the Japanese Camera and Imaging Products Association (CIPA) that produces statistics on digital cameras revised its estimate of the production of digital still cameras for January 2006 onwards by 8.4% to just over four million units and replaced the detailed PDF file of statistical data with the corrected numbers on 3 April 2006.[1] This is quite a significant adjustment for someone trying to track market size and growth in this sector. The Research in Action box gives an example of what you might find using an electronic search engine.

RESEARCH IN ACTION — DATA CAN BE FISHY!

Secondary data are abundant online. All one needs is a good search engine and a little imagination. Suppose you are interested in a statistical overview of aquaculture (fish farming) as part of an environmental analysis for a prospective entrepreneurial business venture in Northern Ireland.

Google.com can supply the bait! Go to www.google.com, enter "fishing and statistics Northern Ireland" in the search window, and press search. Google will recommend several sites. One is the Northern Ireland Statistics and Research Agency (NISRA) with the URL http://www.nisra.gov.uk/. There you will find a list of publications and statistics including a link to agriculture, fishing and forestry. Clicking on this link takes you to another page that permits you to select a statistics link. This, in turn, will allow you to click through to the site of the Department of Agriculture and Rural Development at http://www.dardni.gov.uk/econs/stats.html. Searching through this site will allow you to find numerous interesting statistics on the fishing industry including downloadable Excel or PDF files of data. Amongst these are the production of commercial shellfish farms and the salmon and trout production by commercial fish farms in Northern Ireland. Since the data are charted over a number of years, this would be useful in plotting and analysing trends in the marketplace.

It is surprising how easy it is to find volumes of information from reputable sources on even the seemingly most obscure topics if one is prepared to spend a little time and think in a logical and structured way. ■

Exhibit 5-2 provides a list of some useful external secondary data sources clustered into various groupings. The list includes important and reliable sources, but the almost limitless supply of secondary data sources means the search has only begun. Efforts must now focus on identifying the best sources. For example, a Google™ search on "unemployment statistics for European Union

Source	Description obtained from the Web site
Governmental agencies	
www.un.org	Official site of the United Nations that includes an extensive database of information on international treaties, humanitarian and nongovernmental directories. Video clips of General Assembly meeting can also be accessed via the site.
http://Europa.eu	The portal site for the European Union that provides links to related databases about member states and about the evolution of the legislative framework of the Union.
www.statistics.gov.uk	The Office of National Statistics is the UK government department that is responsible for producing a wide range of economic and social statistics. This site also provides the UK census data in downloadable formats.
www.insee.fr	The National Institute for Statistics and Economic Studies is the French equivalent of the UK Office of National Statistics. It is responsible for providing census and other national data concerning French society and business.
Nongovernmental agencies	
www.ngo.org	A site that serves as the homepage for global nongovernmental organizations associated with the United Nations. Its alphabetic listing of NGOs includes organizations relating to refugees, drug abuse, peace and security, sustainable development, human rights and ethics and values to name just a few.
www.ceps.be	As an independent research institute, the Centre for European Policy Studies produces research into issues considered critical for the challenges facing Europe. Reports produced cover economic policy, financial markets, trade affairs, energy, climate and justice.
www.greenpeace.org	The Web site of Greenpeace. A nonprofit organization that does not receive funding from

EXHIBIT 5-2

Secondary Data Sources Available on the Internet

Source	Description obtained from the Web site
	governments or corporations but relies totally on individual and foundation donations. This site provides reports relating to environmental issues that the organization considers important. It is a useful site for obtaining an "environmentalist perspective" on important sustainability issues.
Industry bodies	
www.niauk.org	A trade association and representative body for the British civil nuclear industry that represents over 100 companies including the operators of nuclear power stations and financial and consulting companies. The association's role is to provide information and try to influence public opinion in favour of nuclear energy.
www.efpia.org	The European Federation of Pharmaceutical Industries and Associations has direct membership that includes national pharmaceutical industry associations and individual companies. Its primary objectives are to promote competitiveness and innovation within the industry. Downloadable publications and position papers can be extracted from the site.
www.asstex.it	An Italian Web site that represents companies operating in the Italian textile industry.
www.fisita.com	Web site of the International Federation of Automotive Engineering Societies. Operating in approximately 40 countries, FISITA exists to support the exchange of technical knowledge in the industry. The site includes a search engine for finding technical information on all aspects of vehicle design.
www.epf-fepi.com	The European Property Federation represents private property real estate associations of European Union member states as well as the interests of associations and groups outside the Union that have allied interests. The site

EXHIBIT 5-2

(continued)

Source	Description obtained from the Web site
	provides links to national associations and policy information of a pan European nature.
www.bba.org.uk	The British Bankers Association is the major trade association for banks operating in the UK. It does not have any regulatory status and it is funded by its member organizations. Amongst other information, the Web site provides data on banking codes, publications, dormant accounts and statistical releases that are available in various downloadable formats.
Commercial providers	
http://money.cnn.com	The investor research centre of CNN. This site provides information on the US and world financial markets.
www.bloomberg.com	Bloomberg provides current and historical market information that is particularly well used by the financial sector. While considerable data is available on the public site, full access requires that one sign up to the professional service.
www.reuters.com	Reuters is a worldwide provider of news and information that is sourced by many professional reporters and used extensively by the global financial markets. With approximately 200 bureaux around the world, Reuters produced two-and-a-half-million news items in 2004.
Library search engines	
www.hoovers.com	A database of over 16 million international public and private companies that provides enhanced company and industry information and access to financial statement data for many of them.
www.emeraldinsight.com	One of the world's largest providers of management journals and online support for libraries. Articles are provided in either abstract or as full text documents. The database includes over 100 full-text journals and reviews from approximately 300 management journals.

EXHIBIT 5-2

(continued)

Source	Description obtained from the Web site
www.lexisnexis.com	An excellent source for identifying current events as reported in newspapers and business periodicals. Access to government statistics is also provided as well as some private statistical tables.
www.proquest.com	ProQuest™ is a data provider that has agreements with thousands of publishers worldwide. It gives access to books, periodicals, newspapers and dissertations in various formats. ProQuest Information and Learning currently provides over five billion pages of information spanning 500 years.

EXHIBIT 5-2

(continued)

member states" results in 6,480,000 hits. Narrowing this search down by requesting that all hits include the exact word combination "official statistics" still produces 208,000 hits. Clearly, other criteria must be applied to select the most useful sources for the research at hand.

The potential for large and indiscriminate search results means that experienced researchers often use other platforms and networks to provide focus. A literature review may suggest the sort of data that is available and provide some indication of its quality. Articles and books you have read while doing the literature research should give you references to the sources of secondary data that prior researchers have employed. You should also speak to people who are knowledgeable about the area as they can often help with data that is available. Published guides like indexes and catalogues can also be helpful in finding secondary data. These are often online and available in downloadable format.

Data that are held by companies and other private organizations are sometimes difficult to obtain because they are not commonly made public. As such, you need to locate a key person in the organization who has access to the data and the authority to release them to you. This may require that you pay for them and/or sign an appropriate statement of confidentiality.

ADVANTAGES AND DISADVANTAGES OF SECONDARY DATA

As with all data collected for research purposes, there are a number of advantages and disadvantages that need to be kept in mind when using secondary data sources. These are presented in summary form in Exhibit 5-3 and discussed in some depth below.

Advantages	Disadvantages
• Resource efficiency	• Misalignment of purpose
• Capacity for evaluation	• Access complications
• Potential for comparative analysis	• *Cost*
• *Longitudinal*	• *Familiarity*
• *Cross-sectional*	• *Impact of reporting methods*
• *Contextual*	• Quality concerns
• Avoids respondent fatigue	• *Source*
• Potential for triangulation	• *Data collection methods*
• Potential for new insights	• *Definitions*
	• Age of data

EXHIBIT 5-3

Advantages and Disadvantages of Secondary Data

ADVANTAGES OF SECONDARY DATA

Considerable cost, time and human capital savings can be realized when secondary data are used. **Cost savings** arise because data that have already been collected and compiled into a suitable format present the initial owner with the opportunity to provide them to third parties for considerably less than the original cost. For example, London Business Schools' Risk Management Service is a quarterly publication that contains computed risk measures for thousands of UK companies. The service is used extensively by a wide range of investment professionals and by corporate executives to assess risk and estimate company cost of capital. The large quantities of data and the sophisticated statistical techniques used make it far more cost effective for users to buy the data than try to undertake the necessary research themselves.[2] Even when the purchase price of data equals or slightly exceeds the cost of gathering equivalent primary data, time and personnel savings occur when secondary data sources are utilized.

The time and personnel requirements necessary to design and execute a field study can be considerable. Using existing data sources to replace or supplement primary data collection methods can significantly reduce the length of a research project. Additionally, resource constraints can result in compromises being made when only primary data are considered. Because these compromises can be avoided when secondary sources are used, the quality of secondary data sometimes is higher and leads to an improved research outcome.

Evaluating Secondary Sources

Secondary data sources can be evaluated before being integrated into a research project. Sometimes the methods used by the original researcher are provided with the secondary data and these can be studied to determine if the collection process is appropriate for the anticipated use of the data.

Alternatively, the reputation of the research entity or organization itself can often be relied on as an indication of data quality. For instance, researchers who use raw data, indices or summary statistics provided by national and international statistical services, or by organizations such as the World Bank and European Commission, generally accept that rigorous collection and verification techniques have been applied throughout. The reputation of these organizations is taken as a signal of data quality.

Several forms of **comparative analyses** may be considered crucial for a particular research project. Comparative analysis involves evaluating the accuracy of secondary data by looking at the same data from multiple sources or by evaluating trends to see if there is any questionable data at a particular point in time. Secondary data sources offer the possibility of achieving this when such analyses would otherwise be impossible or prohibitively expensive. **Longitudinal analysis** involves comparing findings across time to identify trends or seasonal patterns. For example, a high fashion company wishing to enhance its understanding of consumer purchase behaviour under various psychographic, demographic and economic conditions would need to supplement its internal sales and CRM data with longitudinal data and time series indices that are generally available from secondary data sources. **Cross-sectional analysis** occurs when a researcher wishes to compare findings across various clusters or market segments at a particular point in time to identify points of difference or similarity in performance or response pattern. Secondary data sources in this type of research may be vital for obtaining comparable data for selected competitors. For example, a researcher employed by Tesco PLC, might use Hoover's UK, a subsidiary of D&B Group, or `http://www.corpreports.co.uk/` to source much of the standardized competitor information necessary to undertake a comparative study identifying the sources of value creation for British retail companies.

Researchers need to ensure they are fully aware of the context within which their research is being done. Secondary data sources play an important role in identifying contextual issues relevant to a particular research agenda. Consider a business that is looking to increase its access to capital for investment and growth purposes. Although management may believe listing on a stock exchange is an obvious solution, contextual issues need to be considered. For example, the historical performance of the firm, its market profile, strategy and short, medium and longer-term financial needs all play a role in determining what exchange it should consider. Secondary data sources can be used to investigate the listing requirements for local and international stock exchanges. But what criteria determine whether a privatized Russian enterprise should select France, the UK or the US for its initial listing? If it selects the US, should it list on the New York Stock Exchange (NYSE), the National Association of Security Dealers Automatic Quotation (NASDAQ) Exchange, the Over the Counter Bulletin Board (OTCBB) or use "Pink Sheets"? These are all contextual issues that must be addressed when making the proper decision.

Unlike behavioural tracking or observation techniques, survey research generally requires considerable time and effort from respondents. Researchers need to create an appropriate response environment (structure, length, location and timing) when conducting survey research as a means of avoiding **respondent fatigue** and ensuring questionnaires are completed diligently. This concern has historically been addressed within the context of single study research design rather than in terms of the fatigue that occurs when individuals find themselves repeatedly surveyed for similar but varied reasons. The growth of the Internet, and the potential it offers to conduct large and sometimes indiscriminate survey type research, has significantly increased how frequently many of us are approached and asked for our opinions. For example, consider the growth in the number of business school ranking surveys that are conducted by the international press and business magazines like the *Financial Times* (`http://rankings.ft.com/`), *Forbes* (`http://www.forbes.com/`), *Business*

Week (http://www.businessweek.com/) and *Karriere* (http://www.karriere.de/), to name just a few. Many of these surveys require that questionnaires be completed by the same generation of alumni and corporate sponsors or employers. Researchers should consider using secondary data sources whenever possible as this can reduce the scale and frequency of questionnaire usage without diminishing the quality of the collected data.

Secondary data can be used as an unobtrusive method to supplement direct survey research and to corroborate its findings. In other words, the researcher should consider whether archived data can be used to confirm that conclusions drawn from the primary collection method are appropriate. Such an approach **triangulates** findings established from the primary collection method and confirms the validity of the research. The approach offers particular advantages when primary data collection methods limit the researcher to small samples where extrapolation to a broader population group might be problematic. Secondary sources may also provide qualitative analyses to supplement quantitative techniques used in primary research or they may present quantitative census or large sample results that corroborate a smaller but more in-depth qualitative research design.

Re-examination of secondary data and the conclusions extracted from these data presents a researcher with the opportunity to develop **new insights**. Although the initial data collection method undoubtedly focused on gathering data relevant to the research objectives and hypotheses, re-examination and analysis may provide additional insight. Using alternative or more recently established frameworks to examine previously collected data can offer further perspectives of value for hypothesis generation or confirmation purposes. Excellent examples of new interpretations of historically compiled data can be found in the fields of economics, finance and medicine. Policy makers regularly review previously collected national statistics on consumption, investment, productivity, trade and inflation and combine them with interest rates and market price indices to develop new insights for monetary and fiscal policy setting purposes. Within the medical field, complex data collected to investigate the carcinogenic properties of certain chemical compounds may subsequently be used in research seeking to investigate their psychological impact.

DISADVANTAGES OF SECONDARY DATA

Data collected with a particular research agenda in mind are gathered using techniques and approaches specifically designed for that purpose. Consequently, they should meet the requirements necessary to draw valid and reliable conclusions. Unfortunately, the same cannot always be said of secondary data and they may therefore be inappropriate for your purposes.

Whenever possible, you should carefully examine the data-collection methods when using secondary data sources to ensure that there is not a misalignment of purpose that makes the data unacceptable. This examination will confirm whether the sampling technique used and questions asked can answer your research questions fully, partially or not at all. If the secondary source offers only a partial solution then combining it with primary data collection approaches may be the preferred solution rather than discarding the secondary source entirely.

Sometimes you may find it difficult to use secondary data because of cost implications, lack of familiarity with various parties that provide the data, or because of the way the data are summarized and the conclusions drawn from it are reported. These **access complications** have been significantly reduced with the growth of the Internet and the tendency for greater transparency by primary data collection agencies. But they have not been eliminated. Some providers freely provide a restricted subset of their data but require that you subscribe for or directly purchase their more comprehensive and better validated datasets. The cost of these higher quality data can be high. Bloomberg (http://www.bloomberg.com/), a leading global provider of financial data, news and analytics, and Emerald (http://www.emeraldinsight.com/), an international electronic management research library database, are two examples of secondary data providers that offer some of the data services free of charge, but require subscription payments for full-range professional access.

Lack of familiarity with the initial motivation and processes followed when gathering the data also represents a potential weakness to using secondary data. Although many government and private-sector collection agencies that provide significant volumes of important secondary data use transparent and well understood techniques and approaches when reporting their data, this is by no means always the case. The growth of the Internet and the ability to search internationally for multiple sources of data has significantly increased the likelihood of not being familiar with key aspects of the secondary data being reviewed. For example, the format used to present historical data on restaurant habits that you could have extracted from an Internet search may not clearly state who the initial provider is and it may disguise the fact that a convenience sample was used. If the purpose of your study is to investigate the pattern of usage of suburban restaurants, a convenience sample developed by interviewing young professionals within the central shopping district at lunch time will under-represent, if not totally ignore, the influence of parents who work in the home.

Most secondary data you access comes in the form of published reports. These reports present the research data in summarized or aggregated form that may not meet the requirements of your research. Definitions of terms and the methods used for aggregation and drawing inferences are well described in most quality reports. But the possibility exists that the included tables and interpretations reflect the biases of the initial researcher rather than an objective interpretation of the gathered evidence. Clearly, the impact of reporting methods on your capacity to interpret and use secondary source reports needs to be considered.

Potential quality concerns with secondary data relate to source, definition of terms and constructs, and the nature of the collection methods. All of these can have a significant impact upon the overall reliability and validity of your research.

Data sourced from supra-national agencies such as the United Nations (http://www.un.org/); national agencies such as the UK Office of National Statistics (http://www.statistics.gov.uk/) and the German Central Bank (http://www.bundesbank.de/); leading nongovernmental bodies such as Medecins sans Frontieres (http://www.doctorswithoutborders.org/); and from major private sector originators and re-distributors of data such as Reuters (http://today.reuters.com/news/home.aspx) are generally considered reliable and of high quality. Other producers of secondary data, however, may have lesser resources and/or an institutional agenda that calls into question the quality and completeness of the data they provide. The quality of your secondary data sources should be carefully assessed and not accepted at face value. This assessment can include an additional search to see how often and by whom the data and the data provider are cited. Broad usage of a particular dataset or provider by other reputable researchers is an important signal of quality.

Attention needs to be paid to the definitions used for various constructs in the initial research. Even reliable sources of secondary data can produce poor quality research if the original definitions and constructs are inappropriate for the current study. For instance, is the service quality construct summarized in a published report defined and measured using the original SERVQUAL construct of Parasuruman, Zeithaml and Berry (1988)[3] or the SERVPERF construct of Cronin and Taylor (1992)[4]? Whatever approach was used, could this have an impact upon your study? These types of questions need to be asked whenever secondary data are used as a key component of a particular study.

Finally, the age of the secondary data needs to be considered. No matter how legitimate the original study, the passage of time may have changed how data need to be gathered to measure constructs or how relationships are defined. The age of the secondary data are also influenced by the time between collection and the publication of the summarized results. For example, national census studies are sometimes considered problematic because of the significant lag between successive studies and because of delays in publishing the comprehensive results. Economic trends, demographic and lifestyle changes, and technology evolution also must be considered when using older secondary data. For example, research undertaken into study patterns of university students conducted 20 years ago may be of questionable value because of the development of distance learning technologies over the last decade and their pervasive use today.

RESEARCH IN ACTION

DOES INTERNET ADVERTISING WORK FOR CAR PURCHASES?

IAB Europe is a federation of 15 IAB (Interactive Advertising Bureau) associations and think-tanks set up to help businesses get the most from their advertising budgets. IAB's European network, with more than 2000 member companies, has sister IAB organizations in North and South America, Asia and the Far East.

Dynamic Logic, an IAB Europe affiliate, recently released research that illustrates the impact of the Internet on ad effectiveness in the European car industry. Dynamic Logic noted that in Europe online has become the first place most people look for information when buying a new car. In examining ad campaigns for general patterns they found that when consumers are past the awareness stage and more engaged in the buying process, car advertising is most effective on car-type sites. In fact, advertising on car sites is considerably more effective at improving purchase intent of cars than for other types of products. Since the message reaches consumers while they are further along in the purchase process, it is likely to have a greater persuasive impact because they will be more receptive to messaging about pricing deals and product differentiation.

As a business researcher, how could you use this information for a consultancy assignment with a car company? What other types of secondary information would be helpful in getting a consultancy job with a car company?

For more information on IAB log onto `http://www.IABEurope.ws` ∎

EVALUATING THE QUALITY OF SECONDARY DATA

Secondary data need to be rigorously evaluated so that their advantages can be captured and their disadvantages controlled. The process begins with an investigation of the original provider of the data. But whenever possible it should also include a review of the research design and of the data collection methods that were used. These steps are presented in Exhibit 5-4.

- **Source of the Data**

  Reputation

  Expertise

- **Research design**

  Objective

  Definition of constructs

  Examined relationships

  Report structure

- **Data collection methods**

  Sampling

  Respondent intention and response rate

  Measurement techniques

EXHIBIT 5-4

Evaluating the Quality of Secondary Data

EVALUATING THE SOURCE

A general reputation for ethical and trustworthy behaviour increases the likelihood that the secondary data will have been collected using credible methodologies and appropriate expertise. This expertise may be in-house or obtained through contracting with third parties. Whenever it is clear that third parties have been used, they should also be investigated. If the source of the secondary data is considered suspicious then alternative methods for obtaining required information should be used in spite of possible cost savings and efficiencies that may be realized. This critical approach should be used throughout your appraisal of the secondary data.

EVALUATING THE RESEARCH DESIGN

Once the qualifications of the secondary data provider have been established, particulars of the actual research design need to be examined. Data are always collected with one or more objective in mind. Appreciating this is important in establishing whether the data may be appropriate for an alternative application. The sampling design and measures used for the original research may not be fully applicable to a new study. The value of secondary data is reduced when the definition of the measures used is not consistent with the requirements of the new study. Hypothesized and confirmed relationships presented in published reports also need to be interpreted with the original objective in mind before assuming that these insights are relevant. Relationships examined during the original study from which the secondary data is extracted need to be considered carefully because a slight change of emphasis can affect the validity of secondary data. For example, a study wishing to examine "actual" buyer behaviour in response to certain marketing strategies would find prior research that "inferred" patterns of behaviour from attitudinal responses of limited use.

How the report is written can give additional insight into the appropriateness of the source. Summary tables, frequency diagrams or report conclusions that use unusual group clustering approaches may indicate the initial research was undertaken with a particular political agenda in mind rather than as an unbiased investigation. This can also occur when a study is commissioned inside a commercial organization with the intent of substantiating firmly held management beliefs and justifying a previously decided course of action.

EVALUATING DATA COLLECTION METHODS

Assuming you are satisfied with the quality of the secondary data provider and that the objectives of the initial study make it suitable for your purposes, the final step you need to take to confirm that the data are suitable is to review the data collection methods that were employed. Whenever possible, the sampling frame, response rate and measurement techniques should all be examined when evaluating secondary data.

Although the sample frame may have been ideally suited for the original study, it may not fully suit new research objectives. To the extent that this is the case, raw data and summary statistics should be translated with caution. For example, an earlier study into private vehicle purchasing behaviour undertaken for the sports utility vehicle (SUV) market may have restricted itself to sampling higher income households. This may make it inappropriate as a secondary source for a subsequent study of five-door hatchbacks that are more targeted towards less wealthy individuals and families with small children.

The purpose of a particular research project can influence the state of mind of those surveyed. This can have an impact on the response pattern and the response rate. Two studies with different objectives may ask a similar series of questions but the responses received may differ because of subjects' understanding of the purpose of the study. For example, many readers of this textbook may have been approached by a student surveyor while travelling on their national railway system. Consider how you might respond to a question concerning the visibility of railway staff on trains if the survey is introduced as a means of investigating convenience and cleanliness, versus the response you might give if the survey is introduced as a means of investigating railway security!

Low response rates may also result in biased conclusions because nonrespondents may have a different perspective on the initially researched topic. Research into issues considered sensitive such as abortion, legalization of classes of drugs and immigration are particularly susceptible to this type of bias because those who feel most strongly one way or the other about the issue are more inclined to take the time and effort to complete the research questionnaire and make themselves available for interview. Excellent illustrations of this response bias occur with television and radio telephone studies where the presenter raises a topic and asks people to telephone or email their yes/no response to a particular question.

Correctly measuring topics of interest is extremely important and the difficulty of doing this when gathering primary data is often compounded when secondary data are also being gathered. For example, governance research investigating stakeholder awareness amongst company executives might ideally require a large sample design and the use of questionnaires and interviews. This might, however, be prohibitively expensive. Consequently, the researcher may consider undertaking a content analysis of secondary data sources such as company financial statements and published minutes of company meetings to construct surrogates or proxies for executive awareness of stakeholders. To the extent that these do not actually measure company executive stakeholder awareness, conclusions drawn from the research may suffer from questionable measurement validity.

Measurement validity is difficult to establish with any degree of certainty and judgement is often necessary when using secondary data.[5] Because of this you should investigate the extent to which the approach you intend to follow has been used by prior researchers who have experienced similar difficulties.

The potential for measurement bias when using secondary data exists for a number of reasons. These include changing methods of collecting data over time and deliberate distortion as a result of political agendas, such as those reviewed earlier in the chapter. Technological development has significantly changed the methods commonly used to collect household and other data over the last two decades. For example, Internet shopping and the shift away from cash oriented societies have transformed how companies are able to monitor customer spending behaviour. This means that longitudinal studies by these organizations need to adjust for the changing way the data are gathered over time. Real-time data collection using electronic capture techniques clearly eliminates the recall bias that existed when purchase behaviour was captured by respondents in diary form at periodic intervals.

Measurement bias can also arise when a consistently used technique does not truly measure the topic of interest. For example, inflation data that is computed using a stable basket of goods suffers from this deficiency. Cost of living increases for the typical household in a country will be correctly measured only if the basket of goods used to determine the consumer price index represents the actual purchasing preferences of the average household. Considerable effort is required to determine optimally when to change the basket of goods that is the proxy for living expenditures as well as how to link the prior basket to a new basket so as to retain the longitudinal character of the index.

Distortion can also happen when data are gathered to substantiate a particular perspective or because respondents find themselves wanting to please the researcher or interviewer. The extent to which measurement bias exists because of a deliberate desire to confirm a particular perspective is often difficult to discover when using secondary data precisely because the initial intention is to deceive. Consequently, researchers using secondary data may need to rely on the reputation of the initial researcher or on collaborative evidence obtained through some form of triangulation. Equally deliberate, although less malicious, distortion also occurs when respondents to questionnaires wish to expedite the process or please the researcher. Individual responses to telephone surveys may be biased by the desire of the respondent to terminate the discussion speedily and by the belief that a particular response will achieve that goal. Similarly, surveys conducted about animal welfare, the environment, nuclear power, or the willingness to support marginalized segments of society may result in biased response patterns if not handled with a great deal of care and diligence.

RESEARCH IN ACTION

AN ONLINE RESOURCE FOR BUSINESS INSIGHTS

Looking for an online resource for business insights? Try www.mad.co.uk The mission of this UK-based firm is to provide insightful, thought-provoking information to help you make the right business and career decisions. Their Web site offers editorials, business analysis, comments on brands and career opportunities. To be first with the news, they send out alerts when the news happens. Along with news, mad.co.uk claims it delivers the highest quality analysis. They suggest how it might impact your department, business or industry through analysis and comment from thought-leaders and exclusive research available only to mad.co.uk subscribers. They also publish two newsletters, *DM Weekly* and *Technology Weekly*, as well as a branding programme that features profiles and news on the brands they believe are the gold standard for innovation, originality and integrity in selected business sectors. Finally, mad.co.uk is known for its comprehensive jobs service, with hundreds of vacancies listings. As with their news service, they send subscribers job alerts whenever a position arises that matches their criteria. Subscribers can also access a large network of archived material from leading industry publications such as *Marketing Week*, *Design Week*, *In-Store*, *Creative Review* and *Data Strategy*.

Would this be a good source of secondary data for business research? Explain your answer.

Source: www.mad.co.uk, accessed June 2006. ■

ETHICAL ISSUES WHEN USING SECONDARY DATA

Numerous ethical dilemmas need to be considered when deciding whether to use secondary data. These include attempting to use these data when the specificity of the research question requires that primary data are obtained; insisting on using primary data collection methods when appropriate secondary data are inexpensive or perhaps available at no charge; using secondary data gathered under guarantees of anonymity in a manner that may undermine that initial promise; and using secondary data that have been collected using questionable methods.

Researchers may be considered morally obliged to use secondary data that are appropriate for the research at hand if it can reduce the time and cost of a research project. Equally, they should ensure that data used from other sources are relevant and that they were collected in an appropriate way when drawing inferences or conclusions from it in their own studies.

Commissioned research that does not include a fully specified research design provides an opportunity for increased profitability if compromises are made on the data collection side through an over reliance on secondary data when more focused primary data are really required. Clearly, following this type of strategy is ethically questionable. It is an unwarranted financial expense to the customer if the budget was based on primary data. Moreover, it may represent an unwarranted performance expense for the customer if the conclusions are compromised as a result of the inappropriate use of previously published secondary data.

CONTINUING CASE USING SECONDARY DATA WITH SAMOUEL'S RESTAURANT

Phil Samouel's business consultant suggests that secondary data may be useful in better understanding how to run a restaurant. Based on what you have learned about secondary data that should be true.

What kinds of secondary data are likely to be useful? Conduct a search of secondary data sources for material that could be used in Samouel's restaurant projects. Use Google, Yahoo or other search engines to do so.

- What key words would you use in the employee research?
- What key words would you use in the customer research?

Summarize what you found in your search. ■

SUMMARY

■ Discuss the nature and scope of secondary data

Secondary data are data originally collected for some other purpose but that have relevance for a particular research project. These data, collected from various sources, may appear in summarized form as tables or graphs, or in raw form. Whatever the format, these data may offer significant insight and advantages to the researcher and they should be given serious consideration before attempting to "start form scratch" using primary data collection methods.

In addition to a fundamental classification based upon their quantitative or qualitative nature, secondary data can be classified by source, format and type. They may be obtained from within an organization through its standard information gathering processes or as the result of a prior specific piece of research. Alternatively, they can be sourced from external providers that include the originators of the research as well as organizations that consolidate and distribute data collected by others. These syndicated sources can also play a role in categorizing and quality assuring the original source.

Increasingly, secondary data is being made available in electronic forms. This applies to both written reports and datasets. However, even when provided electronically, some data require further processing before they can be properly analysed. Content analysis techniques that enable researchers to cluster and categorize text have greatly increased the use of written documents as important secondary sources of data.

Finally, secondary data can be classified according to their usefulness for longitudinal and cross-sectional studies. Although data can relate to unique one-off studies, some are longitudinal or cross-sectional in nature. The latter types are important sources for comparative purposes in many fields of business research.

■ Discuss the advantages and disadvantages of secondary data

Advantages to using secondary data include potential savings in cost, time and human capital investment. These savings are not only limited to the researcher. They also apply to respondents because of their potential to reduce respondent fatigue through not asking for redundant information. This can significantly increase response quality. The attractiveness of secondary data as comparative sources for longitudinal, cross-sectional and contextual analyses, as well as their potential for triangulation, should not lead to uncritical application. Secondary sources should always be evaluated before being used because they can present numerous disadvantages.

Lack of familiarity with the secondary source, including some doubt as to original method and purpose, can result in invalid conclusions being drawn. This misalignment can occur even when the original research is of an extremely high calibre. Public reporting methods may deliberately, or merely for brevity purposes, hide key elements of the original sampling and data collection methods and/or the research design.

■ Describe the various sources of secondary data

The Internet has become increasingly important in helping researchers find suitable secondary data sources. The web and today's culture of transparency and disclosure have greatly increased the volume of data that is provided in conveniently searchable form. Supranational agencies, governments, nonprofit organizations and companies increasingly provide information and reports via their Web sites. This does not mean that researchers can limit themselves to investigating sources that are just a click away. Sometimes key internal and external data may be held in more traditional archive formats.

Secondary sources include commercial providers that may be considered as primary gathers or collators of relevant information such as Reuters™ as well as re-sellers or syndicated providers such as Emerald™ that offer convenient search engines to reports and datasets that were originally written and compiled by others. Industry bodies that exist primarily to serve their members are also important and interesting sources of secondary data. But, like some nongovernmental agencies, researchers must be aware of their potential bias when using them as sources of secondary data. Triangulation may be important in these circumstances. Governments and supranational agencies such as the World Bank, International Monetary Fund and the European Commission freely offer significant quantities of statistics across a wide range of topics. These agencies are inclined to provide quite a bit of detail as to their collection and process methodology. This means that researchers can investigate beyond "reputation" to access the appropriateness of these secondary data for a particular study.

■ Evaluate the validity, reliability and potential bias of secondary data sources

Evaluating the quality of secondary data involves investigating the credibility of the originator of the data source, the robustness of the research design and the data collection methods that were employed. In many respects, validating and checking the reliability of secondary sources of data mirrors the requirements for diligent review of a piece of academic research – an assessment needs to be made of purpose, method, collection and analysis.

■ Appreciate the ethical issues that may be associated with secondary data

Ethical issues underlying the use of secondary data may be summarized as "inappropriately using these sources when you should not" and "inappropriately not using them when you should"!

Secondary sources should not be used surreptitiously as a way of avoiding research effort. This is particularly important when there is a misalignment of purpose and the sourced data cannot be expected to address the research problem in an unbiased fashion. Data collected in an inappropriate fashion that involves trapping respondents by misleading them about purpose or compensation or designing sample frames with the intention of influencing the outcome are unethical. Confidentiality and exclusivity should be respected at all times and researchers should confirm that data gathered and analysed for a particular client may be used as a secondary source for another one. Secondary data should be employed when they can robustly answer research questions in a more efficient manner and when confidentiality and conflict of interest concerns are not an issue. ■

Ethical Dilemma

Joshua is part of the research team that is working on the project for Samouel's Greek Restaurant. The deadline for completing his part of the project involving collecting secondary data is tomorrow morning. He has spent several hours searching for information and has found some conflicting information about demographic and economic trends in the neighbourhood where Samouel's restaurant is located. Two of the studies are from what appear to be reputable firms that process and sell studies based on government data. The third study that has findings conflicting with the two nongovernment studies is from a government-sponsored Web site. It is late in the afternoon and he wants to finish so he can meet his friends at the pub tonight. What should he do? Ignore the information from the government-sponsored Web site or stay late and miss going to the pub?

REVIEW QUESTIONS

1. Discuss the pros and cons of using internal versus external sources of secondary data.

2. Data provided by national statistical offices are often classified as being both time series and cross-sectional in nature. Provide some specific illustrations of your country's central statistical data that meet this definition.

3. Provide two specific ways in which using secondary data can reduce instances of respondent fatigue?

4. Discuss any potential disadvantages of using Web sites of organizations such as the Nuclear Industry Association of the UK (NIAUK) or Greenpeace as secondary data sources for an investigation into sustainable energy.

5. How might the disadvantages discussed in question 4 above be controlled?

6. A suggested advantage of secondary data is that it provides access to insights of experienced researchers. Discuss.

7. A Belgian client of an international market research agency has asked it to conduct primary research into consumer perceptions of Internet purchasing of home improvement products. The UK Office of the agency has recently completed a similar study for B&Q (the British DIY home improvement company) that confirmed earlier published

research by the Netherlands based Karwei DIY chain. Should the market research company do the primary research as requested? If so, should it discuss the published findings of the Netherlands company, and the fact that its own research has already confirmed its validity?

DISCUSSION AND APPLICATION EXERCISES

1. Discuss three disadvantages of using secondary data when assessing the impact of compensation on employee commitment in a firm.

2. The capacity to quickly and cheaply search for possible sources of secondary data using the Internet means that you often find vast numbers of possible sources literally in seconds. What methods would you consider using to confirm the quality of secondary data sources that you finally focus on?

3. What secondary data sources would you consider appropriate for use in an investigation into trends in the consumption of wine and beer in the Benelux?

4. A private executive education provider is considering opening a campus in Singapore.
   a. How would you determine the size of the market and its responsiveness to foreign providers?
   b. In what way do you think secondary data sources can be used to investigate the nature of the competition you are likely to be exposed to (benchmarking)?
   c. Can secondary data be used to determine your pricing strategy and, if so, how?

5. A researcher who has collected primary data from a sample of Eastern European economic refugees in London wishes to confirm the validity of her conclusions concerning the pay discrimination that these folk experience. What kind of secondary data might she use to try and triangulate her findings?

6. As part of your investigation into commuters' perception of the service quality provided by London Underground you have found a secondary source giving satisfaction rating of the underground. A review of the methodology employed by this prior study reveals that it was carried out by university students at midday. In what way might these secondary data be inappropriate given the purposes of your study?

INTERNET EXERCISES   W W W

1. Go to the Web site of the European Travel Commission at http://www.etc-corporate.org/. Extract information that you believe would be useful to an individual running a

restaurant like Phil Samouel's Greek Cuisine but one that is located in Italy. How might tourism seasonality and trends impact upon the management of the restaurant?

2. Visit the French National Institute for Statistics and Economic Studies at http://www. insee.fr/en/home/home_page.asp. See if you can find a time series of hourly French wage rates over the last 25 years as well as the consumer price index over the same period. Use these data to plot the nominal and real increase in hourly wages over the 25 years. (Nominal increases use the actual quoted hourly rates while real increases first adjust the actual quoted rates by dividing them by the inflation or consumer price index.) How might these graphs and data prove useful for a French firm?

3. Search the European Union Web site at http://www.europa.eu/ for information on food safety. What information does the site provide on genetically modified food? How might this information prove useful to the European pharmaceutical and agri-food industries?

NOTES

1. http://www.cipa.jp/english/data/dizital.html and http://www.cipa.jp/english/pdf/revise060403.pdf accessed on 26 May 2006.
2. http://www.london.edu/facultyresearch3508.html accessed on 21 May 2006.
3. Parasuraman, A., Zeithaml, V. A. and Berry, L. L. (1988). "SERVQUAL: a Multi-item Scale for Measuring Consumer Perceptions of the Service Quality", *Journal of Retailing*, vol. 64, no. 1, pp. 12–40.
4. Cronin, J. and Taylor, S. (1992). "Measuring Service Quality: a Re-examination and Extension", *Journal of Marketing*, vol. 56, July, pp. 55–68.
5. Denscombe, M. (1998). *The Good Research Guide for Small Scale Social Research Projects*, Buckingham, Open University Press.

CHAPTER 6
CONCEPTUALIZATION AND RESEARCH DESIGN

CONTENTS

LEARNING OUTCOMES

- Understand the role of conceptualization in research.
- Clarify how to develop and test hypotheses.
- Describe the three basic business research designs.
- Explain the difference between cross-sectional and longitudinal studies.

INTRODUCTION

Researchers must make sure managers understand how research leads to improved decision making. One way to do this is to communicate the relationships that will be tested with the research. For many people, a visual representation of the relationships will simplify their understanding and more effectively communicate what is being done in the research. This process is called conceptualization. Once the conceptualization process is completed, the researcher can more accurately select the appropriate research design. In this chapter we first explain how to develop a conceptual model for hypothesized relationships. Then we clarify the difference between qualitative and quantitative research. Finally, we describe the basic types of research designs and when they can best be used.

DEVELOPING A CONCEPTUAL MODEL

An important outcome of your literature review is the development of a conceptual model of the relationships you will be studying. The process of developing a model is called **conceptualization**. Conceptualization involves three tasks: (1) identifying the variables and constructs for your research; (2) specifying hypotheses and relationships; and (3) preparing a diagram (conceptual model) that visually represents the theoretical basis of the relationships you will examine.

IDENTIFY VARIABLES AND CONSTRUCTS

The process of conceptualization begins with the identification of variables and constructs. **Variables** are the observable and measurable characteristics in a conceptual model. Researchers assign values to variables that enable us to measure them. Examples of variables include: sales, brand awareness, production level, purchases, search behaviour, demographic characteristics, and so on. When characteristics are measured with a single question and/or statement we generally refer to them as variables. Variables are linked directly to observable facts that can be verified, such as watching a checkout counter in a shop and observing customers' purchase behaviour, or an individual's age.

When several questions/statements are used in combination to represent a characteristic/concept we often call them a **construct**. A big difference between a variable and a construct is that variables are measured directly but constructs can only be measured indirectly by the several variables, using for example survey questionnaires. Thus, constructs are concepts that represent a higher level of abstraction than variables and are defined on the basis of theory. Examples of constructs used in business are service quality, brand attitude, organizational commitment, likelihood of searching for a new job, trust, satisfaction, leadership, and so on. Each of these constructs would be measured indirectly by several variables and when combined they become a construct.

As a further example of a construct, the following questions all asked together on a questionnaire would be considered a service quality construct.

"How strongly do you agree or disagree that:

- ... firms should have their customers' best interests at heart?

- ... firms should be dependable?

- ... firms should be expected to give customers personal attention?

- ... when firms promise to do something by a certain time they should do so?, and

- ... firms should keep accurate records?''

Thus, the primary difference between variables and constructs is that variables directly measure a single characteristic or attribute at a lower level of abstraction, whereas constructs consist of several related characteristics, and are measured indirectly and characterized by a higher level of abstraction than variables. We discuss constructs in greater detail in Chapter 9 on measurement and scaling.

Types of Variables

When developing a conceptual model, we must think about two types of variables/constructs – independent and dependent. An **independent variable** is a measurable characteristic that influences or explains the dependent variable. A **dependent variable** is the variable you are trying to understand, explain and/or predict. For example, employee job satisfaction would be a dependent variable that is explained by two independent variables – compensation level and quality of supervision. The appropriate hypothesis would then be that higher compensation and better supervision (independent variables) explain/predict higher job satisfaction (dependent variable). Constructs, like variables, are also classified as either independent or dependent.

SPECIFY HYPOTHESES AND RELATIONSHIPS

Researchers often have some preliminary ideas regarding data relationships based on the research objectives. These ideas are derived from previous research, theory and/or the current business situation, and typically are called hypotheses. In statistics a **hypothesis** is an unproven supposition or proposition that tentatively explains certain facts or phenomena. A hypothesis may also be thought of as an assumption about the nature of a particular situation. Business researchers test hypotheses to verify that any relationships thought to exist among the variables being studied are due to true relationships and not chance. Some examples of hypotheses business researchers might test include:

- Organizational commitment is related to supervision, coworkers and satisfaction with the work environment.

- Teenage customers will use more wireless minutes per month if we offer package plans with free downloading of music.

- Share prices are positively impacted by favourable performance announcements.

- Customer loyalty is positively related to product quality, pricing, customer service, purchase convenience, opening hours, and so forth.

- Sales are positively related to the amount spent on advertising, the price of the product or service, and the number of sales representatives.

- The announcement of share splits has a positive impact upon share price.

- Fund managers are unable to time the market and thereby earn superior portfolio returns.

- Emerging stock markets exhibit long-term over-reaction patterns.

How to Develop Hypotheses

Hypotheses are developed prior to data collection, and generally emerge from the literature review, research questions and theory. Researchers use hypotheses to explain and test proposed facts or phenomena. For example, Phil Samouel may want to test the proposition that 70 % of his employees are "proud" to be working at his restaurant. Similarly, he may wish to compare two or more groups of employees, for example, female workers vs. male workers, and determine if there are differences between the two groups. He might also want to use the results of his employee survey to test the proposition that part-time employees are more likely to search for another job than are full-time employees.

Two Important Questions in Hypothesis Development   In developing hypotheses, the researcher must always be concerned about whether the hypotheses can actually be tested. To test a hypothesis, one must be able to identify the group you are focusing on and measure the appropriate variables. Thus, in developing hypotheses researchers constantly must ask: "What group will be examined with the hypothesis?" and "What variables are being tested?" For example, if you want to determine whether older workers (defined as 50 years or older) who have younger supervisors (39 years old or younger) are more likely to search for another job than are older workers with older supervisors, then you must ask specific questions about these variables on your questionnaire. Moreover, in stating your hypotheses you must be specific about which group you are talking about and which variables. Consider the following hypotheses recently posed by one of the authors students in a thesis proposal:

1. Older workers who expect more from their younger supervisors will elicit more effective leadership from their younger supervisors.

2. There is a relationship between the younger supervisor's leadership behaviour and the expectations of the older worker.

To actually test these hypotheses, what groups and what variables are involved? Clearly one must have collected data on older workers with a younger supervisor. But does one also have to have data on older workers with older supervisors? In hypothesis one, to measure the effectiveness of the younger supervisors' leadership do you need data on the leadership behaviour of older supervisors as a benchmark to measure younger supervisor's effectiveness? Moreover, what is meant by "will elicit more effective leadership . . ."? How will this variable be measured? Finally, in the second hypothesis what is meant by "the expectations of the older worker" and how will it be measured? Other questions are possible to ensure these hypotheses can be tested, but these give you an idea of how precise one must be in developing hypotheses.

Correctly stating hypotheses is difficult. The researcher must be specific about the variables being measured and the groups being questioned. Consider, for example, the following hypothesis:

• Older workers' (50+) expectations of their immediate supervisors' leadership behaviours are positively associated with their immediate supervisors' actual leadership behaviours.

In the case of the above hypothesis, data must be collected from only one group – older workers (50 years of age and older). Second, the variables being measured are: (1) what the older worker expects from their immediate supervisor in terms of leadership; and (2) how their immediate supervisor actually behaves as a leader. To test this hypothesis, you must have data that measures leadership expectations and behaviours of immediate supervisors as perceived by older workers. If you devote time to developing good hypotheses this will ensure that data is collected from the correct group of individuals and that the appropriate questions are asked on the survey.

Null and Alternative Hypotheses

Hypotheses sometimes are stated in the null form. The **null hypothesis** is that there is no difference in the group statistics, for example, means, medians, and so on. It is based on the notion that any change or difference is entirely the result of random error. In our older worker example, the null hypothesis would be:

- There is no difference in the leadership behaviours of immediate supervisors of older workers with high leadership expectations versus those with lower leadership expectations.

Statisticians almost always test the null hypothesis. But business researchers often test hypotheses stated in other ways.

Another hypothesis, called the **alternative hypothesis**, states the opposite of the null hypothesis. The alternative hypothesis is that there is a difference between the groups being compared. If the null hypothesis is accepted there is no difference in the groups. But if the null hypothesis is rejected and the alternative hypothesis accepted, the conclusion is there is a change or difference in behaviour, attitudes or some similar measure of the groups.

Directional and Nondirectional Hypotheses

Hypotheses can be stated as directional or nondirectional. If you use terms like more than, less than, positive or negative in stating the relationship between two groups or two variables, then these hypotheses are directional. An example of a **directional hypothesis** would be:

- The greater the stress experienced on the job the more likely an employee is to search for another job.

Another way of stating a directional hypothesis is the "If – Then" approach:

- If employees are given more safety training, then they will have fewer accidents.

Nondirectional hypotheses postulate a difference or relationship, but do not indicate a direction for the differences or relationship. That is, we may postulate a significant relationship between two groups or two variables, but we are not able to say whether the relationship is positive or negative. An example of a nondirectional hypothesis would be:

- There is a relationship between stress experienced on the job and the likelihood an employee will search for another job.

Another example of a nondirectional hypothesis is:

- There is a relationship between organizational commitment and likelihood to search for another job.

Directional and nondirectional hypotheses are both acceptable in business research. The advantage of a directional hypothesis, however, is that you can use a one-tailed statistical test for hypothesis testing instead of a two-tailed test. Indeed, if a two-tailed statistical test is used to test a directional hypothesis it is quite possible the researcher will conclude a relationship does not exist when in fact one does. This is an important concept to understand since most commercially available statistical software, like SPSS, only reports the results of two-tailed tests.

Hypothesis Testing

Hypothesis tests are systematic procedures followed to "accept" or "reject" hypotheses about proposed patterns or relationships. The proposed connections or relationships need to be tested to conclude whether they are true relationships. Researchers can test hypotheses whether they are doing qualitative or quantitative research. When testing qualitative hypotheses researchers look for alternative explanations or negative (opposing) examples that are not consistent with the patterns being tested. If information is gathered that differs from the proposed relationship the hypothesis is rejected. When testing quantitative hypotheses researchers collect quantitative data and apply statistical tests.

The variables and constructs measured in business research have relationships that connect them. A **relationship** is a meaningful link believed to exist between two variables/constructs. For example, lower prices are related to higher sales, bad working conditions are associated with a higher likelihood to search for a new job, and so on. Typically, relationships are identified as meaningful and deserving attention based on theory, business experience or expert judgement. Other examples of relationships we study in business research include:

- Employees are absent from work less often when they have good working conditions.
- Accounts that frequently do not balance should be audited.
- Healthy people exercise more often and eat more nutritious foods.
- Conglomerate firms underperform focused firms with respect to the returns they achieve for shareholders
- Individuals who come from diverse backgrounds have greater natural networking ability.
- Dominant firms in mature markets generate greater proportions of free cash flow.

When we draw the relationships we typically label some of the variables/constructs as independent variables and others as dependent variables. The independent variables have arrows coming out of them. The dependent variables have arrows pointing into them. If arrows are coming into and going out of a variable, then these variables are used as both independent and dependent variables in the same conceptual model.

The logic we use in deciding how to draw the relationships is based on the research hypotheses. Recall that hypotheses are preconceptions regarding the relationships represented in data. Two more examples of hypotheses are:

- Teenage customers will use more wireless minutes per month if we offer package plans with free downloading of music.
- Loyalty is positively related to product quality, pricing, customer service, purchase convenience, opening hours, and so forth.

We test hypotheses such as these to enable us to first confirm that a relationship does or does not exist, and second, to help us better understand relationships.

PREPARE A CONCEPTUAL MODEL

A **conceptual model** is a diagram that connects variables/constructs based on theory and logic to display visually the hypotheses that will be tested. When we draw conceptual models we often represent the constructs/variables with rectangles. We connect the rectangles with arrows that represent the relationships. The arrows are pointed in the direction of the dependent variable in the relationship. The direction of the arrows sometimes indicates a "causal" relationship between the two variables/constructs if the research design is set up to measure causation (an experiment). That is, if the research design specifically measures a "before" and "after" relationship, a causal link can be examined. But if the research measures the relationship of two or more variables at the same point in time then one variable (independent) may be associated with another (dependent) but does not necessarily cause it. In most instances the arrow and its direction do not indicate a causal relationship. Rather, it simply says the two variables are possibly related.

To help you to better understand conceptual models, we have drawn a couple of examples in Exhibits 6-1 and 6-2. The first model has four variables. Three of the variables are demographic measures – age, income and gender. In the model these variables are shown as independent variables because they are predicting the fourth variable – the dependent variable wireless minutes usage. All of these variables are measured with a single question and we think of them as individual variables. Also, no signs (+/−) are shown on the arrows to represent the orientation of relationships between the independent and dependent variables. Therefore, our hypotheses only show there is a relationship between the variables, but not whether the relationship is positive or negative (directional).

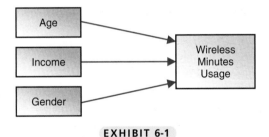

EXHIBIT 6-1

Conceptual Model of Demographics and Wireless Minutes Usage

The conceptual model in Exhibit 6-2 is more complicated. It also has four variables. In this situation, we think of them as constructs because each variable is measured with more than one question. Note that researchers often use the terms variable and construct interchangeably.

To better understand this model, we must define the variables/constructs. First, the construct "Technology Acceptance Climate" is the extent to which employees' ongoing use of the information technology is rewarded, supported and expected within the organization. Although not shown in the model, it is measured with five questions. Second, the construct "Shared Values" represents the feelings and beliefs that form an organization's culture and provide a basis for individuals to understand the organization's functioning and norms for behaviour. Examples of shared values include: customer orientation, entrepreneurial values, adaptive cultural expectations and information sharing norms. Thus, the shared values construct is measured with several questions as well. Third, "Effective Technology Implementation" is how quickly and completely the new information technology is integrated into ongoing operations and "Enhanced Firm Productivity" is higher

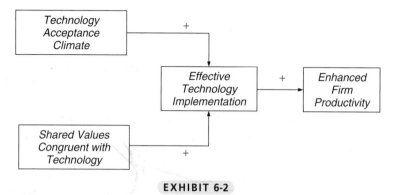

EXHIBIT 6-2

Technology Implementation Model

production output per day. Both of these variables/constructs are measured with several questions as well.

The constructs "Technology Acceptance Climate" and "Shared Values" are independent variables/constructs in our conceptual model. In contrast, the construct "Enhanced Firm Productivity" is a dependent variable. The construct "Effective Technology Implementation" is more complicated in the model because it is both a dependent and an independent variable. In other words, it is a dependent variable because it is predicted by two independent variables (implementation climate and shared values) but it also is an independent variable because it is shown as predicting firm productivity.

Three hypotheses are illustrated by the arrows in this model. They include: "Effective implementation of information technology is positively related to the acceptance climate", "Effective implementation of information technology is positively related to the organisation's shared values", and "Enhanced productivity is positively related to effective implementation of information technology." There is a plus sign (+) by all three arrows so all three relationships are directional and positive.

When you prepare your literature review you should include a written description of your conceptual model as well as an actual drawing of the model. The section of your literature review that describes your model typically is called a **conceptual framework**. The written description integrates all the information about the problem/opportunity in a logical manner, describes the relationships among the variables, explains the theory underlying these relationships, indicates the nature and direction of the relationships, and includes a conceptual model. Exhibit 6-3 provides guidelines on how to prepare a good conceptual framework.

Business researchers could collect empirical data using a questionnaire from a cross-section of firms and test the hypotheses described in the technology implementation model. Indeed, in many instances business research involves collecting information to test hypotheses. Sometimes the research design is qualitative and uses, for example, case studies to test hypotheses. Other times the research design is quantitative and uses surveys to test hypotheses. In the rest of this chapter we describe how to select the appropriate research design to either identify relationships, or if relationships are already known, such as those depicted in the conceptual models, then they can be examined.

- The variables/constructs considered relevant to the study are clearly identified and defined.

- The sources of constructs are clearly identified. If new constructs are developed for the study the process for developing the constructs is explained, and their validity and reliability reported.

- If published constructs are used, their validity and reliability is reported.

- The discussion states how the variables/constructs are related to each other, that is which variables are dependent or independent.

- If possible, the nature (positive or negative) of the relationships as well as the direction is hypothesized on the basis of theory, previous research or researcher judgement.

- There is a clear explanation of why you expect these relationships to exist. The explanation cites theory, business practice or some other credible source.

- A conceptual model or framework is prepared to clearly illustrate the hypothesized relationships.

EXHIBIT 6-3

Guidelines for Preparing Your Conceptual Framework

BASIC RESEARCH DESIGNS

A research design provides the basic directions or "recipe" for carrying out the project. Following the principle of parsimony, the researcher should choose a design that (1) will provide relevant information on the research questions/hypotheses, and (2) will complete the job most efficiently. Once the researcher decides on a study design, the formulation phase of the basic research process is complete.

Recall that the literature review identifies existing themes, trends and relationships between variables. Relevant theories are described and a re-examination or restatement of the preliminary research questions may be necessary. Sometimes the theory is well developed and leads to a formal conceptual framework, including hypotheses to be tested. Other times, the theory is limited or perhaps nonexistent. When hypotheses can be developed, the researcher typically relies on a combination of both qualitative and quantitative approaches to conduct the research. If the topic of interest is a new area, and the theory is not well established, then the researcher will most likely rely on a qualitative approach.

QUALITATIVE VERSUS QUANTITATIVE APPROACHES

Many students fear business research courses because they are associated with maths and statistics. But business research is a discipline that uses statistics. The statistics are used with quantitative data collected from company financial records, sales reports, questionnaires and similar sources. **Quantitative data** are measurements in which numbers are used directly to represent the characteristics of something. Since they are recorded directly with numbers, they are in a form that lends itself to statistical analysis. Chapter 8 describes data collection methods.

Qualitative data represent descriptions of things that are made without assigning numbers directly. Qualitative data are generally collected using some type of unstructured interviews or observation. Focus groups and in-depth interviews are frequently applied qualitative research approaches. Rather than collecting information by assigning numbers, the data are collected by recording words, phrases and sometimes pictures. For example, researchers have asked respondents to describe how they feel about a particular issue, such as globalization, or to tell them a story about a particular event that is important to them. The researcher then analyses the comments on globalization or the event for potential meaning. Exhibit 6-4 compares qualitative and quantitative approaches.

An important point to remember with qualitative research is that hypotheses are developed less frequently. In qualitative research the concern is that if hypotheses are developed they will influence

Description	Quantitative Approach	Qualitative Approach
Purpose:	Collect quantitative data.	Collect qualitative data.
	More useful for testing.	More useful for discovering.
	Provides summary information on many characteristics.	Provides in-depth (deeper understanding) information on a few characteristics.
	Useful in tracking trends.	Discovers 'hidden' motivations and values.
Properties:	More structured data collection techniques and objective ratings.	More unstructured data collection techniques requiring subjective interpretation.
	Higher concern for representativeness.	Less concern for representativeness.
	Emphasis on achieving reliability and validity of measures used.	Emphasis on the trustworthiness of respondents.
	Relatively short interviews (1 to 20 minutes).	Relatively long interviews (1/2 to many hours).
	Interviewer questions directly, but does not probe deeply.	Interviewer actively probes and must be highly skilled.
	Large samples (over 50).	Small samples (1–50).
	Results relatively objective.	Results relatively subjective.

EXHIBIT 6-4

Comparison of Qualitative and Quantitative Approaches

the direction and outcome of the findings. Thus, the literature review in qualitative research leads to a conceptual framework that is examined. But rather than proposing hypotheses, the researcher is guided by the conceptual framework in collecting data to identify concepts and ideas. Thus, the data collection interacts with the conceptual framework to move the research toward its conclusion. At some point in the data collection the researcher begins identifying the common themes and organizing them into patterns. The patterns are then summarized into a set of findings and ultimately conclusions.

The research components that are the strengths of a quantitative study, such as structure and representativeness, are not typical in qualitative research. Qualitative researchers use unstructured interviews as a way of probing deeply into an issue. Since respondents are free to choose their own words, the researcher cannot predict the specific direction of the interview. The lack of structure allows identification of issues that would not be revealed by a structured questionnaire. Respondents who are atypical in some way may be preferred, and individuals highly involved in a situation are especially desirable since new discoveries are often somewhat extreme.

Objectivity is an important component of science. Quantitative approaches provide objectivity in that hypotheses are tested by applying statistical criteria to the measures. Since the respondents provide the numbers, the researcher's opinion does not affect the hypothesis test, although it clearly does influence the design of the questions that are asked in the study. In contrast, qualitative approaches require interpretation. For example, it should be obvious that "cool" clothing usually means the respondent likes it. If clothing is referred to as "funky" or "comfortable", however, is that desirable? These terms represent ambiguity for the researcher when reading an interview transcript. Comfortable could mean clothing that is loose fitting possibly allowing freedom of movement, or it could mean the clothing makes consumers feel comfortable about their bodies;[1] thus, the researcher's judgement is used to resolve the ambiguous meaning. Experienced qualitative researchers are good at resolving ambiguities and use approaches to minimize problems with interpretation. Finally, since judgement is involved, the findings of qualitative approaches can be more difficult to replicate, particularly if the methods followed are not fully documented.

Does subjectivity make qualitative research unscientific and less useful? Absolutely not! Qualitative researchers usually assess inter-rater reliability. **Inter-rater reliability** means that multiple "raters" will evaluate the same qualitative data point. Reliable data exist when the raters agree on their meaning, and this provides an indication that the results can be replicated. This is not often required, however, because most qualitative research is conducted for purposes other than testing hypotheses. It stops short of the testing phase of the scientific method. Since it is discovery oriented, the criticism of subjectivity isn't relevant. Subjectivity becomes a weakness only when researchers try to generalize conclusions based upon a single researcher's opinion.

Some researchers debate the superiority of qualitative research over quantitative research or vice versa. However, this view is near-sighted. A comparison of the two approaches suggests that they complement each other quite well. Qualitative techniques are more often part of an exploratory design. Thus, a very important alliance between the two is that qualitative studies may develop ideas that can be tested with some type of quantitative approach. Effective decision making often requires input from both quantitative and qualitative research approaches.

THREE TYPES OF RESEARCH DESIGNS

Many research designs could be used to study business problems. To simplify your understanding of the different designs, we have grouped them into three types. Researchers generally choose from among (1) exploratory; (2) descriptive; or (3) causal design. An exploratory research project is useful when the research questions are vague or when there is little theory available to guide the development of hypotheses. At times, decision makers and researchers may find it impossible to formulate a basic statement of the research problem. Exploratory research is used to develop a better understanding of a business problem or opportunity. Descriptive research describes some situation. Generally, the situations are described by providing measures of an event or activity. Descriptive research often accomplishes this by using descriptive statistics. Typical descriptive statistics include frequency counts (how many), measures of central tendency like the mean, median or mode, or a measure of dispersion (variation) such as the standard deviation. Statistical tests are used to assess the relationships examined using descriptive statistics. Causal research designs are the most complex. They are designed to test whether one event causes another. For example, does one event X (smoking) cause Y (cancer)? The three basic research designs are explained in greater detail below.

Exploratory Research

Exploratory research is used when the researcher has little information. In other words, exploratory designs are appropriate when the researcher knows little about the problem or opportunity! It is designed to discover new relationships, patterns, themes, ideas and so on. Thus, it is not intended to test specific research hypotheses.

Exploratory research is particularly useful in highly innovative industries. Vodafone, Microsoft, Siemens, TESCO and Apple Computers, for instance, are companies that place a high priority on discovering new ideas from exploratory research. The research not only identifies new technologies, but just as importantly, it is aimed at discovering those technologies that address practical business or consumer needs. Siemens, the German-based telecommunications firm, employs over 40,000 people in research-related positions.[2] Their programmatic exploratory research programme is aimed at discovering potential matches between needs and technologies one, two or three decades in advance.

The importance of exploratory research in product innovation has been described by Swaddling and Zobel as:[3]

> When conducted well, exploratory research provides a window into consumer perceptions, behaviors, and needs. It enables companies to develop successful new products more consistently. This superior understanding of the consumer leads to effective decision-making and recognition of market opportunities, a distinct definition of the business in which your company competes, and a high probability of producing innovative new products that drive extraordinary profits. (p. 21)

Exploratory research was instrumental in helping Apple develop the iPod. From exploratory research, Apple learned that consumers wanted a portable device that could play their favourite songs, at high quality, and store many songs for different occasions (1000+). Exploratory research later helped Apple develop follow up products such as the IPOD Nano and Shuffle. Exploratory research is useful in other situations as well, such as identifying innovative production and management practices, accounting auditing approaches, strategies for diagnosing medical problems, political candidate messages, and incentive compensation systems for managers to increase unit innovativeness.[4]

Exploratory research can take many forms. A literature review can be a useful first step in providing a better understanding of some issue. Literature reviews are conducted by searching through company records, trade and academic journals as well as other sources where research is reported. But a literature review also can be an early part of a descriptive or causal design. Electronic search engines like Google or Yahoo have made the search process simpler. Researchers can enter key terms related to the research question and locate dozens, perhaps hundreds of potential sources containing related research.

Exploratory research relies more heavily on qualitative techniques, although it is possible to use quantitative approaches. The following situations are typical of exploratory designs using qualitative approaches:

- Use of focus groups to identify the factors important in purchasing a new wireless phone.

- Use of in-depth interviews to identify what issues are causing employees to be less productive.

- Case studies to determine what conditions or events are causing companies in a particular industry to have financial problems.

- Videotape or photographs to record the experiences or events impacting the group of individuals being examined.

- Experience surveys to collect information from individuals considered to be knowledgeable on the research topic.

- Document observation and analysis to examine recorded opinions, reports, news stories, and similar secondary data.

- Projective techniques to explore difficult to obtain information, such as motivations or justifications for supporting a less popular or extreme viewpoint.

Descriptive Research

Descriptive research is designed to obtain data that describes the characteristics of the topic of interest in the research. As examples, questions like: Who is likely to be most satisfied? When should we maximize production? How much investment is required? Which brands are most preferred? What advertisements are most effective? How are experience and performance related? and Why do snow skiers prefer the Swiss Alps? . . . can be answered by descriptive research. Descriptive research designs are usually structured and specifically designed to measure the characteristics described in research questions. Hypotheses, derived from theory, usually serve to guide the process and provide a list of what needs to be measured.

Studies tracking seasonal trends are good examples of descriptive studies. A company that brews beer and ale can benefit from seasonality information for numerous reasons. For example, beer and ale sales differ during the year so seasonality information would improve decisions regarding flexible production capacity. Exploratory research might reveal that consumers "feel" more like drinking beer for certain types of occasions and that they prefer beer with certain foods, such as pizza or spicy foods. A research question might ask whether or not beer and ale consumption is seasonal. Further consideration may suggest hypotheses that lager beer sales are highest in the summer, while ale and dark beer sales are highest in the winter. A descriptive study could track monthly sales of each product over a five-year period. The results would describe the seasonality of beer and ale consumption and directly address the hypotheses and research question.

With descriptive studies, data collection usually involves some type of structured process – either observation of data or interviews that ask structured questions. For example, the research may rely on a questionnaire containing specific items that ask respondents to select from a fixed number of choices, or it may involve an individual observing (collecting) financial and/or economic data from government or industry documents. Data may be collected on production processes, stores visited, products or services used, political candidates or issues, employee attitudes, and so on. Bar codes can be scanned to obtain information on the movement of goods, and Web sites can be monitored to determine number of visits, type of information requested, purchase data, and so forth. A descriptive study using scanner data from supermarkets would be able to compare weekly sales of Tabasco hot sauce with and without a price promotion. Unlike exploratory studies, descriptive studies are often confirmatory. In other words, they are used to test hypotheses.

Descriptive studies are generally classified as either cross-sectional or longitudinal. We discuss both in the following paragraphs. Descriptive studies provide a "snapshot" or description of business elements at a given time and are considered *cross-sectional*. Data are collected at a given point in time and summarized statistically. As an example of a cross-sectional study, data could be collected within the European Union to examine different attitudes of individuals from various member countries about the value of obtaining a university degree. Findings of this study could be examined by cross sections of the respondents, such as country of residence, age, gender, rural versus suburban versus city, and so forth. This is a one-shot or cross-sectional study to examine attitudes toward the idea of having a university degree. Most surveys fall into this category.

Sample surveys are good examples of cross-sectional studies. Perhaps you have seen a civil engineer or surveyor examining a piece of land where a new motorway will be built. They are surveying property to describe its characteristics. What are its boundaries and elevation and what are its distinguishing characteristics? Likewise, business researchers survey a sample of business elements in an effort to describe a population's characteristics. When surveying land, the surveyor looks through a transit to take measurements. Generally, business research takes measurements using a questionnaire or some other structured response form. The business elements could be business units, retail outlets, hospitals, salespeople, production workers, brands, products or customers, among others. A key distinguishing feature of cross-sectional studies is that the elements are measured only once during the survey process.

Descriptive statistics based on sample measurements describe the population. Typical statistics include rankings (best to worst), frequency counts (how many), cross-classifications (comparisons of frequencies), group means, correlations and predictions using regression. Each of these is discussed in a later chapter.

Since population characteristics are being inferred from a sample, or subset of the population, cross-sectional descriptive studies must carefully consider how well the selected subset represents the larger population. Researchers assume that the sample characteristics are comparable to those of the population. Error is introduced into the process to the extent that the sample and population are actually different. Thus, for convenience, a researcher may use MBA students as a sample in a study of how managers evaluate subordinates. The MBA students would play the role of managers in the study. Error is introduced to the extent that MBA students are indeed different than practising managers. Sampling approaches and ways to minimize error are discussed in Chapter 7.

Suppose a researcher wanted to study the effect of background music on service quality perceptions. A specific research question deals with whether or not men and women rate background music and service quality similarly. Questionnaires could be used to measure customers' perceptions of background music and service quality using a seven-point scale. A sample of 800 department store customers could be surveyed over a one week period. Answers to the questions could then be used to describe the population's beliefs. After data have been collected results would be tabulated and summarized statistically, and conclusions drawn.

Exhibit 6-5 shows a table containing descriptive, cross-sectional results of a study of the use of music in department stores. Several conclusions are possible from these results. For instance, men rate the store's service quality higher but women like the background music more. Further analysis might show whether or not reactions to the music are related to service quality and perhaps even

	n	Background Music: Mean*	Service Quality: Mean*
Women	500	5.07	6.04
Men	300	4.61	6.22
Overall	800	4.89	6.11

*A seven-point scale was used by shoppers to rate the music and service quality, with 1 = "Unfavourable" and 7 = "Very Favourable."

EXHIBIT 6-5

Department Store Shopper Ratings of Background Music and Service Quality

buying behaviour. Conclusions derived from these results are valid to the extent that the 800 department store shoppers are representative of all department store shoppers. Studies of this type are fairly common and a good example of cross-sectional data.[5]

Longitudinal studies also use a sample to describe business activities. Rather than describing business activities at a single point in time, however, longitudinal data describe events over time. Longitudinal studies are appropriate when research questions and hypotheses are affected by how things vary over time. Unlike cross-sectional studies, longitudinal studies require data to be collected from the same sample units at multiple points in time. The data represent a time series of observations. Longitudinal data enable tracking of business elements so that trends can be observed.

Time is critical to business. Organizations often track employee performance over time. This data enables managers to know how performance varies with time. Similarly, many financial statistics are tracked including all well-known stock exchange indices. In most industrialized nations consumer confidence also is tracked. By analysing these two trends together, we can see how closely the two indices correspond. Is this information useful for making investment decisions? Product sales are usually tracked since many products have seasonal demand, meaning the amount consumed is not constant through time. See the Research in Action boxes to learn about seasonality in beer, wine and alcohol consumption.

RESEARCH IN ACTION — IS THERE A BAD TIME FOR A BEER?

Is beer seasonal? Time and beer are related. Firstly, beer shows a fairly strong seasonal trend. Research shows that beer sales are about 15 % higher during the summer months than they are during the rest of the year. But, it isn't quite that simple. There are spikes in beer sales around the winter holidays. Wintertime beer sales are concentrated around these times. However, time and beer go together in other ways too. Cyclical patterns in demand over long periods of time can be observed. Theoretically, these patterns are due to cyclical patterns in consumer choices for alcoholic beverages. If wine is in, beer is out. And there is even more. Forty per cent of all weekly beer sales are sold in 12 hours, from 4 pm to 10 pm Friday and Saturday.

Both beer companies and retailers tie their promotional efforts to these promotional trends. During these times, copromotions may be used. Research is conducted in a certain area to determine which foods are most often consumed with beer. Promotions might be run on these foods and beer simultaneously to try to make up for the usual drop in sales.

Source: Kelly, B. (1999). ''Beer for All Seasons'', *National Petroleum News*, 91 (August), 34–36. ■

RESEARCH IN ACTION

TRENDS IN LONG-TERM ALCOHOL CONSUMPTION

US Alcohol Consumption per Capita by Beverage

This chart tracks how much alcohol the average American consumes each year. To read this chart, keep in mind that each beverage is only partially alcohol. A typical wine for example is 10 % to 13 % alcohol, spirits (whisky) are 40 % to 50 % alcohol and beer is about 4 % to 6 % alcohol. The chart shows a downturn in spirits consumption over the time period beginning in 1977. Beer consumption also shows a slight decrease, although the average American still consumed 1.25 gallons of alcohol by beer in 1998, which equates to 25 gallons per year. Alcohol consumption via wine displays a peak during the mid 1980s and perhaps the start of an upward trend toward the end of the 1990s. These data might be useful to drinks companies in identifying competitive and market pressures that affect sales and operations. ∎

Longitudinal studies sometimes use a panel to collect data. A **panel** is a fixed sample arranged for the purpose of collecting data. Although panels can include any business element as a unit, they are generally comprised of human elements. With panels, the people involved agree to have repeated measurements taken over an extended period of time. For example, television ratings are derived from a panel of viewers who agree to have their programme selection automatically monitored. Monitoring companies provide each panel member with a meter that is connected to their television. The meter electronically records what channel the TV is tuned to, on what days of the week and at what the time of the day. Some electronic meters also include a "heat sensor" to determine whether the room the TV is located in has humans watching the TV or the family pet! Panel members also record their TV watching habits in a diary. The diary is used to record demographics and other personal details about the household.

Panel surveys collect data from the same group of respondents over a period of time. A large pool of panel members is recruited and when they are involved in a survey they record their responses in a diary. Information on panel members, such as demographic and household characteristics, is collected and used to determine which individuals are used for a particular survey. Panels can represent any group of individuals, from various types of consumer groups to business groups such as doctors, lawyers, CEOs and so forth. One online example is a panel of children ages 6 to 14 that can be viewed at www.kidzeyes.com. Typically, the research company that maintains the panel will randomly select individuals as a representative sample to participate in a particular survey. Sometimes panel members are asked the same questions over time, in which case it is called a longitudinal panel study. At other times, the questions are only asked once. Traditional methods of data collection have been by post, telephone, personal interviews and fax. But electronic data collection is rapidly increasing for panel surveys. Also, panel surveys can be either self-completion or interviewer assisted. An advantage of panel data is response rates are fast and substantially higher than other methods of data collection. See the Research in Action box to learn more about the emergence of electronic panel surveys.

RESEARCH IN ACTION

DECISION ANALYST, INC. ENTERS INTERNET PANEL SECTOR IN A BIG WAY!

Decision Analyst, Inc. is a leader in using technology to collect data. President Jerry Thomas believes the future of marketing research belongs to the Internet. In the US over 60 % of adults currently have access to the Internet at home or work, and Internet users represent over 70 % of total US purchasing power and are rapidly becoming representative of the US population. Other countries, such as the UK, Germany, France, the Netherlands, Australia and Scandinavia are similar in terms of Internet access and usage.

As a global leader in Internet-based research, Decision Analyst has conducted hundreds of online surveys via their worldwide Consumer Opinion Online panels of more than 3.5 million consumers in the US, Canada, Europe, Latin America and Asia, as well as their specialty panels of technology professionals, physicians, executives, and contractors. Based on its own experiences as well as observations from other professionals, Decision Analyst believes Internet-based surveys provide higher-quality data, and are faster and less costly than telephone surveys. For more information on this innovative company visit their Web site at: www.decisionanalyst.com. ∎

CAUSAL RESEARCH

Causal research tests whether or not one event causes another. Does X cause Y? More precisely, a causal relationship means a change in one event brings about a corresponding change in another event. **Causality** means a change in X (the cause) makes a change in Y (the effect) occur! There are four conditions researchers look for in testing cause and effect relationships:[6]

1. Time sequence – the cause must occur before the effect.

2. Covariance – a change in the cause is associated with a change in the effect. In other words, the two variables are related to one another.

3. Nonspurious association – the relationship is true and not due to something else that just happens to affect both the cause and effect. This requires that other potential causes be controlled or eliminated.

4. Theoretical support – a logical explanation exists for why the cause and effect relationship exists.

The following example illustrates these four conditions. Suppose a researcher is testing whether or not a change in compensation systems causes a change in employee turnover. Firstly, the time sequence condition means the researcher must study changes in turnover occurring after the compensation system is altered. Since a change cannot affect what happened in the past, it is illogical to suspect that a change in the compensation plan announced and implemented in July 2007 caused employees to resign from their jobs in December 2006.

Secondly, the researcher examines whether or not a change in compensation is systematically related to employee turnover rates. This is done by comparing turnover rates before and after changes.

Thirdly, even if a relationship is observed, is there something else going on at the same time that could explain any observed changes? For example, what if a competing firm opened a new facility at the same time data were collected? Would any changes in turnover be caused only by the compensation system changes or also by the increased demand for labour brought about by the competition?

Fourthly, a theoretical explanation is needed. A change in compensation may affect how workers feel about their jobs, which will affect whether or not they will continue working for the company. Causality can be established to the extent that these conditions are met.

Decision makers are helped by known cause and effect relationships. Knowing something enables them to predict what will happen if they effect some change. Causality is a powerful concept. Thus, causal designs require very precise execution. Moreover, they can be complex, expensive and often take a long time from planning to execution.

RESEARCH IN ACTION

DO MOBILE PHONE USERS WANT ADVERTISEMENTS?

The mobile phone video download market is expected to increase 800 % by 2010. Some consumers prefer free downloads supported by advertisements whilst others prefer to pay a small monthly fee for commercial-free programmes. The big appeal of mobile phone advertising is to communicate with the youth market. Most of this segment spends little time reading or viewing traditional mediums, like TV, newspapers and magazines. The medium appears particularly good for products like music and movies, which the youth market consumes a lot of. For example, Maiden Group, PLC, a UK-based advertising company, promoted a new album by rock band Coldplay using 30-second spots featuring interviews with musicians and clips from their music videos. To ensure a higher quality sound, the clips were adjusted to better match mobile phone technology. The clips were used in six London train stations and large video advertising screens told mobile phone users to switch on their Bluetooth phones to receive a message. The album became a No. 1 hit in the UK and the ad agency plans to use the approach with other promotions for this segment. Similarly, in Plaza Cataluña, in Barcelona, Nike installed a huge outdoor ad featuring tennis player Rafael Nadal, and powered with Bluetooth technology. By using their Bluetooth cell phone connection, users could download the new Nike Pro TV spot and an exclusive Nadal screensaver.

How do you feel about cell phone advertising? What research design would you use to determine consumers reactions to mobile phone advertising?

Sources: Enid Burns, ''Users Prefer Ad-Supported Video'', 11 January 2006, http://www.clickz.com/news/article.php/3576816. Enid Burns, ''Mobile Video Market Set for Growth'', 28 March 2006, http://www.clickz.com/stats/sectors/entertainment/article.php/3579236. ''Wireless Phone Advertising Has Promise'', *Mobile Advertising, Brands and Affinity Marketing*, Reed Business, www.instat.com. Paul Korzeniowski, ''Cell Phones Emerge as New Advertising Medium'', www.technewsworld.com, and http://www.marketingdirecto.com/noticias/noticia.php?idnoticia=16532, accessed April 2006. ∎

USING SEVERAL RESEARCH DESIGNS

Researchers often use more than one research design in a single project. It is quite common to collect secondary data to help decide if primary data needs to be gathered. Similarly, we often conduct exploratory research using qualitative approaches before moving on to quantitative research using descriptive designs. For example, the National Health Service (NHS) may want to relocate its health clinics to better serve users. But it may not know how the decision is made to use a particular clinic or what factors are considered. To learn about these factors the NHS may first conduct focus groups and follow this exploratory research with descriptive research to determine which findings are valid for the overall population of clinic users.

Selecting the right research design depends upon the research questions and objectives. If the research question involves primarily discovery or clarification of some issue, an exploratory design is best. Research questions that emphasize the description of some quantity, the relative amounts of some variable or the extent to which some variables are related probably calls for a descriptive design. On the other hand, exploratory research may be used to help design a questionnaire for a descriptive research project. Finally, if the research question hopes to establish cause and effect then a causal design with an experiment is appropriate.

RESEARCH IN ACTION

HOW CAN EUROPE KEEP OLDER WORKERS EMPLOYED LONGER?

The European Commission has gone on record urging the European Union to make better use of the potential of its older workers. Increased life expectancy means that people have greater opportunities to fulfil their potential over a longer lifespan, and their employment will be a key factor in maintaining living standards. The European Commission says that the number of workers between the ages of 20 and 29 will fall by 11 million, or 20 %, during the period 1995–2015, while the number of people between 50 and 64 will increase by 16.5 million, or more than 25 %. Over the next 20 years the population above the standard retirement age, 65 years, will increase by 17 million. Companies are going to have to learn how to manage older workers, because there are going to be a lot more of them.

Summits in Stockholm and Barcelona in 2001 and 2002 adopted targets of 50 % for the employment rate for individuals in the 55–64 age group. But progress toward achieving these targets has been disappointing and employment for this age group remains at about 40 %. A Commission report has suggested the following conditions will reinforce the employment of older workers:

- appropriate financial incentives;

- continuing access to training;

- good health and safety conditions at work;

- flexible forms of work organization;

- effective labour market policies; and

- improved quality in work.

What kind of research should be undertaken to determine how Europe can make better use of it older workers?

Sources: `http://europa.eu.int/comm/employment_social/news/2004/mar/ ip_04_295_en.html`. Zwick, S. (2000). "Not Over the Hill Yet!", *Time Europe*, 156(7). "Rethinking the Role of Older Workers: Promoting Older Worker Employment in Europe and Japan", `http://www.aarp.org/research/work/employment/ib77_workers.html`. "Europe Needs to Make Better Use of its Older Workers", `http://www.sheilapantry.com/ oshworld/news/2004/200403.html`, accessed June 2006. ∎

CONTINUING CASE   SAMOUEL'S GREEK CUISINE

A business consultant with experience in the restaurant industry was hired to assist Phil and his brother. After an initial consultation, the business consultant recommended a comprehensive assessment of the restaurant. The assessment would focus on three areas. The first area was the actual operations of the restaurant. The proposed variables to be investigated in this first project included:

- prices being charged,

- menu items being offered,

- interior decorations and atmosphere,

- customer counts at lunch and dinner, and

- average amount spent per customer.

The second area of study involved better understanding of Phil's employees. To do so, the consultant recommended a research project to obtain information regarding the work environment at the restaurant and how employees felt about working there. Variables to be examined on the employee project include:

- relationship with supervisor,

- relationship with co-workers,

- compensation,

- training,

- job satisfaction, and

- classification characteristics for employees.

The third area would be to learn more about Samouel's and Gino's customers. Variables to be examined on the customer project include:

- food quality,

- customer contact employees,

- pricing,

- atmosphere,

- dining out habits, and

- customer characteristics.

Results from examining these three areas will be used to prepare a business plan to compete with Gino's Italian Ristorante.

1. Do the three research projects proposed by the consultant include all the areas that need to be researched? If not, which others need to be studied?

2. Is there other information that needs to be collected in the project on restaurant operations?

3. Should other variables be examined in the employee and customer projects? If yes, what specifically should these variables be?

4. What kind of research design would be most appropriate for the three projects – exploratory, descriptive, causal, or more than one type of research design? Justify your choice. ■

SUMMARY

■ **Understand the role of conceptualization in research**

An important outcome of your literature review is the development of a conceptual model of the relationships you will be studying. The process of developing a model is called conceptualization. Conceptualization involves three tasks: (1) identifying the variables and constructs for your research;

(2) specifying the hypotheses and relationships; and (3) preparing a diagram (conceptual model) that visually represents the theoretical basis of the relationships you will examine.

Researchers often have some preliminary ideas regarding data relationships based on the research objectives. These ideas are derived from previous research, theory and/or the current business situation, and are typically called hypotheses. In statistics a hypothesis is an unproven supposition or proposition that tentatively explains certain facts or phenomena. A hypothesis also may be thought of as an assumption about the nature of a particular situation. Business researchers test hypotheses to verify that any relationships found in the variables being studied are due to true relationships and not chance.

■ Clarify how to develop and test hypotheses

Researchers can test hypotheses whether they are doing qualitative or quantitative research. When testing qualitative hypotheses researchers look for alternative explanations or negative (opposing) examples that are not consistent with the patterns being tested. If information is gathered that differs from the proposed relationship the hypothesis is rejected. When testing quantitative hypotheses researchers collect quantitative data and apply statistical tests. Researchers often develop conceptual models to communicate their hypotheses and the relationships between variables visually. The models visually represent a conceptual framework for the research. Research reports include a written description of the conceptual framework that integrates information about the problem/opportunity in a logical manner, describes the relationships among the variables, explains the theory underlying these relationships, and indicates the nature and direction of the relationships.

■ Describe the three basic business research designs

A research design is selected based upon the scientific method. If the researcher knows little about the topic of interest, then an exploratory design is the best approach. Exploratory designs are discovery oriented. Descriptive research is designed to obtain data that describes the characteristics of the topic of interest in the research. If the researcher wants to develop frequencies of some variables, or describe basic relationships, a descriptive design is probably called for. If the researcher is interested in testing whether one variable causes another, then a causal design should be used.

■ Explain the difference between cross-sectional and longitudinal studies

Descriptive studies generally are classified as either cross-sectional or longitudinal. Descriptive studies provide a "snapshot" or description of business elements at a given time and are considered cross-sectional. Cross-sectional and longitudinal studies both use a sample to describe business activities. Cross-sectional studies describe business activities at a single point in time. In contrast, longitudinal studies describe events over time. Thus, longitudinal studies are appropriate when research questions and hypotheses are affected by how things vary over time.

Ethical Dilemma

Gastro Experiences is a retailer specializing in cooking and kitchen products. The research firm they have hired has suggested they conduct an experiment using a causal research design to determine which air freshener could be used in their outlets to get customers to shop longer and buy more. They are planning to test an all-natural brand of products scented with vanilla, cinnamon apple and orange citrus. The researcher conducting the experiment tells Gastro Experiences' management team not to tell the employees or customers because it will bias the results. Should this be an ethical concern to management?

REVIEW QUESTIONS

1. What is a conceptual framework?
2. What is the difference in the null and alternative hypothesis?
3. What are the major differences in the three types of research designs?
4. How does the researcher select the best design?
5. Can more than one design be used in the same research project?

DISCUSSION AND APPLICATION ACTIVITIES

1. Write two hypotheses for a research project on how to motivate employees in an organization. Be sure the hypotheses can actually be tested by making sure you clarify the group that will be interviewed and the variables to be measured.
2. You are a regional manager for 20 FCUK retail stores. Your monthly reports indicate a large number of employees are quitting in five of your stores but very few in the other 15 stores. What kind of research design would be best to identify the problem and potential solutions to reduce the loss of employees in the five stores?

INTERNET EXERCISES   WWW

1. Go to this Web site http://www.socialresearchmethods.net/kb/desdes.htm and scroll down to the section on "minimizing threats to validity". Prepare a summary report on how to improve validity of research designs.
2. Go to www.greenfield.com What can you learn from this Web site? How will this Web site help business researchers?
3. Go to http://us.lightspeedpanel.com What does this company do with its Web site? Take the poll on the Web site and prepare a report explaining what you learned about business research.

NOTES

1. Teresko, J. (1997). "Research Renaissance", *Industry Week*, 246 (6/9), 139–50.
2. Ibid.
3. Swaddling, J. D. and Zobel, M. W. (1996). "Beating the Odds", *Marketing Management*, 4 (Spring/Winter), 20–34.
4. Holthausen, R. and Larcker, D. F. (1995). "Business Unit Innovation and the Structure of Executive Compensation", *Journal of Accounting and Economics*, 19 (May), 279–304.
5. For a review of similar studies, see: Chebat, J.-C., Chebat, C. G. and Vaillant, D. (2001). "Environmental Background Music and In-Store Selling", *Journal of Business Research*, 54 (November): 115–24.
6. Hunt, S. (1983). *Marketing Theory: The Philosophy of Marketing Science*. Homewood, IL, Irwin.

CHAPTER 7
SAMPLING APPROACHES

CONTENTS

LEARNING OUTCOMES

- Understand the key principles of sampling in business research.
- Appreciate the difference between the target population and the sampling frame.
- Recognize the difference between probability and nonprobability sampling procedures.
- Describe different sampling methods commonly used by business researchers.
- Determine the appropriate sample size for various situations encountered in practice.

INTRODUCTION

Data are essential for business research irrespective of whether an investigation is quantitative or qualitative in nature. The data can be obtained in a number of ways. Ideally the researcher would like to collect data from all members of a population under investigation. This is known as a **census**. But in most situations this is not feasible. Therefore a sample of the population is drawn.

A **sample** is a relatively small subset of the population. It is drawn using either probability or nonprobability procedures. Whether a probability or nonprobability approach is used, careful consideration of sampling design issues is necessary in selecting the sample.

Probability sampling is typically used in quantitative research. This involves a selection of a representative sample from the population using a random procedure to ensure objectivity in selecting the sample. The findings from the sample data can then be generalized to the population with a specified degree of accuracy.

Nonprobability sampling is typically used in qualitative research. Judgement is used to select the sample in qualitative research. Findings from the sample can be used to describe, discover and develop theory. Whilst the findings may be used to generalize to the population this cannot be done with a specified degree of accuracy.

Sample size is an important consideration in both quantitative and qualitative research. For example, a sufficiently large sample is required to generalize to the population. In contrast, when using a qualitative approach to develop theory on organizational behaviour a small number of cases may be sufficient.

In this chapter we discuss the basics of sampling. This includes what sampling is, the different probability and nonprobability sample designs, and the determination of sample size. Examples are given to illustrate their use in practice.

SAMPLING

Sampling design is part of the basic business research process. The sampling design process involves answering the following questions: (1) Should a sample or a census be used? (2) If a sample, then which sampling approach is best? (3) How large a sample is necessary? In answering these questions, the researcher must always consider ways to minimize error that might occur due to the sampling process.

Business research involves collecting information to improve decision making. Collecting information involves contacting people who are knowledgeable about a particular topic. We refer to the group of knowledgeable people as a **population** or **universe**. A population, therefore, is the total of all the **elements** that share some common set of characteristics. The elements in a population can be people, supermarkets, churches, hospitals, and so on. But all the elements must share a set of common characteristics. A census investigates all the elements in the population. In contrast, a sample investigates a small subset of the population to derive conclusions about the characteristics of the population.

While it may be possible to conduct a complete census of the population, business researchers seldom do. Contacting the entire population generally would be costly and time consuming. It often is difficult if not impossible to locate all the elements (people, objects, businesses, and so on). Also, use of the elements may destroy them. For example, quality control tests of products such as medicine, chemicals, light bulbs, and so on, always use sampling because the testing destroys the product.

Properly selected samples provide information that is sufficiently accurate to be used in business decision making. With probability sampling, business researchers at minimum are able to calculate the error associated with a particular sampling design and can make decisions with this knowledge in hand. With nonprobability sampling, researchers are not able to calculate the error but have made informed judgements in an effort to obtain usable sample information.

In the case study for this book, Phil Samouel had to make sampling decisions for his survey of customers. Before conducting the survey, Phil had to define his research problem. His Greek restaurant is reasonably successful, but not as successful as he initially expected. Gino's Italian Ristorante, his major competitor, is doing much better in attracting and retaining customers. Phil would like to know why. To fully understand this situation, he must know both customer and employee perceptions. He decided to conduct a survey of customers of both restaurants, as well as a survey of his employees. The customer surveys used exit interviews and the employee survey consisted of completing interviews with as many employees as possible within the prespecified period of time.

Phil Samouel concluded that taking a census by collecting information from every element (individual) in the target population would be impossible. In the case of the customer survey, it would require getting information from all potential restaurant customers in London. But since London has a population of over seven million, a census is not realistic. A census is feasible if the population is small and relatively easy to contact in a short period of time. For example, many business-to-business populations are small (for example, CEOs of motor companies or agents for financial services companies). But with consumer studies, in most instances the population is large and some form of sampling is necessary.

A sample must be **representative** of the population from which it is drawn. In other words, the sample should mirror characteristics of the population, thereby minimizing the error associated with sampling. Use of an appropriate sampling design should achieve this objective.

THE SAMPLING PROCESS

Representative samples are generally obtained by following a set of well-defined procedures. These include the following steps:

1. Defining the target population.
2. Choosing the sampling frame.
3. Selecting the sampling method.
4. Determining the sample size.
5. Implementing the sampling plan.

We discuss each of these steps in the following paragraphs.

Business researchers must assist their clients in making decisions on each of these steps. But a lot of help is available from companies that specialize in working with researchers to obtain a representative sample. One of the most well known sampling vendors is described in the Research in Action box.

RESEARCH IN ACTION

SURVEY SAMPLING GOES ONLINE

For over 24 years, Survey Sampling Inc. (SSI) has provided business researchers, marketers, pollsters and survey organizations with samples. Realizing the research possibilities available through the Internet, SSI (www.surveysampling.com) now utilizes Web surveys, as well as the more traditional methods of contacting respondents such as telephone, post, or personal interviews. To conduct Web surveys successfully, SSI has learned that many factors, including hardware, software, questionnaire design and appropriate sampling have to be taken into consideration. With this in mind, SSI has filled the need for email samples (eSamples) with two types of eSampling services, SurveySpot™ Panel and SSI-LITe eSamples (Low Incidence Targeted Sampling).

SSI's SurveySpot™ Panel provides researchers with access to a multi-sourced Internet panel of people interested in participating in online research. Because SurveySpot™ records come from many sources, including banner ads, online recruitment methods and RDD (Random Digit Dialing) telephone recruitment, this service can deliver higher response rates than can be obtained using other sources. SurveySpot™ panelists can be targeted by education, ethnic group, gender, income, occupation and race – and family members living in the same household can be targeted by age and gender.

SSI-LITe eSamples are designed to allow researchers to conduct directional research, particularly when low incidence segments of the population are being targeted. Panelists can be targeted by hundreds of lifestyle categories including Advertising, Education, Family, Health, Hobbies, Internet and Travel.

Both SurveySpot™ and SSI-LITe records come from many sources and panelists are recruited through a variety of permission-based techniques. Files are created from self-reported, respondent-specific information, which gives researchers the advantage of reaching the exact targets they are after because the respondent has reported their particular interest. Further, since the panelists have agreed to being contacted with email messages concerning specific areas of interest, they are never "spammed" when receiving an eSample survey invitation.

The process for SSI's eSampling is quite simple. When a researcher secures SSI services, SSI will invite panelists, selected according to prequalifying requirements, via email to participate in a survey located on the researcher's Web site. SSI does not collect the data, since the company works within a noncompete position in the marketing research process. All data are collected at the researcher's own Web site. SSI can handle the infrastructure, servers, hardware, software and timing of the study. SSI also is equipped to handle random selection of prizewinners and administration of monetary rewards.

With the addition of Web surveys, SSI is continuing its mission to provide quality samples for research projects. Through eSamples, SSI offers researchers a low cost per completed interview with national and international samples targeted by demographics, lifestyles and topic of interests. ∎

DEFINING THE TARGET POPULATION

The research objectives and scope of the study are critical in defining the target population. The **target population** is the complete group of objects or elements relevant to the research project. They are relevant because they possess the information the research project is designed to collect. Other practical factors may influence the definition of the target population. These include knowledge of the topic of interest, access to elements (individuals, companies, and so on), availability of elements and time frame. Elements or objects available for selection during the sampling process are known as the **sampling unit**. Sampling units can be people, households, businesses, or any logical unit relevant to the study's objective. When the sampling plan is executed, sampling units are drawn from the target population to use in making estimates of population characteristics. Exhibit 7-1 defines a target population for a survey of employees of a regional bank who participate in an incentive plan.

Element:	Employees with incentive pay
Sampling Unit:	Customer service representatives and branch managers
Extent:	All branch locations in the Paris region
Time:	March 2007

EXHIBIT 7-1

A Target Population for Employees with Incentive Pay

CHOOSING THE SAMPLING FRAME

The sampling frame provides a working definition of the target population. A **sample frame** is a comprehensive list of the elements from which the sample is drawn. Examples of sampling frames are the Yellow Pages listing of restaurants, the telephone directory listing of individuals, a company's internal database listing its employees and/or customers, electronic directories available on CD-ROM or on the Internet, and even university registration lists. A sampling frame, therefore, is as complete a list as possible of all the elements in the population from which the sample is drawn.

Ideally, a sampling frame is an accurate, complete listing of all the elements in the population targeted by the research. In reality, a sampling frame often is flawed in a number of ways:

- it may not be up to date;
- it may include elements that do not belong to the target population;
- it may not include elements that do belong to the target population;
- it may have been compiled from multiple lists and contain duplicate elements as a result of the manner in which the list was constructed.

Before drawing a sample from the sampling frame list, the researcher therefore must confirm the list's accuracy irrespective of its origin. This will be discussed further in the next section dealing with sampling design issues.

SELECTING THE SAMPLING METHOD

Selection of the sampling method to use in a study depends on a number of related theoretical and practical issues. These include considering the nature of the study, the objectives of the study, and the time and budget available.

Traditional sampling methods can be divided into two broad categories: probability and nonprobability. **Probability** methods are based on the premise that each element of the target population has a known, but not necessarily equal, probability of being selected in a sample. In probability sampling, sampling elements are selected randomly and the probability of being selected is determined ahead of time by the researcher. If done properly, probability sampling ensures that the sample is representative.

With **nonprobability** sampling, the inclusion or exclusion of elements in a sample is left to the discretion of the researcher. In other words, not every element of the target population has a chance of being selected into the sample. Despite this, a skilful selection process should result in a reasonably "representative" sample. By representative we mean it represents the researcher's judgement of what she or he wants but is not based on chance. The most common types of sampling methods are shown in Exhibit 7-2.

Probability	Nonprobability
Simple Random	Convenience
Systematic	Judgement
Stratified	Snowball/Referral
Cluster	Quota
Multi-Stage	

EXHIBIT 7-2

Types of Sampling Methods

RESEARCH IN ACTION / ONLINE SAMPLING METHODS

The big switch to online advertising as part of the media mix continues across Europe. Research from the Interactive Advertising Bureau Europe (www.iabeurope.ws) indicates that European online advertising spend exceeded €4bn in 2005 for the first time. In some markets more than 5% of the country's spend on advertising already goes into online, and the proportions continue to grow as more and more firms discover the power of Internet advertising as both a branding and direct marketing medium. It is not surprising that businesses are examining online advertising with audiences across the continent spending 15% of their "media time" online. But online marketing involves more than advertising, it supports every aspect of a customer's journey – from raising awareness of a brand through the sale itself, and even into service after the sales.

Search engine ads have become a popular approach to acquiring new customers. But other formats are also driving the growth of online advertising. A new generation of Web banners is using sophisticated "behavioural targeting" techniques to understand viewers' interests and to provide tailored messaging. For example, television-style commercials can now easily be rebroadcast online, the creative power of the "rich media" formats can display commercial messages across the entire Web page, and affiliate marketing is extending the reach of online retailers, thus giving customers more choice.

As you read the rest of this chapter, reflect on what kind of sampling method you would recommend for businesses wishing to learn more about the potential for their business using online marketing? Explain your decision.

For more information on IAB log onto `http://www.IABEurope.ws` ∎

PROBABILITY SAMPLING

In drawing a probability sample the selection of elements is based on some random procedure that gives elements a known and nonzero chance of being selected thereby minimizing selection bias. Probability sampling usually involves taking large samples considered to be representative of the target population from which they are drawn. Findings based on a probability sample can be generalized to the target population with a specified level of confidence. The most commonly employed probability sampling techniques are described in the following paragraphs.

Simple Random Sampling

Simple random sampling is a straightforward method of sampling that assigns each element of the target population an equal probability of being selected. Drawing names from a hat or selecting the winning ticket from a container in a raffle are examples of simple random sampling. It is easy to draw names or numbers from a hat when you draw a sample from a small population. But when the target population is large, other approaches are necessary.

One popular method of simple random sampling is random digit dialing with telephone surveys. This technique is used because it overcomes the bias introduced when telephone directories do not include recent listings or unpublished numbers. Unfortunately, it has the disadvantage of creating nonworking numbers as well as the problem of refusals to answer a phone. Indeed, telemarketing has created a huge refusal rate problem in the UK. Ten years ago, business researchers were able to complete telephone interviews using a sample to completion ratio of 4 to 1 (completion ratio = start with a total sample of 200 listings to complete a sample of 50; i.e., 150 refused, would not answer phone, and so on). Today this ratio is often 10 to 1 (start with 5,000 listings to complete 500 interviews). Part of the problem is certainly that potential respondents are not at home, or there may be lack of time or interest in the topic. But technology such as caller ID and other issues such as simply not wanting to be bothered are having a substantial impact on telephone refusal rates.

The procedure for drawing large samples involves the following steps:

1. Sequentially assign a unique identification number to each element in the sampling frame.

2. Use a random number generator to identify the appropriate elements to be selected into the sample.

3. Ensure that no element is selected more than once.

Software packages like SPSS will execute the above steps for you. If the determined sample size is sufficiently large, the resulting sample will be representative of the target population. In the Data Analysis box we illustrate the SPSS click-through sequence to draw a random sample of 50 cases from 100 of Samouel's customers in our restaurant database. If you are not familiar with SPSS go to the book's Web site (www.wileyeurope.com/college/hair) and we provide a more detailed explanation of how to use the software.

DATA ANALYSIS

USING SPSS TO SELECT A RANDOM SAMPLE FOR SAMOUEL'S GREEK RESTAURANT

Our sampling objective is to draw a random sample of 50 customers of Samouel's Greek Cuisine who were interviewed in the survey. Each of the 100 interviews represents a sampling unit. The sampling frame is the list of 100 customers of Samouel's included in the restaurant database (to access this list, sort the data so Samouel's Customers are first. To do so, follow this sequence: DATA → SPLIT FILE → Compare Groups, highlight X_{28} and move it to Groups based on box, and click OK.) The SPSS click through sequence to select the random sample is: DATA → SELECT CASES → RANDOM SAMPLE OF CASES → SAMPLE → EXACTLY → 50 CASES → FROM THE FIRST 100 CASES → CONTINUE → OK. In the preceding sequence you must click on each of the options and place 50 in the 'cases' box and 100 in the from the 'first_cases' box. The customers (cases) not included in the random sample are indicated by the slash (/) through the case ID number on the left side of your computer screen.

Any subsequent data analysis will be based only on the random sample of 50 customers of Samouel's restaurant. For example, the table below shows the number and percentage of occasional, somewhat frequent and very frequent customers of Samouel's restaurant who were included in the sample. Data in the frequency column indicates we selected 27 occasional, 10 somewhat frequent, and 13 very frequent, for a total of 50 customers. This table is an example of what you get when you use the SPSS software. Another random sample of 50 customers may yield slightly difference frequencies.

X_{18} – Frequency of Patronage

	Frequency	%	Cumulative %
Occasional Customer	27	54.0	54.0
Somewhat Frequent Customer	10	20.0	74.0
Very Frequent Customer	13	26.0	100.0
Total	50	100.0	

Systematic Sampling

Systematic sampling is a process that involves randomly selecting an initial starting point on a list, and thereafter every nth element in the sampling frame is selected. For example, suppose you have a list of 10,000 students who attend a particular university and you want a sample of 500 students. Your sampling objective is a representative cross-section of the student body. To draw the sample you must determine the sample size and then calculate the sampling interval. The **sampling interval** is the number of population elements between each unit selected for your sample. In this case, the sampling interval is 20 (10,000 students/sample of 500 = 20). To draw the sample, you randomly select a number between 1 and 20 as a starting point. For example, say you randomly choose 7, then the sample would be the sampling elements numbered 7, 27, 47, 67 and so on. Similarly, in the Data Analysis box we tell you how to develop a systematic sampling procedure to survey Samouel's restaurant customers.

DATA ANALYSIS

SELECTING A SYSTEMATIC RANDOM SAMPLE FOR SAMOUEL'S GREEK RESTAURANT

Over the past four years, Phil Samouel has compiled a listing of 1,030 customers arranged in alphabetical order. A systematic sample of 100 customers' opinions is his research objective. Having decided upon a sample size of 100 to be selected from the sampling frame of 1,030 customers, Phil calculates the size of the interval between successive elements of the sample dividing the sampling frame size by the desired sample size (1,030/100 = 10.3). In situations like this, where we end up with a decimal instead of a round number, you ignore the decimal to be sure of a minimum sample of 100. Thus, we have effectively partitioned the sampling frame into 100 intervals of size 10. From the numbers in the interval of 1 to 10, we then must randomly select a number to identify the first element for the systematic sample. If, for example, that number is 4, then we begin with the 4th element in the sampling frame and every 10th element thereafter is chosen. The initial starting point is the 4th element and the remaining elements selected for the sample are the 14th, 24th, 34th and so on until the final element chosen is the 1,024th. This will result in a sample of 103 customers to be interviewed in the survey.

■

Systematic sampling produces representative data if executed properly. To work properly, the sampling interval must divide the sampling frame into relatively homogeneous groups. If there is a cyclical sequence to the sampling frame instead of a random sequence, systematic sampling will not work. For example, alphabetical listings are considered random and not cyclical. In contrast, if we wanted to do weekly interviews with Samouel's customers and our interval was 7, the sample would produce biased information because we would always interview on the same day of the week. To be truly random, we must conduct interviews across at least several different days of the week. Similarly, if our list of 1,030 Samouel's customers is arranged according to frequency of dining and the first 100 names on the list eat at Samouel's at least once a week and the remaining 930 eat at Samouel's an average of four times a year, we would have a problem using systematic sampling. If the sampling interval is 10 and our sample size is 103, then our sample would under-represent the frequent customers (only 10 frequent customers) and over-represent the less frequent customers (93 nonfrequent customers). Thus, we must know ahead of time if there are underlying systematic patterns in the data so we can account for them in our sampling plan.

Stratified Sampling

Stratified sampling requires the researcher to partition the sampling frame into relatively homogeneous subgroups that are distinct and nonoverlapping, called strata. The researcher usually does the stratification on the basis of some predetermined criteria that may be the result of his or her past experience, or could even be specified by the client. For example, in his survey Phil Samouel may wish to stratify his customers on the basis of a characteristic such as age, marital status, family size, income levels, frequency of patronage, levels of satisfaction or some combination of these.

The researcher determines the total sample size as well as the required sample sizes for each of the individual strata. For example, the total sample size might be 400 and the four individual strata might each have a sample size of 100. The stratified sample is the composite of the samples taken from the strata. Elements for the stratified sample usually are selected either by drawing simple random or systematic samples of the specified size from the strata of the target population. With stratified sampling, elements must be selected from all the strata of the total sample. When done properly, stratified sampling increases the accuracy of the sample information but does not necessarily increase the cost. In practice a stratified sample is selected in one of two ways – proportionately stratified sampling or disproportionately stratified sampling. Descriptions of these two approaches follow:

In **proportionately stratified sampling**, the overall sample size will be the total of all the elements from each of the strata. The number of elements chosen from each strata is proportionate to the size of a particular strata relative to the overall sample size. So if we have a stratum that is 25 % of the target population then the size of the sample for that stratum will be 25 % of the total sample. For example, if we use proportionately stratified sampling to select a sample of males and females at a university with 10,000 students, and 6,000 students are females and 4,000 students are males, then the overall sample would include 60 % females and 40 % males.

In **disproportionately stratified sampling** the sample elements are chosen in one of two ways. One approach involves choosing the elements from each stratum according to its relative importance. Relative importance is usually based on practical considerations such as the economic importance of the various strata. For example, if Samouel's restaurant is located in an area dominated by older individuals who dine out less frequently, then sampling a higher proportion of younger customers who dine out more often would be viewed as more important to him. This is illustrated in the far-right column of information shown in the Continuing Case box.

With disproportionately stratified sampling based on economic or other reasons, the sample size from each stratum is determined independently without considering the size of the stratum relative to the overall sample size. The more important a particular stratum is considered, the higher will be the proportion of the sample elements from the stratum.

CONTINUING CASE   SAMOUEL'S GREEK CUISINE

Which is better... proportionate or disproportionately stratified samples?

Phil Samouel, owner of Samouel's Greek Cuisine restaurant, has a list of 3,000 potential customers broken down by age. His business consultant has determined through the use of a statistical formula that a proportionately stratified sample of 200 will produce information that is sufficiently accurate for decision making. The number of elements to be chosen from each stratum using a proportionate sample based on age is shown in the fourth column of the table. But, if the consultant believes it is necessary that the sample size in each stratum be relative to its economic importance, and the 18 to 49 age group are the most frequent diners and spend the most when dining out, then the number of selected elements would be disproportionate to stratum size as illustrated in the fifth column. The numbers in the disproportionate column would be determined based on the researcher's judgment of each stratum's economic importance.

Age Group	Number of Elements in stratum	% of Elements Stratum	Number of Elements Selected for the Sample	
			Proportionate Sample Size	Disproportionate Sample Size
(1)	(2)	(3)	(4)	(5)
18–25	600	20	$40 = 20\%$	$50 = 25\%$
26–34	900	30	$60 = 30\%$	$50 = 25\%$
35–49	270	9	$18 = 9\%$	$50 = 25\%$
50–59	1020	34	$68 = 34\%$	$30 = 15\%$
60 and Older	210	7	$14 = 7\%$	$20 = 10\%$
Total	**3000**	**100**	**200**	**200**

Should the consultant recommend proportionate or disproportionate sampling? Should the decision be based on economic importance, or some other criteria?

Another approach to selecting a disproportionately stratified sample considers the variability of the data within each stratum. Elements from each stratum are selected based on the relative variability of the elements. Strata with high relative variability will contribute a higher proportion of elements to the total sample. Similarly, the lower the variability of a stratum the lower will be its proportional representation in the total sample. For example, assume a university with 10,000 students has 50% male students and 50% female students. We know that almost all the males drink beer and there is wide variation in beer-drinking habits, with some drinking beer every day and a very small number who do not drink beer at all. On the other hand, only a small proportion of the female students drink beer and not very often (the female students prefer wine), so there is not much variation in their beer consumption patterns. In this example, we would sample a larger number of male students in our survey so we could more accurately represent male beer consumption patterns. Since female students do not vary much in their beer consumption habits, the smaller sample of females should still accurately represent their behaviour.

Cluster Sampling

In **cluster sampling** the target population is viewed as made up of heterogeneous groups called clusters. Examples of clusters are ethnic groups, companies, households, business units or geographic areas. We now illustrate the use of cluster sampling with an example.

The most frequently used type of cluster sampling is geographic area sampling. For example, assume you want to interview managers of banks in south London, UK. The researcher could obtain a list of post code areas in which banks are located: each area is then a cluster. The clusters to be sampled would be randomly selected and then all bank managers or a random sample of managers of banks would be interviewed in each of the selected clusters. This process generally works well and produces representative data. The procedure for taking a cluster sample is as follows:

1. Define the cluster characteristics in a way that ensures the clusters are unambiguously identified in the target population. In this manner, the total number of clusters in the population will be known ahead of time.

2. Decide on how many clusters to sample.

3. Choose the cluster(s) in a random manner.

4. Obtain a sampling frame for the chosen clusters.

5. Decide whether to conduct a census on the chosen cluster(s) or whether to take a probability sample from the cluster(s).

6. If a probability sample is desired, determine the total sample size. If more than one cluster will be used then the sample size should be allocated appropriately. This is generally done on a proportionate sampling basis.

The Continuing Case example explains how Phil Samouel might use a cluster sampling process to identify the relevant customers to interview.

CONTINUING CASE   SAMOUEL'S GREEK CUISINE

Cluster Sampling of Restaurant Customers

Phil Samouel would like to know the perceptions of his weekend customers because the average bill size is £110. In contrast, the average bill of weekday customers is only £65.

For this research project a cluster is defined as customers who dine at the restaurant on weekends. This will result in 52 clusters (one for each week) from which a random sample of clusters (weekends) can be drawn. One of two possible options may be followed. The first option is that all customers from the selected clusters can be interviewed. In this case a census is conducted. The second option is that elements (customers) can be drawn from the selected clusters by one of the above probability sampling methods, or by one of the nonprobability approaches discussed in the following paragraphs.

Which approach is most realistic and why? What problems are associated with each approach?

Multi-stage Sampling

Multi-stage cluster sampling involves a sequence of stages. These stages are illustrated by the following example. The problem is to investigate the views of medical practitioners in the UK concerning the use of medical software to assist in patient diagnosis. The first stage is to select a random sample of regions in the UK. The regions are the clusters. The second stage is to select a random sample of hospitals from the selected regions, and then either collect information from all medical practitioners from the chosen hospitals or a random sample from within each of the chosen hospitals. Even more complex multi-stage sampling is possible.

NONPROBABILITY SAMPLING

In nonprobability sampling the selection of sample elements is not necessarily made with the aim of being statistically representative of the population. Rather, the researcher uses subjective methods such personal experience, convenience, expert judgement and so on to select the elements in the sample. As a result, the probability of any element of the population being chosen is not known. Moreover, there are no statistical methods for measuring the sampling error for a nonprobability sample. Thus, the researcher cannot generalize the findings to the target population with any measured degree of confidence, which is possible with probability samples. This does not mean nonprobability samples should not be used. Indeed, in some situations they may be the preferred alternative. The most frequently used nonprobability sampling methods are now described.

Convenience Sampling

A **convenience sample** involves selecting sample elements that are most readily available to participate in the study and who can provide the information required. For example, when exit interviews are used with restaurant customers they are chosen on the basis of having just finished a meal at the restaurant. Similarly, when a college professor interviews students at his university they represent a convenience sample. Convenience samples are used because they enable the researcher to complete a large number of interviews quickly and cost effectively. But they suffer from selection bias because the individuals interviewed are often different from the target population. Thus, it is difficult and dangerous to generalize to the target population when a convenience sample is used.

Judgement Sampling

A **judgement sample**, sometimes referred to as a **purposive sample**, involves selecting elements in the sample for a specific purpose. It is a form of convenience sample in which the researcher's judgement is used to select the sample elements. Sample elements are chosen because the researcher believes they represent the target population, but they are not necessarily representative. An example of a judgement sample might be a group of experts with knowledge about a particular problem or issue; that is, physicians who specialize in treating diabetes might be interviewed in a survey to learn about the most effective ways to convince diabetics to adopt good diets and exercise properly. The advantages of judgement samples are their convenience, speed and low cost.

Quota Sampling

Quota sampling is similar to stratified random sampling. The objective is for the total sample to have proportional representation of the strata of the target population. They differ from stratified sampling in that the selection of elements is done on a convenience basis.

In quota sampling the researcher defines the strata of the target population, determines the total sample size, and sets a quota for the sample elements from each stratum. In addition, the researcher specifies the characteristics of the elements to be selected, but leaves the actual choice of elements to the discretion of the person collecting the information. Thus, while quota sampling ensures proportionate representation of each stratum in the total sample, the findings from the sample cannot be generalized because the choice of elements is not done using a probability sampling method. As with judgement sampling, the advantages of quota samples are their convenience, speed and low cost.

Snowball Sampling

A **snowball sample**, also called a **referral sample**, is one where the initial respondents typically are chosen using probability methods. Then the researcher uses the initial respondents to help identify the other respondents in the target population. This process is continued until the required sample size is reached. Snowball sampling uses referrals to facilitate the location of rare populations or those where a list does not exist. For example, the 2006 FIFA World Cup football games were held in Germany. The games were previously held in 2002 in Korea/Japan. There is a list of individuals who purchased tickets, but no list of who actually attended the games. The situation is complicated further because of the fact that many companies purchased multiple tickets either for their own employees or for resale. If the organizing committee wanted to conduct a survey of individuals who attended the 2002 games in order to better plan for the 2006 games, the list available would not be very accurate. An effective approach might be to use the names available, contact those individuals, and ask them for referrals to other individuals or groups that attended the games. This is a particularly good approach when the target population is narrow, such as identifying individuals who frequently attend the World Cup versus those who go less frequently.

DETERMINE SAMPLE SIZE

Efficient sample sizes can be drawn from either large (infinite) populations or small (finite) populations. Below, we discuss the determination of the sample size for both cases.

SAMPLING FROM A LARGE POPULATION

Researchers often need to estimate characteristics of large populations. To achieve this in an efficient manner, it is necessary to determine the appropriate sample size prior to data collection.

Determination of the sample size is complex because of the many factors that need to be taken into account simultaneously. The challenge is to obtain an acceptable balance between several of these factors. These include the variability of elements in the target population, the type of sample required, time available, budget, required estimation precision, and whether the findings are to be generalized and, if so, with what degree of confidence.

Formulas based on statistical theory can be used to compute the sample size. For pragmatic reasons, such as budget and time constraints, alternative "ad hoc" methods often are used. Examples of these are: sample sizes based on rules of thumb, previous similar studies, one's own experience or simply dictated by what is affordable. Irrespective of how the sample size is determined it is essential that it should be of a sufficient size and quality to yield results that are seen to be credible in terms of their accuracy and consistency.

When statistical formulas are used to determine the sample size three decisions must be made: (1) the degree of confidence (often 95%); (2) the specified level of precision (amount of acceptable error); and (3) the amount of variability (population homogeneity). The degree of confidence (confidence level) typically is based on management or researcher judgement. Historically a 95% confidence level (<0.05 chance of the estimated population parameter being incorrect) has been used, but a lower confidence level is acceptable where less risk is involved. Managerial and/or researcher judgement also is involved in determining the level of precision. The level of precision is the maximum acceptable difference between the estimated sample value and the true population value.

The third decision relates to the variability, or homogeneity, of the population. The variability of the population is measured by its standard deviation. If the population is homogeneous it has a small standard deviation. For example, the standard deviation in the age of college students is small and therefore requires a relatively smaller sample size. But if the population is heterogeneous, such as people attending a Premier Football League game, then a relatively large sample is necessary because the standard deviation in the age of this population is larger. In practice, it is unlikely the true standard deviation is known. Thus, the researcher typically uses an estimate of the standard deviation based on previous similar studies or a pilot study.

If you have information on these three factors, the sample size can be calculated as follows:

$$\textbf{Sample size (SS)} = [\textbf{DC} \times \textbf{TV}/\textbf{DP}]^2$$

Where:

> **DC** (Degree of Confidence) = the number of standard errors for the degree of confidence specified for the research results.
> **TV** (True Variability) = the standard deviation of the population.
> **DP** (Desired Precision) = the acceptable difference between the sample estimate and the population value.

Note that the above formula does not include the population size. This is because, except with finite populations, the size of the population has no impact on the determination of sample size. Specifically, a sample size of 500 is equally useful in understanding the opinions of a target population of 15 million as it is for one of 100,000. This is always true for "large" populations.

The calculated sample size does not necessarily ensure the sample is representative of the target population. The extent to which a sample is representative is dependent upon the process used in the selection of the elements. A representative sample is more likely to be achieved through probability rather than nonprobability sampling. Two examples of how to determine sample size are provided in Exhibits 7-3 and 7-4. In Exhibit 7-3 we illustrate how to determine sample size for estimating a mean through the use of two cases. In Exhibit 7-4 we show you how to estimate the sample size when you are dealing with a small population.

Case 1: Using a Rating Scale

Phil Samouel asked his research consultant to estimate the appropriate sample size considering the rating scale questions that will be asked on his survey of restaurant customers. The researcher must determine the sample size that will estimate the true perceived mean score for the characteristics of the restaurants (for example, food quality, reasonable prices, and so on) to a desired level of precision and to a specified level of confidence. To do so, the researcher must consider all three elements in the sample size formula – the degree of variability in the population as measured by the standard deviation, the acceptable level of precision, and the specified level of confidence. The researcher is likely to proceed as follows:

The first component of the sample size formula that must be decided upon is the true variability. Generally speaking, the true variability as measured by the standard deviation is not known. In most cases, therefore, it will have to be estimated either through the use of a pilot test sample or by some subjective method, such as the researcher's past experiences with similar types of questions.

It is also necessary to make some assumptions about the properties of the distribution of responses to the questions. In general, it is assumed that the measure for the characteristics to be estimated follows a normal distribution. In Phil Samouel's study the characteristics are measured with a 1 to 7 rating scale. This gives a range of six units $(7 - 1 = 6)$. Once we know the range, we estimate the standard deviation of the rating scale by dividing the range by 4 $(6/4 = 1.5)$. The division by 4 is based on the assumption that the distribution of the responses to the restaurant characteristics questions is normal. When we have a normal distribution business researchers typically use a confidence interval of plus or minus 2 standard errors (95 %). When plus or minus 2 standard errors is used the range of standard errors is 4. Hence, we divide the range of responses by 4 to get the estimated standard deviation.

In consultation with the client the researcher generally determines the acceptable level of precision and the desired level of confidence. Suppose that the precision is specified as 1/3 of a unit on the rating scale. This means the sample estimate should be accurate within 1/3 of a unit. A confidence level of 95 % is desired.

We now have sufficient information to calculate our sample size using the formula:

Sample Size = [(degree of confidence required × variability)/(desired precision)]^2
Sample Size = [(2 × 1.5)/(0.33)]^2 = 82.6

Thus, 83 is the minimum sample size the researcher should aim for in order to meet the specified precision and confidence goals.

Case 2: Using a Ratio Scale

Consider the case where we wish to estimate the average monthly expenditure on eating out. Although, the true standard deviation (variability) is unknown a pilot test study of 30 customers provides an estimate of the unknown standard deviation of €14. We want

EXHIBIT 7-3

Estimating the Sample Size for a Mean

to be 95 % confident that our estimate of the mean monthly expenditure on eating out is within €2 of the true population mean. Assuming the distribution of expenditures follows a normal distribution then the sample size is determined as follows:

Sample size = [(degree of confidence required × variability)/(desired precision)]^2
Sample size = [(2 × 14)/(2)]^2 = 196

We should aim for a sample of at least 196 to meet our preset criteria of an efficient sample size.

EXHIBIT 7-3

(*continued*)

RESEARCH IN ACTION

WILL BIOMETRIC IDS BE ACCEPTED BY CUSTOMERS?

Cash point fraud and theft costs banks in excess of €300 million in losses every year. In an effort to reduce this, banks have examined fingerprints and eye scanning for identification. Customers in some countries, such as the UK, have resisted fingerprint identification because they associate it with police detection and are reluctant to submit fingerprints when they are not charged with a crime. Similarly, many people believe the eye is too vulnerable for an invasive search approach like iris eye scanners to be used regularly. As a result, banks and other businesses have been searching for an authentication method acceptable to customers.

For several years, Japanese manufacturer Hitachi has been selling biometric scanners that check customer's finger and palm veins for ID purposes at banks. Now it is hoping to enter the European market. The system not only can use biometric identification with false acceptance less than 0.0001 %, but can designate a particular finger as a "duress" signal. Thus, if a customer is being forced to withdraw cash they simply place the previously identified "duress" finger on the scanner and it alerts authorities within less than half a second that a problem exists.

How do you feel about submitting your finger and palm vein pattern to banks or other businesses for identification purposes? What kind of research design and sampling method is best to ensure valid results for a study to determine customer acceptance to the use of this technology?

Source: Glover, T. (2006). "Hitachi Launches Biometric ID to Stop Cashpoint Fraud", *The Business*, www.thebusinessonline.com, 30 April 2006, p. 1, "I've got a biometric ID card", http://news.bbc.co.uk/1/hi/uk/3556720.stm, and "Speeding up the Checkout Line with Biometrics", http://www.informationweek.com/story/ IWK20020313S0060, accessed June 2006. ■

SAMPLING FROM A SMALL POPULATION

In the previously described formula the size of the population has no impact on the determination of the sample size. This is always true for "large" populations. When working with small populations, however, use of the above formula may lead to an unnecessarily large sample size. If, for example, the sample size is larger than 5% of the population then the calculated sample size should be multiplied by the following correction factor:

$$N/(N + n - 1)$$

Where:

N = population size

n = the calculated sample size determined by the original formula.

Thus, the adjusted sample size is:

Sample Size = [(specified degree of confidence × variability)/(desired precision)]^2
×[N/N + n − 1]

Use of this formula is illustrated in Exhibit 7-4.

Suppose a bank has 5,000 ATMs installed in the UK; the bank wishes to establish their users' views of this service. A researcher they commissioned estimates the required sample size given their agreed criteria is 750. This sample size is 13% of the population and is larger than is necessary for an efficient sample size. In this case the sample size correction factor needs to be applied as illustrated below:

Adjusted Sample Size = 750 × [5000/(5000 + 750 − 1)] = 653

The reduction in the sample size could lead to significant savings in time and costs.

EXHIBIT 7-4

Estimating Sample Size Adjusted by the Correction Factor

Business researchers working with clients who serve the business-to-business market are also sampling from a small population. That is, the number of customers for a company selling to the business sector may be several hundred or less. This contrasts to the several thousand customers for a company selling to consumers. In this situation the question arises: "What is an adequate sample size?" This is because using a sample size formula can result in a sample size that cannot be achieved. In this type of situation it is typical to interview 10% to 20% of the total number of individuals in the population. Also, a minimum sample size of 30 is recommended and larger if possible. In all situations dealing with sample sizes this small it is necessary to examine the characteristics of the sample respondents to ensure they are reasonably representative. That is, do the respondents represent all types of customers, such as larger and smaller businesses, or only one type? If all types of customers are not represented in sufficient numbers, then the findings must be interpreted accordingly.

Many issues must be considered in selecting the best sampling method and the proper sample size. Consider the issues posed in the Research in Action on women's usage of the Internet.

RESEARCH IN ACTION

ONLINE USAGE PATTERNS CHANGING THROUGHOUT EUROPE?

Recent research shows women throughout Europe using the Internet almost as much as men. Men spend an average of 11 hours per week online while women spend nine hours per week. But women are increasing their web usage at a faster rate than men. Where are women spending less time – reading magazines? The increase in Internet usage among women is mostly among the 16–24 age group, which includes young professional women and those with young children. The Web sites visited most often by women include travel, banking, shopping and auction. Based on this research, the implication is that advertisers in Europe must consider how women's shopping habits and use of different media is changing if they are to be successful in communicating with this segment. The research was based on 7,000 random telephone interviews with 1,000 respondents from the UK, Germany, France, Spain and the Nordic countries, and 500 respondents each from Belgium and the Netherlands.

Is the sample size for this study sufficient to produce reliable findings? What kind of research design would answer the question as to why women are increasing their web usage faster than men?

Sources: Enid Burns, ''Euro Women to Outpace Men Online in Near Future'', 29 March 2006, http://www.clickz.com/stats/sectors/broadband/article.php/3595241, http://www.eiaa.net/, ''EIAA Digital Women Report 2006'', http://www.eiaa.net/. ∎

IMPLEMENT SAMPLING PLAN

The researcher implements the sampling plan after all the details of the sampling design have been agreed upon. The target population has been defined, the sampling frame has been chosen, the sampling method has been selected, and the appropriate sample size determined. If the sampling unit is companies, then the types of companies must be specified as well as the titles and perhaps names of the individuals that will be interviewed. Many details must be decided on before a final sample plan is accepted and implemented because once the data is collected it is too late to change the sampling design.

CONTINUING CASE   SAMOUEL'S GREEK CUISINE

Which sampling method is best?

The business consultant hired by Phil Samouel has recommended a survey of his customers and his employees. The consultant has also recommended a survey of Gino's customers. Samouel has a total of 77 employees. Some work full-time and others work part-time.

Samouel is open seven days a week for lunch and dinner and so is Gino. The consultant is considering both probability and nonprobability sampling methods as ways to collect customer data.

1. Is a sampling method needed for the employee survey? Why?

2. Which of the sampling options is best for the survey of Samouel's customers? Why?

3. What are some possible ways to collect data from Gino's customers? Recommend a sampling method you believe will work best.

SUMMARY

■ **Understand the key principles of sampling in business research**
The key issues in sampling are to identify the target population, the sampling frame, and the method of sampling. Generally, a researcher seeks to draw a "representative" sample from the target population using either probabilistic or nonprobabilistic procedures. Access to and participation of respondents whether they are companies or individuals is therefore an important consideration to ensure that the sample size is credible, efficient and representative.

■ **Appreciate the difference between the target population and the sampling frame**
Before beginning sampling it is necessary for us to identify all of the elements of interest to our study. These elements could be individuals or objects such as companies, or even events. These elements are the target population. In practice there may not be an exhaustive list of these elements, so we make use of one or more lists that provide a "good" proxy for the population. It is this proxy that forms the sampling frame from which we draw the sample.

■ **Recognize the difference between probability and nonprobability sampling procedures**
The difference between the two sampling approaches is simple. For probability sampling methods the chances of selection of elements into a sample are known. In contrast, for nonprobability sampling methods the chances of selection are not known. Also, to infer from a sample to a population probability sampling must be used.

■ **Describe different sampling methods commonly used by business researchers**
Probability sampling, generally used in large-scale surveys, is based on a random procedure for selecting elements from the target population. If the sample size is sufficiently large the sample selected should be representative. Probability sampling approaches include: simple random sampling, systematic sampling, stratified sampling, cluster sampling and multi-stage sampling. Each one of these sampling designs has advantages and disadvantages that must be considered before selecting a particular approach. If executed properly probability sampling enables you to make generalizations about the population with a specified degree of confidence.

Nonprobability sampling, generally used in exploratory research, involves selecting elements into the sample based on convenience, judgement, referral or quotas, without attaching probabilities to the elements in the target population. For such samples it is difficult to ensure they are representative and thus the findings cannot be generalized to the population with a specified degree of confidence.

■ **Determine the appropriate sample size for various situations encountered in practice**
To determine the sample size three pieces of information are needed. These are: the degree of confidence necessary to estimate the true value; the precision of the estimate, and the amount of true variability present in the data. In practice the researcher and client discuss and agree upon the desired level confidence and the precision of the estimate. Further, since the true variability is unlikely to be known, it typically is estimated based on judgement or through a pilot study. ■

Ethical Dilemma

Mark Stephenson is an account manager for a business research firm. At the request of a local hospital's marketing director, he submits a proposal to conduct a patient satisfaction survey. His opinion is the sample should be random and collected either by phone or the Internet. After his presentation to the marketing director and the hospital chief executive, the marketing director asks Mark to use exit interviews to collect the data instead. She explains that her boss feels exit interviews are just as valid and will save the hospital money.

What should Mark do?

REVIEW QUESTIONS

1. What is the difference between a sample and a population?

2. Why use sampling methods instead of interviewing the population?

3. What are the steps in the sampling process?

4. What is the difference between probability and nonprobability sampling?

DISCUSSION AND THINKING ACTIVITIES

1. Discuss the difficulties researchers face in defining the target population and its associated sampling frame. Comment with examples on how you would overcome these.

2. In which situations is nonprobability sampling preferred to probability sampling? Comment with examples.

3. For each of the probabilistic sampling designs illustrate their use with examples.

4. What considerations need to be taken into account when determining the appropriate efficient sample size?

5. Would you prefer to use a sample of 20,000 voters or 2,000 voters to describe voting behaviour in national elections? Explain with reasons your choice.

INTERNET EXERCISES   W W W

1. Go to the Google or Yahoo search engines and type in the words population and sampling. Prepare a brief summary of what you find.

2. Go to the following Web sites: www.surveysystem.com/sscalc.htm and www.svys.com. Use the functions on the Web sites. Prepare a brief report of what the Web sites do and how they work. Include you comments as to how useful these Web sites would be to the business researcher.

3. Go to the following Web site: http://random.mat.sbg.ac.at/links. Use the functions on the Web site to prepare a brief report of what the Web site does and how it works. Include your comments as to how useful this Web site would be to business researchers.

CHAPTER 8
METHODS OF COLLECTING PRIMARY DATA

CONTENTS

LEARNING OUTCOMES

- Provide an overview of the different data collection methods.
- Describe differences between qualitative and quantitative data collection.
- Understand the differences between observation and interview methods.
- Explain the role of the various interview methods in obtaining data.
- Assess the use of self-completion versus interviewer-completed surveys.

INTRODUCTION

Researchers describe and explain phenomena that exist in the business world. To do so they examine, for example, demographics, behaviour, attitudes, beliefs, life-styles and expectations of consumers and/or organizations. To complete this task, researchers must have data. Data are collected by means of one or more of the following: interviews, observation and/or questionnaires. Once data are obtained, it is analysed and becomes the basis for informed decision-making, which in turn helps to reduce the risk of making costly errors.

Data collection requires considerable knowledge and skills. We provide an overview of qualitative and quantitative data collection methods in this chapter. This stage of the research process is very important because once the data is collected, you cannot return to an earlier step to correct decisions that led to limitations in the study. At that point, the only choice is to collect the data again after correcting the problem and this can be expensive and sometimes impossible.

DATA COLLECTION METHODS

The type and amount of data to be collected depends upon the nature of the study together with its research objectives. If the study is exploratory the researcher collects narrative data through the

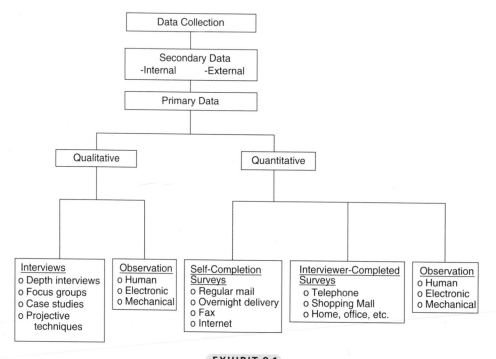

EXHIBIT 8-1

Primary Data Collection Methods

use of focus groups, personal interviews, or by observing behaviour or events. This type of data is referred to as qualitative. Such studies typically involve the use of smaller samples or case studies. But if the study is descriptive or causal the researcher is likely to require a relatively large amount of quantitative data obtained through large-scale surveys or by accessing electronic databases.

Until recently, face-to-face interviews, telephone surveys, mall intercepts, and mail surveys were the primary methods of data collection. Information technology is revolutionizing data collection, however, and large amounts of data, both qualitative and quantitative, can be obtained and integrated into databases relatively fast and at a very low cost compared to more traditional methods. These new methods include computerized questionnaires administered over the Internet, electronic capture of data at the point of sale, and electronic "conversations or discussions" both internally over an intranet and externally over the Internet. Indeed, globally electronic methods of collecting data now account for over 30% of all data collection.

The various data collection approaches are depicted in Exhibit 8-1. The process of data collection begins by examining secondary data. A limited amount of data may have already been collected through informal observation and interviews, or by scanning easily accessible information. But now the process becomes much more formal. The initial objective is to determine whether the research objectives can be achieved using secondary data. If they can, there is no need to collect primary data. The secondary data collection process involves examining internal data sources as well as external data. We discussed secondary data earlier in Chapter 5. The focus here is on the collection of primary data.

When the research objectives cannot be achieved with secondary data, primary data must be collected. Primary data collection methods can be divided into two types – qualitative and quantitative. An overview of both types is provided in the rest of this chapter.

QUALITATIVE DATA COLLECTION

There are two broad approaches to qualitative data collection – observation and interviews. If the objective of your research is to examine the behaviour of people or events, then observation is the appropriate method. On the other hand, if your objective is to understand why something happens then you will need to interview people. We discuss observation and interviews as methods of qualitative data collection in this section.

OBSERVATION

Observational data are collected by systematically recording observations of people, events or objects. Observational data can be obtained by use of human, electronic, or mechanical observation. An observational approach results in either narrative or numerical data. If narrative data is collected, it typically involves researchers preparing written descriptions of behaviour, behaviour recorded on an electronic medium such as audio or videotape, or information obtained from an electronic database (e.g., a blog). If numerical data is gathered, it would involve either a trained observer recording events using a structured questionnaire, or a device that counts or tracks specific actions. For example, a researcher may study fruit-, vegetable-or meat-selection behaviour in a supermarket by having an observer record the amount of time between the approach of the individual and the decision to purchase a particular item, whether the item is picked up or turned over, and so forth. This information could be recorded on a questionnaire along with purchase information.

Similarly, Phil Samouel might evaluate the competence of the waiters in his restaurant on a number of predetermined criteria.

Today, however, probably the most widespread use of observational data collection is either through scanning of purchases in supermarkets, drugstores, or other retail outlets, or over the Internet when companies observe an individual's click-through behaviour. But what you may not realize is that when you phone a business and are informed the call may be recorded for quality control monitoring and training, what often happens is the recording is being used to collect observational data. Recording of such calls provides a rich source of qualitative data for assessing company procedures, employee performance, and customer comments.

A disadvantage of observation is there is no opportunity to observe any unseen thoughts or attitudes. For example, if behaviour is being observed in a supermarket we do not know the vegetable or fruit customer's attitude, hunger level or whether the purchase is for her/his own consumption. In contrast, a primary advantage of observational data is its **unobtrusive** approach. Unobtrusive means the respondent is unaware of his/her participation in a research project. Because individuals being observed have had no interaction with a researcher, such as instructions or a questionnaire, they cannot be influenced by any activities associated with collecting data. Thus, observational data collection avoids interview bias since no instructions are given or questions asked.

Does this unobtrusive approach violate the research participant's right to privacy? Or is it possible the participant can be harmed in any way? If the behaviour being observed is typically performed in public with the likelihood that others may notice, it is unlikely the person's privacy has been violated, or that they will be harmed. But, observations of human behavior for research purposes should avoid recording the person's name. This is another way in which privacy is protected. On the other hand, private acts should not be observed. For example, retail store dressing rooms should not be used to collect observational data even though the data might be very useful in understanding how and why people buy clothes.

As a general rule, individuals do not know their behaviour is being observed. But, occasionally researchers may choose to request the participation of respondents in an observational study. As an example, mall shoppers may be given a GPS (Global Positioning System) transmitter that allows their behaviour to be tracked throughout the mall. This provides researchers with useful information on shopping patterns. Researchers hope shoppers will forget they have the device so it will not influence their behaviour. Similarly, GPS technology is being used to observe the location and driving patterns of commercial trucks and buses, railroads, and school buses. GPS technology is expected to be standard equipment on most new vehicles within five years.

Ethnographic research and content analysis are two special forms of the observational approach. We discuss both in the following paragraphs.

Ethnographic Research

Ethnographic researchers prefer to interpret behaviour through observation of actual life experiences. Researchers typically will spend long periods of time with a respondent, and then write narratives that describe the respondent's behaviour. For example, a researcher studying heavy beer consumption may actually spend days or weeks with a "heavy" beer consumer to try and discover all the needs addressed by beer consumption.[1] Similarly, a researcher may actually spend weeks or months as an "employee" in a workplace in an effort to understand the organization and the behaviour of its employees. Ethnographic approaches to observation often are referred to as participant-observer research.

Ethnographic observational studies sometimes pay consumers to place small video cameras in their homes or cars.[2] For example, 3-M paid consumers to track their in-home movements via video in an effort to understand better how its Ergo hand-held electronic Internet appliance would be used. This eventually led to the belief that people would use it differently than they do the Internet via a computer. Similarly, Moen, one of the largest plumbing fixture manufacturers in the world, got permission to videotape people in their showers! This enabled them to discover several aspects of shower behaviour that people couldn't or wouldn't voice. For example, they noticed that many women used a faucet handle for balance while shaving their legs. Findings like these enabled Moen to design shower fixtures that improve your shower experience! We discuss ethnographic methods more in Chapter 11.

Content Analysis

Content analysis obtains data by observing and analysing the content or message of written text. Examples of text where content analysis typically is used include reports, contracts, advertisements, letters, blogs, open-ended questions on surveys, in-depth interviews and similar content. Through systematic analysis as well as observation, the researcher examines the frequency that words and main themes occur and identifies information content and characteristics embedded in the text. The end result often is to quantify qualitative data.

The initial content analysis may count word or phrase frequency. For example, a researcher could analyse transcripts from employment interviews. The transcripts are typically analysed by software that counts the frequency of occurrence of words and expressions. One successful application of content analysis has been in discovering expressions that indicate a dishonest response. A job candidate with a high count of short negative expressions such as "never" and "nothing," or a high number of qualifiers such as "kind of" or "I don't think," may be classified as dishonest.[3] Moreover, "kind of" and "sort of" may both be interpreted as "hedging". An initial content analysis may reveal many words that have essentially the same meaning. If this occurs, categories of 'common meaning' are developed.

Researchers have used content analysis to discover the primary theme and purpose of business codes of ethics. Codes of ethics are available as secondary data for many large public firms. Content analyses of codes found in the *Fortune* 500 database and *Business Review Weekly* database provide an interesting comparison among British, Australian and American codes of ethics. For example, the themes that were identified suggested that codes are directed either toward owners, management or all employees of an organization. Themes emerging most often involve employee conduct, community involvement and customer treatment. Activities identified most often include gift giving and receiving, conflicts of interest and accurate record keeping. Relatively few passages described specific guidance on what is acceptable. The themes were similar across the UK, Australia and the US But UK codes contained more community welfare references and Australian and US codes contained more references to customer treatment and equal opportunity.[4]

Content analysis is frequently used to interpret text interviews. It also is commonly used to discover themes and orientations of media programs and advertising. Given the visual nature of advertising, content analyses often involves identifying the frequency of themes expressed both in words and in pictures.[5] For example, television commercials directed at teenagers in the US were analysed using content analysis and it was determined that teens are exposed to over 14,000 ads a year containing sexual references. Similarly, news and other types of television programs are analysed to determine the amount and type of violence included. Indeed, even video and computer games are examined to determine and classify their content.

INTERVIEWS

An **interview** is where the researcher "speaks" to the respondent directly. Interviews are particularly helpful in gathering data when dealing with complex and/or sensitive issues, and when open-ended questions are used to collect data. Interviews also enable the researcher to obtain feedback and to use visual aids if the interviews are face-to-face. For example, respondents might be shown a new corporate logo, a new corporate mission statement, building designs, automobile styles and colours, and so on, and asked to comment. Finally, interviews are flexible in where they can be conducted (at work, home, or in malls, etc.) and researchers can increase participation rates by explaining the project and its value.

To get the cooperation of the interviewee in a face-to-face interview, and thereby obtain quality information, the interviewer must make every effort to create a relaxed atmosphere within which to conduct the interview. Once this has been achieved, interviewers will ask the respondents to describe the situation or phenomenon of interest, followed by: "Why?" "How?" "When?" "Where?" and "Who?" questions. For example, if Phil Samouel wanted information about the food being served in his Greek restaurant, he might ask customers "What do you think about the quality of my food?" If their response is "We think it is very good." Then he would follow-up by asking "Why do you say that?" as well as ask them to give examples such as: I really like the special of the day or a particular desert is very good. In this way, Phil can really begin to understand what customers think about the food in his restaurant. In short, Phil can get "actionable" information for his business plan, not just general information that is of little value in taking corrective actions. In formulating questions for interviews, therefore, always ask yourself: "Will the answers I get to this question help me make a better decision about a particular business approach?" If not, do not ask them!

Interviews can vary from being highly unstructured to highly structured. Unstructured interviews are generally conducted using a very flexible approach. In contrast, the interviewer controls structured interviews in a consistent and orderly manner. Whether structured or unstructured, interviewing can take a variety of forms such as face to face or telephone.

Structured Interviews

For **structured interviews** the interviewer uses an interview sequence with predetermined open-ended questions. For each interview, the interviewer is required to use the same interview sequence and to conduct the interview in exactly the same way to avoid biases that may result from inconsistent interviewing practices. Additionally, a standardized approach will ensure responses are comparable between interviews.

Each respondent is provided with an identical opportunity to respond to the questions. The interviewer may collect the responses in the form of notes or may tape record the interview. Taping should only be done with the permission of the interviewee. If the interview is not tape recorded, it is good practice to provide the interviewee with a copy of the interviewer's notes after they are completed as this will help ensure the interview is captured accurately.

Semi-structured interviews

Sometimes **semi-structured interviews** are used. Here researchers are free to exercise their own initiative in following up an interviewee's answer to a question. For example, the interviewer may want to ask related, unanticipated questions that were not originally included. This approach may result in unexpected and insightful information coming to light, thus enhancing the findings.

Semi-structured interviews have an overall structure and direction, but allow a lot of flexibility to include unstructured questioning. Perhaps the best-known semi-structured interview approach is the **focus group**. Focus groups are semi-structured interviews that use an exploratory research approach and are considered a type of qualitative research. Focus groups are unstructured because the moderator allows participants to answer questions in their own words and encourages them to elaborate on their responses. But focus groups also are structured in that the moderator has a list of topics and/or questions to guide the discussion.

Focus groups are relatively informal discussions among eight to twelve respondents. Respondents usually share something in common. They may all have the same job, work for the same company, be a customer of the same bank or do the same household chores. This common ground is usually very much involved in the discussion. Unlike other survey approaches, a random sample is neither required nor desired.

Focus groups are guided by a **moderator** who encourages discussion and keeps the group "on track," meaning they don't stray too far from the primary topic. A good moderator is a key to a successful focus group. Good moderators possess some or all of the following characteristics:[6]

1. Personable – the moderator should have good conversation and people skills. Focus group participants need to feel comfortable discussing the subject matter with this person. The moderator must be comfortable in encouraging comment from quiet respondents and suppressing comments from any dominant participants.

2. Attentive – focus groups usually last 60–120 minutes. The moderator has to pay close attention the entire time and allocate time so that all topics are covered.

3. Professional training – focus group moderators usually have a background in communications, psychology, advertising or marketing research.

4. Well organized – the moderator should be prepared to lead the discussion in a logical sequence. A focus group outline is an essential part of this process. The outline is a discussion guide that lists all key discussion points that should be covered by the group. It's a good idea to get input from key decision makers in constructing this outline.

5. Objective – the moderator should not let his/her opinion interfere with the interview in any way. A moderator who has a very strong opinion on the subject matter may very well lead the discussion toward a personally desirable outcome. Sometimes, this effect is unintentional. This is why it's often advisable to have an outsider conduct the focus group interview. A good moderator may not even require a great deal of knowledge about the situation to be effective. It's difficult for moderators to be leading when they have no opinion.

6. Listens – generally, the less a moderator says the better the focus group. The key is getting the respondents to discuss the issues without having to individually ask each to answer every question. A quiet moderator is less likely to be leading.

The Research in Action box tells you what focus groups revealed as important reasons for selecting a family-style restaurant.

RESEARCH IN ACTION

IT'S ALL ABOUT THE QUALITY OF THE FOOD!

One of the authors was asked to conduct a series of focus groups in seven different geographic areas. The client was a large chain of family-style restaurants that wanted to know what motivated customers to come to a particular restaurant. The information would help management better understand patronage behavior and be used in developing an advertising and promotion campaign. Eleven unique reasons were identified in the focus groups. They are listed below:

Reason:	Percent of Time Mentioned:
• Quality of food.	88 %
• Variety of menu items.	51 %
• Expected cost of meal.	39 %
• Convenient locations.	34 %
• Friendly service.	31 %
• Nutritious food.	19 %
• Speed of service.	17 %
• Competent, knowledgeable employees.	17 %
• Atmosphere.	15 %
• Portion size.	14 %
• Special promotions, coupons and discounts.	9 %

Two focus groups were held in each geographic area and a total of 137 individuals participated. How valid are these findings? How can they be used? Can they be generalized to the overall market for family-style restaurants? ■

Focus groups are used across all business disciplines. For example, focus groups can be instrumental in developing ideas related to supervisory issues, including compensation systems and flexible work scheduling.[7] Focus groups also have played a role in developing professional certification programs in finance and accounting.[8]

Politicians frequently use focus groups. Focus groups are useful in discovering potential issues that can reinforce or build a candidate's image. In the US, focus groups are used in Presidential campaigns, in most campaigns for the US Senate and in many statewide elections. They are particularly useful when the public's opinion is very diverse. President Clinton's administration relied on focus groups through his entire term.[9] Tag lines and phrases were developed from focus group sessions that communicated the intended messages effectively. American politicians aren't the only ones using focus group research. Australian politicians successfully used input from focus groups to position candidates and policies based on tax issues.[10]

Making decisions based solely on focus group research is risky. Focus groups are discovery-oriented. The group size is very small. Thus, the results are much less likely to represent those of the population. Sometimes opinions are very dependent upon a particular group's chemistry. Researchers usually recommend two or three focus groups at a minimum to try and find consistent opinions. Therefore, conclusions drawn from focus groups are best tested using another more confirmatory approach. The Research in Action box describes two blunders that occurred because decisions were made based only on focus groups.

RESEARCH IN ACTION

THE AZTEC AND THE CRUISER – A TALE OF TWO "BLUNDERS"

Businesses sometimes make decisions based solely on an exploratory design. However, it increases the risk. It is usually a situation where the need for expediency takes priority over further confirmatory research. The story below illustrates risks associated with this approach.

When a company introduces a new product, there are two ways to go wrong. One, the company can overestimate demand. Second, the company can underestimate demand. Both cause problems but certainly the latter situation is preferable to the former. The Chrysler PT Cruiser suffered from the latter problem. Focus group research suggested it was the kind of design that consumers would either love or hate. Thus, based on the proposition that the car did not have broad appeal, it entered into a niche car strategy. Chrysler developed production capacity for 60,000 vehicles in the first model year. They took orders for 120,000 vehicles in the first year. Thus, many customers were disappointed in the wait or settled for another vehicle. They are now trying to double production capacity.

Likewise, Pontiac conducted many focus groups discussing the Aztec. Consumers had a lot of positive things to say about the concept. Pontiac was enthused and developed production capacity for 80,000 vehicles in the first model year. The focus groups failed, however, to fully communicate the product's design. During the first model year, Pontiac sold 20,000 Aztecs. If you are looking for a deeply discounted vehicle, think Aztec! Research conducted afterwards trying to identify the source of the low sales volume suggests consumers think it is ugly, and not in a cute sort of way as some would say about the PT Cruiser.

Could further confirmatory research have avoided these blunders? Perhaps. Has Chrysler put enough effort into studying the situation to warrant doubling production capacity? It is unclear. This decision depends on new research questions including, "Will the demand remain high when the novelty wears off or when me-too competitors make it not so novel?"

Source: Kobe, G. (2001). "How Focus Groups Failed Aztec, PT Cruiser", *Automotive Industries*, 181 (February), 9. ∎

There are hundreds of research firms worldwide specializing in focus group research.[11] Focus group interviews generally require human and physical resources aside from a moderator. A support staff is needed to recruit participants, who are usually paid (£50 − £100) for their time and participation. People are needed to coordinate the group and provide basic hospitality. Focus group interviews are usually recorded. A typical focus group room includes a one-way mirror and recording equipment. Focus group sponsors generally observe the interview through the mirror and the entire session is audio taped and/or videotaped. Respondents should be informed about the recording and given an option not to participate should they object. By now it should be no surprise that focus groups are expensive. A typical focus group session costs about £3,000 − £4,000 to conduct including a fee for analysis and report preparation.

Technological developments are providing additional focus-group opportunities. Electronic focus groups are conducted using password protected Web site bulletin boards. A moderator posts a question and waits for participants to respond. If the group gets off course, or once enough discussion on a topic has been obtained, the moderator will post a new comment. Generally, this process will go on for a week to a month. Electronic focus groups are not seen as a replacement for traditional focus groups. While they are useful in obtaining large quantities of highly elaborate responses, they are even more expensive than a traditional focus group (about £9,000) and they are often unable to capture the real-time face-to-face interactions of participants.[12]

Unstructured Interviews

An **unstructured interview** is conducted without the use of an interview sequence. This allows the researcher to elicit information by engaging the interviewee in free and open discussion on the topic of interest. A particular advantage of this approach is the researcher has the opportunity to explore in depth issues raised during the interview.

Unstructured interviews are a type of qualitative research. They are used when research is directed toward an area that is relatively unexplored. By obtaining a deeper understanding of the critical issues involved, the researcher is in a better position to not only better define the research problem, but also to develop a conceptual framework for the research. This will then form the basis for subsequent empirical research to test the ideas, concepts and hypotheses that emerge.

The Research in Action box provides and example of how a corporate policy on document shredding might be developed. An in-depth semi-structured interviewing approach was used instead of focus groups because it was believed employees would not be as open in their comments in a focus group setting.

RESEARCH IN ACTION

DEVELOPING COMPANY POLICIES REQUIRES EFFORT!

All large accounting firms have a policy on shredding of documents. One would think such policies would be specific and well thought out. The Andersen/ENRON situation indicates this is not necessarily true. A smaller accounting firm retained one of the authors to conduct unstructured interviews with employees. The purpose of the interviews was to obtain information to assist in updating and improving its document-shredding policy.

The interviews were conducted individually and anonymity was guaranteed. In-depth interviews were used instead of focus groups because it was anticipated employees would be more open and honest with their comments if interviewed separately instead on in a focus-group setting. Information was requested on how the policy had been applied in the past, if it had worked well, were their situations in which they had any doubts about whether the policy was appropriately applied, how it could be improved, and so forth. Since more than 40 individuals had to be interviewed and the responses tabulated, the process took several weeks and a substantial amount of time. But several gaps in the old policy were identified and management felt the outcome, a substantially improved policy, was worth the effort. ∎

Depth Interviews

A **depth,** or **in-depth interview**, is an unstructured one-to-one discussion session between a trained interviewer and a respondent. Respondents are usually chosen carefully because they have some specialized insight. For example, a researcher exploring employee turnover might conduct a depth interview with someone who has worked for five different restaurants in a period of two years. Like a focus group, the interviewer first prepares an outline that guides the interview (this is the structured part of an in-depth interview). Also like a focus group, the responses are unstructured. Indeed, a depth interview allows much deeper probing than does a focus group. **Probing** means that a researcher delves deeply into a response to identify possibly hidden reasons for a particular behavior. The "why, why, why" technique (asking Why? several times) is a popular probing technique.

Depth interview participants are usually more comfortable discussing potentially sensitive topics. For example, employees are far more likely to be candid in discussing their superiors' behaviours in a one-to-one setting than among a dozen coworkers. Some consumer issues also fall into the sensitive category. Consumers may discuss hygiene, financial or sexual preference issues more readily in a depth interview than in a focus group setting. Likewise, executives and top managers are more comfortable in a one-to-one setting. You might imagine that a focus group of product design engineers from Honda, Toyota, Mercedes and Ford might be a very quiet session.

Like focus groups, depth interviews can be very useful in clarifying concepts. Researchers need an operational definition for something before they can measure it. For example, what does a work climate of "trust and responsibility" mean? Depth interviews proved useful in identifying observable workplace events that employees identified with coworker responsibility. Depth interview participants indicated that the "CYA" principal (cover "yourself") is associated with low trust in the workplace. Depth interviews also have been used with restaurant employees to examine issues such as hiding tips to prevent them from being shared with coworkers and the effects of stress on workplace behavior including food preparation and wholesomeness.

Depth interviews generally are more expensive than focus groups. Since the interviews are one-on-one as opposed to one-on-12, fees charged by the interviewer are multiplied. The interviewer may spend 12 hours with only six respondents. Further, since more text is generated, more analysis time is generally required. This adds up to a higher bill. Exhibit 8-2 compares and contrasts depth interviews and focus groups.

Benefits of Exploratory Research	Focus Groups	Depth Interviews
Helping to form hypotheses. Discussion provides clarity of thought aiding in expressing researchable propositions.	★★★★★	★★★★★
Identifying salient attributes of some situation. This might be some important product or job characteristic.	★★★★★	★★★★★
Aiding measurement in future studies by providing an operational definition of some concept.	★★★★★	★★★★★
Identifying usage patterns.	★★★★	★★★
Identifying key sources of difficulties for respondents.	★★★★	★★★★★
Identifying novel ideas.	★★★★★	★★★
Concept testing of new ideas. Present the idea for refining and guessing initial reactions.	★★★★★	★★
Discussing sensitive issues.	☹	★★★★★
Identifying personal problems of respondents.	☹	★★★
Effective in testing hypotheses.	☹	☹
An economical form of exploratory research	☹	☹

[a]Here are some of the things that can be accomplished with focus groups and/or depth interviews. The number of stars listed indicates how effective a technique is in producing the benefit listed. Five stars = highly effective; fewer stars = less effective. A frown indicates the technique is ineffective in producing a benefit.

EXHIBIT 8-2

Comparison of Focus Groups and Depth Interviews.[a]

Projective Techniques

Focus groups, depth interviews and surveys all involve some type of interview process. Both the researcher and the respondent are actively engaged. When we conduct interviews there is always a risk the interview process itself will influence respondents. Perhaps respondent comments are not entirely accurate. The inaccuracy may be because of incomplete recall, a suppression of information because of social concerns or an unwillingness to provide an accurate response to the question. There are some things people simply will not tell an interviewer.

Projective data can be collected in an interview as well. In **projective interviewing**, the researcher presents the respondent with an ambiguous stimulus. For example, the interviewer may provide the respondent with a stick-man cartoon showing a grocery store employee eating an apple in the store. The respondent, a grocery store employee, is then asked to complete the picture in words and/or images. Since the respondent is describing another person and not him/herself, the researcher is more confident the explanation is true. For example, a respondent is more likely to mention whether or not the apple was purchased or pilfered. This picture-completion type of exercise is known as **thematic apperception**. As with all projective approaches, the researcher will infer that the characteristics applied to the ambiguous figure actually reside within the respondent. Thus, projective approaches are a good way to discover hidden motivations. Other projective approaches include sentence completion, word association, balloon test and role playing. The Research in Action box describes a classic study that used the projective technique approach.

RESEARCH IN ACTION

ARE INSTANT COFFEE DRINKERS REALLY THAT BAD?

Suppose you found a grocery list that contained the following items: a loaf of bread, 5 lbs of flour, an 8 oz jar of Maxwell House Instant Coffee, 2 lbs of ground beef, a 15 oz can of cling peaches. How would you describe this person? This projective approach was applied by a researcher studying the reasons people select instant versus ground coffee. A group of respondents were asked to respond to a list of this type. Another group responded to a list identical in all respects with the exception that instant coffee was replaced by ground coffee. The respondents were asked to describe the woman who purchased these groceries in as much detail as possible, based on nothing but the list. While the ground coffee purchaser generally received positive responses, the instant coffee buyer was often described as "lazy," "living alone," "a poor homemaker," "careless with her money" and even as "an old maid"! This led to the theory that the process of purchasing and making instant coffee was not as fulfilling as making coffee in a more traditional way. Keep in mind that these data were collected 56 years ago. Do you think things have changed?

Source: Haire, M. (1950). "Projective Techniques in Marketing Research", *The Journal of Marketing*, 14 (April), 649–656. ∎

Case Studies

Case studies focus on collecting information about a specific event or activity – often a particular firm or industry. The logic of conducting a case study is that in order to obtain a complete picture of the entire situation one must examine a real-life example. This enables the researcher to identify interactions between all the variables in a real-life setting.

Several decisions are necessary in case studies. The first is the unit of analysis. That is, what will be the focus of the study? Will it be the company as a whole, a division of the company, a particular department, or perhaps even a project that is being implemented by the company. A second decision is the time frame to be studied. When does the study period begin and when does it end? Incorrect decisions on either of these issues could invalidate the study's findings. When comparisons are made of one company, event or activity, the situation becomes even more complex. For example, it would not be appropriate to compare a family business to a publicly traded one, just as it would not be appropriate to compare a situation in the year 2007 with one that occurred in 1997. Comparisons are necessary, but the situations must be comparable.

QUANTITATIVE DATA COLLECTION

Quantitative data collection involves gathering numerical data using structured question-naires or observation guides to collect primary data from individuals. The data range from beliefs, opinions, attitudes, behaviour and lifestyles to general background information on individuals such as gender, age, education and income, as well as company characteristics like revenue and number of employees. Business researchers often refer to quantitative data collection as survey research. When the research project involves collecting information from a large sample of individuals, survey research is the best approach. An important consideration with surveys is that respondents clearly know information about their behaviour and/or attitudes is being collected. Thus, it is always possible this may influence their responses and create response bias.

Methods of collecting quantitative survey data fall into three broad categories – self-completion, interviewer-completion and observation. **Self-completion** methods include mail surveys, Internet/electronic surveys, drop-off/pick up, and similar approaches. **Interviewer-completed** methods involve direct contact with the respondents through personal interviews either face-to-face or via telephone. Observation studies that are quantitative involve collecting a large amount of numerical data, such as studying individuals' click-through behaviour on the Internet or purchase behaviour using scanner methods. The primary difference in observation techniques between qualitative research and quantitative research is that qualitative observation involves mostly the recording of narrative information, whereas quantitative observation approaches involve counting and numerical information on behaviour, actions or events instead of narrative.

As noted earlier, personal interviews, whether structured or unstructured, are often used to obtain detailed qualitative information from a relatively small number of individuals. This approach is sometimes referred to as an in-depth survey. On the other hand, structured questionnaires are used to collect quantitative data from large numbers of individuals in a relatively quick and convenient manner. Finding a company to assist in conducting a survey is a lot easier with the Internet as the Research in Action box on Quirks.com shows.

RESEARCH IN ACTION

QUIRKS.COM – YOUR ONLINE SOURCE FOR RESEARCH SERVICES

For over 15 years Quirk's Research Review has been producing a monthly print magazine that reports on research trends and techniques in a simple and straightforward manner to promote the value of research. The company's Web site (www.quirks.com) is designed to encourage the use, understanding and value of research, while providing free access to as many research resources as possible. On the Web site business researchers can search for and purchase over 40,000 research reports from more than 350 publishers.

The site also allows researchers access to archived articles from the magazine, including case histories on successful research projects, discussion of research techniques, the statistical use of data in marketing research and other topics relevant to the research industry. Some of the directories available online include the Researcher

SourceBook™ which contains listings of more than 7,300 firms providing marketing research products and services; listings of world wide focus group facilities; and listings of more than 300 data processing and statistical analysis firms. For example, if you log on to the Web site, key in London and focus group facilities, it will give you a listing and contact information for 11 different companies. After using the online directories to locate a firm, business researchers can then use the online Request For Proposal forms to send project parameters directly to a particular firm.

Another unique feature of the site is the Job Mart page that allows researchers to view or post research-related employment opportunities and view or post online resumes. From job postings and case studies to directories and a glossary of research terms, Quirks.com offers marketing and business research professionals the tools, information and solutions to most any research questions they might face. ■

SELF-COMPLETION SURVEYS

Self-completion approaches to collecting data use structured questionnaires. A structured questionnaire is a predetermined set of questions designed to capture data from respondents. It is a scientifically developed instrument for measurement of key characteristics of individuals, companies, events and other phenomena. Good survey research requires good questionnaires to ensure accuracy in the data.

In conducting a questionnaire-based study there are a number of inter-related activities that must be considered. These include: the general design of the questionnaire, validation of the questionnaire by pretesting, and the method by which the questionnaire is administered.

Questionnaire surveys generally are designed to obtain large quantities of data, usually in numerical form. A questionnaire consists of a standard set of questions with answers to the questions often limited to a few predetermined mutually exclusive and exhaustive outcomes. Mutually exclusive means each answer has a separate response category while exhaustive means a response category has been included for every possible answer. Questionnaire wording is very important to the accuracy of the information collected, and in Chapter 10 we give you guidelines on how to deal with this topic as well as other questionnaire design considerations.

Questionnaires are frequently completed without a researcher present. The assumption is that respondents have the knowledge and motivation to complete them on their own. It does, however, mean the topic, design and format must be sufficiently appealing that respondents actually complete and return the questionnaire. Examples of self-completion questionnaires include surveys given to theatre patrons either before or after the show, or perhaps at intermission, "tabletop" surveys at restaurants or in doctors' offices, and questionnaires sent by auto dealerships following service visits.

Self-completion questionnaires are delivered to respondents several ways. Traditional approaches include mail and fax surveys. More recently, electronic delivery approaches are being utilized. A major problem with any kind of self-completion questionnaire is the loss of researcher control. You typically do not know whether the intended person completed the questionnaire, if respondents answer the questions in the sequence they are formatted in, or whether they asked for input from others. Any of these can introduce response bias. But perhaps the biggest problem with this type of questionnaire is the low response rate raising the question of whether those who responded are representative of the target population for the research project.

Mail Surveys

Surveys delivered to respondents via regular mail, fax and overnight delivery are typically thought of as **mail surveys**. Some mail surveys are short, others are quite long, as many as five or six pages, and in some instances booklets requesting extensive information are used. With fax surveys the researcher has few options. The major limiting factor is that only individuals with fax machines can be surveyed. For business surveys this is not much of a problem, but few consumers have a fax machine at home.

With traditional mail and overnight delivery, however, decisions must be made on the envelope, cover letter, length, and incentive. All of these factors impact the response rate in some way. Attractive envelopes and stationery, well-written cover letters and reasonable length questionnaires will all increase response rates. With longer surveys, an incentive will increase responses. While overnight delivery is a costly alternative, it often is used in business-to-business surveys if the budget permits. Prior agreement to participate generally is obtained over the phone. But actual delivery to the respondent is by overnight (Federal Express, DHL Express, Emery, etc.) because experience has shown that overnight packages are delivered to the respondent's desk and bypass traditional "gatekeepers" such as secretaries. If time is a factor, then traditional mail is not a good alternative. Generally speaking, researchers must allow at least three weeks for individuals to respond. But even then in most instances it will be necessary to send follow-up reminders to achieve a sufficient sample size, and this will take another two or three weeks. Some suggested approaches to increase mail survey response rates are summarized in the Research in Action box.

RESEARCH IN ACTION

HOW TO INCREASE POSTAL SURVEY RESPONSE RATES

Below are some suggested ways to increase response rates in mail surveys:

Approach	Examples
Preliminary contact	Letter, email or phone call ahead of time.
Personalization	Individually typed and addressed letter, personal signature, etc.
Response deadline	Provide a due date in the letter.
Appeals	Convince respondent survey is important and has some social or other important value.
Sponsorship	Survey is sponsored by an important organization, such as a national trade organization or prestigious university.

Approach	Examples
Incentives	Nonmonetary gifts like summary of findings or a ballpoint pen. Monetary incentive like a £1.00 to buy a cup of coffee.
Questionnaire Length	Print on both sides of the paper and make no longer than four pages.
Type of Postage	Special commemorative stamp. Sending overnight delivery such as FedEx will bypass "gatekeepers" for business surveys, if the budget permits. Always include a postage-paid envelope to return the questionnaire.
Follow-ups	Send follow-up reminders such as postcard. Sometimes respondents lose the questionnaire so sending a letter with a second copy can help.

Source: Adapted from Conant, J., Smart, D. and Walker, B. (1990) "Mail Survey Facilitation Techniques: An Assessment and Proposal Regarding Reporting Practices", *Journal of the Market Research Society*, 32(4), 569–580. ∎

To conduct mail surveys you must have a list. If you are surveying your own customers or other individuals with whom you already have a relationship, a list will be available. If you are soliciting information from other individuals or organizations, however, it will be necessary to purchase a list from a direct marketing company. Several large companies sell lists. The Research in Action box tells you about the services of one of the larger UK direct marketing companies.

RESEARCH IN ACTION

DIRECT MARKETING CAMPAIGNS FOR INDIVIDUALS AND ORGANIZATIONS

Fox Media is one of the largest UK direct marketing companies. It uses a variety of methods to develop lists of Business-to-Business and Business-to-Consumer mailing lists covering both UK and worldwide prospects. It notes that with direct mail representing over half of all the mail received by the average UK consumer in a typical week, it represents an excellent method of efficiently contacting potential customers. It's proprietary modelling approaches help to identify lists that have the greatest potential to produce high response rates and enable the identification of highly targeted segments. It also offers e-mail and mobile marketing capabilities which offer additional potential benefits such as interactivity and often much lower costs. Legislation such as the UK Data Protection Act and the Privacy and Electronic Communications Regulations needs to be adhered to, but there is still enormous scope for effective implementation of direct marketing campaigns.

For more information on Fox Media, see their Web site at: `http://ourworld.compuserve.com/homepages/foxmedia/cont.htm`, accessed June 2006. ∎

Electronic

Several approaches are used to complete electronic, self-completion questionnaires. The traditional approach is to deliver a computer diskette to the respondents. The questionnaire is programmed on the diskette and respondents simply place the diskette in their computer, follow the instructions, and when completed return the diskette to the research company. But email and 'web-hosted' Internet have replaced this approach in recent years.

Email surveys are popular, inexpensive, can be completed in a short period of time, and generally produce high quality data. But web-hosted Internet surveys have more flexibility. To maintain anonymity of respondents and increase response rates, **web-hosted Internet surveys** typically are created and hosted by an independent research company on their own server (computer). But companies sometimes host them on an in-house server. The greater flexibility of Internet surveys is due to the questionnaires being located on the "in-house" server that can include manipulations not possible in email surveys in which the questionnaire is located on the client/respondent side (i.e., it is sent to the respondent and is completed on their own PC). Access to web-hosted surveys can be controlled by password to ensure only qualified respondents complete the survey according to specified instructions. Respondents are contacted and asked to participate, and then given a unique password. In general, Internet surveys provide quick responses and high-quality data. But they can be expensive due to Web site programming costs. When evaluating the option of an Internet data collection approach, researchers must be careful that the profile of Internet users includes their targeted respondents. For example, 60-plus consumers are less likely to respond to Internet surveys.

Another method of self-completion interviews is the **kiosk survey**. A self-contained kiosk is located in a high traffic area and individuals sign on to obtain information and submit survey information. Drug stores use them to dispense medical information. Supermarkets use them to provide recipes and related information for food purchases. Conferences and trade shows use them at hotels to collect and disperse information, and fuel stops on highways use them to collect and disperse travel information. The main problem is the lack of control over who can use a kiosk to fill out questionnaires. But they do provide 24/7 access to information and ability to collect data.

INTERVIEWER-COMPLETED SURVEYS

Interviewer administered questionnaires are completed either face-to-face or over the telephone. Face-to-face and telephone interviews are the most prevalent methods of collecting interviewer-completed survey data.

Personal versus Telephone Interviews

Personal interviews involve direct face-to-face contact with respondents. Telephone interviews are not face-to-face, but can still be very effective. Telephone interviewing generally is faster and less expensive than personal interviews, but lacks the ability to use visuals and generally respondents will not tolerate as long an interview as in a face-to-face situation. Telephone surveys do enable greater control, however, particularly when conducted from a central facility under a supervisor's monitoring.

The objectives of the research can impact the decision on which method of administering questionnaires is best. Exhibit 8-3 summarizes the advantages and disadvantages of the major methods of administering survey questionnaires.

CONTINUING CASE   SAMOUEL'S GREEK CUISINE

Choosing the best data collection method

The business consultant hired by Phil Samouel has recommended a survey of his customers and his employees. The consultant has also recommended a survey of Gino's customers. For the survey of Samouel's employees, the consultant has said there are several options. One is to give all employees a copy of the questionnaire and ask them to return it to Phil. A second option is to give employees a copy of the questionnaire and ask them to return it to the consultant. The third option is to require all employees to come to a meeting and complete the questionnaire. He says there are other alternatives, but they are probably too expensive.

For the survey of Samouel's customers, the consultant has suggested a couple of approaches for collecting the data. One approach involves asking customers to complete the questionnaires at their table either before or after they get their food. Another is to stop them on the way out of the restaurant and ask them to complete a questionnaire. A third option is to give it to them and ask that they complete it at home and mail it back. A fourth option is to load software on the computer, write a program to randomly select customers, and when they pay their bill give them instructions on how to go to a Web site and complete the survey. The last option, however, is most expensive because it is expensive to do the computer programming to set the survey up on the Internet.

The consultant has been brainstorming with other restaurant industry experts on how best to collect data from Gino's customers. He does not yet have any options he feels comfortable suggesting to Phil.

1. Which of the data collection options is best for the employee survey? Why?

2. Which of the data collection options is best for the customer survey? Why?

3. What are some possible ways to collect data from Gino's customers? Recommend a method you believe will work best. ■

Methods of Administration	Advantages	Disadvantages
Through the post, fax, drop off, etc. Involves sending the questionnaire to predetermined respondents with a covering letter. Generally used when there is a large number of geographically dispersed respondents.	• Wider access and better coverage • Provides anonymity • Relatively low cost • Large sample size • Respondents complete questionnaire at own pace	• Questionnaire must be simple • Low response rate • Points of clarification are not possible • Follow-up of nonresponse is difficult
In person Requires face-to-face contact with respondents. Generally makes use of smaller samples to gather opinions and when dealing with sensitive issues.	• Establish empathy and interest in the study • Can probe complex issues • Clarify respondents' queries • High response rate	• Expensive in time and cost • May lead to interviewer bias • Difficult to obtain wide access • Relatively small sample size
Over the telephone A form of personal interviewing which is used to obtain information quickly. Generally used to gain access to respondents that are geographically dispersed.	• Provides personal contact • Wide geographic coverage • Easy and quick access • Can be done with the aid of a computer	• Short interview time • Limited to listed telephone owners • Can be expensive
Electronic Administered via the intranet and Internet through the use of email. An increasingly popular method for collecting data.	• Easy to administer • Global reach • Fast data collection and analysis • No interviewer bias	• Loss of anonymity • Low cost • Can be complex to design and program • Limited to computer users

EXHIBIT 8-3

Advantages and Disadvantages of Methods of Administering Survey Questionnaires

SUMMARY

■ **Provide an overview of the different data collection methods**

There are many different data collection methods. The selection of a particular data collection method can influence the accuracy and reliability of data. Therefore, it is very important to select the correct method. Data collection can be divided into two types: qualitative and quantitative. Both methods can be used to capture narrative and/or numeric data using observation, trained interviewers and/or technology. Electronic data collection approaches are emerging as one of the most efficient and cost-effective means of collecting data. But traditional methods will continue to have their role long into the future.

■ **Describe differences between qualitative and quantitative data collection**

Qualitative data are is usually captured in narrative form and is used to describe human behaviour or business phenomena. Quantitative data, on the other hand, is captured through the use of various numeric means, such as scales. Qualitative approaches to data collection are frequently used at the exploratory stage of the research process. Their role is to identify and/or refine research problems that may help to formulate and test conceptual frameworks. In contrast, quantitative approaches to data collection are often used when we have well defined research problems or theoretical models. Validation of these concepts and models usually involves the use of data obtained from large-scale questionnaire surveys.

■ **Understand the differences between observation and interview methods**

Data are obtained through observation and/or interviews. Observation data are collected through a systematic approach to recognizing and recording occurrences associated with people, events, behaviour and objects. Collection of such data can be achieved through trained observers or through mechanical or electronic means like videos, scanning at checkout counters, or other electronic methods. Observation data can be narrative, graphic or numeric.

A survey usually involves the collection of large amounts of quantitative data through the use of self-completion and interviewer-completed questionnaires, or through observation using structured guides. Questionnaires can include both closed-ended and opened-ended questions, which yield numeric and narrative respectively. In cases where narrative data are obtained, they can be converted to numbers through coding techniques. An example of this is content analysis.

■ **Explain the role of the various interview methods in obtaining data**

An interview is the interaction between interviewer and interviewee through face-to-face, telephone or computer dialogue. Interviews are an appropriate means for gathering complex and sensitive information, or where a lot of elaboration is necessary to understand concepts. It is important that an interview be conducted in a relaxed and friendly atmosphere.

The nature of the interview can range from being highly unstructured to highly structured. Highly unstructured interviews do not require an interview schedule and this makes free and open dialogue between interviewer and interviewee possible. On the other hand, a highly structured interview requires an interview schedule of prepared questions to be followed when conducting the interview. In both types of interviews care must be taken to avoid biases and inconsistencies in the data collected.

Focus group interviews and depth interviews are both important discovery-oriented exploratory research tools. Depth interviews are preferable when a respondent may be more open in a private setting as opposed to a group setting. Focus groups are preferable when the group dynamics will not hinder comment. In fact, the group dynamics often encourage discussion.

■ **Assess the use of self-completion versus interviewer-completed surveys**

Surveys collect data using questionnaires. When the questionnaires are completed by the individual taking the survey it is referred to as self-completion. When the questionnaires are completed by having an interviewer ask the individual the questions it is referred to as an interviewer-completed survey.

A questionnaire is a means of obtaining data that are not already available in written or electronic form as secondary data, or cannot easily be obtained by observation. An example of data that cannot be obtained readily by observation is feelings or beliefs. Data generated by a questionnaire generally are referred to as primary data.

A questionnaire can be unstructured, semi-structured or highly structured. Irrespective of its structure, a questionnaire must produce accurate and reliable data amenable to statistical analysis using software packages such as SPSS. Key to achieving these objectives is the design and development of the questionnaire. ■

Ethical Dilemma

Midway through a series of focus groups about the new mobile data package a regional telecommunications company is planning to offer, the research firm tells the product manager, Salvador Andretti, that customer response has been overwhelmingly positive. Salvador reported the early feedback to his boss who was excited because the company needs a new product that can help boost company sales before the end of the year if bonuses are to be paid. In anticipation, Salvador decides to observe the final focus group himself. While observing, he begins to sense that the focus group facilitator is leading the subjects toward favourable responses. He fears the research is flawed but still believes the product will be popular with consumers. He is also aware that if he reschedules the focus groups with a new facilitator he will not have the data his boss needs to make the final decision about releasing the product until the first quarter of next year. If you were Salvador, what would you do? Should you present the focus group findings to your boss without voicing your concerns? Did the researcher act unethically in disclosing the early but incomplete results?

REVIEW QUESTIONS

1. Why would a business researcher want to collect data?

2. What are the main data gathering methods? Comment on their strengths and weaknesses and illustrate their use with examples.

3. What are the advantages and disadvantages of conducting surveys on the Internet?

4. What is the difference between structured and unstructured interviews?

5. What are focus groups and when would the business researcher use them?

DISCUSSION AND THINKING ACTIVITIES

1. An organization is experiencing low morale among its employees. Why and how might survey research be used in this situation?

2. What are the main issues that need to be considered in selecting a method of data collection for a survey of opinions about diversity in the workplace?

3. What type of questions would one expect to find on a survey of opinions about business ethics? Illustrate with examples their purpose, wording and coding. Would the topics in a business ethics survey differ from a survey of political ethics?

4. How would you go about creating a relaxed and friendly atmosphere during an interview? Give examples.

5. Go to the Web site for this book as www.wileyeurope.com/college/hair. Click on the link to "Bar Soap Focus Groups" and review the list of bar soap purchase criteria that was identified in the focus groups. Rank the criteria from most important to least important in deciding which brand of soap to purchase. Now click on "Ranking Answer" to see if your answers are the same as the original sample. Can you think of any criteria were not identified? If so, send and email to one of the authors of this book to see if they agree. Their email addresses are provided on the home page of this Web site.

6. How have recent technology developments facilitated data collection?

7. "Bias in data collection cannot be avoided." Give your view on this statement and suggest ways to minimize bias.

8. Critique the following methods of data collection.
   a. A shopping mall places interviewers in the parking lot every Saturday to ask where they live and the two to three stores they came to visit on this shopping trip.
   b. To evaluate the popularity of a new television series, the BBC invited people to call a number and vote yes, they would watch it again, or no, they would not watch it again. Each caller was charged £2.00.
   c. A supermarket recently completed a major renovation. To obtain customer reactions, the checkout personnel placed a short questionnaire into each customer's grocery bag while putting the groceries in.

INTERNET EXERCISES   WWW

1. Go to www.acnielsen.com and www.infores.com. Prepare a report on what these two companies are saying about their latest scanner-based technology.

2. Use an Internet search engine such as Yahoo or Google. Conduct a search using the words "data collection". Prepare a report summarizing what you found.

3. Go to the Geo Investor Web site at: http://www.geoinvestor.com/statistics/unitedkingdom/economicdata.htm. Identify reports related to data collection and prepare a report on what you learned.

4. The UK Office of National Statistics (ONS) conducts surveys that report on the current labour force and work history, status and so forth. Go to www.bls.gov http://www.statistics.gov.uk/statbase/tsdataset.asp?vlnk=496&More=Y and prepare a report summarizing the information available at this Web site and the methods used to collect the data.

5. The Web site for the Princeton University Survey Research Centre is located at: http://www.wws.princeton.edu/psrc/index.html. Go to this Web site and prepare a report summarizing the types of information located on there and why it might be of interest to business researchers.

NOTES

1. Woodside, A. G., and Wilson, E. J. (1995). "Applying Long Interview in Direct Marketing Research", *Journal of Direct Marketing Research*, 9(1), 37–65.
2. Khermouch, G. (2001). "Consumers in the Mist", *Businessweek*, 3721(2/26), 92–93.
3. Hunt, W. (1995). "Getting the Word on Deception", *Security Management*, 39 (June), 26–27.
4. Robin, D. P., Gialourakis, M. F. David, F. and Moritz, T. E. (1989). "A Different Look at Codes of Ethics", *Business Horizons*, 32(1), 66–73; Farrell, B. J. and Cobin, D. M. (1996). "A Content Analysis of Codes of Ethics in Australian Enterprises", *Journal of Managerial Psychology*, 11(1), 37–56.
5. Lawrence, J. and Berger, P. (1999). "Let's Hold a Focus Group", *Direct Marketing*, 61 (December), 40–44. Greenbaum, T. L. (1993). *Handbook of Focus Group Research*. New York, Lexington.
6. Maynard, M. L. and Taylor, C. R. (1999). "Girlish Images Across Cultures: Analyzing Japanese versus US Seventeen Magazine Ads", *Journal of Advertising*, 28 (Spring), 39–49.
7. Lussier, R. N. (1995). "Flexible Work Arrangement from Policy to Implementation", *Supervision*, 56 (September), 10.
8. *Internal Auditor* (1997). "EAR Focus Groups Target ISO 14,000", 54 (June), 8.
9. Hunter, P. (2000). "Using Focus Groups in Campaigns: A Caution", *Campaigns and Elections*, 21 (August), 38–41.
10. Walsh, M. (1999). "Focus Groups Set a New Agenda", *Bulletin with Newsweek*, 117(2/9), 7.
11. See *Marketing News*, 36 (March 4) for a directory of focus group firms and facilities. Also go to www.quirks.com.
12. James, D. (2002). "This Bulletin Just In: Online Research Technique Proving Invaluable", *Marketing News*, 36(March 4), 45–46.

CHAPTER 9
MEASUREMENT AND SCALING

CONTENTS

LEARNING OUTCOMES

- Understand the role of concepts in business research.
- Explain the notion of measurement.
- Provide an overview of the types of measurement scales.
- Distinguish between reliability and validity.

INTRODUCTION

Measurement is an important issue in business research. We must correctly measure the concepts we are examining. Otherwise, our interpretations and conclusions will not be accurate. To ensure the accuracy of our findings, we must consider how we measure as well as whether our measures are valid and reliable.

Measurement is a common occurrence for most people. School entrance examinations are measuring devices. So are employment tests. While in school exams measure achievement. Similarly, quarterly and annual reviews at work measure our progress. In a group setting, measurement is involved if we count the number of individuals, classify them as either male or female, or judge them as introverted or extroverted. Similarly, when we purchase car insurance or take a test to get a drivers' licence, measurement is involved. These are only a few examples of measurement in our everyday lives. In most instances we take the measurement process for granted. We seldom think about how we measure and the accuracy of the measurement. This chapter examines some of the more important issues we need to be aware of in measurement.

WHAT IS A CONCEPT?

A **concept** is a mental abstraction or idea formed by the perception of some phenomena. The idea is a combination of a number of similar characteristics of the concept. The characteristics are the variables that collectively define the concept and make measurement of the concept possible. Indeed, together they indirectly measure the concept which is also referred to as a construct. For example, the variables listed below were used to measure the concept/construct of "customer interaction".[1]

- This customer was easy to talk with.
- This customer genuinely enjoyed my helping her/him.
- This customer likes to talk to people.
- This customer was interested in socializing.
- This customer was friendly.
- This customer tried to establish a personal relationship.
- This customer seemed interested in me, not only as a salesperson, but also as a person.

By obtaining scores on each of the individual variables, you can indirectly measure the overall concept of customer interaction. The individual scores are then combined into a single score, according to a predefined set of rules. The resultant score is often referred to as a scale, an index or a summated rating scale. In the previous example of customer interaction, the individual variables were scored using a 5-point scale, with 1 = Strongly Disagree and 5 = Strongly Agree.

Suppose the research objective is to identify the characteristics (variables) associated with a theory of restaurant satisfaction. The researcher is likely to review the literature on satisfaction, conduct both formal and informal interviews, and then draw on his or her own experiences to identify characteristics like quality of food, quality of service and value for money as important components of a conceptual model of restaurant satisfaction. Logical integration of these characteristics then provides a theoretical framework and/or a conceptual model, which can facilitate empirical investigation of the concept of restaurant satisfaction.

MEASUREMENT IN BUSINESS RESEARCH

Measurement is a fundamental concept of business research. To understand business research, or really any concept, we must be able to measure it. Without measurement, it is difficult if not impossible to comment on business behaviour or phenomena. This is because we subconsciously measure something when we say something about it. For example, if we buy an ice cream cone and say it tastes good we are measuring. We are saying this tastes good compared to other flavours we have tasted previously. Similarly, if we say an employee is lazy, or irresponsible, or uncooperative, we are measuring.

Managers are interested in measuring many aspects of business. Supervisors measure employee performance, motivation, staff turnover rates, and other performance indicators. Accountants measure profits and losses, assets and liabilities, depreciation, and so on. Marketing managers measure awareness of a particular shop or restaurant, favourable or unfavourable perceptions of various characteristics such as service quality, portion size or food taste, brand preference, volume of sales through traditional "bricks and mortar compared to online", and so on. The more effectively managers measure these business aspects the better their decisions.

MEASUREMENT DIFFICULTIES

When we think of measurement, most of us think in terms of our own experiences. How fast am I driving or how high is that airplane flying? Similarly, how much do I weigh or how tall am I? Measurement of things like this is easy because these things are not very complex. It is easy to use a ruler or set of scales to measure height or weight. In contrast, when we attempt to measure attitudes, opinions or perceptions it is much more difficult. Often we do not have precise definitions of concepts, such as satisfaction. Instead, we have to develop new scales (questions) to measure a concept because we do not have tools like rulers or speedometers to measure concepts precisely.

In business research we work with concepts that can range from being simple and concrete in nature to those that are extremely complex and abstract. Therefore, one of the first things we have to do is develop "precise" definitions of the concepts we examine in our research, thereby ensuring there is no ambiguity in their interpretation. In this book we use the terms "concept" and "construct" interchangeably. Recall that a concept is a mental abstraction or idea formed by the perception of some phenomena. Examples of concepts in business include job satisfaction, job commitment, brand awareness, brand loyalty, service quality, image, risk, channel conflict, empathy, strategic orientation, executive values, motivation to search online, and so on.

Consider concepts such as "age" and "income" as opposed to "satisfaction" and "competence of employees". For "age" and "income" there will, generally speaking, be agreement as to their definition because they are directly observable and represent facts. But for "satisfaction" and "competence of employees" there is unlikely to be a common interpretation of their meaning, and they can only be measured indirectly. The more complex and abstract the concept is, for example "executive values", the more we need to provide an explicit definition.

Once we have defined the concepts, we must still be sure we measure them properly. The measurement process involves specifying the variables that serve as proxies for the concepts (constructs). A **proxy** is a variable that represents a single component of a larger concept and taken together several proxies are said to measure a concept. Proxies are also referred to in business research as indicator or manifest variables because they indirectly measure constructs. Identification of proxy variables (indicators) is very important because the variables provide the numerical scores used to measure concepts in quantitative terms. The Research in Action box shows examples of the proxy variables for several concepts – source credibility, financial and performance risks and pricing perceptions.

RESEARCH IN ACTION

PROXY VARIABLES ARE IMPORTANT IN BUSINESS RESEARCH

Business researchers often use proxy variables to measure concepts or constructs for their research. Some examples of frequently measured constructs include source credibility, risk perceptions, pricing, and so forth. The proxy variables shown below were used in surveys conducted to better understand customer behaviour. Excerpts from the study are reported but the entire scale can be viewed in the original article.

Source Credibility Check

A six-item seven-point scale was used. Respondents were asked to rate the spokesperson on each of the following:

Trustworthy – Not Trustworthy

Open-minded – Not Open-minded

Good – Bad

Expert – Not Expert

Experienced – Not Experienced

Trained – Untrained

Perceived Financial Risk

A three-item seven-point scale was used. Respondents were asked:
"Considering the potential investment involved, for you to purchase the Hito VCR would be":

Not risky at all – Very risky

"I think the purchase of the Hito brand VCR would lead to financial risk for me because of the possibility of such things as higher maintenance and/or repair costs":

Improbable – Very probable

"Given the potential financial expenses associated with purchasing the Hito brand VCR, how much overall financial risk is associated with purchasing the Hito brand VCR?"

Very little risk – Substantial risk

Perceived Performance Risk

A three-item seven-point scale was used. Respondents were asked:

"How confident are you that the Hito brand VCR will perform as described?"

Very confident – Not confident at all

"How certain are you that the Hito brand VCR will work satisfactorily?"

Certain – Uncertain

"Do you feel that the Hito brand VCR will perform the functions that were described in the advertisement?"

Do feel sure – Do not feel sure

Message Framing Check

Respondents were provided an aided-recall question:
"How did the spokesperson in the advertisement rate most of the features of the Hito VCR?"

Hito rated superior to Toshiba _____
Toshiba rated superior to Hito _____

Price Check

Respondents were asked the following question using a seven-point scale.
"The price of the Hito VCR is":

Very high – Very low

Source: Grewal, D., Gotlieb, J. and Marmorstein, H. (1994). "The Moderating Effects of Message Framing and Source Credibility on the Price-Perceived Risk Relationship," *Journal of Consumer Research*, 21 (June), pp. 145–53. ∎

Variables that are relatively concrete in nature, such as gender, age, height, household income, food prices and even social class, are relatively easy to define and thus can be measured in an objective and fairly precise manner through observation, questioning or the use of a "calibrated" instrument, such as a ruler. The following examples illustrate how we might measure the demographic variables mentioned above.

Gender

Suppose we need to know the gender of a customer. There is really no need for a definition of gender as people have a clear understanding of the concept. We determine the gender of a person either by observation or in a survey by including a question asking the respondent to state their gender. Thus, a simple concept like gender can be measured "without" error, assuming it is recorded correctly. The measurement involves assigning numerical scores to the outcome of the gender variable, such as "1" for male and "0" for female. Note the assignment of numbers is arbitrary and could just as easily be "1" for female and "0" for male.

Dining Out Expenditures

Now consider having to measure the average weekly eating out expenditures of a family. Again, the concept is easily understood and not in need of an explicit definition. To measure this concept all we need do is to include a question in our survey that asks the respondent to state his or her family's average weekly expenditure on eating out. In this case while the respondent will be clear as to what is being asked he or she is likely to find it difficult to give a very precise answer. In this case measurement of the variable can be achieved by assigning a number on a continuum with lower limit of "0". There still will be some error because the individual will be responding based on recall of a previous period (assuming he or she did not keep a record of the expenditures). But ideally the error will be minimal because the concept is easily understood.

Total Family Wealth

Contrast the examples above on gender and dining out expenditures with the concept of "total family wealth". It is highly unlikely there is a common understanding of the concept of "total family wealth". The understanding will depend upon how well we define the concept. The definition can include tangible variables like cash, property, stocks and bonds, and even cars, as well as intangible variables like education, health and so on. In this case, a definition of the concept "total family wealth" will be complex incorporating a combination of some or all of the variables considered as being manifestations or indicators of total family wealth. In addition, measurement of the concept will involve the use of a series of questions to represent the variables that make up the concept. Then, a numerical response to each of the questions is obtained from each participant in a survey. An overall measure of the concept usually is determined by combining the individual scores either by calculating their sum or their average. The amount of error associated with this question will depend upon how precise the researcher was in defining the concept and its individual variables.

The preceding examples demonstrate the definitional and measurement problems confronting business researchers. Concepts such as gender and expenditure, for example, are easily defined and objectively measured in absolute terms. In contrast, concepts that are complex and abstract in nature, for example, "wealth", "satisfaction", "organizational commitment" and "image" are relatively difficult to define and measure objectively. To measure such concepts researchers are likely to use subjective measures that include perceptions, attitudes, beliefs, opinions and values. In the next section we describe how complex concepts like the above can be measured.

HOW TO MEASURE CONCEPTS

Measurement involves assigning numbers to a variable according to certain rules. The assigned numbers must reflect the characteristics of the phenomenon being measured. For example, if we are measuring how important food quality is in the selection of a restaurant we might say the number "5" represents very important and the number "0" represents not important at all. In this case, the "rule" is a higher number means something is relatively more important and a lower number means it is relatively unimportant.

There are four levels of measurement available to the researcher. The levels determine the sophistication of the measurement employed. The researcher must decide on the level of measurement to be used before the research is conducted. Such a decision also is influenced by the nature of the concept. For example, the respondent must be willing and able to provide information at the level sought. This may not be true if the researcher is asking questions about sensitive issues like sexual orientation, birth control use, medical condition, or even income. Similarly, if data are obtained by observation, the way the variable can be measured will depend on the situational context and the ability of the observer to accurately record the observed behaviour. For example, if we are measuring purchases "online" this is very easy because all of the information is collected from transactions online. Similarly, measurement of scanner data at a checkout counter is easy because the information is automatically collected and stored in a computer database. On the other hand, if we watch people walk out of a cinema and try to observe whether or not they enjoyed the film we have more difficulty. It is much more difficult to measure a quality such as enjoyment accurately via observation.

As you may recall, the business consultant hired by Phil Samouel recommended an employee survey as well as a customer survey. It would be very difficult if not impossible to interview Gino's employees because he would not permit it. Therefore, the employee survey is based on a sample of Samouel's employees. The employee survey questionnaire is shown in Exhibit 9-1. We use it to illustrate several points on questionnaire design in this chapter and in Chapter 10.

Measurement is achieved through the use of scales. A **scale** is a measurement tool that can be used to measure a question with a predetermined number of outcomes. These outcomes can be directional or categorical (labels). For example, a yes/no scale measures a directional outcome – either yes or no. Other examples of such a scale might measure whether an employee agrees or disagrees with a supervisor or company policy, or likes or dislikes a particular product or service. For some scales the number of distinct outcomes can be more than two. For example, a question on industry type would represent more than two outcomes and might include categories for financial, manufacturing, retailing, and so on. In this case the outcome/response is strictly a label.

In contrast, when scales are continuous they not only measure direction or classification, but intensity as well. Examples of such scales are time to complete task, age of an investment project, preference or importance using more than two outcomes, etc. Thus, in addition to measuring agree/disagree, a continuous scale can measure the intensity of agreement, such as strongly agree or somewhat agree. Furthermore, the intensity of the scale can vary with a three-point scale measuring little intensity while a ten-point scale provides the opportunity for measuring a great deal of respondent variation in intensity of feeling.

TYPES OF SCALES

The four levels of measurement are represented by different types of scales: nominal, ordinal, interval and ratio. Variables measured at the nominal or ordinal level are discrete and referred to as either categorical or nonmetric. Variables measured at the interval or ratio level are continuous and referred

Hello. My name is _____ and I work for DSS Research. As you know, Phil Samouel has hired my company to conduct a survey of its employees to better understand the work environment, and suggest improvements as needed. The survey will only take a few minutes and it will be very helpful to management in ensuring the work environment meets both employee and company needs. All of your answers will be kept strictly confidential. In fact, once the questionnaires are completed they will be taken to my office and kept there.

1. "Are you currently an employee of Samouel's restaurant?"   _____Yes   _____ No

2. "Do you have any questions before you take the survey?"   _____Yes   _____ No

If they are currently employed by Samouel's restaurant and do not have any questions, hand them the survey and ask them to complete it. Tell them to ask you if there is any thing they do not understand.

WORK ENVIRONMENT SURVEY

Please read all questions carefully. If you do not understand a question, ask the interviewer to help you.

Section 1: Perceptions Measures

Listed below is a series of statements that could be used to describe Samouel's Greek Cuisine restaurant. Using a scale from 1 to 7, with 7 being "Strongly Agree" and 1 being "Strongly Disagree", to what extent do you agree or disagree that each statement describes your work environment at Samouel's:

1. I am paid fairly for the work I do.	Strongly Disagree Strongly Agree 1 2 3 4 5 6 7
2. I am doing the kind of work I want.	Strongly Disagree Strongly Agree 1 2 3 4 5 6 7
3. My supervisor gives credit and praise for work well done.	Strongly Disagree Strongly Agree 1 2 3 4 5 6 7

EXHIBIT 9-1

The Samouel's Employee Questionnaire

4. There is a lot of cooperation among the members of my work group.	Strongly Disagree Strongly Agree 1 2 3 4 5 6 7
5. My job allows me to learn new skills.	Strongly Disagree Strongly Agree 1 2 3 4 5 6 7
6. My supervisor recognizes my potential.	Strongly Disagree Strongly Agree 1 2 3 4 5 6 7
7. My work gives me a sense of accomplishment.	Strongly Disagree Strongly Agree 1 2 3 4 5 6 7
8. My immediate work group functions as a team.	Strongly Disagree Strongly Agree 1 2 3 4 5 6 7
9. My pay reflects the effort I put into doing my work.	Strongly Disagree Strongly Agree 1 2 3 4 5 6 7
10. My supervisor is friendly and helpful.	Strongly Disagree Strongly Agree 1 2 3 4 5 6 7
11. The members of my work group have the skills and/or training to do their job well.	Strongly Disagree Strongly Agree 1 2 3 4 5 6 7
12. The benefits I receive are reasonable.	Strongly Disagree Strongly Agree 1 2 3 4 5 6 7

EXHIBIT 9-1

(*continued*)

Section 2: Relationship Measures
Please indicate your view on each of the following questions:

13. I have a sense of loyalty to Samouel's Restaurant.	Strongly Disagree Strongly Agree 1 2 3 4 5 6 7
14. I am willing to put in a great deal of effort beyond that normally expected to help Samouel's restaurant to be successful.	Strongly Disagree Strongly Agree 1 2 3 4 5 6 7
15. I am proud to tell others that I work for Samouel's restaurant.	Strongly Disagree Strongly Agree 1 2 3 4 5 6 7
16. How likely are you to search for another job in the next six months?	7 = Extremely Likely 6 = Very Likely 5 = Somewhat Likely 4 = Neither – about 50–50 3 = Somewhat Unlikely 2 = Very Unlikely 1 = Extremely Unlikely
17. How long have you been an employee of Samouel's restaurant?	1 = Less than One Year 2 = One year to three years 3 = More than three years

Section 3: Classification Questions
Please indicate the number that classifies you best.

18. **Your Work Type**

a	Full Time
1	Part-Time

19. **Your Gender**

0	Male
1	Female

EXHIBIT 9-1

(*continued*)

20. **Your Age in Years**	1	18 – 25
	2	26 – 34
	3	35 – 49
	4	50 – 59
	5	60 and Older

21. **Performance**	1	Very Low Performance
	2	Somewhat Lower Performance
	3	Average Performance
	4	Somewhat Higher Performance
	5	Very High Performance

Thank you very much for your help. Please give your questionnaire to the interviewer.

EXHIBIT 9-1

(*continued*)

to as either quantitative or metric. In the following paragraphs we discuss the different measurement scales in more detail.

NOMINAL SCALE

A **nominal scale** uses numbers as labels to identify and classify objects, individuals or events. For example, when an athlete is assigned a number this is a nominal scale. When we use a nominal scale each number is given to only one object (individual). Numbers used in this manner serve as a label to identify the netball players. In business research, nominal scales are used to identify individuals, job titles or positions, brands, shops and other objects. To illustrate this point consider the following example:

A survey of diners poses the following question:

Are you happy with the service at Samouel's Greek Cuisine?   Yes/No

In this case the restaurant is the object and the measured characteristic is happiness with the service. The predetermined categories are "happy" or "not happy" as reflected by the nominal scale with two discrete scale points – yes or no. In this case each respondent can be placed in one of the two categories – yes I am happy or no I am not happy. The Samouel's employee survey shown in Exhibit 9-1 has two nominal questions – X_{18} – Work Type and X_{19} – Gender.

Nominal scales are not limited to just two categories. For example, we may characterize the restaurant according to ownership type – sole ownership, partnership or corporation. Similarly, we might measure occupation with a nominal scale using the categories teacher, banker, doctor, lawyer, and so forth. A requirement for a nominal scale is that its categories are mutually exclusive and exhaustive of all possibilities. This means each category must be different (no overlap) and all possible categories must be included.

To ensure all possible categories are considered, researchers typically use an "Other" category. But care must be taken to ensure that not too many respondents choose the other category. More than 15% response to an "Other" category usually is considered too high. In such cases we must learn more about why individuals are choosing the other category. For example, it is typical to indicate "Please Specify _____" beside the other category. We can then determine how individuals are responding and create another category to represent the responses that make up a large portion of the other responses.

Nominal scales are the lowest level of measurement. Data analysis is restricted mostly to counts of the number of responses in each category, calculation of the mode or percentage for a particular question, and use of the Chi-square statistic.

ORDINAL SCALE

An **ordinal scale** is a ranking scale. It places objects into a predetermined category that is rank ordered according to some criterion such as preference, age, income group, importance, etc. This scale enables the researcher to determine if an object has more or less of a characteristic than some other object. But it does not enable the researcher to determine how much more or less of the characteristic an object has. The following example illustrates this point:

A survey of diners poses the following question:

Regarding your visits to restaurants in the last month, please rank the following attributes from 1 to 4, with "4" being the most important reason for selecting the restaurant and "1" being the least important. Please ensure no ties.

Food quality	[ ]
Atmosphere	[ ]
Prices	[ ]
Employees	[ ]

If we tabulated the results of the survey of restaurant selection factors and found that 40% of the respondents assigned a "4" to food quality, 30% a "4" to atmosphere, 20% a "4" to prices, and 10% a "4" to employees, then we would know that relatively speaking food quality is the most important reason, followed by atmosphere, prices and employees. Thus, employees would be the least important reason for selecting a restaurant. This same question is used in the Samouel's and Gino's customer survey shown in Chapter 10.

The points on an ordinal scale do not indicate equal distance between the rankings. For example, the difference between a ranking of "3" and "4" is not necessarily the same as the difference between a ranking of "1" and "2". But we do know that a ranking of "4" is better than "3", just not how much better. In summary, ordinal scales allow entities to be placed into groups that are ordered.

A higher level of analysis is possible with ordinal data than is possible with nominal data. We can now calculate the median as well as percentages. We also can use Spearman rank–order correlation statistics.

INTERVAL SCALE

An **interval scale** uses numbers to rate objects or events so that the distances between the numbers are equal. Thus, with an interval scale differences between points on the scale can be interpreted and compared meaningfully. The difference between a rating of "3" and "4" is the same as the difference between a rating of "1" and "2". An interval scale has all the qualities of nominal and ordinal scales, plus the differences between the scale points is considered to be equal. Therefore, in addition you can compare the differences between objects.

With an interval scale the location of the zero point is not fixed. Both the zero point and the units of measurement are arbitrary. The temperature scale is frequently mentioned as an example of an interval scale. For the Centigrade scale, a $1°C$ increase in temperature has the same meaning anywhere on the scale but it is not true to state that $2°C$ is twice as hot as $1°C$. The explanation for not being able to state "$2°C$ is twice as hot as $1°C$" is that the origin or zero point for the centigrade scale is arbitrarily set at $0°C$.

When researchers use interval scales in business, they attempt to measure concepts such as attitudes, perceptions, feelings, opinions and values through the use of rating scales. **Rating scales** typically involve the use of statements on a questionnaire accompanied by precoded categories, one of which is selected by the respondent to indicate the extent of their agreement or disagreement with a given statement. To illustrate the use of rating scales, consider the following typical statement on a questionnaire:

Please indicate the extent of your agreement or disagreement with the following statement by circling the appropriate number

	Strongly Disagree	Disagree	Neither Agree Nor Disagree	Agree	Strongly Agree
Samouel's restaurant is a fun place to go	1	2	3	4	5

Strictly speaking, the above rating scale is an ordinal scale. It has become customary in business research, however, to treat the scale as if it were interval. Empirical evidence that people treat the intervals between points on such scales as being equal in magnitude provides justification for treating them as measures on an interval scale. To further illustrate this point, let us consider the following responses:

Response 1:

	Strongly Disagree	Disagree	Neither Agree Nor Disagree	Agree	Strongly Agree
Samouel's restaurant is a fun place to go	(1)	2	3	4	5

Response 2:

	Strongly Disagree	Disagree	Neither Agree Nor Disagree	Agree	Strongly Agree
Samouel's restaurant is a fun place to go	1	(2)	3	4	5

Response 3:

	Strongly Disagree	Disagree	Neither Agree Nor Disagree	Agree	Strongly Agree
Samouel's restaurant is a fun place to go	1	2	(3)	4	5

Firstly, the responses can be ordered in terms of strength of agreement. Response 1 strongly disagrees, response 2 disagrees, and response 3 neither agrees nor disagrees. Secondly, we observe that respondent 1 is one unit away from respondent 2, who in turn is one unit away from respondent 3. Also, respondent 3 is two units away from respondent 1. Thirdly, we cannot conclude the rating point "2" is twice the intensity of rating point "1" in terms of strength of agreement. Similarly we cannot conclude that the strength of agreement of respondent 3 is three times that of respondent 1. All we can conclude is that respondent 1 disagrees with the statement by two units more than respondent 3.

In summary, the numbers on an interval scale possess all the properties of nominal and ordinal scales and also allow for objects (respondents) to be compared in terms of their differences on the scale. When constructing rating scales the researcher arbitrarily chooses the origin or anchor point of the scale. In the preceding example the scale ranged from 1 to 5. But it could just as easily have ranged from 0 to 4. Moreover, it was a five-point scale but it also could have been a seven-point or ten-point scale.

The Samouel's employee survey questionnaire has several interval scales. First, all 12 statements that represent the work environment perceptions are measured using a seven-point Likert-type interval scale. Similarly, the questions that measure organizational commitment to Samouel's restaurant ($X_{13} - X_{15}$) are considered interval scales.

Interval scales include the properties of both nominal and ordinal scales. Therefore, data obtained using an interval scale are amenable to the same calculations as the earlier mentioned scales but also can handle more sophisticated calculations such as the mean, standard deviation and Pearson's product-moment correlation coefficient.

RATIO SCALE

A **ratio scale** provides the highest level of measurement. A distinguishing characteristic of a ratio scale is that it possesses a unique origin or zero point, which makes it possible to compute ratios of points on the scale. The bathroom scale or other common weighing machines are examples of ratio scales because they have absolute zero points. When comparing one point to another, for example, you can say that a 200-kilogram person is twice as heavy as a 100-kilogram person. The following example is a ratio scale as it might be used in business research. Consider the question:

How many children are there in your household?

A response of "0" to the question can only be interpreted in one way. Namely, that there are no children in the household. On the other hand, if we compare two responses, e.g., a response of "2" with a response of "4", we can conclude that the number of children in the household are "2" and "4", respectively. Further, we can state that the first household has fewer children than the second household by two children. Finally, we can compute the ratio "(4/2) = 2" and conclude that the second household has twice as many children as the first. Ratio scales possess all the properties of the other scales plus an absolute zero point. In terms of statistics, we can compute the coefficient of variation as well as the standard deviation and product-moment correlation.

FREQUENTLY USED MEASUREMENT SCALES

Broadly speaking, there are two types of scales – metric and nonmetric. **Metric scales** often are referred to as quantitative and **nonmetric** as qualitative. Nominal and ordinal scales are nonmetric and interval and ratio scales are metric. Business researchers use several types of metric and nonmetric scales. Exhibit 9-2 lists the various types of metric and nonmetric scales that are most frequently used in business research.

```
┌─────────────────────────────────────┐
│  Metric                              │
│      • Summated Ratings (Likert)     │
│      • Numerical Scales              │
│      • Semantic Differential         │
│      • Graphic Ratings               │
│                                      │
│  Nonmetric                           │
│      • Categorical                   │
│      • Rank Order                    │
│      • Sorting                       │
│      • Constant Sum                  │
└─────────────────────────────────────┘
```

EXHIBIT 9-2

Types of Measurement Scales

METRIC SCALES

We describe each of the types of metric scales and give examples in the following paragraphs.

Summated Ratings Scale

A **summated ratings scale** attempts to measure attitudes or opinions. Summated scales often use a five-point or seven-point scale to assess the strength of agreement about a group of statements. For each point on the scale you develop a label to express the intensity of the respondent's feelings. There are several statements that typically all relate to a single concept, such as opinions about a company or product. When you sum the scales for all the statements it is referred to as a summated ratings scale. When you use the scale individually it is referred to as a **Likert scale**. An example of a Likert scale is: **When I hear about a new restaurant I eat there to see what it is like**

Strongly Agree	Agree Somewhat	Neither Agree or Disagree	Disagree Somewhat	Strongly Disagree
1	2	3	4	5

A seven-point Likert scale also can be used as well as only a three-point scale. The more points you use the more precision you get with regard to the extent of the agreement or disagreement with a statement. An example of a seven-point scale is:

Gino's Italian Ristorante has a wide variety of menu choices

Strongly Agree	Agree Somewhat	Agree Slightly	Neither Agree or Disagree	Disagree Slightly	Disagree Somewhat	Strongly Disagree
1	2	3	4	5	6	7

Likert-type scales are also used to measure other concepts in business research such as importance or intensions. Examples of intensions and importance measures using Likert-type scales are shown below:

How likely are you to look for another job in the next six months?

Very Unlikely	Somewhat Unlikely	Neither Likely or Unlikely	Somewhat Likely	Very Likely
1	2	3	4	5

How important are credit terms in selecting a vendor to do business with?

Very Unimportant	Somewhat Unimportant	Neither Important or Unimportant	Somewhat Important	Very Important
1	2	3	4	5

Question X_{16} on the Samouel's employee questionnaire is an example of this type of scale, but it uses a seven-point scale instead of a five-point scale.

Numerical Scales

Numerical scales have numbers as response options, rather than verbal descriptions. The numbers correspond with categories (response options). For example, if there are seven response positions the scale is called a seven-point numerical scale. This type of scale can be used to assess the level of agreement or disagreement. But it is often used to measure other concepts, such as important/unimportant, essential/not essential, likely/unlikely, satisfied/dissatisfied, and so on. An example follows using the phrasing with an "important/not at all important" question:

> Using a 10-point scale, where 1 is not at all important and 10 is very important, how important is _____ in your decision to do business with a particular vendor?

You fill in the blank with an attribute, such as reliable delivery, product quality, complaint resolution, competitive pricing, credit terms and so forth.

Numerical scales are frequently used to measure behavioural intentions. Typical concepts examined with this type of scale include intention to buy, likelihood of seeking additional information, likelihood of seeking another job (turnover), likelihood of visiting a particular Web site, probability of investing in a particular stock, and so forth. Scales that measure behavioural components of an individual's attitudes ask about a respondent's likelihood or intention to perform some future action.

We noted earlier that Likert-type scales can be used to measure intentions and/or likelihood. A method other than Likert-type or numerical scores for measuring likelihood uses descriptive phrases such as the following examples:

Example 1:

How likely is it that you will pursue your MBA in the next three years?

___ I definitely will pursue my MBA in the next three years.

___ I probably will pursue my MBA in the next three years.

___ I might pursue my MBA in the next three years.

___ I probably will not pursue my MBA in the next three years.

___ I definitely will not pursue my MBA in the next three years.

Example 2:

How likely is it that you will look for another job in the next six months?

___ **Extremely Likely**

___ **Very Likely**

___ **Somewhat Likely**

___ **Neither – about a 50 – 50 chance**

___ **Somewhat Unlikely**

___ **Very Unlikely**

___ **Extremely Unlikely**

The choice of a particular method of measuring behavioural concepts depends upon the nature of the group being measured and the researcher's preference. All of the approaches are considered acceptable. An example of how a numerical scale has been used in business research is reported in the Research in Action box.

RESEARCH IN ACTION

MEASURING SERVICE QUALITY EXPECTATIONS IN BUSINESS RESEARCH

Recent research studies indicate that an increasingly important consideration for businesses is how their customers feel about the service they receive from the companies they do business with. Service quality has been measured extensively in many industries in an effort to better understand customer perceptions and develop effective ways to treat customers. Below are examples of a frequently used approach for measuring customer expectations and perceived service quality.

Instructions:

Please think of the kind of company that would deliver excellent service quality – the kind of company with which customers would be pleased to do business. Please indicate the extent to which you think such a company would possess the characteristic described by each statement. If you feel a characteristic is "not at all essential" for an excellent company, then say the number "1" for the statement. If you feel a characteristic is "absolutely essential" for excellent companies, say "7". If your feelings are less strong, give me one of the numbers between 1 and 7. There are no right or wrong answers – all we are interested in is a number that truly reflects your feelings regarding companies that deliver excellent quality service to their customers.

When customers have a problem, an excellent company will show
a sincere interest in solving it.   ____

Would you say this characteristic is not at all essential, absolutely essential, or somewhere in between? Remember, a "1" is not at all essential,
a "7" is absolutely essential, or you could select a number anywhere in
between 1 and 7 that you feel represents your feelings about excellent
companies.

Employees of excellent companies will give prompt service to customers.   ____

Excellent companies will have the customers' best interests at heart.   ____

Employees of excellent companies will have the knowledge to answer
customer questions.   ____

Excellent companies will perform services right the first time.   ____

Excellent companies will give customers individual attention.   ____

Materials associated with products and services (such as pamphlets or
statements) will be visually appealing in excellent companies.   ____

Employees of excellent companies will never be too busy to respond to
customer requests.   ____

Do you think asking questions like the above can be helpful to businesses? What other
questions might be asked?

Source: Parasuraman, A., Zeithaml, V. and Berry, L. (1985). "A Conceptual Model of
Service Quality and Its Implications for Future Research", *Journal of Marketing*, Fall,
p. 44. ∎

Semantic Differential Scale

A semantic differential scale is another approach to measure attitudes. Both five-point and
seven-point scales are used depending on the level of precision desired and the education level of
the targeted population. The distinguishing feature of semantic differential scales is the use of bipolar
end points (or anchors) with the intermediate points typically numbered. The end points are chosen
to describe individuals, objects or events with opposite adjectives or adverbs. Respondents are asked
to check which space between a set of bipolar adjectives or phrases best describes their feelings
toward the stimulus object. An example of how you might use the semantic differential to rate a
supervisor follows.

"My supervisor is. . . ."

Courteous	____	____	____	____	____	Discourteous
Friendly	____	____	____	____	____	Unfriendly
Helpful	____	____	____	____	____	Unhelpful

Supportive	——	——	——	——	——	Hostile
Competent	——	——	——	——	——	Incompetent
Honest	——	——	——	——	——	Dishonest
Enthusiastic	——	——	——	——	——	Unenthusiastic

As another example, let's consider Phil Samouel's Greek Cuisine restaurant. Based on observing his customers, Phil Samouel believes a particular personality type eats at his restaurant. To confirm this he identifies a number of personality characteristics that could describe restaurant customers. A semantic differential format is then used to collect data from his customers. For example,

Instructions:

A number of personality characteristics that can be used to describe people are shown below. Notice that each feature has an opposite. Please look at each characteristic and then rate yourself according to whichever end of the scale you feel best applies. For example, if you think you are more modern you would place a mark on the modern end of the scale that most closely fits you. On the other hand, if you think you are more traditional then you would place a mark on this end of the scale. Please rate yourself on every feature and try to be as honest about yourself as possible.

Traditional	—	—	—	—	—	Modern
Self-confident	—	—	—	—	—	Not Confident
Reserved	—	—	—	—	—	Sociable
Outgoing	—	—	—	—	—	Introverted
Liberal	—	—	—	—	—	Conservative
Sophisticated	—	—	—	—	—	Down to Earth

Semantic differential scales are easy to understand and are considered a metric measure. The difficulty in using this type of scale is being able to come up with adjectives that are opposite. The Research in Action box provides and example of how the semantic differential scale was used to measure "product complexity".

RESEARCH IN ACTION

HOW BUSINESS RESEARCHERS CAN HELP COMPANIES BE MORE EFFECTIVE IN SELLING THEIR PRODUCTS AND SERVICES

Companies need to know how their customers perceive the products and services they are selling. Business researchers can help them to better understand customer perceptions so salespeople are more effective in communicating benefits. Below is an example of how some researchers have measured customer perceptions of some issues important in purchase decisions. The research used a five-point semantic differential as a measurement scale. To use the scale, researchers would place the name of the product or service being studied in the blank space.

Survey instructions: Using the rating scale shown below, please circle one number for each set of factors listed. The numbers have no specific values and are only designed to represent a continuous scale between the high and low definitions provided for each factor. Circle the number that reflects your opinion of where _____ falls on such a continuum.

Standardized Product	1	2	3	4	5	Differentiated Product
Technically Simple	1	2	3	4	5	Technically Complex
Easy to Install/ Use	1	2	3	4	5	Specialized Installation/Use
No After Sales Service	1	2	3	4	5	Technical After Sales Service
No Consequential Adjustment	1	2	3	4	5	Large Consequential Adjustment

What are some examples of product characteristics that might be measured using a semantic differential scale like the above?

Source: McCabe, D. (1987). "Buying Group Structure: Constriction at the Top", *Journal of Marketing*, 51 (October), 88–89.

Graphic Ratings Scale   A **graphic ratings scale** is one that provides measurement on a continuum in the form of a line with anchors that are numbered and named. The respondent gives their opinion about a question by placing a mark on the line. Sometimes the mid-point is labelled and sometimes it is not. An example of how this scale might be used to assess restaurant perceptions follows:

On a scale from "0" to "10" how would you rate the atmosphere of Samouel's Greek Cuisine restaurant?

Graphic rating scales are used in other types of business research as well. An example of how this type of scale could be used to examine the concept of organizational commitment follows. Notice that the mid-point is not labelled and that numbers are not placed beside the scales. Respondents simply mark an "X" on the line at the appropriate place.

I talk about this company to my friends as a great place to work.

Strongly
Disagree

Strongly
Agree

├───┤

I really care about the future of this company.

Strongly
Disagree

Strongly
Agree

├───┤

For me this is the best of all companies to work for.

Strongly
Disagree

Strongly
Agree

├───┤

NONMETRIC SCALES

Nonmetric scales often are referred to as comparative scales. A distinguishing feature of a comparative scale is that responses to the questions are evaluated relative to each other rather than independently. These scales are considered ordinal measurement tools because objects are evaluated in a rank-ordered manner, often reflecting preference or importance. The following examples illustrate the variety of comparative scales.

Categorical Scale

Categorical scales are nominally-measured opinion scales that have two or more response categories. When there are more categories the researcher can be more precise in measuring a particular concept. Categorical scales often are used to measure respondent characteristics such as gender, age, education level, product type, industry sector, and so on. But they also can be used to measure other concepts, as follows:

How satisfied are you with your current job?

[ ]   **Very Satisfied**
[ ]   **Somewhat Satisfied**
[ ]   **Neither Satisfied nor Dissatisfied**
[ ]   **Somewhat Dissatisfied**
[ ]   **Very Dissatisfied**

How interested are you in learning more about what is expected of you in your new job assignment?

[ ]   **Very Interested**
[ ]   **Somewhat Interested**
[ ]   **Not Very Interested**

Rank Order Scale

Individuals often place items or alternatives in a rank order. A **rank order scale** is an ordinal scale that asks respondents to rank a set or objects or characteristics in terms of preference, similarity, importance or similar adjectives. An example of a rank order scale using importance follows:

Please rank the following five attributes on a scale from "1" (the most important) to "5" (the least important) in searching for a job.

Job Attributes	Ranking
Pay	
Benefits	
Coworkers	
Flexible Scheduling of Work Hours	
Working Conditions	

This scale measures only relative importance. That is, the importance of each job attribute relative to the other attributes. If pay is ranked highest in a sample survey we only know that relatively speaking it is higher. But we do not know how much higher.

Sorting

Sorting scales ask respondents to indicate their beliefs or opinions by arranging objects (items) on the basis of perceived similarity or some other attribute. Sorting also can be used to rank order objects. It is particularly useful when there are a large number of objects. To use this scale, you prepare a card for each object and write the object on the card. Then give the cards to the respondents and ask them to arrange the cards in the order of their preference or importance. For example, let's say you wanted to rank order students' preferences for taking courses from different areas of study. There are many fields of study, including accounting, finance, management, information systems, psychology, marketing, education, law and so on. You would give respondents a stack of cards with the names of the fields of study you want them to compare and ask them to stack them in the order of their preference for each of the fields of study. The technique is particularly useful in ranking the importance of objects because it prevents respondents from giving all objects a high rating, as often happens when rating scales are used.

Constant Sum Scale

With a **constant sum scale** respondents are asked to divide a constant sum over several categories to indicate, for example, the relative importance of the attributes. For example, suppose DHL wants to determine the importance of several attributes in the selection of an overnight delivery service. Respondents might be asked to allocate 100 points across the following attributes to indicate their relative importance.

Attribute	Score
On-Time Delivery	
Price	
Tracking Capability	
Invoice Accuracy	
Sum	**100**

Generally speaking, the constant-sum scale can be used only with respondents that are well educated. When respondents follow instructions the results approximate an interval scale. But the technique becomes increasingly difficult as the number of attributes increases. Unfortunately, the likelihood of the scores not adding up to 100 can be a problem.

Another example of a constant-sum scale follows. It demonstrates how data could be collected to determine the relative importance of components of a compensation package.

Suppose your monthly salary is €3,500. Think of an ideal compensation plan to meet your needs. How much would you like to allocate to each type of benefit. Please be sure that the points allocated among the benefits sum to 100.

Benefits	Score
Life Insurance	
Disability Insurance	
Savings	
Salary	
Retirement	
Sum	**100**

The constant-sum scale provides both a ranking and the magnitude of relative importance of each attribute. For the previous example, if salary is given a score of 40 and life insurance is given a score of 20, then we know salary is much more important than is health insurance. It should be noted that some analysts consider this scale to be metric while others consider it nonmetric.

PRACTICAL DECISIONS WHEN DEVELOPING SCALES

Several practical decisions are necessary when developing scales. They include: number of scale categories, odd or even number of categories, balanced or unbalanced scales, forced or nonforced choice, and nature and degree of verbal description.

NUMBER OF SCALE CATEGORIES

Should your scale have three, five, seven or ten categories? From a research design perspective, the larger the number of categories the greater the precision of the measurement scale. But, with more categories it is more difficult to discriminate between the levels, and respondents face greater difficulty in processing the information. Thus, the desire for a higher level of precision must be balanced with the demands placed on the respondent.

Respondents must be reasonably well educated to process the information associated with larger numbers of categories. For example, children probably can only use three-point scales, but with high school or comparable education a seven-point scale is acceptable. College educated individuals typically can respond to a ten-point scale. Likewise, individuals with experience in responding to scaling questions can respond to more categories of discrimination. But individuals exposed to scaling questions less often, from countries where interviewing is not commonplace, can more easily respond to scales with fewer categories. Generally speaking, from the researcher's perspective you would prefer to use no fewer than five categories. This is because respondents frequently avoid the extremes and a five-point scale, for example, may effectively become a three-point scale.

NUMBER OF ITEMS TO MEASURE A CONCEPT

Concepts should be measured using scales with multiple items. When this is done the scales are referred to as multi-item scales. A **multi-item scale** consists of a number of closely related individual statements (items or indicators) whose responses are combined into a composite score or summated rating used to measure a concept. But is two items enough or should the researcher use ten or even 20 items to measure a concept? The general guideline is the statements need to be closely related, represent only a single construct, and must completely represent the construct to be measured with the multi-item scale. In the author's experiences, a minimum of three items is necessary to achieve acceptable reliability but it is common to see at least five to seven items, and sometimes more.

RESEARCH IN ACTION

MOTIVATION TO SEARCH ONLINE BEFORE PURCHASE

Retailers nowadays recognize that most customers engage in an extensive information search online before purchasing high-value goods. So before making a strategic marketing decision the retailers would like to understand customer behaviour, particularly their motivation to search online. The key issue for the market researcher is how to develop a reliable and valid scale for "motivation to search online". To achieve this, the researcher needs to engage in both qualitative and quantitative analysis. The qualitative element is exploratory in nature. The focus is to identify the key questions that will form the domain of the scale. The domain comprises of two major dimensions: the psychology of motivation to search and the ability to obtain, assimilate and process information.

How does one address this problem? An initial step is to investigate what is already known about this area and whether such a scale already exists. If none exists or those that do exist are deficient, then a process of scale development is required.

If you were given the assignment to define and operationalize the concept of "motivation to search online" how would you proceed? The references below will help in this task.

Sources: Punj, G. N. and Staelin, R. (1983). "A Model of Consumer Information Behavior for New Automobiles", *Journal of Consumer Research*, 9, 366–80.

Schmidt, J. B. and Spreng, R. A. (1996). "A Proposed Model of External Consumer Information Search", *Journal of the Academy of Marketing Science*, 24(3), 246–56.

Rose, S. (2006). *Online Consumer Information Search: An Empirical Investigation*, Unpublished DBA, Henley Management College, UK. ∎

ODD OR EVEN NUMBER OF CATEGORIES

The mid-point typically represents a neutral position when an odd number of categories is used in a scale. This type of scale is used when, based on the experience or judgement of the researcher, it is believed that some portion of the sample is likely to feel neutral about the issue being examined. On the other hand, if the researcher believes it is unlikely there will be many neutral respondents or wants to force a choice on a particular issue, then an even number of categories should be used.

BALANCED OR UNBALANCED SCALES

Scales can be either balanced or unbalanced. With a **balanced scale** the number of favourable and unfavourable categories is equal. With an **unbalanced scale** the number of favourable and unfavourable categories is unequal. Examples of balanced and unbalanced scales follow:

Balanced:

To what extent do you consider TV shows with sex and violence to be acceptable for teenagers to view?

___ **Very Acceptable**

___ **Somewhat Acceptable**

___ **Neither Acceptable or Unacceptable**

___ **Somewhat Unacceptable**

___ **Very Unacceptable**

Unbalanced:

___ **Very Acceptable**

___ **Somewhat Acceptable**

___ **Unacceptable**

Unbalanced scales are used when the researcher expects responses to be skewed toward one end of the scale. For example, in satisfaction studies it is common for respondents to give very favourable responses. Therefore, researchers may choose to use an unbalanced scale to the positive end to provide an opportunity for more variation in the responses. This is an example of how the research problem should be considered in deciding whether to use a balanced or unbalanced number of scale categories.

It should be noted, however, that unbalanced scales can create bias in the responses by giving more options toward one end of the scale. For example, in the previous unbalanced acceptable/unacceptable scale the two options for acceptable and one option for unacceptable would result in more acceptable responses than with a balanced scale.

FORCED OR NONFORCED CHOICE

With a **forced choice scale** respondents are forced to make a choice. There is no mid-point that can be considered a neutral or no opinion category. If many respondents are likely to have not formed an opinion about a particular issue then a forced-choice scale will make them respond in one direction or another. It will, for example, make them respond either favourably or unfavourably, likely or unlikely, agree or disagree, aware or unaware, and so on. If a respondent selects the middle category when they have "no opinion" or are "neutral" this will cause error in the responses. In such cases it is better to use a forced-choice scale and provide a "no opinion" option. No opinion response categories typically are placed at the far right end of the scale, as follows:

Very Unlikely					Very Likely	No Opinion
1	2	3	4	5	6	_____

CATEGORY LABELS FOR SCALES

The scales we discussed included three types of situations – verbal labels, numerical labels and unlabelled choices. Some researchers prefer only scales with verbal labels, typically because they believe it helps respondents give more precise answers. Using numerical labels gives some guidance to respondents on label interpretation, but less than verbal labels. Numerical labels are helpful because they tend to make responses more closely resemble interval data.

Numerical labels and unlabelled scales are used when researchers have difficulty in developing appropriate verbal descriptions for the middle categories. This typically occurs when the number of scale points exceeds seven. A compromise is to label the end points and the middle category if one uses an odd number of scale points. Examples of the three types of scale labelling follow:

Verbal Label
How important is the size of the hard drive in selecting a laptop PC to purchase?

Very Unimportant	Somewhat Unimportant	Neither Important or Unimportant	Somewhat Important	Very Important
1	2	3	4	5

Numerical Label
How likely are you to purchase a laptop PC in the next six months?

Very Unlikely				Very Likely
1	2	3	4	5

Unlabelled
How important is the weight of the laptop PC in deciding which brand to purchase?

Very Important				Very Unimportant
___	___	___	___	___

CRITERIA FOR ASSESSING MEASUREMENT SCALES

Before using the scores from any concept (construct) for analysis, the researcher must ensure the variables (indicators) selected to represent and measure the concept do so in an accurate and consistent manner. Accuracy is associated with the term **validity** while consistency is associated with the term **reliability**. The most common criteria for assessing the accuracy and consistency of scales are displayed in Exhibit 9-3.

Our concern in selecting scales for questionnaires is on the quality of the measurement obtained. A scientific study must always address these two issues – reliability and validity. When these issues are addressed properly measurement error is reduced. Measurement error occurs when the values obtained in a survey (observed values) are not the same as the true value. For example, if you ask a respondent to answer the following question:

> Using a ten-point scale where 1 is poor and 10 is excellent, how does Samouel's Greek Restaurant rate on competitive prices?

Reliability

- Test-retest reliability
- Alternative-forms reliability
- Internal consistency reliability

Validity

- Content validity
- Construct validity
    - Convergent validity
    - Discriminant validity
- Criterion validity
    - Concurrent validity
    - Predictive validity

EXHIBIT 9-3

Criteria for Assessing Measurement Scales

You have measurement error if the response is "8" when in fact the true answer is "6". Measurement error is the result of: interviewer bias or errors, data input errors, respondent's misunderstanding or misrepresentation, and so forth. In conducting business research we always strive to reduce measurement error as much as possible. Measurement error is minimized when the observed numbers accurately represent the characteristics being measured and nothing else.

RELIABILITY

A survey instrument (questionnaire) is considered reliable if its repeated application results in consistent scores. This is contingent upon the definition of the concept being unchanged from application to application. Reliability is concerned with the consistency of the research findings. Reliability is important no matter what form the question takes, but is most frequently associated with multi–item scales. Multi-item scales consist of multiple items (variables, indicators) representing a concept. A single item is one statement or question that respondents evaluate as part of the entire concept.

If the instrument is a multi–item scale then for it to be reliable the scores (ratings) for the individual questions (items) that comprise the scale should be correlated. The stronger the correlations the higher the reliability of the scale will be. Similarly, the weaker the correlations the more unreliable the scale will be. Exhibit 9-4 is an example of a multi-item scale that was used to measure the construct "confirmation of expectations". To be reliable as a scale, the questions must be answered by respondents consistently in a manner that is highly correlated. If they do not, the scale would not be reliable.

Purpose: Measures the extent to which a distributor rates the performance of a manufacturer as being up to expectations.

Instructions

Following is a list of supplier (manufacturer) characteristics that might be important to your operations. Please indicate how well _____ has performed relative to the original level you expected them to perform at for each item listed. Circle the number that most accurately reflects your belief.

1 = Much worse than expected
2 = Somewhat worse than expected
3 = About as expected
4 = Somewhat better than expected
5 = Much better than expected

1.	Product quality	1	2	3	4	5
2.	Reliable delivery	1	2	3	4	5
3.	Quality of advertising	1	2	3	4	5
4.	Pricing	1	2	3	4	5
5.	Technical support	1	2	3	4	5
6.	Order processing speed	1	2	3	4	5
7.	Credit terms	1	2	3	4	5
8.	Problem resolution	1	2	3	4	5
9.	Salesforce call frequency	1	2	3	4	5
10.	Responsiveness of salesforce	1	2	3	4	5

Note: The name of the supplier is placed in the blank.

Source: Excerpt adapted from Cronin, J. J., Jr. and Morris, M. H. (1989). "Satisfying Customer Expectations: The Effect of Conflict and Repurchase Intentions in Industrial Marketing Channels", *Journal of Academy of Marketing Sciences*, 17 (Winter), 41–49.

EXHIBIT 9-4

Confirmation of Expectations of a Distributor

Test-Retest Reliability

Test–retest reliability is obtained through repeated measurement of the same respondent or group of respondents using the same measurement device and under similar conditions. Results are compared to determine how similar they are. If they are similar, typically measured by a correlation coefficient, we say they have high test-retest reliability.

Several factors cause problems with the use of test-retest reliability. The first time respondents take a test (survey) may influence their response the second time they take it. Also situational factors such as how one feels on a particular day may influence how respondents answer the questions, and something may change in the time between repeated usage of the test. Finally, it often is very difficult and sometimes impossible to have the same respondents take a survey twice.

Alternative Forms Reliability

Alternative forms reliability can be used to reduce some of these problems. To assess this type of reliability the researcher develops two equivalent forms of the construct. The same respondents are measured at two different times using equivalent alternative constructs. The measure of reliability is the correlation between the responses to the two versions of the construct.

Internal Consistency Reliability

This type of reliability is used to assess a summated scale where several statements (items) are summed to form a total score for a construct. For example, one could assess the internal consistency reliability of a satisfaction construct with the following three items:

1. **How satisfied are you with Samouel's Greek Cuisine restaurant?**
2. **How likely are you to return to Samouel's Greek Cuisine in the future?**
3. **How likely are you to recommend Samouel's Greek Cuisine to a friend?**

Each of the above three statements measures some aspect of the satisfaction construct. Responses to the statements should be consistent in what they indicate about Samouel's restaurant. That is, a respondent who is very satisfied should be very likely to return in the future and very likely to recommend the restaurant to a friend. The Research in Action box shows how businesses are using multi-item scales to measure the satisfaction construct.

RESEARCH IN ACTION
MULTI-ITEM CONCEPTS ARE WIDELY USED IN BUSINESS RESEARCH

If you think only academic researchers use multi-item concepts, think again. Burke, Inc., one of the largest business research firms in the world, developed the "Secure Customer Index" to use in customer satisfaction and retention projects. The index is a three-item scale that asks respondents about satisfaction, likelihood to purchase or return in the future, and likelihood of recommending a particular business to others. The three items (indicators) are measured using a five-point Likert-type scale. Secure customers are those respondents who choose a five on all three items. It typically is measured in terms of the percentage of customers that check the "top box" (5) of a particular item. Burke has had good success using this approach on satisfaction studies with their clients.

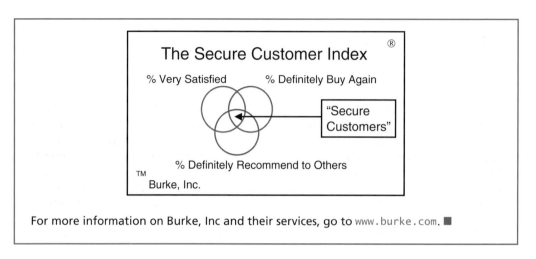

For more information on Burke, Inc and their services, go to www.burke.com. ■

There are two types of internal consistency reliability. The simplest is **split–half reliability**. To determine split-half reliability, the researcher randomly divides the scale items in half and correlates the two sets of items. A high correlation between the two halves indicates high reliability. The second type of internal consistency reliability is **coefficient alpha**, also referred to as Cronbach's alpha. To obtain coefficient alpha you calculate the average of the coefficients from all possible combinations of split halves. Coefficient alpha ranges from 0 to 1. Your can use the guidelines in Exhibit 9-5 as rules-of-thumb to interpret alpha values. Researchers generally consider an alpha of 0.7 as a minimum, although lower coefficients may be acceptable depending on the research objectives.

RULES OF THUMB ABOUT CRONBACH-ALPHA COEFFICIENT SIZE*

Alpha Coefficient Range	Strength of Association
<0.6	Poor
0.6 to <0.7	Moderate
0.7 to <0.8	Good
0.8 to <0.9	Very Good
≥0.9	Excellent

*If alpha >0.95, items should be inspected to ensure they measure different aspects of the concept.

EXHIBIT 9-5

The Continuing Case box tells you how to use SPSS to calculate Cronbach's alpha for three of the perceptions variables on the Samouel's and Gino's questionnaire.

CONTINUING CASE   USING SPSS TO CALCULATE CRONBACH'S ALPHA

We can use SPSS to calculate Cronbach's alpha for the variables in the customer database. Questions X_6 on employee friendliness, X_{11} on employee courteousness, and X_{12} on employee competence are characteristics that reflect different aspects of employee quality. The Cronbach alpha can be used to determine whether the three items, combined into a single index, capture in a consistent manner the quality of employees. To perform a Cronbach-alpha analysis using SPSS, the click-through sequence is as follows: ANALYZE → SCALE → RELIABILITY. Scroll down and highlight X_6 – Friendly Employees, click on the arrow box to move it into the Items box. Repeat this procedure for X_{11} – Courteous Employees and X_{12} – Competent Employees. Next click on "OK" to run the program. The resulting output follows:

RELIABILITY ANALYSIS – SCALE (ALPHA)

Reliability Coefficients
N of Cases = 200.0   N of Items = 3
Alpha = 0.8176

The Alpha value of 0.82 is "very good". Thus, we conclude that the three items can be combined to measure the quality of restaurant employees in a consistent manner.

Where else might you calculate reliability in either the employee or customer surveys? A copy of the customer survey is included in Chapter 10.

Words of Caution on Reliability

An acceptable level of reliability indicates respondents are answering the questions in a consistent manner. Good research requires acceptable reliability. The following guidelines can be used to ensure reliability in your scales:

1. The minimum number of items in a scale to measure a particular concept should be at least three.

2. The items included in the scale must be positively correlated. Where negative correlations arise between items:
   – Check the wording of the questions and if a question is negatively worded then the scores for that question must be "reverse coded". By "reverse coded" we mean that on a five-point scale a "1" is recoded "5", a "2" is recoded as a "4" and so on. You can use the RECODE function in SPSS to do this.
   – Should the "negative wording" check fail, then remove the offending item from the scale.

3. Items in a scale that are correlated with other items in the scale at a level lower than 0.30 should be evaluated for removal from the scale.

VALIDITY

Validity is the extent to which a construct measures what it is supposed to measure. For example, if you want to know a family's disposable income this is different from total household income. You may start with questions about total family income to arrive at disposable income, but total family income by itself is not a valid indicator of disposable income. A construct with perfect validity contains no measurement error. An easy measure of validity would be to compare observed measurements with the true measurement. The problem is we very seldom know the true measure. To assess measurement validity we use one or more of the following approaches:

- content validity
- construct validity
- criterion validity

Content Validity

Establishing the **content** or **face validity** of a scale involves a systematic but subjective assessment of a scale's ability to measure what it is supposed to measure. Validation, in general, involves consulting a small sample of typical respondents and/or experts to pass judgement on the suitability of the items (indicators) chosen to represent the construct. This is a commonly used validation method in business research. Generally speaking, content validity is not considered an adequate measure of validity and business researchers typically go on to assess either construct or criterion validity.

To illustrate content validity, let's consider the construct of job satisfaction. A scale designed to measure job satisfaction should include items on compensation, working conditions, communication, relationship with co-workers, supervisory style, empowerment, opportunities for advancement, and so on. If any one of these major areas does not have items to measure it then the scale would not have content validity.

Construct Validity

Construct validity assesses what the construct (concept) or scale is in fact measuring. To assess construct validity you must understand the theoretical rationale underlying the measurements you obtain. The theory is used to explain why the scale works and how the results of its application can be interpreted.

To assess construct validity two checks have to be performed. The checks are convergent and discriminant validity. **Convergent validity** is the extent to which the construct is positively correlated with other measures of the same construct. **Discriminant validity** is the extent to which the construct does not correlate with other measures that are different from it. These are objective tests, based on numerical scores, of how well the construct conforms to theoretical expectations.

Convergent Validity Establishing convergent validity of a scale requires that the following be done:

Step 1: **Based on theory and experience, identify another established construct that is claimed to measure the same concept as the one being validated.**

Step 2:   **Obtain scores on both constructs and compute the correlation between the scores.**

If the scores are highly correlated then it is concluded that convergent validity is evident.

Discriminant Validity   Establishing the discriminant validity of a construct requires a similar set of steps:

Step 1.   **Based on theory and experience, identify a construct that is claimed to be different from the concept being validated.**

Step 2.   **Specify the manner in which the two scales representing the constructs are expected to differ. It is expected that the scores resulting from administering the scales on the same respondents will be uncorrelated.**

Step 3.   **Obtain scores on both scales and compute the correlation between the scores.**

If the correlation is low then we conclude the construct exhibits discriminant validity.

Criterion Validity

Criterion validity assesses whether a construct performs as expected relative to other variables identified as meaningful criteria. For example, theory suggests employees who are highly committed to a company would exhibit high job satisfaction. Thus, correlations between measures of employee commitment and job satisfaction should be positive and significant. If this is so, then we have established criterion validity for our construct. Similarly, when we measure the construct of customer loyalty, a criterion for validating it would be the construct satisfaction. Very loyal customers should be highly satisfied with the business.

To establish criterion validity we need to show that the scores obtained from the application of the scale being validated are able to predict scores obtained on a theoretically identified dependent variable, referred to as the criterion variable. One or both of two-types of criterion validity checks can be performed. These checks are referred to as concurrent and predictive validity.

Concurrent Validity

To demonstrate **concurrent validity** of a construct some prespecified association must be established between the scores on the construct being validated and the scores on a dependent variable as determined by theory. The scores of both variables are obtained at approximately the same point in time and should be highly correlated. For example, Samouel's highly satisfied customers also should be frequent patrons of his restaurant.

Predictive Validity

Predictive validity assesses the ability of a construct measured at one point in time to predict another criterion at a future point in time. The other criterion can be either another individual variable or a multi-item scale. Thus, for a construct to have predictive validity it must be possible to predict future values of a dependent variable from scores obtained on the construct being tested. So, predictive validity differs from concurrent validity in that the scores on the dependent variable are obtained some time after the scores for the construct that is being validated. Validity is established if the scores are highly correlated. An example of predictive validity would be assessing whether the Graduate Management Admissions Test (GMAT) is a valid predictor of performance in graduate school in business.

HOW TO DEVELOP A SCALE

In developing a scaling approach, we must consider the underlying theory as well as the reliability and validity of the scale. We also must consider the level of measurement (nominal, ordinal, interval and ratio), any problems that might arise administering the scale, and the respondent's knowledge of the research issues. Our research objective is that the scale will be theoretically valid, reliable and include the highest level of measurement possible. Moreover, respondents must be able and willing to respond to questions accurately and must not have negative attitudes regarding a particular issue being examined.

Consider the following problem that may concern our restaurant owner. Phil Samouel is interested in determining the image of his restaurant. A prerequisite to doing this is the development of a scale to measure the concept "image". The process of developing a scale involves a number of steps:

1. Definition of the concept or concepts to be measured.
2. Identification of the components of the concept.
3. Specification of a sample of observable and measurable items (indicators or proxy variables) that represent the components of the concept.
4. Selection of the appropriate scales to measure the items.
5. Combination of the items into a composite scale, sometimes referred to as an instrument, which in turn serves as a means of measuring the concept.

Concept:	Satisfaction		
Components:	**Quality of Food**	**Quality of Service**	**Price of Meals**
Items/Questions:	1. The food served must be of the highest quality.	1. When I visit a restaurant I expect its employees to be courteous.	1. When I visit a restaurant for a special occasion price is not important to me.
	2. The food served must be fresh.	2. I expect prompt service from a restaurant.	2. I am prepared to pay more for specialty dishes.
	3. The menu should offer a wide range of choices.	3. I expect the restaurant staff to be knowledgeable about the menu offerings.	3. When taking the family out to a restaurant price is important to me.

EXHIBIT 9-6

Potential Components of the Concept "Restaurant Satisfaction"

6. Administer the scale to a sample and assess respondent understanding.

7. Confirm scale reliability and validity.

8. Revise scale as needed.

The scale obtains perceptions of different components of the concept being measured. For example, components of the concept "restaurant image" might include assessments of the employees, food, atmosphere, and so on. Each of these components should have several indicators to measure them. A rule-of-thumb is each component should have a minimum of three items to be adequately measured. For example, measuring the image of a restaurant involves acquiring perceptions on such characteristics as the friendliness of the staff, parking facilities, the physical layout of the restaurant, the prices and so on. Similarly, measuring the concept of satisfaction with the restaurant involves several components. Possible components of the satisfaction concept are illustrated in Exhibit 9-6.

In developing an instrument to measure a concept, we generally look for previously developed scales. This is because scale development is difficult and time consuming. Fortunately, in the last 25 or 30 years many excellent scales have been developed and published. Several sources of scales are described in the Research in Action box.

RESEARCH IN ACTION

WHERE TO FIND SCALES TO MEASURE RESEARCH CONCEPTS?

Researchers like to use previously published scales in their research. This saves them a lot of time and effort in their own research. Sometimes these scales are used exactly as they were previously developed. Other times small modifications are made to the original instrument to more closely fit the needs of the specific research objectives. Several valuable sources of previously used scales are listed below. References are organized by the relevant discipline.

Organizational Behaviour and Management

Price, James L. (1997). *Handbook of Organizational Measurement*, International Journal of Manpower, 18 (4, 5, 6) www.mcb.co.uk.

This is a reference handbook and research tool that focuses on constructs to measure organizational behaviour. It includes 28 separate chapters reporting on constructs that measure a wide variety of work behaviours. Examples of constructs include: absenteeism, commitment, communications, innovation, involvement, compensation, power, productivity, technology, turnover and others.

Management Information Systems (MIS)

Two Web sites provide measures of constructs associated with user reactions to computer systems.

`www.ucalgary.ca/~newsted/surveys.html`. This Web site provides listings of constructs and attributes relevant to information systems research. All measures in the database were published in research journals.

`www.misq.org/archivist/home.html`. This Web site is affiliated with MIS Quarterly and includes data and measures from articles published in the journal.

Marketing

Bearden, W. O. and Netemeyer, R. (1998). *Handbook of Marketing Scales*, 2nd edn. Thousand Oaks, CA, Sage Publications.

This book has information on over 130 scales, including a definition of the scale, type of scale and number of scale points, how scale was developed, including the sample, and evidence of validity and reliability. It includes the following types of scales: individual traits such as opinion leadership and innovativeness, values such a social responsibility and materialism, involvement and information processing, reactions to advertising stimuli, performance of business firms, social agencies, and the marketplace, including ethical issues, and sales, sales management and inter-intrafirm issues.

Bruner, G. and Hensel, P. (1998). *Marketing Scales Handbook*, Chicago, IL, American Marketing Association.

This handbook includes scales in three primary areas: consumer behaviour, advertising and sales force, and general. Specific examples include assertiveness, aggressiveness, arousal, brand switching, brand loyalty, complaining behaviour, convenience, curiosity, information seeker, innovativeness, opinion leadership, risk, satisfaction, store image, novelty, source credibility, acceptance of coworkers, alienation from work, channel conflict, customer orientation, and so on. It reports scale name, origin, reliability and validity, etc. for almost 600 scales.

General

Robinson, J. P., Shaver, P. R. and Wrightsman, L. S. (1991). *Measures of Personal and Social Psychological Attitudes*, San Diego, CA, Academic Press.

This book contains published scales in 11 different areas: response bias, subjective well-being, self-esteem, social anxiety and shyness, depression and loneliness, alienation and anomie, trust and human nature, authoritarianism, sex roles, and values. Over 150 scales are reviewed and summarized.

Buros Institute of Mental Measurements Web site, which allows the user to search, locate and obtain reviews of published tests and measurements. `www.unl.edu/buros` ∎

SUMMARY

■ **Understand the role of concepts in business research**

In business research we examine concepts of varying degrees of complexity. These concepts describe business phenomena that we must understand and explain to make effective decisions. Successful research requires clearly delineated definitions of concepts to avoid ambiguity in measuring them. In defining concepts, the researcher will draw upon established theory, literature and business experience.

■ **Explain the notion of measurement**

Measurement involves quantifying the outcomes of variables by assigning numbers to the outcomes according to some preset rules. Managers measure many aspects of business, including employee performance and satisfaction, motivation, turnover, and profits. The measurement process involves specifying the variables (indicators) that serve as proxies for the concepts. Variables that are relatively concrete in nature, such as gender and age, are easy to define and measure. But many concepts are much less precise and more difficult to measure accurately.

■ **Provide an overview of the different types of measurement scales**

To measure business phenomena we use four types of scales: nominal, ordinal, interval and ratio. Nominal and ordinal scales are nonmetric variables. Interval and ratio scales are metric measurement tools.

Data analysis for nonmetric variables is limited. For nominal data only counts, percentages and the mode can be computed. For ordinal data, we can compute the percentiles, median and range. Data analysis is much more extensive for metric variables. In addition to the above, it is possible to compute means, standard deviations and other statistics.

When measuring a complex concept, we typically use multi-item scales where the individual items of the scale collectively capture different aspects of the concept. The multi-item scale index is a composite derived from the scores on its individual questions or statements.

■ **Distinguish between reliability and validity**

Before using a multi-item scale, the researcher must perform certain essential checks to ensure that the items selected to represent and measure a concept do so in an accurate and consistent manner. Accuracy is associated with the term validity while consistency is associated with the term reliability. ■

Ethical Dilemmas

Centroid Systems, Ltd.

Five years ago, when a new CEO was hired, a business research firm conducted an organizational climate survey for Centroid Systems, Ltd. Since that time the new CEO has reorganized departments and tightened budgets. As a result company performance has improved and shareholders are happy. Richard Johnson, Centroid's human resources director believes employees are also feeling better about their work environment. To measure the changes, Richard decides to conduct another organizational climate survey. However, in order to save money, Richard decides to conduct the survey himself using the questionnaire and scale that was used in the previous survey without consulting the original research firm. Is this unethical?

Nutrix, Ltd.

Nutrix, Ltd, the maker of dietary healthcare supplements, has recently launched a new marketing campaign for Slender, an herbal supplement to increase weight loss. According to the product marketing materials, in an experiment conducted by Nutrix, people using Slender lost 5% more weight than those using a placebo. In addition, the people using Slender reported none of the side effects such as increased heart rate commonly reported to be caused by other weight loss products. As the product has gained popularity, critics have begun to attack the company's claims arguing that Nutrix's research is not comprehensive enough because it fails to measure the long-term effects of Slender. In fact, according to critics, most people who use the product report that they are unable to maintain the weight loss after they quit taking Slender. Many also report experiencing withdrawal symptoms such as migraine headaches. Nutrix stands by their research, which shows the product is a safe weight-loss alternative, arguing that since patents are not available on herbal supplements the company cannot afford expensive, long-term studies. What do you think? Is the short-term measurement of effects adequate? Or should Nutrix be required to conduct long-term experiments before releasing its products?

REVIEW QUESTIONS

1. What is a "concept" in business research?

2. How do we measure concepts?

3. What is the difference between metric and nonmetric scales? Give an example of each.

4. What is reliability? How does it differ from validity?

5. What are steps to follow in developing a scale?

DISCUSSION AND THINKING ACTIVITIES

1. Why would a business researcher want to measure concepts?

2. What key issues need to be considered by the business researcher in defining a concept? Illustrate this through a concept that you are familiar with.

3. What considerations need to be taken into account in determining the level of measurement of variables?

4. Make a list of concepts that college students might want to learn more about? Prepare a list of indicators (statements) for each concept. Decide on the type of measurement scale you will use and justify your selection.

5. **SPSS Application:** We are interested in measuring a concept labelled "work environment". From the list of variables in the Samouel's employee database select those you believe will collectively capture restaurant work environment. Assess the reliability of your chosen items in measuring this concept.

6. **SPSS Application:** Identify the work environment variables from the Samouel's employee survey. Select the six statements covering coworkers and supervision and calculate their reliability using SPSS. What did you find?

7. The Samouel's employee questionnaire has three indicators of organizational commitment (variables 13, 14 and 15). Develop a more comprehensive measure of organizational commitment covering areas not included in that questionnaire.

INTERNET EXERCISES   www

1. Complete a survey at the following Web site and prepare a report on your experience. http://future.sri.com/vals/valshome.html

2. Go to www.icpsr.umich.edu/gss. Find the General Social Survey and prepare a report telling what it is. How does it compare to the Yankelovich MONITOR that can be found at www.yankelovich.com?

3. VALS is a Values, Attitudes and Lifestyles survey that has been conducted for many years by SRI International. The VALS approach is well known and respected as a profiling approach that groups Americans based on questions about their values and lifestyles. Go to their Web site at http://future.sri.com, click on VALS and complete the survey for yourself. Prepare a brief report on what you found.

NOTE

1. Williams, K. C. and Spiro, R. L. (1985). "Communication Style in the Salesperson-Customer Dyad", *Journal of Marketing Research*, 12, 434–42.

CHAPTER 10
QUESTIONNAIRE DESIGN

CONTENTS

LEARNING OUTCOMES

- Understand that questionnaire design is difficult and why.
- Explain the steps involved in designing an effective questionnaire.
- Recognize how the method of data collection influences questionnaire design.
- Understand the types of questions and how they are used.
- Describe the major sections of the questionnaire and how they relate to each other.

INTRODUCTION

Few managers dispute the value of accurate information in improving decision making. The purpose of business research is to provide managers with accurate information, often from surveys. But information from surveys is accurate only if the questionnaire is properly designed. Many individuals believe questionnaires are easy to design. But those with experience in designing questionnaires know this is not true. Indeed, experienced researchers can easily make mistakes in questionnaire design if they overlook essential steps, such as pretesting.

This chapter describes the importance of careful questionnaire design and suggests an approach for developing good questionnaires. Specific guidelines to be followed at each stage in the design process are provided. But, unfortunately, few of the guidelines hold in all situations. Indeed, many individuals believe questionnaire design is more of an art than a science.

QUESTIONNAIRES

Questionnaire design is only one phase of several business research steps that are all interrelated. But it is a very important phase because data collected with questionnaires are used to improve decision making. A **questionnaire** is a prepared set of questions (or measures) used by respondents or interviewers to record answers (data). That is, questionnaires are a structured framework consisting of a set of questions and scales designed to generate primary data. When designing a questionnaire, researchers must realize that there will be only one opportunity to interact with respondents since a reasonable interval of time is necessary before the same respondent can be contacted again, and then it should generally involve either another topic or a different approach to the same topic. We review the essentials of questionnaire design in this chapter, but entire books have been written on the topic. For those who wish to review more extensive coverage of questionnaire design we refer you to the Research in Action box for additional sources of information on this topic.

RESEARCH IN ACTION

THE ART AND SCIENCE OF QUESTIONNAIRE DESIGN

Is questionnaire design an art or a science? We say it is both. We refer you to the following sources for more detailed treatment of this important topic. The sources are organized into practical and theoretical categories.

Practically-Oriented Books

Berdie, D. and Anderson, J. (1974). *Questionnaires: Design and Use.* Metuchen, NJ, Scarecrow Press.

Fink, A. (1995). *How to Ask Survey Questions.* Thousand Oaks, CA, Sage Publications.

Patten, M. (1998). *Questionnaire Research.* Los Angeles, CA, Pyrczak Publishing.

Payne, S. (1951). *The Art of Asking Questions.* Princeton, NJ, Princeton University Press.

Peterson, R. (2000). *Constructing Effective Questionnaires.* Thousand Oaks, CA, Sage Publications.

Theoretically-Oriented Books

Belson, W. (1981). *The Design and Understanding of Survey Questions.* London, Gower.

Schuman, H. and Presser, S. (1981). *Questions and Answers in Attitude Surveys.* New York, Academic Press.

Sudman, S. and Bradburn, N. (1982). *Asking Questions.* San Francisco, CA, Jossey-Bass. ■

There are two methods other than questionnaires to record data. One is an interview guide and the other is an observation guide. Both are much less structured than questionnaires. An **interview guide** specifies the topics to cover, the questions to be asked, the sequence of questions/topics, and the wording of the questions (which is fixed), but there are no scales for measuring concepts. The role of the interviewer is to explain the survey, motivate the respondent to answer, make sure the respondent understands the questions, and probe for clarification or elaboration of open-ended questions. **Observation guides** are used to record data that are observed. They indicate what the observer is to look for and provide a place to record the information. The initial structure of the guide is based on the conceptual framework for the research, but during the data collection process it may expand to include new information that emerges.

STEPS IN THE QUESTIONNAIRE DESIGN PROCESS

The final outcome of a well-constructed questionnaire is reliable and valid data if the related phases of the research are executed well. To develop questionnaires that produce reliable and valid data, you must follow a systematic process, such as that shown in Exhibit 10-1. We discuss each of the steps in this chapter. Guidelines are given on the best approach for designing questionnaires. Similarly, examples of specific types of questions are provided. Finally, the questionnaire used for the customer survey in the Samouel and Gino case study is shown in Exhibit 10-2. We will use it to illustrate many of the above issues.

Step 1: *Initial Considerations*

- Clarify the nature of the research problem and objectives.
- Develop research questions to meet research objectives.
- Define target population and sampling frame (identify potential respondents).
- Determine sampling approach, sample size and expected response rate.
- Make a preliminary decision about the method of data collection.

Step 2: *Clarification of Concepts*

- Ensure the concept(s) can be clearly defined.
- Select the variables/indicators to represent the concepts.
- Determine the level of measurement.

Step 3: *Determine Question Types, Format and Sequence*

- Determine the types of questions to include and their order.
- Check the wording and coding of questions.
- Decide on the grouping of the questions and the overall length of the questionnaire.
- Determine the structure and layout of the questionnaire.

Step 4: *Pretest the Questionnaire*

- Determine the nature of the pretest for the preliminary questionnaire.
- Analyse initial data to identify limitations of the preliminary questionnaire.
- Refine the questionnaire as needed.
- Revisit some or all of the above steps, if necessary.

Step 5: *Administer the Questionnaire*

- Identify the "best practice" for administering the type of questionnaire utilized.
- Train and audit field workers, if required.
- Ensure a process is in place to handle completed questionnaires.
- Determine the deadline and follow-up methods.

EXHIBIT 10-1

Steps to be Followed in the Design of a Questionnaire

Screening and Rapport Questions

Hello. My name is _____ and I work for Whitehall Research. We are talking to individuals today/tonight about dining out habits.

1. "Do you occasionally dine out in restaurants?"   ____Yes   ____ No

2. "Did you just eat at Samouel's/Gino's?"   ____Yes   ____ No

3. Is your annual household income £20,000 or more?   ____Yes   ____ No

4. "Have you completed a restaurant questionnaire for our company before?"   ____Yes   ____ No

If person answers "Yes" to the first three questions and "No" to the fourth question, then say:
We would like you to answer a few questions about your experience today/tonight at Samouel's/Gino's restaurant, and we hope you will be willing to give us your opinions. The survey will only take a few minutes and it will be very helpful to management in better serving its customers. We will pay you £5.00 for completing the questionnaire.

   If person says yes, give them a clipboard with the questionnaire on it, briefly explain the questionnaire, and show them where to complete the survey.

DINING OUT SURVEY

Please read all questions carefully. If you do not understand a question, ask the interviewer to help you.

Section 1: Perceptions Measures.

Listed below is a set of characteristics that could be used to describe *Samouel's Greek Cuisine/Gino's Ristorante*. Using a scale from 1 to 7, with 7 being "Strongly Agree" and 1 being "Strongly Disagree", to what extent do you agree or disagree that *Samouel's/Gino's* has:

1. Excellent Food Quality	Strongly Disagree Strongly Agree 1 2 3 4 5 6 7
2. Attractive Interior	Strongly Disagree Strongly Agree 1 2 3 4 5 6 7

EXHIBIT 10-2

The Samouel and Gino Customer Questionnaire

3. Generous Portions	Strongly Disagree Strongly Agree 1 2 3 4 5 6 7
4. Excellent Food Taste	Strongly Disagree Strongly Agree 1 2 3 4 5 6 7
5. Good Value for the Money	Strongly Disagree Strongly Agree 1 2 3 4 5 6 7
6. Friendly Employees	Strongly Disagree Strongly Agree 1 2 3 4 5 6 7
7. Appears Clean and Neat	Strongly Disagree Strongly Agree 1 2 3 4 5 6 7
8. Fun Place to Go	Strongly Disagree Strongly Agree 1 2 3 4 5 6 7
9. Wide Variety of Menu Items	Strongly Disagree Strongly Agree 1 2 3 4 5 6 7
10. Reasonable Prices	Strongly Disagree Strongly Agree 1 2 3 4 5 6 7
11. Courteous Employees	Strongly Disagree Strongly Agree 1 2 3 4 5 6 7
12. Competent Employees	Strongly Disagree Strongly Agree 1 2 3 4 5 6 7

EXHIBIT 10-2

(*continued*)

Section 2: Selection Factors.

Listed below are some factors (reasons) many people use in selecting a restaurant where they want to dine. Think about your visits to fine dining restaurants in the last 30 days and please rank each attribute from 1 to 4, with 4 being the most important reason for selecting the restaurant and 1 being the least important reason. There can be no ties so make sure you rank each attribute with a different number.

Attribute	Ranking
13. Food Quality	
14. Atmosphere Prices	
15. Prices	
16. Employees	

Section 3: Relationship Measures.

Please indicate your view on each of the following questions:

17. How satisfied are you with Samouel's restaurant?	Not Satisfied At All Very Satisfied 1 2 3 4 5 6 7
18. How likely are you to return to Samouel's restaurant in the future?	Definitely Will Not Return Definitely Will Return 1 2 3 4 5 6 7
19. How likely are you to recommend Samouel's restaurant to a friend?	Definitely Will Not Recommend Definitely Will Recommend 1 2 3 4 5 6 7
20. How often do you eat at Samouel's restaurant?	1 = Occasionally (Less than once a month) 2 = Frequently (1 – 3 times a month) 3 = Very Frequently (4 or more times a month)

EXHIBIT 10-2

(*continued*)

21. Have you seen any advertisements for Samouel's restaurant in the last three months?

_____ Yes   _____ No (Skip to Q #24)

22. Which ad did you see? (Interviewer: show respondent the three ads)

_____ Ad #1   _____ Ad #2   _____ Ad #3

23. Please rate each of the ads, using a seven-point scale, with 1 = Poor and 7 = Excellent.

Ad Ratings: _____ Ad #1   _____ Ad #2   _____ Ad #3

24. How long have you been a customer of Samouel's/Gino's?   _____ Months

Section 4: Classification questions.

Please indicate the answer that classifies you best.

25. Your Gender

0	Male
1	Female

26. What is your age in years?   _____

27. What is your total annual household income? £_____

Interviewer Record:

28. Samouel's customer = 0; Gino's customer = 1

Thank you very much for your help. Please give your questionnaire to the interviewer and you will be given £5.00.

Note: There were two forms of the questionnaire. One had questions that referred to Samouel's and the other referred to Gino's.

EXHIBIT 10-2

(continued)

INITIAL CONSIDERATIONS

Before developing a questionnaire the researcher must be clear as to exactly what is being studied and what is expected from the study. This means the research problem must be clearly defined, project objectives must be clarified, and research questions agreed upon. If these tasks are completed properly, it is much more likely the research questions will be accurately answered. Once these are in place the questionnaire can be designed.

Developing questions is one of the critical early tasks in questionnaire design. When an initial list of questions is developed, they must be evaluated to determine if answers to these questions will provide the information needed to make a decision, understand a problem, or test a theory. The more specific the questions the easier they are to evaluate. For example, several possible research questions are listed below:

- Is sexual harassment a problem in this organization?

- Do employees in this organization support diversity in the workplace?

- Does religious affiliation influence support for human cloning?

- What are the most important factors influencing the purchase of a laptop computer?

- Do you agree with President Bush's policies on eliminating terrorism?

The preceding questions provide an initial start for the researcher, but a final evaluation requires them to be stated even more specifically. As an example, with the sexual harassment question the researcher would want to clarify what kinds of sexual harassment problems exist, how often they occur, if employees understand what harassment means, and so forth. This level of specificity is necessary if training is to be implemented to resolve any potential problems.

When the preliminary list of questions to be included in the questionnaire has been agreed upon, the researcher must evaluate them from the respondent's perspective. Firstly, can the respondents understand the questions? This is particularly important when respondents are children, are less familiar with a particular research topic, or if the study examines technical issues. Along with understanding the questions, one must consider whether the potential respondents have the knowledge to answer the questions. If the research is designed to understand the purchase decision process for software in an organization, then those who will be asked to respond to the questions must be knowledgeable about this process. Finally, respondents must be willing to answer the questions. If the questions focus on sensitive topics, or if answering the questions might reveal an organization's competitive advantage, it is likely to be difficult if not impossible to obtain answers. Evaluation of questions in terms of respondents' ability and willingness to answer questions is an important early step in questionnaire design.

To enable the researcher to evaluate questions from the respondent's perspective, the target population for the study must be specified. If the target population is not precisely defined, the researcher cannot evaluate the questions. It is at this point that the researcher considers to what extent respondents can be contacted and convinced to respond. If the survey must obtain information from a group of CEOs of large companies, or from physicians or even school children, this may be very difficult to accomplish. It also can influence the method of data collection and questionnaire administration. For example, to determine children's preferences for various shapes and tastes of biscuits shaped like animals, one company chose to observe which biscuits children ate and in which order rather than to ask them questions. Similarly, because different methods of questionnaire administration (for example, telephone versus personal) can influence the nature of responses the method used must be carefully considered, particularly when questionnaires include attitude and behaviour questions.

In addition to respondent capabilities, the researcher needs to consider whether the questions can be answered using a self-completion approach or if an interviewer-assisted approach is necessary. To some extent this is related to the potential respondents because some may be able to successfully answer self-completion questionnaires while others may not. For example, educational background, language capabilities such as vocabulary level, prior experience completing questionnaires, age of respondents and cultural issues related to responding can be important, particularly when these are different from the researcher's.

Researchers must be concerned not only with whether respondents will answer a particular question, but whether they will respond accurately. Potential respondents may refuse to answer questions on sensitive issues, or because they consider the question an invasion of their privacy. But what is sensitive or an invasion of privacy to one group may not be the same with another group. For example, in a recent survey of US teenagers they willingly answered questions regarding personal experiences with various types of sexual practices, whereas older individuals are very reluctant to answer such questions. With questions of such a sensitive nature, however, all groups of respondents are likely to under report their personal experiences.

Respondents may not answer a question because it is perceived to be too long or too difficult to answer. In contrast, respondents may willingly respond but do so in a manner they perceive to be "socially responsible". For example, if asked about alcohol consumption an individual who drinks "daily" will almost always identify themselves as an "occasional" drinker, if they answer the question at all. Similarly, if asked about "belief in God" few individuals will deny such a belief. Finally, respondents may answer by guessing a response simply because they want to be helpful. Close consideration of all these issues is very important in minimizing error in data collected with questionnaires.

CLARIFICATION OF CONCEPTS

In designing the content, structure and appearance of a questionnaire a number of aspects need to be taken into account. Firstly, the concepts (constructs) to be measured must be identified, clearly defined, and then a method of measurement found. Secondly, decisions on other questions to include, such as classification and outcome information (for example, intention to search for a job or likelihood to visit a particular Web site), types and wording of questions, questionnaire sequence and general layout must be made by the researcher. As a general rule, only questions relevant to the research objectives should be included. When done properly, these decisions will result in a questionnaire with a high response rate and minimal error. They also will ensure the necessary kind of data analysis can be used.

If the questionnaire requires attitudinal or opinion questions about a particular concept, the indicators and the level of measurement must be determined. For example, if management wants to better understand employee turnover, it would include questions related to the work environment, pay, benefits, coworkers, job expectations, role clarity, supervisory style, and so forth. Information on each of these topics could help clarify issues impacting employee turnover. Moreover, the target population must be considered in determining how to measure the indicators. When step 2 (clarification of concepts) has been completed, the researcher should have a list of potential questions to address the research objectives.

The Samouel's employee survey addressed some of these issues associated with job satisfaction and employee turnover. Recall from Chapter 9 that the first section of the employee questionnaire asked questions about the work environment. Four topics were included: supervision, compensation, co-workers and overall satisfaction. Three indicators (statements) were included for each of these topics. Indicators on organizational commitment and likelihood to search for another job also were included. Thus, several concepts were measured in the Samouel's employee questionnaire.

DETERMINE QUESTION TYPES, FORMAT AND SEQUENCE

To achieve a high response rate and a high quality of responses, the researcher must pay particular attention to the length of the questionnaire as well as the manner in which the questions are structured, sequenced and coded. This will also facilitate the data collection and statistical analysis.

Typically, in gathering information through questionnaires we make use of different types of questions. The form of these questions and the order in which they appear in the questionnaire is very important. The types of questions and their order in the questionnaire depend upon the nature of the topic, how the questionnaire is administered, the target population's ability and willingness to respond, the type of statistical analysis and similar factors. We now describe what we believe to be the most important considerations.

Closed versus Open-ended Questions   In broad terms, two forms of questions are used in questionnaires. The two types are known as **closed** and **open–ended** questions. With closed questions the respondent is given the option of choosing from a number of predetermined answers. An open-ended question places no constraints on respondents who are free to answer in their own words. Examples of open and closed questions follow:

Open-Ended Questions

- What do you think about the National Health Service?
- Which mutual funds have you been investing in for the past year?
- How are the funds you are investing in performing?
- What do you think of airport security?

Closed Questions

- Did you check your email this morning?   ___Yes   ___ No
- Do you believe Enron senior executives should be put in jail?   ___Yes   ___ No
- Should the UK adopt the euro or keep the pound?
    - Adopt the euro   ___
    - Keep the pound   ___
- Which countries in Europe have you travelled to in the last six months?
    - Belgium   ___
    - Germany   ___
    - France   ___
    - Holland   ___
    - Italy   ___
    - Switzerland   ___
    - Spain   ___
    - Other (please specify)   _____
- How often do you eat at Samouel's Greek Cuisine restaurant?
    - Never   ___
    - 1–4 times per year   ___
    - 5–8 times per year   ___
    - 9–12 times per year   ___
    - More than 12 times per year   ___

Open-ended questions are relatively easy to develop because the researcher does not have to specify the answer alternatives ahead of time. Indeed, in instances where the researcher does not know the answer alternatives (for example, exploratory research) open-ended questions are the only possibility. Open-ended questions also are useful when the researcher believes the alternatives may influence the answer, or for "unaided recall" and "top-of-mind" awareness questions. For example, to determine unaided recall or awareness the researcher might ask: "When you think of banks in your area, which one comes to mind first?" Open-ended questions often follow an initial question, whether that question is open-ended or closed. In response to the earlier question about banks, when a bank is mentioned, the researcher might follow up with the question "And is there a second bank that comes to mind?" Similarly, an open-ended question might follow a closed question like the following:

On a scale from 1 to 10, where 1 is "Not at all Customer Oriented" and 10 is "Very Customer Oriented", how customer-oriented do you consider Barclays Bank to be?

Following the response to this question, the interviewer would then ask the question:

Why do you say that?

Open-ended questions provide rich information and often insight into responses. But respondents need to be articulate and willing to spend time giving a full answer. The main drawback to open-ended questions is that it takes a great deal more time and effort to understand the responses. In self-completion questionnaires open-ended questions should be used sparingly.

The design of closed questions is more difficult and time consuming than designing open-ended questions. This means closed questions typically are more expensive to design. But closed questions can be precoded making data collection, data input and computer analysis relatively easy and less expensive. Closed questions typically are used in quantitative studies employing large-scale surveys. All the questions in the Samouel's and Gino's customer and employee surveys are closed. This makes it easy for the answers to be placed in a data file and analysed. Note also that the process of creating the data file has been greatly simplified because all of the answers have been precoded.

Questionnaire Sections   After the researcher decides the types of questions to ask, the preliminary questionnaire structure must be determined. The structure follows a three-part sequence of **questionnaire sections**. The questions in the initial section are referred to as opening questions. The middle section has questions directed specifically at the topics addressed by the research objectives. The final section includes the classification questions that help the researcher to better understand the results. The Research in Action box shows a typical example of the three questionnaire sections as used in the hospitality industry.

RESEARCH IN ACTION   SERVICE QUALITY DRIVES COMPETITIVE STRATEGIES IN THE HOSPITALITY INDUSTRY

Almost all types of businesses in the hospitality industry, from hotels to restaurants and entertainment facilities, are realizing the importance of service quality as a competitive strategy. To improve service quality, businesses must have data for decision-making. To obtain those data, they rely on customer surveys. The following is a typical example of a questionnaire a hotel might use to collect this type of data.

Guest Satisfaction Survey

Thank you for your recent stay at _____! Because we value your business, we would like your opinion as to how well we meet our goal of delivering excellent service to you every time you visit. A postage-paid envelope has been included for you to return your completed questionnaire.

Sincerely

Jens E. Jorgensen

Senior Vice President, Customer Relations

Please check the boxes as requested.

1. Were you a recent guest at _____ in ____city? ___Yes ____No

2. Was this your first visit to this particular hotel? ____Yes ____No

3. Was this your first visit to any of our hotels? ____Yes ____No

4. What was the primary reason for your stay?

    ____Business

    ____Pleasure

    ____Both business and pleasure

Please think of your stay at this hotel when completing the following questions.

5. How did you make your reservation?

    ____0800 number (Continue with Q. 6)

    ____Called hotel directly (Continue with Q. 6)

    ____Travel agent (Skip to Q. 7)

    ____Web site (Skip to Q. 7)

    ____Someone else made my reservation (Skip to Q. 7)

    ____Did not have a reservation (Skip to Q. 7)

6. If you made an advanced reservation, please rate the person you spoke with using a report card grade, where "A" is "Excellent" and "F" is "Poor".   Circle the correct response.

	Excellent				Poor
How quickly was the call answered?	A	B	C	D	F
How courteous was the person you talked to?	A	B	C	D	F
How knowledgeable was the person you talked to?	A	B	C	D	F

7. Was the type of room you requested available?   ____Yes   ____No

For the following questions, please rate your satisfaction with the hotel you stayed at using a report card grade where "A" is "Excellent" and "F" is "Poor". Circle the correct response. If a question is not applicable to your stay, please circle the NA response.

	Excellent				Poor	
8. Check-In						
Exterior appearance of hotel	A	B	C	D	F	NA
Appearance of lobby	A	B	C	D	F	NA
Speed of check-in	A	B	C	D	F	NA
Courtesy of front desk staff	A	B	C	D	F	NA
Knowledge of front desk staff	A	B	C	D	F	NA
Hotel Staff						
Knowledgeable hotel staff	A	B	C	D	F	NA
Helpful housekeeping staff	A	B	C	D	F	NA
On-time wake up call	A	B	C	D	F	NA
Courtesy of hotel staff	A	B	C	D	F	NA
Guest Room						
Cleanliness of room	A	B	C	D	F	NA
Cleanliness of bathroom	A	B	C	D	F	NA
Cleanliness of carpet	A	B	C	D	F	NA
Cleanliness of bed linens	A	B	C	D	F	NA
Comfort of the bed	A	B	C	D	F	NA
Quietness of room	A	B	C	D	F	NA
Bathroom supplies sufficient	A	B	C	D	F	NA
Adequacy of phone equipment	A	B	C	D	F	NA
Working order of TV, radio, etc.	A	B	C	D	F	NA
Working order of heating and AC	A	B	C	D	F	NA
Other Facilities						
Condition of pool/spa	A	B	C	D	F	NA
Cleanliness of pool/spa	A	B	C	D	F	NA
Cleanliness of exercise facility	A	B	C	D	F	NA
Variety of exercise machines	A	B	C	D	F	NA
Convenience of business centre	A	B	C	D	F	NA
Usefulness of business centre	A	B	C	D	F	NA

9. What one thing could we have done to make your stay more satisfactory?

_____

_____

_____

10. Thinking of your overall experience at this hotel, how would you rate each of the following using a report card grade where "A" is "Excellent" and "F" is "Poor". Circle the correct response.

	Excellent				Poor
Overall condition/appearance of hotel	A	B	C	D	F
Overall staff service	A	B	C	D	F
Overall stay	A	B	C	D	F

11. If you were to return to this area, how likely would you be to stay at this hotel using a report card grade where "A" is "Very Likely" and "F" is "Very Unlikely". Circle the correct response.

Very Likely				Very Unlikely
A	B	C	D	F

12. If a friend were planning a trip to this area, how likely would you be to recommend this hotel using a report card grade where "A" is "Very Likely" and "F" is "Very Unlikely". Circle the correct response.

Very Likely				Very Unlikely
A	B	C	D	F

Classification Information

13. How many nights during the last year did you stay at a hotel? _____

14. What is your gender? _____Male _____Female

15. What is your age?

_____ Under 25

_____ 25 – 34

_____ 35 – 49

_____ 50 – 64

_____ 65 and over

16. Which category best describes your total annual household income before taxes?

_____ Under £30,000

_____ £30,000 – £45,000

_____ £45,001 – £60,000

_____ £60,001 – £90,000

_____ £90,001 – £150,000

_____ £150,001 and over

If you have additional comments, please use a separate sheet of paper and mail them with your survey. Your comments are important to us. ■

Opening Questions   The first questions on a questionnaire are referred to as **opening questions**. Usually the first couple of opening questions are designed to establish rapport with respondents by gaining their attention and stimulating their interest in the topic. It is typical to ask the respondent to express an opinion on an issue that is likely to be considered important, but still relevant to the study. Opening questions should be simple and nonthreatening, such as the following:

- Tell me about a film (or television programme) you have recently seen?
- What is your favourite pub? Why is this your favourite pub?

While rapport questions must be simple and easy to answer, they still must be relevant to the topic being researched.

Screening questions, sometimes referred to as filtering questions, are another type of opening question. They are used to ensure that respondents included in the study are those that meet the predetermined criteria of the target population. They may also be in the form of **skipping questions** that direct respondents to the appropriate section of the questionnaire. This ensures the respondent will not be required to answer irrelevant questions. An example of a screening question for a financial services telephone survey follows. It was used to ensure that the most knowledgeable individual in the household responds to the survey.

Tonight we are talking with individuals who are 18 years of age or older and have 50 % or more of the responsibility for banking decisions in your household. Are you that person? ___Yes ___No

If people say yes, they continue with the survey. If they say no, then the interviewer asks for the person who meets those criteria.

To summarize, the main objective of the opening questions is to include relevant participants and to create an atmosphere that encourages participation. Under no circumstances should the opening questions be of a sensitive nature. Note that the Samouel's and Gino's customer survey opening questions were easy to answer, relevant, and made sure the respondents had eaten at the restaurant and had not previously completed a questionnaire. The question about income may, however, be threatening to some individuals.

Research Topic Questions   The second group, referred to as **research topic questions**, includes those designed to provide information on the topic being researched. This series of questions typically asks about things such as attitudes, beliefs, opinions, behaviours and so on. These questions usually are grouped into sections by topic, because respondents then find it is easier to respond. It also helps to maintain interest and avoid confusion. Moreover, since early questions can influence responses to later questions, the nature of question sequencing is to ask general questions early and more specific ones later. Moving from general to specific questions is referred to as a **funnel approach**. Note that with the Samouel's and Gino's customer questionnaire, the questions were organized by logical sections, starting with opinions about the restaurant. People like to give their opinions so it will be easy to get them to answer these questions. The ranking of selection factors requires more thought so these questions were placed second. The ranking questions were also placed here because it minimizes the likelihood of the earlier perceptions questions influencing answers to the relationship measures. Finally, the classification questions were at the end of the questionnaire, with the income question being the very last one.

Branching Questions   **Branching questions** are used to direct respondents to answer the right questions as well as questions in the proper sequence. Branching questions enable respondents to skip irrelevant questions or to more specifically explain a particular response. An example of a branching question follows:

- Have you heard or seen any advertisements for wireless telephone service in the past 30 days?
- If no, go to question 10.
- If yes, were the advertisements on TV or radio or both?
- If the advertisements were on TV or both, go to question 6.
- If the advertisements were on radio go to question 8.
- For both questions 6 and 8, the next question would be:
  - Were any of the advertisements for Vodaphone?
- If yes for Vodaphone, then ask:
  - What did the advertisement say?
- If no, go to question 10.

The main disadvantage of funnel questions is the possibility that respondents will become confused when the questionnaire is self-completion. For this reason, they work best with interviewer-administered questionnaires. This is particularly true with computer-assisted interviewing, where funnel questions can easily be used with both open-ended and closed questions.

Classification Questions   With the exception of screening questions, demographic and socio-economic type questions used for classification of respondents should be placed at the end of the questionnaire. The reason for placement at the end is that **classification questions** often seek information of a more personal nature, for example age and income, and if asked early on may affect the nature of responses to subsequent questions or even result in nonparticipation. Being at the end does not mean classification questions are less important. Putting them there is simply an effort to increase response and reduce error.

Because many classification questions are considered sensitive or an invasion of privacy, researchers have found that a funnel approach can be used to increase the response rate. Below is an example of how funnelling might be used with the income question.

- Is your total annual household income above or below £30,000?

- If the answer is below £30,000, then the next question might be: Is your total annual household income above or below £20,000?

This process can continue until the answer is as precise as the researcher would like it to be. In the above example, however, it would probably stop at this point if the response were "above" because knowing the annual household income is between £20,000 and £30,000 is generally as precise as the researcher needs.

PREPARING AND PRESENTING GOOD QUESTIONS

Converting research objectives into questions that will be understood and correctly answered by respondents is not an easy task. As noted earlier, entire books have been written on this topic. To assist you in preparing good questions, we suggest you observe the following guidelines.

Use Simple Words Questions must be in a language familiar to the respondent. Avoid using jargon or technical terms unless absolutely necessary. In situations where technical terms must be used it is "good practice" to provide definitions for all words where misunderstandings could occur. The Research in Action box provides an example of why questionnaire wording is important yet so difficult.

RESEARCH IN ACTION

SO YOU THINK YOUR RESPONDENTS UNDERSTAND YOUR QUESTIONS?

Recently a survey was conducted by the United Nations using a sample from several different countries. The question asked was:

"**Would you please give your opinion about the food shortage in the rest of the world?**"

The survey was a huge failure. Why?

- In Africa they did not know what *food* meant.

- In Western Europe, they did not know what *shortage* meant.

- In Eastern Europe they did not know what *opinion* meant.

- In South America they did not know what *please* meant.

- And in the United States, they did not know what *the rest of the world* meant.

Note: The authors do not know the source or authenticity of this question. A former student sent the example to them. We included it because we believe it makes an important point in a humorous way. ■

Be Brief Questions should be short and to the point, and if possible not exceed one line. The longer a question is the more likely it will be misunderstood by respondents. Long questions have higher nonresponse rates and produce more error in responses. The higher error is a result of respondents tending to answer long questions before fully reading them because they are in a hurry to complete the questionnaire.

Avoid Ambiguity Wording should be clear, concise and avoid vagueness and ambiguity. Questions are ambiguous when they contain words that are unfamiliar to respondents or the words can have more than one meaning. These include words such as: often, frequently, sometimes, occasionally, generally, normally, good, bad, fair, poor and so forth. An example of a poorly worded, ambiguous question follows:

How often do you consider your supervisor to be fair with all her/his subordinates?
- ___ **Never**
- ___ **Occasionally**
- ___ **Quite Often**
- ___ **All the Time**

The words *consider* and *fair* both can be interpreted very differently. Moreover, the response alternatives can mean different things to different respondents. Finally, to eliminate ambiguity, researchers often quantify vague alternatives. For example, if a researcher is investigating church attendance the question could be worded:

How often do you attend church?
- ___ **Regularly**
- ___ **Often**
- ___ **Occasionally**
- ___ **Never**

But this wording is clearly ambiguous. Three of the four "frequency of attendance" alternatives could mean different things to different respondents (never is the only clear one). A much better way to word this question is:

How often do you attend church?
- ___ **Every Week**
- ___ **1 – 3 times a month**
- ___ **Once a month**
- ___ **Between 2 and 12 times a year**
- ___ **Never**

Open-ended questions typically are more ambiguous than closed questions. For example, consider the following question:

Do you like orange juice?

If a parent answered this question with a simple "Yes" and the interviewer does not follow with a probing question like "Why?" there are at least two possible interpretations to the Yes answer. One is the parent personally likes orange juice. But another possibility is the parent likes orange juice because he/she believes it is healthy for his or her children to drink.

With open-ended questions, it sometimes can be useful to provide respondents with some help in answering questions. An **aided question** is one that provides the respondent with a stimulus that jogs the memory, whereas **unaided questions** do not have a stimulus. Stimulus information in aided questions should be neutral in nature to avoid biasing the response. For example, a researcher may aid the respondent by asking for a recall on the most recent visit to a restaurant. Instead of just saying "Where did you last eat out?" which is an un-aided question, the researcher might say: "When you ate out the last time did you go to Samouel's Greek Cuisine, Gino's Ristorante, Juban's Creole Restaurant, The Swan Pub, or somewhere else?" The latter question phrasing is called an aided-response question.

Avoid Leading Questions **Leading questions** imply that a particular answer is correct or lead a respondent to a socially desirable answer. This sometimes is referred to as "framing" the question to encourage a particular response. The Research in Action box provides an example of how framing can bias responses.

RESEARCH IN ACTION

FRAMING YOUR QUESTIONS CAN INTRODUCE BIAS!

On a Saturday morning in spring one of the authors was out working in the garden. A group of young folks got out of a van and began knocking on doors to solicit participation in a survey of exercise-related topics. They were students from a small university doing a class project for a local health club. The students were pleasant and polite in soliciting participation, and upon agreement to participate they began asking the questions on the survey. About halfway through the survey they said the following:

When people were asked this question in the past, 90 % said "Yes". "Do you think belonging to a health club motivates people to exercise?" Yes or No?

The author refused to answer the question and proceeded to inform the student interviewers that they did not ask if he believed belonging to a health club motivates people to exercise. They, in essence, asked: "How willing are you to give a response that differs from 90 % of the others who have responded to this question in the past?" The young people were shocked, but courteous. The author then informed them if they would like to learn how to design valid questionnaires they should take his research methods course at the university where he worked. ■

Avoid Double-Barrelled Questions   **Double-barrelled questions** include two or more issues and make interpretation difficult, and often impossible. For example, it is not uncommon to see questions like the following on a survey:

To what extent do you agree or disagree with the following statements:

- Harrod's employees are friendly and helpful.

- Harrod's employees are courteous and knowledgeable.

When questions like the above are used, it is impossible to know which of the two adjectives a respondent is reacting to. Moreover, respondents do not know how to answer if they have a different opinion about the two descriptors.

Be Careful About Question Order and Context Effects   Questions should be asked in a logical order that is organized by topics. Early questions should be general in nature and later ones more specific to minimize **position bias** introduced by the order of the questions. Examples of position bias and how to eliminate it are shown below:

Position Bias

Q-1:   How important are flexible hours in evaluating job alternatives?
Q-2:   What factors are important in evaluating job alternatives?

No Position Bias

Q-1:   What factors are important in evaluating job alternatives?
Q-2:   How important are flexible hours in evaluating job alternatives?

Position bias occurs above because asking the specific question about "flexible hours" before the more general question will cause the respondent to be more likely to include a reference to flexible hours in the general question.

An **order bias** also is possible on questions like the perceptions measures on the Samouel's and Gino's customer survey. Answers to questions posed early in a survey can influence how respondents answer the later questions. For example, the first question is on the food quality at Samouel's/Gino's. If a respondent "Strongly Agrees" with the first (or early) question then all later questions in that section are likely to be nearer the "Strongly Agree" end of the scale. Similarly, if early opinions toward a question are "Strongly Disagree", then opinions about later questions are more likely to be toward the disagree end of the scale. To avoid this type of order bias, researchers generally rotate the sequence in which respondents are asked a particular question. This is easy to do with telephone or Internet surveys. But with self-completed surveys, like postal surveys or the self-read and complete ones used with the Samouel's and Gino's case study, the only way to overcome this is to have two or more versions of the questionnaire with a different sequence of the questions in a particular section.

A **context effect** occurs when the position of a question relative to other questions influences the response. Marsh and Yeung[1] reported contextual effects when they studied "global self-esteem" as measured by questions like "I feel good about myself" or "Overall, I have a lot to be proud of". They noted that if the question "I feel good about myself" is positioned on the questionnaire where the other statements refer to academic situations, then respondents will respond in terms of how they feel about themselves academically. But if the same question is positioned near other statements that refer to an individual's physical condition, they are more likely to answer the "I feel good about myself" relative to how they feel about themselves physically.

Check Questionnaire Layout   Presentation, spacing and layout of the questions can influence responses. This is particularly true with postal, Internet or other self-completion questionnaires. In Exhibit 10-2 shown previously note that the questions on the Samouel's and Gino's questionnaire have been grouped into sections. Each section has a clearly marked heading and, where required, specific instructions on how to answer the questions. Finally, care was taken to avoid splitting a question over two pages.

PREPARE CLEAR INSTRUCTIONS

Almost all questionnaires have instructions of some sort. Self-completion and interviewer-assisted questionnaires are likely to include instructions in the following areas:

Self-Completion Instructions

- Introducing and explaining how to answer a series of questions on a particular topic.

- Transition statements from one section (topic) of the questionnaire to another.

- Which question to go to next.

- How many answers are acceptable, for example, "Check only one response." Or "Check as many as apply."

- Whether respondents are supposed to answer the question by themselves, or can consult another person or reference materials.

- What to do when the questionnaire is completed, for example, "When finished, place this in the postage paid envelope and return it."

Interviewer-Assisted Instructions

- How to increase respondent participation.

- How to screen out respondents who are not wanted and still keep them happy.

- What to say when respondents ask how to answer a particular question.

- When concepts may not be easily understood, how to define them.

- When answer alternatives are to be read to respondents (aided response) or not to be read (unaided response).

- How to follow branching or skip patterns.

- When and how to probe.

- How to end the interview.

Whether instructions are used in self-completion or interviewer-assisted questionnaires, they always must be clear, concise and consistent throughout the questionnaire. Researchers often make instructions bold, italicized or all capital letters to distinguish them from questions and to increase the likelihood they will be easily understood.

With the growth of the Internet, several online support facilities have emerged to assist researchers in designing questionnaires. The Web site addresses of several vendors are provided in the Research in Action box. Many of these Web sites are helpful, particularly in the mechanical aspects of questionnaire design. But none of them can replace the knowledge and judgement of a researcher experienced in questionnaire design.

RESEARCH IN ACTION

ONLINE SOFTWARE REVOLUTIONIZES QUESTIONNAIRE DEVELOPMENT

Need some help to develop a questionnaire? Researchers are increasingly turning to resources on the Internet. Below are some of the better Web sites providing help in the design of questionnaires and the collection of data online.

Decision Analyst www.decisionanalyst.com	This research company has an Internet-based panel of over 3 million individuals, plus several specialty panels of physicians, attorneys, etc. They provide online assistance in questionnaire development.
Perseus Development www.perseusdevelopment.com	Their Survey Solutions XP Standard is and easy and cost effective way to gather information on the Web. It handles multiple choice, ranking, and scaling questions as well as open-ended one. Its questionnaire design wizard provides good flexibility for skip patterns and randomization.
SPSS www.spss.com	SPSS Data Entry Builder enables users to create and execute customized surveys on the Web, phone or paper, and save data to a central file accessible by password.
Socratic Technologies www.sotech.com	The Socratic Web Survey[SM] system operates on a CATI-like platform. It allows for quota controls and skip patterns as well as randomization of lists and attributes. Other features make it very flexible and comprehensive, including a system for handling multiple languages on international surveys.
Survey Builder www.surveybuilder.com	A survey design Web site that helps you to develop customized web-based surveys. Relatively user-friendly and offers free trial.

SurveyPro.com `www.surveypro.com`	This site claims that its breakthrough technology creates ''on the fly'' email surveys and forms in less than 5 minutes. Their format includes radio buttons, check boxes and data entry fields. Students and faculty are offered free access to use this site for surveys.
The Survey System `www.surveysystem.com`	A comprehensive software package that is simple enough for occasional users but powerful and flexible enough for business research professionals. The system is written in a modular format so the researcher can purchase only the modules needed.
Websurveyor `www.websurveyor.com`	This online survey software claims the user can create professional questionnaires and have immediate and ongoing access to your results. You can analyse, filter, export and report data online.
Survey Monkey `www.surveymonkey.com`	This company says it has a single purpose: to enable anyone to create professional online surveys quickly and easily. It is easy, but the claim of anyone is a stretch.

PRETEST THE QUESTIONNAIRE

No questionnaire should be administered before the researcher has evaluated the likely accuracy and consistency of the responses. This is achieved by **pretesting** the questionnaire using a small sample of respondents with characteristics similar to the target population. Respondents should complete the questionnaire in a setting similar to the actual research project. Moreover, they should be asked probing questions about each part of the questionnaire, from instructions to scaling to format to wording, to ensure each question is relevant, clearly worded and unambiguous. Asking questions such as these is relatively easy with consumer surveys because generally there is a large number to question. But with employee surveys there often is a small number of individuals to choose from and you do not want to include too many in the pretest. In such cases, researchers may choose to have the questionnaire evaluated by other experts or by individuals as similar to the employees as possible.

The pretesting approach depends upon several factors. When a research topic is new to a researcher the questionnaire should always be pretested. But even if the researcher has extensive experience with a topic if the questionnaire will be used with a different group of respondents it must be pretested. Clearly, if a researcher has used a questionnaire in England and is asked to use it in the US it must be pretested. And of course, if the questionnaire were translated into French for use in France it must be extensively pretested. But, even a questionnaire used in one geographic location of the UK, such as southern England or London, would need to be pretested if it were to be used in Scotland or Ireland. Finally, longer questionnaires are more likely to need more extensive pretesting and pretesting always is required if the mode of administration has changed, such as using an Internet approach to administration instead of the telephone.

How large should the sample size be in a pretest? The smallest number would likely be four or five individuals and the largest number no more than about 30. In the authors' experiences pretest sample sizes larger than 30 typically do not provide substantial incremental information for use in revising the questionnaire. Sample size is covered in more detail in Chapter 7.

Based on feedback from the pretest, including the coding and analysis of the responses to individual questions, the questionnaire may require some refinement. The pretest may have to be undertaken several times, using a different set of respondents, depending upon the nature and extent of revisions suggested, before the researcher feels confident to proceed with the main survey. In situations where multi-items scales are used to measure concepts, this process at minimum provides a check of face validity.

ADMINISTER THE QUESTIONNAIRE

There are five major ways of administering a questionnaire in order to collect data. These include:

1. Through the post, including overnight delivery.
2. Via fax.
3. In person.
4. Over the telephone.
5. Electronically via disk, email or hosted Internet Web site.

For each of these approaches, there is an accepted "best practice" to increase the likelihood of higher response rates and quality responses to the questions. Each of these ways of administering a questionnaire was discussed in Chapter 8. But the final decision on how to administer the questionnaire cannot be made until the questionnaire has been pretested and agreed upon.

CONTINUING CASE   EVALUATING SAMOUEL'S AND GINO'S CUSTOMER SURVEY QUESTIONNAIRES

The questionnaire used in the customer surveys was introduced earlier in this chapter. Review the questionnaire looking at the ease of completion, sequence of questions, topics covered, scaling, and so on. Does the questionnaire flow well? Is the sequence of questions correct? Are any topics missing that should have been included? List any questions that need to be rewritten. Give suggestions on how to rewrite them to overcome any weaknesses. ◼

SUMMARY

◼ **Understand that questionnaire design is difficult and why**

Few managers dispute the value of accurate information in improving decision making. The purpose of business research is to provide managers with accurate information, often from surveys. But information from surveys is accurate only if the questionnaire is properly designed. Many individuals believe questionnaires are easy to design. But those with experience in designing questionnaires know this is not true. Indeed, experienced researchers can easily make mistakes in questionnaire design if they overlook essential steps, such as pretesting. In designing a questionnaire researchers must realize there will be only one opportunity to interact with respondents since a reasonable interval of time is necessary before the same respondent can be contacted again, and then it generally should involve either another topic or a different approach to the same topic. For this reason, a great deal of care must be taken to ensure the questionnaire will produce reliable and valid data.

◼ **Explain the steps involved in designing an effective questionnaire**

In developing a questionnaire careful planning and a systematic approach are necessary to ensure the data collected are accurate. Clear definitions of concepts and how they might be communicated and measured are prerequisites for the design of a "good" questionnaire. Consideration must be given to the readability, presentation, structure and length of a questionnaire because previous research has shown that these affect response quality and rate. Finally, researchers also must be cautious about the type of questions used, their wording, and the coding of the responses.

◼ **Recognize how the method of data collection influences questionnaire design**

There are five major ways of administering the questionnaire: post, including overnight delivery, fax, in-person, telephone and electronic (Internet or disk). Each of the approaches has an accepted best practice. The method chosen must be appropriate for the study and yield an acceptable response quality and rate.

◼ **Understand the types of questions and how they are used**

Typically, in gathering information through questionnaires we make use of different types of questions. The form of these questions and the order in which they appear in the questionnaire is very important. The types of questions and their order in the questionnaire depend upon the nature of the topic, how the questionnaire is administered, the target population's ability and willingness to respond, the type of statistical analysis and similar factors. Sometimes open-ended questions are best, while other times closed questions best achieve the research objectives. Similarly, rating scales are used sometimes while other times dichotomous questions are better.

■ **Describe the major sections of the questionnaire and how they relate to each other**
After the researcher decides the type of questions to ask, the preliminary questionnaire structure must be determined. The structure follows a three-part sequence. The initial questions are referred to as opening questions. The middle section has questions directed specifically at the topics addressed by the research objectives. The final section includes the classification questions which help the researcher better understand the results. ■

Ethical Dilemma

Shelly Appleby graduated from college in May and has just started working for a marketing research firm. She has been doing a great job and as a reward her supervisor asks her to write the survey questions for a telephone survey of customer perceptions about local supermarket chains. She turns in her questions and is told by her supervisor that they looked good and only required minor editing. One month later, Shelly is included in the meeting to present the results to the grocery store that commissioned the survey. During the meeting, Shelly notices that the survey questions had been altered and, in her opinion, slanted to produce positive results about the client's shops. When she mentions her thoughts to her supervisor, her supervisor explains that while objectivity is fine in the academic world, in the real world, the most important thing is to make the client happy. Shelly disagrees with her supervisor. What should she do?

REVIEW QUESTIONS

1. What are the steps to follow in questionnaire design?
2. What is the difference between closed and open-ended questions? Give an example of each.
3. What is an opening question and why would a business researcher use one.
4. What is a classification question?
5. What are the guidelines for preparing good questions?
6. Why pretest a questionnaire?

DISCUSSION AND THINKING ACTIVITIES

1. How does the researcher know which questions should be included in a questionnaire?

2. Design an open-ended questionnaire to obtain college students opinions about diversity on campus.

3. Design a closed questionnaire to obtain college students opinions about binge drinking on campus. Include questions to determine whether respondents themselves are binge drinkers?

4. Pretest the binge-drinking questionnaire prepared in question 3 on 8–10 students. Prepare a report on your findings.

5. How can questionnaire design help to minimize error in research data?

6. Go to the Web site for this book (www.wileyeurope.com/college/hair). Click on the link for the survey of public houses and brewers in London. Could this questionnaire be used in the US? If yes, how would it have to be changed, if at all? What is your opinion of the structure, layout and wording of the questionnaire?

7. Go to the Web site for this book (www.wileyeurope.com/college/hair). Click on the link to the restaurant "Neighbourhood Survey." Would you complete and return this survey? Why or why not? Are there questions that should have been asked that were not included on the survey? Identify any questions you feel were unnecessary and could be deleted. Prepare a report on your conclusions about this survey.

8. Go to the Web site for this book (www.wileyeurope.com/college/hair). Click on the link to the "Binge Drinking" survey questionnaire. Evaluate the questionnaire in terms of wording, question sequence, layout and scales. Pay particular attention to the definition of binge drinking and comment on its validity and possible influence on answers to the questions.

9. **SPSS Application:** We are interested in measuring a concept labelled "work environment". From the list of variables in the Samouel's employee survey database select those you believe will collectively capture work environment. Assess the reliability of your chosen items in measuring this concept. Are there any weak or confusing items that relate to this concept?

10. **SPSS Application:** We are interested in measuring a concept labelled "restaurant atmosphere". From the list of variables in the Samouel's and Gino's customer survey database select those you believe will collectively capture restaurant atmosphere. Assess the reliability of your chosen items in measuring this concept.

INTERNET EXERCISES   W W W

1. Go to the Surveypro.com Web site. Use the software to design a questionnaire to obtain student evaluations of college professors. See www.surveypro.com.

2. Go to www.google.com. Type in the phrase "questionnaire design" and conduct a search. What did you find? Try this with www.yahoo.com. How did it differ?

3. Complete a survey on one of the following Web sites and prepare a report that evaluates the questionnaire.
   a. www.survey.net
   b. www.cc.gatech.edu/gvu/user_surveys/

4. Go to the Web site located at www.customersat.com. Prepare a report on what you learned about customer satisfaction surveys.

NOTES

1. Marsh, H. W. and Yeung, A. S. (1999). "The Liability of Psychological Ratings: The Chameleon Effect in Global Self-Esteem", *Personality and Social Psychology Bulletin*, 25, 49–64.

PART IV
ANALYSIS AND
INTERPRETATION OF DATA

CHAPTER 11
BASIC DATA ANALYSIS FOR QUALITATIVE RESEARCH

CONTENTS

LEARNING OUTCOMES

- Clarify when qualitative research is best at achieving your research objectives
- Understand the different approaches to conduct qualitative research.
- Explain the importance of managing qualitative data.
- Describe the process for analysing qualitative data.

INTRODUCTION

Business research involves a lot more than numbers and statistics. Some researchers have criticized qualitative research as being "soft", lacking rigour and being inferior. Measurement and quantifying findings does not ensure that business research is useful or more accurate. What increases the likelihood of good research is a careful, thoughtful, knowledgeable approach whether qualitative or quantitative research methods are used. Indeed, we advocate using both qualitative and quantitative approaches in the same research in many instances because they each have their role and together enhance the research outcomes.

In this chapter we first review the basic differences between qualitative and quantitative research. Next we describe the process for analysing qualitative data. This includes the interrelationships between data collection, data reduction and data display. We end the chapter with an overview of how to draw conclusions and to verify your findings.

UNDERSTANDING QUALITATIVE RESEARCH

To understand qualitative data analysis we must first understand qualitative research. Qualitative research can be characterized in many ways. But among the most important is that it is discovery oriented, uses the data to generate ideas, and is based on inductive reasoning. **Inductive reasoning** is how effective an individual is in identifying patterns within a large amount of data. When researchers use an inductive approach they are attempting to build their theory or conceptual framework from the data they collect. The opposite approach referred to as **deductive reasoning**, works from the more general to the more specific and involves descriptive or confirmatory aspects. It starts with an idea or conceptual framework, and then uses the data to better understand and narrow that down into more specific hypotheses that can be tested. We narrow down even further by obtaining observations to assess the hypotheses. This process may ultimately enable us to test the hypotheses with specific data obtained in quantitative research – a confirmation (or not) of our original idea or theory. Thus, qualitative research emphasizes the development of hypotheses while quantitative research focuses on testing hypotheses.

A qualitative research approach is the most appropriate and indeed the only way of achieving some research objectives. Situations in which qualitative research is the preferred method include: (1) where little is known about a research problem or opportunity; (2) where previous research only partially or incompletely explains the research question; (3) if current knowledge involves complex or evolving phenomena that need to be organized or simplified to examine further; (4) if the researcher needs to more fully understand phenomena to clarify patterns and themes; and (5) if the primary purpose of the research is to propose a conceptual/theoretical framework that represents current reality and could eventually be tested with quantitative research. For example, if the research goal is to identify the issues and concerns of older workers with a younger supervisor, then a qualitative approach is preferred. But, if previous research proposes some likely relationships involving older workers with a younger supervisor and the goal is to determine whether older workers expect more from their younger supervisors, then a survey using a quantitative approach is best.

APPROACHES TO QUALITATIVE RESEARCH

Many approaches are available to conduct qualitative research. Four of the most widely used are discussed in this section.

Phenomenology is a qualitative research method that studies human experiences and consciousness. It is the study of "phenomena", or how things appear in our experiences, the ways we experience things, and therefore the meanings things have in our experiences. Phenomenological studies examine conscious experiences from the first person (interviewer or observer) point of view, and ranges from experiences involving perceptions, thoughts, desires, memories, emotions and imagination to bodily awareness and social interactions. These studies sometimes are referred to as "lived experiences" because they focus on how human behaviour is shaped by relationships with one's physical environment, including objects, people and situations. A specialized field of phenomenology is **hermeneutics**, which attempts to understand and explain human behaviour based on an analysis of stories people tell about themselves.

Ethnography is the qualitative description of human socio-cultural phenomena, based on field observation. An ethnographic approach typically focuses on a community of individuals, selecting participants expected to represent an overview of the activities of the community. The community is not necessarily based on geography, and can be defined in terms of an individual's work or leisure-time setting, or some other criteria. Data is collected by a participant-observer, who actually becomes part of the community and observes other participants. Nonobserver participants are asked to identify other individuals representative of the community, and snowball sampling is used to obtain a sufficient number of individuals to represent all areas relevant to the investigation. Participants are interviewed several times, using information from previous participants to obtain clarification and deeper responses when interviewed the second, third or perhaps fourth time. Typical questions asked include: "What is happening?" and "Tell me about what is going on here?"

Grounded theory is a process involving a set of steps that if carefully executed is thought to "guarantee" that the outcome will be a good theory. Thus, the general goal of grounded theory research is to construct theories in order to understand phenomena. The researcher poses questions about how experiences change over time or what the stages of change are, and thereby creates, elaborates on, and sometimes validates theory. Examples of questions used in a grounded theory approach include: "Tell me about the process of . . . ?" and "How is this different from . . . ? Grounded theory procedures are neither statistical nor quantitative, and begin by focusing on an area of study and then gathering data from a variety of sources, including respondent interviews, observation, field notes or diaries. Once gathered, the data are analysed using coding and theoretical sampling procedures. When completed, theories are generated based on interpretive procedures and summarized in a report. Although grounded theory has been developed and principally used within the field of sociology, it also has been used successfully by researchers in a variety of different disciplines, including business, education, medicine, political science and psychology.

Case studies are a documented description of a particular person, group, organization, activity or event. Actions taken by individuals or groups in the case are described, and their reactions, responses and effects on other participants are compared in order to draw conclusions. The main event or activity is described extensively but smaller events may be highlighted for their relevance. Data are typically obtained from personal interviews, focus groups and/or company histories. Rather than using large samples and following rigid procedures to examine activities or variables, case study methods involve an in-depth, longitudinal examination of an activity or event, referred to as a case. Case studies provide a systematic way of looking at events, collecting data, analysing information, and reporting the findings. By conducting case studies researchers hope to gain a better understanding of why an event happened as it did and what might be important to look at in future research. Case studies enable researchers to learning about complex events through extensive description and contextual analysis. They most often are used to develop hypotheses rather than to test them.

The Research in Action box provides an example of how observation can be used to collect qualitative data.

RESEARCH IN ACTION

MYSTERY SHOPPERS OBSERVE WHETHER HOSPITALITY PROVIDERS HAVE STANDARDS

In recent years, competition has been strong among luxury hotels. To ensure that their facilities meet customers' expectations, hotel chains and other hospitality businesses have been hiring consultants to check them out. Registering under assumed names, these mystery shoppers act like eccentric guests, examining and reporting on service, staff competence, cleanliness, food quality, responsiveness, and so on. For example, they typically check out the rooms, order room service, eat in the restaurant, ask advice from the concierge, and visit toilets in public areas. In fact, one of the interesting findings is that the men's rooms in public areas are typically cleaner than the women's, probably because most hotel managers are men and therefore visit the men's toilet more often. The goal of these consultants is to help hospitality providers to transform their business so they are truly guest-centered, exceeding customer expectations, providing memorable experiences, and encouraging loyalty.

Which qualitative approach is used to collect these data? How should patterns or themes be identified in the analysis phase? Could the identified themes impact data collection?

Sources: http://www.hotel-online.com/News/PR2005_1st/Jan05_StandardsReview.html, http://www.hospitalityperformance.com/, accessed June 2006. ■

MANAGING QUALITATIVE DATA

Qualitative data generally originate from two sources – field generated data and found data. **Field generated data** typically come from interviews or focus groups in the field and consists of words and phrases in textual format. In contrast, **found data** are from existing sources like newspaper articles, speeches, diaries, advertisements, audio and video records, and so forth. Data management presents different challenges depending upon the source of the qualitative data.

Field generated data must be transcribed into a textual format to enable qualitative analysis. Researchers differ in their resources, assumptions and objectives, and what is actually transcribed into text will differ depending on each of these. For example, it is expensive to transcribe field notes so researchers with a limited budget may choose to transcribe only portions of their notes based on their assumptions about its relevance to their research objectives. Even if voice-recognition software is used with audio or video formats the possibility exists for errors to enter text files. Thus, qualitative researchers using field generated data must consider this issue when designing their study and incorporate methods to minimize error.

The issue of what is actually analysed in qualitative research can be difficult for found data too. The reason is that today society is producing so much data/information, and the search techniques have improved so much, that it is impossible to include even a small portion of what is being generated about a particular topic. Qualitative researchers have access to literally millions of sources of information on a particular topic and must use some criteria for deciding what to examine in their research. For example, if one submits the key words "case study" to a Google search the result is 611,000,000 entries. Clearly it is impossible to examine all of this information.

Managing data in qualitative research is even more important because of the interactive nature of qualitative data collection and analysis. In other words, since qualitative data analysis can lead to changes in data collection as the study evolves, the researcher must have a plan of how to manage the data before beginning the study. Decisions made early in the process of conducting qualitative research about how to manage the data can have consequences later in the study. These decisions typically are of two types – how to deal with information overload, since qualitative researchers often generate large amounts of data, and what criteria to use in deciding which data are relevant to the study and must be included, and which can be overlooked.

Computers are increasingly providing a great deal of help to qualitative researchers in managing not only their data, but their ideas. The software facilitates a wide range of approaches to managing data using document names, themes, definitions, memos, codes, shapes, colours, and so on. Even if computer software is used to manage qualitative data, researchers will always need to have quick and easy access to the original data to verify patterns, themes and conclusions.

ANALYSING QUALITATIVE DATA

The objective of qualitative data analysis is to identify, examine, compare and interpret patterns and themes. Recall that in quantitative data analysis, the process of data collection and analysis follows a set of steps that may involve revisiting earlier steps, but often involves a step-by-step sequence. In contrast, qualitative analysis involves a "loop-like" process in which the data is revisited regularly as new questions and connections emerge, or as the overall understanding of the research situation emerges. Indeed, with qualitative research data collection and analysis often are concurrent, with new analysis steps initiating additional data collection which in turn stimulates other analysis processes. Thus, with qualitative research data collection, analysis and theory development are closely related. Unless the purpose of the research is to elaborate on or extend existing theory, the researcher begins with an idea and allows the theory to emerge from the data.

When analysing data in qualitative research, the following questions should be continually asked:

1. What themes and common patterns are emerging that relate to the research objectives?

2. How are these themes and patterns related to the focus of the research?

3. Are there examples of responses that are inconsistent with the typical patterns and themes?

4. Can these inconsistencies be explained or perhaps be used to expand or redirect the research?

5. Do the patterns or themes indicate additional data, perhaps in a new area, need to be collected? If yes, then proceed to collect those data.

6. Are the patterns and themes consistent with other research? If yes, continue to collect data as planned. If not, assess how this impacts the validity of the study.

To conduct qualitative analyses, researchers must understand coding. **Coding** is the process of assigning meaningful numerical values that facilitate understanding of your data. The purpose of coding is the enable the researcher to simplify and focus on meaningful characteristics of the data. To properly code the researcher must be very familiar with the data. If the researcher was not the observer or the one who conducted the interviews, the coding is much more difficult and requires more work.

Before starting the analysis, the researcher must code the data. Coding data begins with selecting the coding units. Examples of **coding units** include words, phrases, themes, items, images, graphics, photographs, and so on. In selecting coding units you may only want to identify whether or not a particular item is present in the data. But you may also want to calculate the number of times a word or item appears, the proportion of time or space representing a particular topic or theme, or the position of an item (unit) within a particular document. The end result of coding, therefore, is to enable the researcher to link data with topics, themes, concepts, ideas and other higher order abstractions so the data can be manipulated, organized and eventually categorized.

To clarify the process of qualitative data analysis, it is helpful to review the framework developed by Miles and Huberman.[1] Their steps in qualitative analysis are shown in Exhibit 11-1. They include data collection, data reduction, data display, drawing conclusions, and verification of findings.

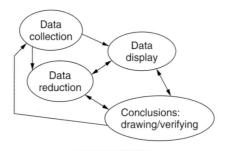

EXHIBIT 11-1

Steps in Qualitative Data Analysis

DATA REDUCTION

When qualitative data are collected, they need to be organized and reduced. **Data reduction** involves selecting, simplifying and transforming the data to make it more manageable and understandable. The process requires choices about what should be emphasized, minimized and eliminated from further study. Initial decisions are guided by predetermined research questions, but the analyst continuously looks for new meanings and relationships. Thus, data reduction is guided by the relevance of the emerging themes and patterns to the study's research questions. But if new directions appear fruitful they are pursued. The objective is to reduce your data to a manageable amount whilst at the same time not eliminating anything that is relevant to your research. The Research in Action box illustrates the process of data reduction.

DATA DISPLAY

A second step in the process of qualitative data analysis is data display. **Data display** goes beyond data reduction by organizing the information in a way that facilitates drawing conclusions. The process of data display helps qualitative researchers to organize information and view it in a way that enables them to identify linkages and develop explanations that relate their findings to existing theory. During the data-display process, higher order themes or patterns are likely to be extracted from the data. Examples of higher order displays are frequently mentioned phrases, charts and/or diagrams linking several themes or phrases, or perhaps a matrix that arranges patterns in a logical manner. Building upon the data reduction process described in the Research in Action box about European software companies, it is likely that the knowledge sharing methods will be implemented differently in each of the participating software firms. Factors such as the size of the company, management's support of the idea of developing software for the Asian market, and how receptive each company's culture is to new ideas will influence the extent of knowledge sharing. During the data display step, the qualitative analyst would identify how and why knowledge sharing resulted in greater receptivity to developing software for the Asian market. The end result of the data display step might be a preliminary conclusion that acceptance of the idea of developing software for the Asian market was quicker and more extensive in companies where management was more supportive of pursuing new opportunities, and much slower in larger, highly structured firms.

RESEARCH IN ACTION / DATA REDUCTION AND DISPLAY GENERATES INFORMATION SHARING METHODS

US and Japanese firms have been market leaders in developing world-class information-technology (IT) products. In contrast, with the exception of SAP, a German software company, European firms have been slow to leverage their existing contacts to facilitate penetration of Asian software markets, particularly the packaged computer software market. In fact, European complacency threatens to erase the future competitiveness of the entire western European software sector.

The EU Commission funded a study in which Chief Information Officers from leading software companies in member countries were assembled to discuss ways to motivate companies to pursue this market more aggressively. One of the questions posed was "What can be done to facilitate sharing of knowledge about the need to pursue the Asian market?" Extensive qualitative responses were offered and the data reduction process involved developing a list of knowledge-sharing methods. But the process went beyond the development of a list, with participants actually indicating which of the methods they believed would be most effective and why. To complete the data reduction process, the relative frequency with which different knowledge-sharing methods were mentioned was examined, as well as the level of support for each approach. Thus, data reduction involved identifying the approaches likely to be most effective in sharing knowledge among major software companies in Europe, and this led to data display which extracted information about the importance of the various knowledge-sharing methods. ∎

DRAWING AND VERIFYING CONCLUSIONS

The third step in qualitative data analysis is drawing conclusions and verifying their accuracy through cross checking. **Drawing conclusions** involves deciding what the identified themes and patterns mean and how they help to answer the research questions. Qualitative researchers begin drawing conclusions when data collection begins, not when it is complete. They ask questions such as "What does this mean?" "Is it consistent or inconsistent with other data or theory", "Are patterns or themes emerging?" and so on. **Verification** involves checking and re-checking the data to ensure the initial conclusions are realistic, supportable and valid. Recall that validity in quantitative research is the extent to which a construct measures what it is supposed to measure. In qualitative research, validity involves assessing the extent to which the conclusions that have been drawn are logical, believable, justified by the data and patterns identified and supportable even when there are alternative explanations.

The process of drawing and verifying conclusions is driven by the objective of looking for and ultimately identifying the best of several alternative conclusions or explanations, not by looking for a single explanation. To enhance the likelihood that the best conclusion has been drawn, it is advisable to collect data from multiple sources using different approaches. Thus, when possible, if information collected in focus groups, as well as in-depth interviews, was used, and perhaps even information collected through observation, more valid conclusions could be produced. For example, information obtained in focus groups with managing directors of European software companies about how decisions are made to develop software for the Asian market might suggest that group consensus is important. But individual in-depth interviews could reveal that senior management support and knowledge is really more important. Thus, analysing data from multiple sources involves more than deciding who may be right or wrong, or relying on who talks most often or speaks the loudest. It is a much more subtle process of hearing different viewpoints, assessing their plausibility and significance, and ultimately drawing the correct conclusion.

In analysing qualitative data the researcher is often excited about extreme or deviant cases because they may suggest a new direction for data collection or analysis, or an alternative explanation or approach to solving a problem. This contrasts with quantitative research where outliers or extreme cases are typically removed.

Finally, some analysts use computer software to conduct qualitative data analysis. Indeed, there are quite a few packages that have emerged in recent years, all of which have strengths and weaknesses. Before selecting a particular software package the researcher should consider the amount and type of data to be collected, the sources of data, and the anticipated types of analysis. Also, one should understand that software packages are simply a method of more efficiently completing tasks that involve counting or organizing data. They do not develop codes for the data and cannot define themes or phrases to be examined. In summary, even when software is used the researcher cannot skip the intensive intellectual examination and assessment that is required to complete qualitative research properly.

Until recently, examining qualitative data was a manual, time-consuming process. Now there are numerous software packages that can make the task much simpler. Two examples are described in the Research in Action box.

RESEARCH
IN ACTION

QUALITATIVE DATA ANALYSIS: SOFTWARE TO THE RESCUE!

Increasing use is being made of computer software to analyse data that is narrative in form. Such software is often known by the acronym CAQADS (Computer Assisted Qualitative Data Analysis Software). Two examples of such software are Atlas.ti and NVIVO.

ATLAS.ti facilitates qualitative analysis of large amounts of unstructured textual, graphical, audio and video data. That is, data that cannot be meaningfully analysed by numerical or statistical approaches. It offers a variety of tools for accomplishing the tasks associated with a systematic approach to examining unstructured data, including managing, extracting, comparing, exploring and reassembling meaningful segments of large amounts of data in flexible and creative, yet systematic ways. Examples of how it has been used include: X-ray images and microscoped samples in medicine, video taped gestures in anthropology, annotated floor plans in architecture, video archives in history, parts lists in engineering, video archives of historical situations, part lists in engineering, handwriting features in graphology, letters, finger prints, photographs in criminology, and quality assurance in business, and interpretative descriptions of paintings in art. See their Web site http://www.atlasti.com/ for more information about this package.

Another popular computer software package used by researchers is **QSR NVIVO**. It is typically used to analyse text from focus group or interview transcripts, literary documents, nontextual data such as photographs, tape recordings, films, multimedia materials, and so on. It enables the user to index and link several documents in a structured way to produce categorical data in a form useful for further analysis. Using this software, researchers can explore issues, understand or explain phenomena, or develop theories, and a numerical summary of output can be exported to software programs such as SPSS and Excel.

For more information about QSR and its related products, such as NVIVO 7, visit the following Web sites: http://www.qsrinternational.com/index.htm and http://www.datasense.org/ ∎

To use computer-aided content analysis software, the researcher needs an electronic copy of the narrative information. Initial applications of this type of software were mostly in academic or scholarly research. But applied business researchers and industry in general are now finding applications. An example of the use of computer-aided software to examine qualitative interviews asking questions on organizational behaviour and worker productivity is described in the Research in Action.

RESEARCH IN ACTION

APPLICATION OF COMPUTER-ASSISTED QUALITATIVE DATA ANALYSIS SOFTWARE

Researchers interviewed 16 sales managers to identify organizational variables considered important in the effective implementation of sales force automation systems. Responses were transcribed and submitted to computer-aided content analysis. The relative occurrence of key concepts and value-laden terms was tabulated, and categories of themes were developed for each question. A panel of experts then defined the categories by developing a list of key words that described each category. The software searched the entire text of the interviews and placed information into the categories. Then the panel of experts again examined the results to eliminate any information misplaced in a category due to contextual issues. The four questions asked, the categories developed, and the relative percentage of ''hits'' for each category in each question is reported below:

1. What employee behaviours should firms reward, support, and expect if they are interested in effectively implementing and SFA system?

Teamwork	28 %
Computer Skills	35 %
SFA Competence	37 %

2. What kinds of information can SFA provide that would be valuable in terms of helping increase a firm's productivity?

Prospecting	34 %
Account Development	32 %
Buyer Profile	34 %

3. Please describe the kind of organizational culture or shared values necessary to effectively implement an SFA system?

Information Sharing	41 %
Teamwork	33 %
SFA Commitment/Ownership	26 %

4. Please describe issues that might limit or enhance the effectiveness of an SFA system?

Resistance to Change	61 %
Insufficient Support for SFA	39 %

As an example, for question (1), three categories were identified. Their relative importance was 28 % for teamwork, 35 % for computer skills, and 37 % for SFA Competence. The other questions are interpreted in a similar manner. Computer-aided content analysis software enables the business researcher to analyse open-ended responses quickly and confidently, and report the findings in an effective manner.

Source: Pullig, C., Maxham, T. and Hair, J. (2002). "Salesforce Automation Systems: An Exploratory Examination of Organizational Factors Associated with Effective Implementation and Salesforce Productivity", *Journal of Business Research*, 55(5), May, 401–16.

∎

ASSESSING RELIABILITY AND VALIDITY

An important requirement in qualitative research, just as in quantitative approaches, is that the methods used produce reliable findings. In **qualitative research**, **reliability** is the degree of consistency in assignment of similar words, phrases or other kinds of data to the same pattern or theme by different researchers. This is referred to as **inter–rater reliability**. Reliability can also mean the degree of consistency that the same researcher assigns similar observations and interpretations at different points in time. Qualitative researchers must always be aware of and implement appropriate methods to assess reliability.

Questions also arise as to whether qualitative findings can be validated. **Validation in qualitative research** is the extent to which qualitative findings accurately represent the phenomena being examined. With quantitative research, methods for assessing validity involves inserting numbers into formulas and calculating the outcome. But since qualitative research involves generating information that cannot be summarized in the form of numbers, one cannot simply calculate the validity measure for a particular study. This does not mean, however, that the validity of qualitative research cannot be assessed. It means that different methods must be used to assess validity when conducting qualitative research.

Methods for assessing the validity of qualitative research depend upon the approach used. If a case study approach is followed, then validity can be assessed by comparing the outcome of the cases described with the researcher's predictions. If the predictions are accurate, the research is valid. The question of validity then hinges on what is meant by accurate. Qualitative researchers assessing the validity of case studies must therefore adopt a systematic and consistent process to establish and confirm the accuracy of their predictions. For example, qualitative researchers must clearly explain how negative cases are treated in establishing accuracy. In contrast, if the qualitative research involves assigning codes and examining patterns, assessing validity is more difficult. Recommended methods for assessing qualitative research based on coding and pattern identification include the extent of the rapport between the researcher and the participants, the amount of fieldwork involved in collecting the data, the time and procedures involved in the coding process, the proportion of the data associated with the dominant patterns identified compared to the less often mentioned themes, and so forth. In the end, to establish validity effectively, qualitative researchers must document their fieldwork and analysis procedures in a manner than enables others to examine and confirm the validity of their procedures and conclusions.

To ensure reliability and validity of qualitative research, it is helpful to use **triangulation**. There are four possible types of triangulation in qualitative research – researcher, data, method and theory. **Researcher triangulation** involves comparing the methods, analysis and interpretation of different researchers on the same topic. **Data triangulation** requires collecting data from several different sources at different times and comparing it. **Method triangulation** involves conducting similar research using several different methods and comparing the findings, including sometimes using both qualitative and quantitative approaches. Finally, **theory triangulation** is using multiple theories and perspectives to interpret and explain the data. Qualitative researchers cannot use all types of triangulation in a single research project but should be aware of them and know when each method is best.

Several other approaches can also enhance the validity of qualitative research. **Extended fieldwork** involving collection of data over an extended period of time is likely to improve both discovery and interpretation. Interactions involving **participant feedback** and the researcher's interpretations and reflections facilitate insights and interpretation. **External peer review** by other research experts, including those both familiar with the research as well as disinterested parties, can verify interpretations and conclusions. Finally, qualitative researchers can use **pattern matching** where the data are used to predict or suggest particular outcomes and the actual results are evaluated to determine if they fit the predicted pattern. It is not possible or necessary to use all approaches in a single research study. But researchers should use multiple approaches whenever possible and communicate their findings in such a manner that the logical processes by which they were developed are accessible to the reader, the relationship between the actual data and the conclusions about data is explicit, and the claims made in relation to the data are credible and believable.

RESEARCH IN ACTION — MANAGING WORKERS FROM DIVERSE CULTURES

Companies that conduct business across national borders must adapt their strategies to be successful. Among the more frequent adaptations are modifications in organizational processes and systems, such as motivation, leadership and evaluation of workers that often involve examining the company's core values and culture. Researchers have identified six subsystems associated with human performance:

- Performance specifications = expectations of the outputs and standards associated with job goals and feedback regarding outcomes.
- Task support = inputs and procedures that help workers do their jobs.

- Incentives = how workers are motivated to either change or continue their performance.

- Skills and knowledge = the fundamental required to do the job.

- Individual capacity = the worker's intellectual, mental, emotional and physical capabilities.

- Motives = the worker's intrinsic motivation.

In attempting to improve performance, companies must examine assumptions regarding how cultures influence each of the six subsystems. Since national cultural differences may determine the effectiveness of interventions used to improve performance, the assumptions made by managers must be examined through the lens of national cultures.

What kind of qualitative research would be appropriate to better understand which interventions would be most effective in a particular country?

Sources: Hoecklin, L. (1995). *Managing Cultural Differences: Strategies for Competitive Advantage*, Wokingham, Addison-Wesley; Schneider, S. and Barsoux, J. L. (1999). *Managing Across Cultures*, London, Prentice-Hall; and Dean, P. J. (1999). *Performance Engineering at Work*, Washington, DC, International Society for Performance Improvement. ■

CONTINUING CASE   SAMOUEL'S GREEK CUISINE

The role of qualitative research

The business consultant hired by Phil Samouel has recommended two quantitative surveys – one of Samouel's employees and customer surveys for both Samouel's and Gino's. He has not recommended any qualitative research. Phil Samouel is not an expert in research methods, but he does know the difference between qualitative and quantitative research. He is wondering if some kind of qualitative research method should be used to better understand the challenges facing him in improving his restaurant.

Could observation be used to collect qualitative information? If yes, when and how could observation be used? What about focus groups? Are there topics that need to be explored using focus groups? If yes, suggest topics to be used in focus group studies. ▫

SUMMARY

■ **Clarify when qualitative research is best at achieving your research objectives**
A qualitative research approach is the most appropriate and indeed the only way of achieving some research objectives, including: (1) where little is known about a research problem or opportunity; (2) where previous research only partially or incompletely explains the research question; (3) if current knowledge involves complex or evolving phenomena that need to be organized or simplified to examine further; (4) if the researcher needs to more fully understand phenomena to clarify patterns and themes; and (5) if the primary purpose of the research is to propose a conceptual/theoretical framework that represents current reality and could eventually be tested with quantitative research.

■ **Understand the different approaches to conduct qualitative research**
Many approaches are available to conduct qualitative research. Four of the most widely used are phenomenology, ethnography, grounded theory and case studies. Phenomenology is a qualitative research method that studies ''phenomena'', or how things appear in our experiences, the ways we experience things, and therefore the meanings things have in our experiences. Ethnography is the qualitative description of human socio-cultural phenomena that typically focuses on a community of individuals, selecting participants expected to represent an overview of the activities of the community. Grounded-theory is a process involving a set of steps of carefully executed is thought to ''guarantee'' that the outcome will be a good theory. Thus, the general goal of grounded theory research is to construct theories in order to understand phenomena. Case studies are a documented description of a particular person, group, organization, activity or event. Actions taken by individuals or groups in the case are described, and their reactions, responses and effects on other participants are compared in order to draw conclusions.

■ **Explain the importance of managing qualitative data**
Qualitative data generally originate from two sources – field generated data and found data. Field generated data typically come from interviews or focus groups in the field and consist of words and phrases in textual format. In contrast, found data are from existing sources like newspaper articles, speeches, diaries, advertisements, audio and video records, and so forth. Data management presents different challenges depending upon the source of the qualitative data. Field generated data typically comes from interviews or focus groups in the field and consists of words and phrases in textual format. In contrast, found data are from existing sources like newspaper articles, speeches, diaries, advertisements, audio and video records, and so forth. Data management presents different challenges depending upon the source of the qualitative data. Field generated data must be transcribed into a textual format to enable qualitative analysis. Researchers differ in their resources, assumptions and objectives, and what is actually transcribed into text will differ depending on each of these. Qualitative researchers using field generated data must consider this issue when designing their study and incorporate methods to minimize error.

The issue of what is actually analysed in qualitative research can be difficult for found data too because society is producing so much data, and the search techniques have improved so much, that it is impossible to include even a small portion of what is being generated about a particular topic. Managing data in qualitative research is important because decisions made early in the process of conducting qualitative research about how to manage the data can have consequences later in the study.

■ **Describe the process for analysing qualitative data**
The objective of qualitative data analysis is to identify, examine, compare and interpret patterns and themes. Qualitative analysis involves a "loop-like" process in which the data are revisited regularly as new questions and connections emerge, or as the overall understanding of the research situation emerges. Indeed, with qualitative research data collection and analysis often are concurrent, with new analysis steps initiating additional data collection which in turn stimulates other analysis processes. The specific steps in qualitative research include data collection, data reduction, data display, drawing conclusions, and verification of findings. ■

Ethical Dilemma

Stavros Kalafatis is an experienced qualitative researcher with Mayfair Research, Ltd. His company contracted to conduct a series of 20 employee focus groups in five countries to use in completing a training needs assessment for a large industrial manufacturing firm. The budget submitted in the initial proposal, prepared by a former employee of Mayfair, covered only the cost of collecting the data, not transcribing participant comments and preparing a report. When he presented the budget for transcribing the 20 focus group sessions the client said it was too much and suggested that Stavros either transcribe half of the focus group sessions or transcribe only selected portions of all focus groups. What should he do? How could Stavros develop criteria to select which focus groups to transcribe, or which portions?

REVIEW QUESTIONS

1. What are the situations in which qualitative research is the preferred approach?
2. What is the difference between ethnography and grounded theory?
3. What are the steps in analysis of qualitative data? How are they related?
4. Can the validity of qualitative research be determined? If yes, what are some methods to do so?

DISCUSSION AND APPLICATION ACTIVITIES

1. Discuss how data collection, data reduction, data display are interrelated in qualitative research?

2. How can qualitative researchers verify the conclusions they develop from their data?

3. Discuss the role of coding in qualitative data analysis.

4. How does triangulation help qualitative researchers achieve reliability and validity?

INTERNET EXERCISES   W W W

1. Access the Google and Yahoo search engines. Use the key words "interviews" and "case studies". Select five sources of information to rely on in explaining each of these terms in a qualitative research context. After you have identified your five sources, prepare a list of criteria you used to select the five sources. Be prepared to justify the logic and objectivity of your criteria.

2. Go to the following Web site: `http://kerlins.net/bobbi/research/qualresearch/`. Browse this Web site and prepare a report on the resources that are available to qualitative researchers.

3. This Web site `http://www.qualitative-research.net/fqs/fqs-e/debate-3-e.htm` offers debates on the ethical issues associated with qualitative research. Identify two articles on this topic and prepare a report summarizing the issues debated.

NOTES

1. Miles, M. B., and Huberman, A. M. (1994). *Qualitative Data Analysis*. Newbury Park, CA, Sage.

CHAPTER 12
BASIC DATA ANALYSIS FOR QUANTITATIVE RESEARCH

CONTENTS

LEARNING OUTCOMES

- Describe the process for conducting quantitative data analysis.
- Understand the importance of data preparation.
- Explain how descriptive statistics enable you to better understand your data.
- Clarify how to identify and deal with outliers.

INTRODUCTION

Business researchers typically have lots of data to help managers improve their decision making. One of their primary tasks is to convert the data into knowledge. With quantitative research, this means examining the data to identify and confirm relationships. Before quantitative data can be analysed, they must be edited, coded, and in some instances transformed to ensure that they can be properly used in statistical analysis. In discussing quantitative analysis, we begin with the process of data preparation. We then show you how to graphically display data so decision makers can better understand them. For example, if you conducted a survey of Sainsbury's customers you would be able to determine how frequently they shopped in that store, identify which respondents are the most frequent customers compared to the least frequent customers, and perhaps why, and to make comparisons with shoppers at competitive food stores.

In many situations today there are "too many numbers" to look at and identify relationships that might be useful. Information must be developed, therefore, to summarize and describe the numbers. The basic statistics and descriptive analysis covered in this chapter were developed for this purpose. In later chapters we show you more sophisticated methods to use when the simple approaches cannot adequately explain the data relationships.

ANALYSING QUANTITATIVE DATA

Many research projects have numerical data or information that can be quantified to enable research questions to be answered. Recall that quantitative data are measurements in which numbers are used to directly represent the properties of some phenomena. To be useful the data need to be analysed and interpreted. Data analysis in quantitative research involves a series of steps, as shown below:

1. Review conceptual framework and relationships to be studied.

2. Prepare data for analysis.

3. Determine if research involves descriptive analysis or hypothesis testing.

4. Conduct analysis.

5. Evaluate findings to assess whether they are meaningful.

An overview of basic approaches to data examination is provided in this section. The discussion begins with data preparation, which is the initial step in data examination following review of the conceptual framework.

DATA PREPARATION

After data have been collected and before they are analysed, the researcher must examine them to ensure their completeness and validity. Blank responses, referred to as **missing data**, must be dealt with in some way. If the questions were precoded then they can be input into a database. If they were not precoded then a system must be developed so they can be coded for input into the database. The typical tasks are editing, dealing with missing data, coding, transformation, and entering data. We discuss each of these.

Editing

Before survey data can be used they must be **edited**. This means the data must be inspected for completeness and consistency. Some inconsistencies can be corrected at this point. For example, a respondent may have not answered the question on marriage. But in other questions the respondent's answers indicated that he or she had been married 10 years and had three children all under the age of 18. In such cases the researcher may choose to fill in the unanswered marriage question. Of course, this has some risk because the individual may have recently been divorced or in some instances individuals choose to have children but not be married. If this is true, researchers would be introducing bias in the data if they chose to mark the married category. Thus, if possible it is always best to contact individuals to complete missing responses.

Editing also involves checking to see if respondents understood the question or followed a particular sequence that they were supposed to follow in a branching question. For example, assume the researcher is conducting a study about two types of work situations. One situation describes a supportive work environment and the other a work environment with little or no support from management. To verify that a respondent interpreted the description of the work environment properly the researcher may do what is called a **"manipulation" check**. That is, after respondents have answered the questions they are asked to comment on the level of management support in the two work environments. If the respondents indicate both work environments are equally supportive it means they did not understand the differences in the two work situations. In such situations, the researcher may choose to remove those particular respondents from the data analysis because they did not see the difference in the two work environments.

Finally, editing may result in the elimination of questionnaires. For example, if there is a large proportion of missing data then the entire questionnaire may have to be removed from the database. The general rule of thumb for eliminating an entire questionnaire is when the proportion of missing data exceeds 10% of the total responses. Similarly, a screening question may indicate you want to interview only persons who own their own home. But the response on a completed questionnaire may say a particular respondent is a renter. In such cases, the questionnaire must not be included in the data analysis. We talk about how to deal with missing data in the next section.

Missing Data

Business researchers almost always have missing data, whether from surveys or internal sources such as data warehouses. Missing data can impact the validity of the researcher's findings and therefore must be identified and the problems resolved. Missing data typically arise because of data collection or data entry problems. The business researcher must assess how widespread the missing data problem is and whether it is systematic or random. If the problem is of limited scope, the typical solution is to simply eliminate respondents and/or questions with missing data. When missing data are more widespread the researcher must deal with it because by removing respondents with missing data the sample size may become too small to provide meaningful results. In the Samouel's restaurant survey, a total of 71 employee surveys were completed. But seven employee surveys had missing data on one or more of the questions, and the proportion of missing data exceeded 15%. In this case, we chose to simply remove the seven surveys with missing data and work with the remaining 63 interviews.

We will cover two approaches to deal with missing data, although other alternatives are possible.[1] The first approach is to identify the respondents and variables that have a large proportion (10% or more) of missing data points. These respondents and/or variables are then eliminated from the analysis. The second approach is to estimate the missing values by substituting the mean.

Unfortunately this is only appropriate for metrically measured variables. When nonmetric variables have missing data the respondent/question must be eliminated from the analysis in most situations.

One approach to replacing missing values is to calculate the mean and input it to your data file. Another approach is to use the SPSS software which has a procedure for substituting the mean before any data analysis. To do so, go to the Transform pull down menu, scroll down and click on Replace Missing Values. Highlight and move variables with missing data into the box. Several methods of replacement are possible but we recommend you use the default, which is Series mean, and then click OK.

Coding and Data Entry

Responses must be coded either before or after the data are collected. If at all possible, it is best to code them ahead of time. Coding means a number is assigned to a particular response so the answer can be entered into a database. For example, if we are using a 5-point Agree – Disagree scale then we must decide if Strongly Agree will be coded with a 5 or a 1. Most researchers will assign the largest number to Strongly Agree and the smallest to Strongly Disagree; e.g., a 5 = Strongly Agree and a 1 = Strongly Disagree, with the points in between being assigned 2, 3 or 4. A special situation arises when the researcher has a two-category variable like gender. Some researchers use a coding approach that assigns a 1 = male and a 2 = female. But we recommend that in such instances a coding approach be used that assigns a 1 to one of the categories and a 0 to the other category. This enables greater flexibility in data analysis and is referred to as using dummy variable coding. We discuss this approach in Chapter 14.

When interviews are completed using a computer-assisted approach, the responses are entered directly into the database. When self-completed questionnaires are used it is good to use a scanner sheet because then responses can be directly scanned into the database. In other instances, however, the raw data must be manually keyed into the database using a PC. Most popular software includes a data editor similar to a spreadsheet that can be used to enter, edit and view the contents of the database. Missing values typically are represented by a dot (.) in a cell so they must be coded in a special way as was indicated earlier.

Human errors can occur when completing the questionnaire, when coding it or during data entry. Therefore, at least 10% of the coded questionnaires as well as the actual database typically are checked for possible coding or data entry errors. Selecting questionnaires to be checked usually involves a systematic, random sampling process.

Data Transformation

Data transformation is the process of changing the original form of data to a new format. This is typically done to understand the data more easily or achieve some other research objective. For example, with measurement scales we often have both negatively and positively worded statements. In such cases, the researcher typically will reverse code the questions that are negatively worded so a summated scale can be calculated to interpret the results. That is, if a 5-point scale is used a 5 will be transformed to a 1, a 4 to a 2, and so on (a 3 does not have to be changed). Another situation that might require transformation is when data are collected on the respondent's age. Generally less response bias is associated when respondents are asked what year they were born in rather than how old they are. In such cases, the researcher would simply transform the birth year into the age of the respondent.

Researchers may also choose to collapse or combine adjacent categories of a variable in a way that reduces the number of categories. For example, the age variable may be collapsed to respondents aged 30 years and younger, versus those older than 30 years. Similarly, a 7-point Agree – Disagree scale may be reduced to a 3-point scale by combining the 5, 6 and 7 responses and the 1, 2 and 3 responses. The 4 responses would remain the middle or neutral category.

Another important data transformation involves creating new variables by re-specifying the data with logical transformations. For example, we may choose to combine Likert- scales into a summated rating. This would involve combining the scores (raw data) for several attitudinal statements into a single summated score. The **summated score** for a three-statement attitude scale is calculated as shown below:

$$\text{Summated score} = \text{variable } 1 + \text{variable } 2 + \text{variable } 3$$

Another approach the researcher could use is to calculate the **average summated score**. This involves calculating the summated score and then dividing it by the number of variables. When this approach is used the new transformed, composite variable is comparable in scaling to the original scale. For example, if we had three 5-point statements the summated score might be $4 + 4 + 5 = 13$. But if we used the average summated score the result would be $4 + 4 + 5 = 13/3 = 4.3$. The SPSS software calculates summated scores as shown in the Data Analysis box.

DATA ANALYSIS | USING SPSS TO CALCULATE SUMMATED AND AVERAGE SUMMATED SCORES

The work environment statements on the Samouel's employee survey include three measures related to the supervisor. They are variables X3, X6 and X10. To calculate the summated score, load the employee survey data (Employee Survey N = 63.sav). The click-through sequence is: TRANSFORM → COMPUTE. First type a variable name in the Target Variable box. In this case we are calculating a summated score for the supervisory statements so let's use the abbreviation SUMSUP for Summated Supervisor. Next click on the Numeric Expression box to move the cursor there. Look below at the buttons and click on the parenthesis to place it in the Numeric Expression box. Now highlight variable X_3 and click on the arrow box to move it into the parenthesis. Go to the buttons below and click on the plus (+) sign. Go back and highlight variable X_6 and click on the arrow box to move it into the parenthesis. Again click on the plus (+) sign. Finally, go back and highlight variable X_{10} and click on the arrow box to move it into the parenthesis. Next click on "OK" and you will get the summated score for the three variables. You can find it as a new variable at the far right-hand side of your data editor screen.

To calculate the average summated score, you follow the same procedure as before. This time you must type a different Target Variable name than used before. Let's use the abbreviation ASUMSUP to indicate average summated supervisor rating. After you have moved all three variables into the parentheses and before you click on OK you click the cursor to place it after the parentheses. Next go to the buttons below the Numeric Expression box and click on the slash sign (/= the division sign) to place it after the parenthesis. Now again go to the buttons below the Numeric Expression box and click on 3. You click on 3 because you are calculating the average of the three variables. Next click on "OK" and you will get the average summated score for the three variables. You can find it as a new variable at the far right-hand side of your data editor screen. ∎

DATA ANALYSIS USING DESCRIPTIVE STATISTICS

Quantitative data analysis involves one of two approaches: (1) using descriptive statistics to obtain an understanding of your data, or (2) testing hypotheses using statistical tests. In the rest of this chapter we provide an overview of descriptive data analysis. Chapters 13 and 14 describe the major statistical methods that can be used to test hypotheses.

Graphics and charts help you to understand and describe your data more easily. They also more effectively communicate complex issues and make your business research reports more visually appealing. We show you how to use frequency distributions, histograms, bar charts, pie charts and line charts, as well as measures of central tendency and dispersion.

THE FREQUENCY DISTRIBUTION

Business researchers often answer research questions based on a single variable. For example, the researcher may need to answer questions such as the following:

1. How likely is it that the employees of a particular business will search for another job? For example, are they very likely, somewhat likely, or not likely at all to search for a new job in the next six months?

2. What percentage of the patrons of a restaurant should be classified as very frequent, somewhat frequent, or infrequent users? For example, if you interview a sample of individuals as they leave a Quick Hamburger restaurant, what percentage of them come to the restaurant frequently versus infrequently?

3. What is the geographic location of customers? For example, are there more owners of Mercedes in Germany than in the US?

Questions like these can be answered by examining a table that describes the data. The table is called a frequency distribution. **Frequency distributions** examine the data one variable at a time and provide counts of the different responses for the various values of the variable. The objective of a frequency distribution is to display the number of responses associated with each value of a variable. Typically, a frequency distribution shows the variable name and description, the frequency counts for each value of the variable, and the cumulative percentages for each value associated with a variable.

Let' use our Samouel's and Gino's employee survey database to illustrate a frequency distribution. Exhibit 12-1 shows three questions from the employee survey used in many of the examples in this chapter. Note that employees were asked to indicate their feelings about working at Samouel's restaurant by responding to a 7-point Agree/Disagree scale. In the examples question 13 is labelled "Loyalty", question 14 is labelled "Effort" and 15 is labelled "Proud".

Please indicate your view on each of the following questions:

13. I have a sense of loyalty to Samouel's Restaurant.	Strongly Strongly Disagree Agree 1 2 3 4 5 6 7
14. I am willing to put in a great deal of effort beyond that normally expected to help Samouel's restaurant to be successful.	Strongly Strongly Disagree Agree 1 2 3 4 5 6 7
15. I am proud to tell others that I work for Samouel's restaurant.	Strongly Strongly Disagree Agree 1 2 3 4 5 6 7

EXHIBIT 12-1

Employee Survey Questions Used As Examples

The frequency distribution for variable X_{15} – Proud is shown in Exhibit 12-2. In the frequency distribution table, the first column with numbers in it shows the various responses (ratings) to the question. For example, responses to this question were on a 7-point scale, but the lowest rating was a 4 and the highest was a 7. The second column, labeled Frequency, is the count of the number of times a particular rating was given by respondents. In this example, a rating of 5 was given by 28 respondents. The third column, Percent, shows the percent of all respondents (N = 71) selecting the value for this variable. For example, 39.4% of the respondents gave a rating of 5 on this question (28/71 = 39.4%). The fourth column, Valid Percent, displays the percent of valid responses (N = 69). In other words, the percentage of "responses", not the percent of "respondents." For the survey there were eight respondents that had missing data on one or more of the questions. But, for this question (X_{15}) there were only 2 respondents (2.8%) with missing data. If there is no missing data the percentages in the Percent and Valid Percent columns will be the same. Cumulative Percent, the last column, is the cumulative percentage from the top to the bottom based on the valid response column. The cumulative percentage is simply the sum of the Valid Percents. In this survey, 55.1% of the respondents gave a rating of 5 or below.

Frequency distributions have many uses in business research. Frequency distributions are used to describe the responses to a particular variable by displaying the counts and percentages both before and after adjustment for nonresponses (missing data). A frequency distribution can be used to perform an "eye-ball" check of the data, and to easily determine the amount of nonresponse, if any. If a rating appears in the frequency distribution that is not a valid response the researcher can also determine when there are data inaccuracies. For example, seeing a zero on the frequency distribution in Exhibit 12-2 (where a 1–7 scale was used) would indicate a problem with the data since that rating was not possible given the coding of this variable. Cases in which ratings are out of range would be investigated and corrective actions taken. The researcher also can examine the data

X$_{15}$ – Proud

Valid Responses	Frequency	Percent	Valid Percent	Cumulative Percent
4	10	14.1	14.5	14.5
5	28	39.4	40.6	55.1
6	21	29.6	30.4	85.5
Definitely Agree = 7	10	14.1	14.5	100.0
Total	69	97.2	100.0	
Missing	2	2.8		
Total	71	100.0		

EXHIBIT 12-2

Frequency Distribution For Variable X$_{15}$ – Proud on Employee Survey With Missing Data

for each variable to see if there are any outliers – cases with extreme values that may distort the total picture. For example, an individual who eats at a Quick Hamburger restaurant more than 10 times each week would be likely to be so unusual the person may be considered an outlier.

HISTOGRAMS

A frequency distribution also provides evidence of the shape of the distribution for the variable. Are most of the responses on the high or low end of the response values? A vertical bar chart, or **histogram**, can be constructed from the information in the frequency distribution and the shape of the actual data as presented in the histogram can be compared to the expected shape. Exhibit 12-3 is a histogram for the proud variable (X$_{15}$). It shows that most employees of Samouel's restaurant are moderately proud to be working there. That is, most of the employees gave a 'Proud' rating of five, six or seven. A normal curve (bell-shaped) is superimposed over the histogram to facilitate comparison of the actual distribution with the normal curve. The distribution in this example conforms reasonably well to a normal curve. At the lower right hand corner of the graph the mean, standard deviation and sample size are indicated. Note the sample size is 69. This indicates there is missing data on this variable for two respondents.

The results shown above would be of interest to Phil Samouel, owner of Samouel's Greek Cuisine. But a comparison of the satisfaction of his customers with those of Gino's would also be of interest to him. By making this comparison he could determine if there are differences in the satisfaction levels of the customers of the two restaurants. The question used to measure satisfaction on the Samouel's and Gino's customer surveys is shown in Exhibit 12-4.

The frequency tables in Exhibit 12-5 show the customer satisfaction ratings for the two restaurants. Note that you can now compare the satisfaction ratings for the two restaurants. First go to the Frequency column and look at the Total for both Samouel's and Gino's. You will see that each total is 100 – the number of customers interviewed at each restaurant that had no missing data on their questionnaires. Now let's look at how the two customer groups responded to this question. To the far right is a column labeled Cumulative Percent. If you look at the third from the top

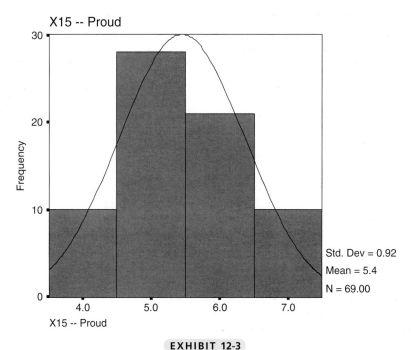

EXHIBIT 12-3

Histogram for Employee "Proud" Variable With Missing Data

Please indicate your view on the following question:

15. How satisfied are you with Samouel's/ Gino's restaurant?	Not Satisfied At All	Very Satisfied
	1 2 3 4 5 6 7	

EXHIBIT 12-4

Customer Survey Question Measuring Satisfaction

---

number in this column you will see the number 68.0 percent for Samouel's. This is the percentage of satisfaction ratings of 5.0 or lower. But when you look at Gino's you see that only 35% of his customers gave a satisfaction rating of 5 or below. These numbers tell us that Gino's customers are more satisfied than are Samouel's customers. How do we know this? It is based on the fact that Gino's customers give higher ratings on the satisfaction variable (X_{17}) than do Samouel's customers. For example, as noted earlier 68% of Samouel's customers rate his restaurant a 5 or below, while only 35% of Gino's customers rate his restaurant 5 or below. Information such as this can be very useful to business researchers, owners and managers.

X₁₇ – Satisfaction

X₂₅ – Competitor		Frequency	Percent	Valid Percent	Cumulative Percent
Samouel's	3	10	10.0	10.0	10.0
	4	42	42.0	42.0	52.0
	5	16	16.0	16.0	68.0
	6	24	24.0	24.0	92.0
	Highly Satisfied = 7	8	8.0	8.0	100.0
	Total	100	100.0	100.0	
Gino's	4	7	7.0	7.0	7.0
	5	28	28.0	28.0	35.0
	6	27	27.0	27.0	62.0
	Highly Satisfied = 7	38	38.0	38.0	100.0
	Total	100	100.0	100.0	

EXHIBIT 12-5

Frequency Table Comparing Samouel's and Gino's

Visual comparisons using a histogram of the satisfaction ratings of the two restaurants make it even easier to compare the ratings. A histogram simply takes the information in a frequency table and displays it in a chart. We quickly see from Exhibit 12-6 that Samouel's has very few ratings of 7 (Highly Satisfied) and Gino's has many. Moreover, Samouel's has many ratings of 4 while Gino's has very few ratings of 4. Thus, it is easy to see that Gino's customers are more highly satisfied than are Samouel's.

BAR CHARTS

Bar charts show the data in the form of bars that can be displayed either horizontally or vertically (the only difference between a bar chart and a histogram is that there is no space between the bars in a histogram). Bar charts are very useful for showing both absolute and relative magnitudes, and for comparing differences. Exhibit 12-7 is an example of a vertical bar chart for the distribution of responses to a question in the Samouel's employee survey (X₁₅ – Proud). The question asked how proud an employee is that she/he worked at Samouel's restaurant. Respondents rated the question using a 7-point scale where 7 = Definitely Agree and 1 = Definitely Disagree. For example, the frequency (10) for the value of Definitely Agree = 7 is the vertical bar on the right side of the chart. This chart shows that a moderately high proportion of Samouel's employees are proud to work there (a high proportion of employees responded with a five, six or seven on the 7-point scale). Note that none of the responses were lower than a four on the 7-point scale.

PIE CHARTS

Pie charts display relative proportions of the responses. Each section of the pie is the relative proportion. That is, the pie sections are shown as a percentage of the total area of the pie. In

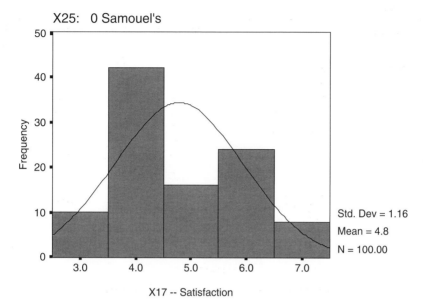

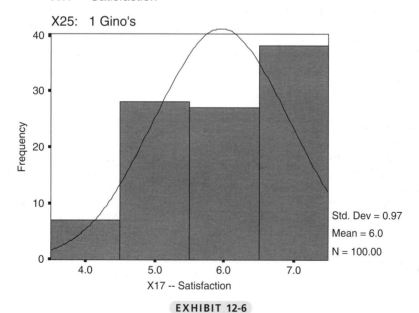

EXHIBIT 12-6

Histograms Comparing Samouel's and Gino's Restaurants

Exhibit 12-8 there is a pie chart for variable X_{15} – Proud in the Samouel's employee survey. Generally, six or seven sections in a pie chart are considered the maximum possible, and three to four is ideal.

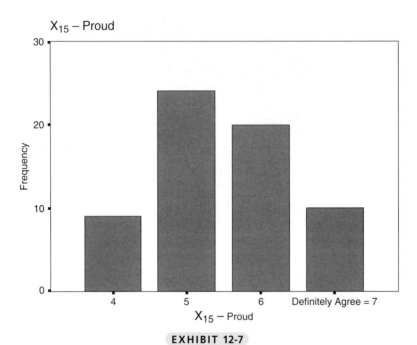

X_{15} – Proud

EXHIBIT 12-7

Bar Chart and Frequency Table for Variable X_{15} – Proud to Work at Samouel's

X_{15} – Proud

Response	Frequency	Percent	Valid Percent	Cumulative Percent
4	9	14.3	14.3	14.3
5	24	38.1	38.1	52.4
6	20	31.7	31.7	84.1
Definitely Agree = 7	10	15.9	15.9	100.0
Total	63	100.0	100.0	

   The pie chart is another way to present data visually. The proportion of Samouel's employees that indicated they were very proud to work there (responded with a 5, 6 or 7) was very high – over 80%. Check out the Research in Action box for an interesting historical perspective on the pie chart.

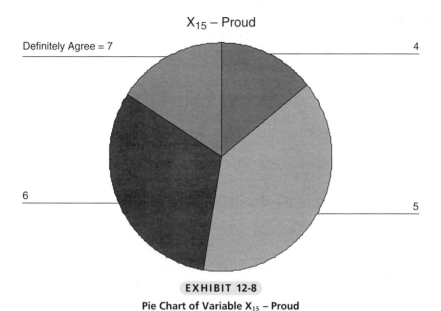

EXHIBIT 12-8

Pie Chart of Variable X$_{15}$ – Proud

RESEARCH IN ACTION

FLORENCE NIGHTINGALE AND THE PIE CHART

Florence Nightingale is best remembered as the mother of modern nursing. Few realize, however, that she also occupies a place in history for her use of graphical methods to convey complex statistical information.

After witnessing deplorable sanitary conditions in the Crimea, she wrote *Notes on Matters Affecting the Health, Efficiency and Hospital Administration of the British Army* (1858), which included colourful polar-area diagrams where statistics being represented were proportional to the area of a wedge in a circular diagram. These charts visually illustrated that far more deaths were attributable to nonbattle causes such as unsanitary conditions than to battle related causes.

With this information, Nightingale helped to promote the idea that social phenomena could be objectively measured and subjected to mathematical analysis. And through this statistical approach, Nightingale convinced military authorities, Parliament and Queen Victoria to carry out her proposed hospital reforms – which resulted in a decline in the mortality rate for soldiers.

As Nightingale demonstrated, statistics provided an organized way of learning and led to improvements in medical and surgical practices. She also developed a Model

Hospital Statistical Form that could be used to collect and generate consistent data and statistics. She became a Fellow of the Royal Statistical Society in 1858, an honorary member of the American Statistical Association in 1874 and has been acknowledged as a "prophetess" in the development of applied statistics.

Sources: www.math.yorku.ca/SCS/Gallery/flo.html, http://en.wikipedia.org/wiki/ Pie_chart, and http://mathworld.wolfram.com/PieChart.html, accessed June 2006. ■

The numbers and percentages in our restaurant examples show how customers and employees rate various aspects of the restaurant operations. Because numbers were involved, frequency distributions, bar charts and pie charts all can be used to display descriptive statistics. We next discuss the normal curve and then measures of central tendency and dispersion.

THE NORMAL DISTRIBUTION

One of the most useful distributions for business researchers is the normal distribution, also called the normal curve. The **normal distribution** describes the expected distribution of sample means as well as many other chance occurrences. For sufficiently large samples (typically a sample size of 30 or more), the normal curve is symmetrical, bell shaped and almost all (99%) of its values are within plus/minus three standard deviations from its mean. An example of a normal curve is shown in Exhibit 12-9. Note that 68% of the values are within plus/minus one standard deviation and 95% are within plus/minus two standard deviations. The normal distribution is particularly important because it provides the underlying basis for many of the inferences made by business researchers who collect data using sampling. For example, recall that the mean satisfaction rating for Samouel's customers was 4.8 and the standard deviation was 0.116. Using this information we can be 95% confident that the average satisfaction rating for all of Samouel's customers is between a low of 4.57 and a high of 5.03 (two standard deviations around the mean).

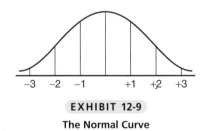

EXHIBIT 12-9

The Normal Curve

MEASURES OF CENTRAL TENDENCY

Frequency distribution tables are easy to read and provide a great deal of basic information about your data. Many times, however, researchers need to summarize and condense information to better understand it. Measures of central tendency can be used to do this. The mean, median, and mode are measures of central tendency. Measures of central tendency locate the centre of the distribution as well as other useful information.

Mean

The **mean** is the arithmetic average, and is one of the most commonly used measures of central tendency. For example, if you are interested in knowing the daily consumption of soft drinks, you can calculate the mean (average) number soft drinks an individual drinks each day. The mean can be used when your data is measured with either an interval or a ratio scale (also called metric). The data typically shows some degree of central tendency with most of the responses distributed close to the average, or mean value.

In most instances the mean is not sensitive to data values being added or deleted. For this reason, statisticians say it is a "robust" measure of central tendency. If extreme values (referred to as outliers) occur in the distribution, however, the mean can misrepresent the true characteristics of the data. For example, suppose you ask four individuals how many Cokes they drink in a single day. Respondent answers are as follows: Respondent A = 1 coke; Respondent B = 10; Respondent C = 5; and Respondent D = 6. In addition, you have observed that respondents A and B are females and respondents B and C are males. With this knowledge, you now can compare consumption of Cokes between males and females. Looking at the females first (Respondents A and B) we calculate the mean number of Cokes to be 5.5 (1 + 10 = 11/2 = 5.5). Similarly, looking at the males next (Respondents C and D) we calculate the mean number of Cokes to be 5.5 (5 + 6 = 11/2 = 5.5). We could conclude there are no differences in the consumption patterns of males and females if we consider only the mean number of Cokes consumed per day. But if we consider the underlying distribution, it is obvious there are some differences. The two females are at the extremes while both males are in the middle of the distribution. Drawing conclusions based only on the mean can distort our understanding of the Coke consumption patterns of males and females in situations like the above. Of course, we must also consider that in the example above we were referring to a small sample and as the sample size increases the ability to accurately infer to the larger population improves. So sample size must be considered as well in drawing conclusions about distributions and their characteristics, such as means.

The mean is most often used with interval or ratio data (metric). But as noted above, when extreme values occur within the data the mean can distort the results. In those situations, the median and the mode should be considered to represent your research findings.

Median

The next measure of central tendency, the **median**, is the value that is in the middle of the distribution. In other words, the median is the value below (and above) which half the values in the sample distribution fall. For this reason, it is sometimes referred to as the 50th percentile. For example, let's assume you interviewed a sample of individuals about the number of soft drinks they drink in a typical week. You might find the median number of soft drinks consumed is 10, with the number of soft drinks consumed above and below this number being the same (the median number is the exact middle of the distribution). If you have an even number of data observations, the median is the average of the two middle values. If you have an odd number of observations, the median is the middle value. The median is the appropriate measure of central tendency for ordinal data.

Mode

The **mode** is the measure of central tendency that identifies the value that occurs most often in the sample distribution. For example, the typical individual may drink an average of three Cokes per day, but the number of Cokes that most people drink is only two (the mode). The mode is the value that represents the highest peak in the distribution's graph. The mode is the appropriate measure of central tendency for data that is nominal (categorical).

EXAMPLES OF MEASURES OF CENTRAL TENDENCY

The statistics table in Exhibit 12-10 contains the measures of central tendency for the 63 employee surveys with no missing data. Note that the mean is 5.49, the median is 5.0, the mode is 5 and there is no missing data. Since this variable is measured on a 7-point scale, with 1 = Definitely Disagree and 7 = Definitely Agree, this shows that employees feel very proud to work at Samouel's (the middle of the 7-point scale = 4).

X_{15} – Proud		
N	Valid	63
	Missing	0
Mean		5.49
Median		5.00
Mode		5

EXHIBIT 12-10

Measures of Central Tendency for X_{15} – Proud Statistics

Next look at the histogram in Exhibit 12-11. We have imposed a normal curve on the chart to enable you to compare the responses to it. The chart visually shows you the lowest point on the 7-point scale for X_{15} – Proud is 4 and the highest is 7. It also shows the distribution is fairly normal and does not represent a problem.

MEASURES OF DISPERSION

Measures of central tendency seldom give a complete picture of a sample distribution. For example, if The Gaucho Grill in London collects data about customers' attitudes toward a new steak sandwich, you could calculate the mean, median, and mode of the distribution of answers. But you also might want to know if there is much variability in the respondent's opinions about the steak sandwich. For example, recall our discussion of the mean and Coke consumption where males and females averaged the same consumption, but females were very high and very low in the distribution and males were in the middle. If The Gaucho Grill's survey of attitudes toward the new steak sandwich is very consistent (little variation) and on the positive end of the scale, they would likely be pleased. On the other hand, if the responses varied from the very low extreme (negative) to the very high extreme (positive) they would want to investigate the new sandwich more before adding it to their menu. Specifically, they would want to know why there are negative responses (very low extreme) and what could be done to eliminate or minimize them. You can learn more about this problem by examining the measures of dispersion associated with the distribution of sample responses on the customer survey.

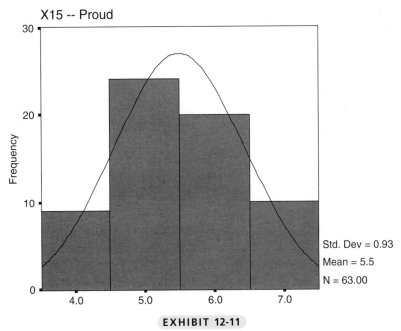

EXHIBIT 12-11

Histogram with Normal Curve for X₁₅ – Proud

   Measures of dispersion describe the tendency for sample responses to depart from the central tendency. Calculating the dispersion of the data, or how the responses vary from the mean, is another means of summarizing the data. Typical measures of dispersion used to describe the variability in a distribution of numbers include the range, the variance, the standard deviation, skewness and kurtosis.

Range

The **range** is the simplest measure of dispersion. It defines the spread of the data and is the distance between the largest and the smallest values of a sample frequency distribution. We also can define the range by saying it identifies the end-points of the sample distribution. For example, if The Gaucho Grill's survey of opinions about a new steak sandwich asked the likelihood of purchasing the sandwich using a 10-point scale and the highest likelihood rating is 8 and the lowest rating is 1, the range is seven ($8 - 1 = 7$).

Variance

To determine how far away a respondent is from the mean we can calculate individual deviation scores for each respondent. If the deviation scores are large, we will find that the distribution has a wide spread or variability. The problem with deviation scores is that when we try to calculate an average deviation for all respondents the positive deviation scores always cancel out the negative ones, thus leaving an average deviation value of zero. To eliminate this problem we can square the deviation scores and then calculate the average. The result is a measure called the **variance**. It is useful to describe the variability of the distribution and is a very good index of the degree of dispersion. The variance is equal to zero if each and every respondent in the distribution is the same as the mean. The variance becomes larger as the observations tend to differ increasingly from each other and from the mean.

Standard Deviation

The variance is used often in statistics. But it does have a major drawback. The variance is a unit of measurement that has been squared. For example, if we measure the number of Cokes consumed in a day and wish to calculate an average for the sample of respondents, the mean will be the average number of Cokes and the variance will be in squared numbers. To overcome the problem of having the measure of dispersion in squared units instead of the original measurement units, we use the square root of the variance, which is called the standard deviation. The **standard deviation** describes the spread or variability of the sample distribution values from the mean, and is perhaps the most valuable index of dispersion.

To obtain the squared deviation we square the individual deviation scores before adding them (squaring a negative number produces a positive result). Once the sum of the squared deviations is determined, it is divided by the number of respondents minus 1. The number 1 is subtracted from the number of respondents to help produce an unbiased estimate of the standard deviation. If the estimated standard deviation is large, the responses in a sample distribution of numbers do not fall very close to the mean of the distribution. If the estimated standard deviation is small, you know that the distribution values are close to the mean.

Another way to think about the estimated standard deviation is that its size tells us something about the level of agreement among the respondents when they answered a particular question. For example, in Samouel's employee survey, respondents were asked to indicate their loyalty and pride about working at Samouels Greek Cuisine (X_{13} and X_{15}) using a 7-point scale. If the estimated standard deviation of these two variables is small (<1.0) it means the respondents were very consistent in their opinions about working at Samouel's. In contrast, if the estimated standard deviation of these two variables is large (>3.0) then there is a lot of variability in their opinions.

One final concept to be clarified is the standard error of the mean. The standard deviation of the sampling distribution of the mean is referred to as the **standard error of the mean**. When we have information on the population we can determine the standard deviation. Since we seldom have population information we typically draw a sample and estimate the standard deviation. When we draw only one sample we refer to this as the estimated standard deviation. When we draw many samples from the same population we have a sampling distribution of all the possible values of the sample means. The standard deviation of this distribution of means is the standard error of the mean.

Skewness and Kurtosis

We often are interested in the shape of our distribution. Two measures we typically look at are skewness and kurtosis. **Skewness** measures the departure from a symmetrical (or balanced) distribution. In a symmetrical distribution the mean, median and mode are in the same location. A distribution that has respondents stretching toward one tail or the other is called skewed. When the tail stretches to the left (smaller values) it is negatively skewed. When the tail stretches to the right (larger values) it is skewed positively. When a distribution is symmetrical the skewness is zero, and the larger the number the larger the skewness. With a positive skew we get a positive number and with a negative skew we get a negative number. When skewness values are larger than +1 or smaller than −1 this indicates a substantially skewed distribution.

Kurtosis is a measure of a distribution's peakedness (or flatness). Distributions where responses cluster heavily in the centre are peaked. Distributions with scores more widely distributed and tails further apart are considered flat. For a normal curve the value of kurtosis is zero. A large positive value means the distribution is too peaked while a large negative value means the distribution is too flat. A curve is too peaked when the kurtosis exceeds +3 and is too flat when it is below −3.

Measures of central tendency and dispersion can reveal a lot about the distribution of a set of numbers from a survey. Business researchers often are interested, however, in solving research problems involving more than one variable at a time. We will explain how to do this in later chapters.

EXAMPLES OF MEASURES OF DISPERSION

The measures of dispersion for X_{15} − Proud on Samouel's employee survey are shown in Exhibit 12-12. The highest response on the 7-point scale is a 7 (maximum) and the lowest response is a 4 (minimum). None of the respondents gave a 1, 2, or 3 on this question. The range is calculated as the distance between the smallest and the largest values in the set of responses and is three (7 − 4 = 3). The standard deviation is 0.931 and the variance is 0.867. A standard deviation of. 931 on a 7-point scale is relatively small and indicates the responses are reasonably close to the sample mean of 5.49.

X_{15} − Proud	
Valid N	63
Missing	0
Std. Deviation	.931
Variance	.867
Skewness	.086
Std. Error of Skewness	.302
Kurtosis	−.809
Std. Error of Kurtosis	.595
Range	3
Minimum	4
Maximum	7

EXHIBIT 12-12

Measures of Dispersion for X_{15} − Proud Statistics

OUTLIERS

An outlier is a respondent (observation) that has one or more values that are distinctly different from the values of other respondents. Like missing data, outliers can impact the validity of the researcher's findings and therefore must be identified and dealt with as well. Outliers may result from data collection or data entry errors. Data collection or data entry outliers typically are identified and corrected in the data-cleaning phase of the research project. Another type of outlier may be an accurate observation that represents the true characteristics of the population, but still distorts the findings. For example, if we calculated the average net worth of the households located in the neighbourhood where Bill Gates of Microsoft lives, the resulting average would be much higher with Gates included as opposed to being eliminated, because his extremely high net worth makes him an outlier. Certainly Gates neighbours are wealthy, but they have a far smaller net worth than does he. In this situation, the question would be "Is the average net worth of households in Bill Gates' neighbourhood more representative with him included or excluded?" The answer here is it depends upon the research objectives. The true average would include Bill Gates. But removing him would be much more representative of the typical net worth in the neighbourhood. See the Research in Action box to demonstrate this point.

RESEARCH IN ACTION   IS BILL GATES AN OUTLIER?

Bill Gates lives in Medina, Washington near Seattle. The number of households in the town of Medina is 1,206. His net worth and that of the next two most wealthy individuals in his town is shown below. The net worth for his town changes dramatically when he is removed from the calculation of average net worth of the town of Medina. It changes even more when the other two individuals are removed from the calculation.

Is Bill Gates an outlier?

Individual	Net Worth – $	Source
Bill Gates	46.0 billion	Microsoft
Jeff Bezos	5.1 billion	Amazon.com
Craig McCaw	2.0 billion	Telecommunications

Number of households, Medina, Washington $= 1,206$
Average Net Worth (1206 households) $= \$44,253,482$
Average Net Worth (remove Bill Gates) $= \$6,115,934$
Average Net Worth (remove top three) $= \$224,189$

Source: Calculated from *Forbes*, 2003 and US Census data.■

A final type of outlier is a respondent(s) that has one or more values that are unique, but there is no apparent reason (with the Bill Gates example we knew the reason, here we do not). In cases like this, if the researcher cannot determine the outlier represents a valid segment of the population it must be removed. For more information on the nature of outliers and how to deal with them see.[2]

CONTINUING CASE   USING DESCRIPTIVE STATISTICS
                        WITH THE SAMOUEL'S RESTAURANT
                        EMPLOYEE SURVEY

As you learned in Chapter 9, the employees of Samouel's Greek Cuisine were interviewed as part of the research studies conducted by the consultant. On the Web site of this text (www.wileyeurope.com/college/hair) there is a dataset that has the responses of the employee survey. It is named Employee Database_UK edition. Start your computer, load the SPSS statistical software, and download the database from the Web site. While you are getting the employee survey database, download and save the customer survey titled Customer Database_UK edition.

   When the employee database is loaded, run bar charts for the following variables – X_4, X_6, X_{13}, X_{16}, and X_{21}. What did you learn about Samouel's employees? Are there some indications that Phil Samouel should be concerned about? If yes, explain why. ■

SUMMARY

■ **Describe the process for conducting quantitative data analysis**

Many research projects have data that can be quantified to enable research questions to be answered. Quantitative data are measurements in which numbers are used to directly represent the properties of some phenomena. To be useful the data need to be analysed and interpreted. Data analysis in quantitative research involves the following series of steps: (1) review conceptual framework and proposed relationships; (2) prepare data for analysis; (3) determine if research involves descriptive analysis or hypothesis testing; (4) conduct analysis; and (5) evaluate findings to assess whether they are meaningful.

■ **Understand the importance of data preparation**

After data have been collected and before they are analysed, the researcher must examine them to ensure its validity. Blank responses, referred to as missing data, must be dealt with in some way. If the questions were precoded then they can simply be input into a database. If they were not precoded then a system must be developed so they can be input into the database. The typical tasks involved are editing, dealing with missing data, coding, transformation, and entering data.

■ **Explain how descriptive statistics enable you to better understand your data**

Descriptive statistics such as graphics and charts help you to more easily understand your data. They not only add clarity but also impact to research reports. The most often used charts and graphs include frequency distributions, bar charts, pie charts and line charts.

Measures of central tendency enable researchers to summarize and condense information to better understand it. The mean, median and mode are measures of central tendency. Measures of central tendency locate the centre of the distribution as well as other useful information.

Measures of dispersion describe the tendency for responses to depart from the central tendency (mean, median and mode). Calculating the dispersion of the data, or how the responses vary from the mean, is another means of summarizing the data. Typical measures of dispersion used to describe the variability in a distribution of numbers include the range, the variance, the standard deviation, skewness and kurtosis.

■ Clarify how to identify and deal with outliers

When you have outliers, as well as observations with missing data, you must decide whether to retain or eliminate them. The most conservative approach is to eliminate them to avoid distorting or misrepresenting your findings. If you retain them, you must have a valid reason for doing so. This is also true if you decide to replace the missing data with an estimate of the value and then retain them in your analysis. Retaining observations with missing or replaced data is risky and must be done cautiously. ■

Ethical Dilemma

Ann Webster is a sales analyst for Sainsbury's. The company is planning its annual meeting and Ann's boss has asked her to prepare visuals for the company's performance presentation. The company president is planning to downplay the fact that the company's overall sales are slipping by focusing on the performance of the company's top five stores. Therefore, Ann is asked to prepare separate bar charts for each of the top stores listing the sales quarters in ascending order and to prepare a bar chart of the overall sales figures with sales quarter in descending order. Although the data will be factual, Ann realizes that the graphics could mislead board members. What should she do?

REVIEW QUESTIONS

1. What are the steps in analysing qualitative data?

2. Why is it necessary to prepare data before analysing them?

3. How can frequency distributions help us to better understand our data?

4. How do measures of central tendency differ from measures of dispersion?

5. What is an outlier?

DISCUSSION AND APPLICATION ACTIVITIES

1. Why would the business researcher want to use charts and graphs?

2. What is the value of measures of central tendency and dispersion?

3. Why are missing data and outliers a problem?

4. **SPSS Application:** Examine all the variables in the employee database using histograms, skewness and range to determine if you have any problems with the data.

INTERNET EXERCISES   WWW

1. The SPSS statistical software package has a home page at www.spss.com. Go to their Web site and identify and summarize the statistical techniques that can be used with the activities in this chapter.

2. The home page for the American Statistical Association is www.amstat.org. Go to their Web site and identify and summarize the career options that one might have if they are interested in statistics.

3. Go to www.yankelovich.com. Prepare a report summarizing the MONITOR. How can business researchers use the data from this research?

4. Go to www.acop.com. Prepare a report summarizing the Web site and the types of surveys being completed.

5. Go to http://www.shodor.org/interactivate/activities/piechart/. Prepare a report explaining how the information helps you to better understand pie charts.

NOTES

1. Hair, J. F., Black, B. Babin, B., Anderson, R. and Tatham, R. (2006). *Multivariate Data Analysis*, 6th edn. London, Prentice-Hall.
2. Ibid.

CHAPTER 13
TESTING HYPOTHESES

CONTENTS

LEARNING OUTCOMES

- Understand how to represent hypothesized relationships for testing.
- Clarify the difference between sample statistics and population parameters.
- Describe how to choose the appropriate statistical technique to test hypotheses.
- Explain when and how to use the t-test, ANOVA and Chi square to examine hypotheses.

INTRODUCTION

Data become knowledge only after analysis has confirmed that a set of proposed relationships can be used to improve business decision making. In quantitative research we examine hypothesized relationships to see what kinds of conclusions are appropriate. Examples of relationships that would be of interest to business researchers include:

- The Mercedes division of Daimler–Chrysler wants to confirm what types of individuals will respond favorably to the new Mercedes SL 600 line of cars.

- The *Daily Telegraph* wants information about who reads its newspaper and who does not so it can either add or delete sections to increase circulation.

- Nokia wants to know which factors are likely to increase productivity on its production lines.

- Companies want to know if there is a difference in preference for flexitime in the workplace between female and male workers?

- Organizations would like to know whether offering employee profit sharing schemes will result in higher worker productivity?

In this chapter we first show you several conceptual models of relationships that can be tested using the Samouel's databases. These conceptual models will help you to better understand how relationships in any type of business research can be tested using statistics. Next we review and explain the relationship between sample statistics and population parameters, and how to select the appropriate statistical test. We then cover several univariate and bivariate statistics that can be used to test hypotheses. The software package SPSS is used to illustrate hypothesis testing.

UNDERSTANDING HYPOTHESIZED RELATIONSHIPS

Measures of central tendency and dispersion provide an overview of research results. But researchers often want to test one or more hypotheses. Statistical techniques enable us to determine whether the proposed hypotheses can be confirmed by the empirical evidence. Consider the two conceptual models for the Samouel's Employee database shown in Exhibit 13-1. The models are based on organizational behaviour theory and display relationships between a single dependent variable and two independent variables. The dependent variable for Model a. is Loyalty and it is measured by a single variable (X_{13} in the dataset). The dependent variable for Model b. is Intention to Search and it too is measured by a single variable (X_{16} in the dataset). Both models have the same independent variables – supervision and workgroups. Recall from our earlier discussion that constructs typically are made up of several variables. Constructs are preferable in testing hypotheses because the multiple variables are more valid and reliable measures of a concept. When you examine the Samouel's employee database, you will see that the supervision construct is measured by three variables – X_3, X_6 and X_{10}, and the work group construct is measured by three other variables – X_4, X_8 and X_{11}. These six variables are not shown in the exhibit but can be found in the listing of variables for the survey in Chapter 9.

The conceptual models display several testable hypotheses. The hypotheses for Model a. are: "More favourable perceptions of supervision and work groups are associated with higher loyalty." The hypotheses for Model b. are: "More favourable perceptions of supervision and work groups are

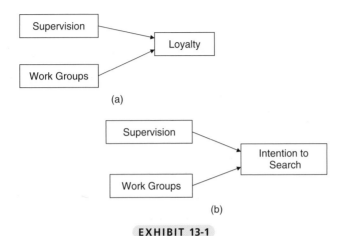

EXHIBIT 13-1

Conceptual Models – Samouel's Employee Survey

associated with lower intention to search for another job." These are directional hypotheses – for Model a. the dependent variable is positively related to the two independent variables, and for Model b. the dependent variable is negatively related to the two independent variables.

In this chapter we will show you how to use statistical tools to test empirically whether hypothesized relationships can be confirmed as being true. We also explain how to determine if these relationships differ between groups, such as male employees versus female employees. Exhibit 13-2 lists the steps in developing and testing quantitative hypotheses.

1. State the null and alternative hypotheses.

2. Make a judgement about the sampling distribution of the population and then select the appropriate statistical test based upon whether you believe the data are parametric or nonparametric.

3. Decide upon the desired level of significance ($p = <0.05$, <0.01, or something else).

4. Collect the data from the sample and compute the appropriate test statistic to see if the level of significance is met.

5. Accept or reject the null hypothesis. That is, determine whether the deviation of the sample value from the expected value would have occurred by chance alone, for example, 5 times out of 100.

6. Evaluate your findings to determine if they are meaningful.

EXHIBIT 13-2

Steps in Hypothesis Development and Testing in Quantitative Research

SAMPLE STATISTICS VERSUS POPULATION PARAMETERS

Inferential statistics helps us to make judgements about the population from a sample. A sample is a small subset of the total number of respondents in a population. For example, in the Samouel's employee survey the sample of 63 respondents is used to project to all of his employees. Similarly, for the customer survey the sample of 100 Samouel's respondents is used to project to all customers of Samouel's Greek Cuisine and the sample of 100 Gino's respondents is used to project to all customers of Gino's Italian Ristorante.

We use different terminology to refer to characteristics of the sample than we do to refer to characteristics of the population. **Sample statistics** are the characteristics computed from the sample. **Population parameters** are the characteristics of the population. We use sample statistics to estimate population parameters because we only have data from the sample. An example of a sample statistic would be: the number of glasses of wine the sample of 100 Samouel's customers said they drink. Similarly, it might be the number of cups of Starbucks coffee consumed by a sample of students in a survey at the London School of Economics, or the percentage of individuals in a sample from Ireland who say they prefer Guinness stout over lager, compared to a sample of Germans who likely would say they prefer lager over ale. The sample statistic is based on the sample data but is used to estimate the population parameter. The actual population parameters seldom are known since the cost to conduct a census of the population is very high.

A **null hypothesis** concerns a population parameter, not a sample statistic. Based on the sample data, the business researcher can reject the null hypothesis or accept the alternative hypothesis. In other words, the researcher can conclude either there is a meaningful relationship between two population variables or there is no meaningful relationship. If there is no meaningful relationship, the researcher would not detect any significant relationship between the two variables.

In business research the null hypothesis is developed so that by rejecting it we accept what we think is correct – the **alternative hypothesis**. Using our Samouel's employee survey data, an example of a null hypothesis is: No relationship exists between supervision and loyalty. The alternative hypothesis is: A relationship exists between supervision and loyalty. In statistical terminology, the null hypothesis is notated as H_0 and the alternative hypothesis is notated as H_1. If the null hypothesis H_0 is rejected then the alternative hypothesis H_1 is accepted.

TYPE I AND TYPE II ERRORS

There is always a risk that the inference a researcher draws about a population from the sample may be incorrect. In business research error can never be completely avoided. Thus, statistical tests the researcher performs to accept or reject the null hypothesis may be incorrect. Two types of errors are associated with hypothesis testing. The first type of error is termed Type I. **Type I error**, referred to as alpha (α), occurs when the sample results lead to rejection of the null hypothesis when it is true. In the Samouel's customer survey, a Type I error would occur if we concluded, based on the sample data, that satisfaction with Samouel's and Gino's is different when in fact it is the same. The probability of this type of error (α), also referred to as the level of significance, is the amount of risk the researcher is willing to accept. Thus, the level of significance is the probability of making an error by rejecting the null hypothesis.

Depending on the situation, business researchers typically consider <0.05 an acceptable level of significance. The proper interpretation of <0.05 is that a researcher is willing to accept the risk of making five errors out of every 100 decisions made as to whether a hypothesis can be accepted or should be rejected. The researcher is willing therefore to accept some risk they will incorrectly reject the null hypothesis. But the level of risk is specified before the research project is carried out.

If the research situation involves testing relationships where the risk of making a mistake is very costly, the researcher would specify a higher level of significance, for example, <0.01. For example, in examining the relationship between two chemicals that might explode, or the failure rate of an expensive piece of equipment, such as an aircraft engine, the researcher would not be willing to take very much risk. On the other hand, when examining behavioural or attitudinal relationships where the risk generally is less costly, then the researcher is willing to take more risk. In some situations, the researcher may even accept a 0.10 level of significance.

The second type of error is referred to as Type II error. **Type II error** occurs when, based on the sample results, the null hypothesis is not rejected when it is in fact false. Type II error is generally referred to as beta (β) error. The researcher specifies the alpha error ahead of time, but the beta error is based on the population parameter (that is, mean or proportion). This concept is summarized in the table below:

	H_0 is true	H_0 is false
Accept H_0	X	Type II
Reject H_0	Type I	X

A third important concept in testing hypotheses for statistical significance is the **statistical power** of the test. The power of a test is the ability to reject the null hypothesis when it in fact the null hypothesis is false. The statistical power of a test can be described as $(1 - \beta)$, the probability of correctly rejecting the null. The probability of a Type II error is unknown, but it is related to the probability of a Type I error. Extremely low levels of α will result in a high level of β error, thus it is necessary to reach an acceptable compromise between the two types of error. Sample size can help control Type I and Type II errors. Generally, the researcher will select the α and the sample size in order to increase the power of the test and to minimize α and β.

HYPOTHESIS TESTING

After the researcher has developed the hypotheses and selected an acceptable level of risk (statistical significance), the next step is to test the hypotheses. In this section we discuss the statistics used to actually test hypotheses. Firstly, we tell you how to select the appropriate statistical technique. Then we discuss the use of the t-test, Chi square and Analysis of Variance (ANOVA) to test hypotheses.

CHOOSING THE APPROPRIATE STATISTICAL TECHNIQUE

When we test hypotheses we are converting data to knowledge. A number of statistical techniques can be used to test hypotheses. The choice of a particular technique depends on (1) the number of variables and (2) the scale of measurement.

Number of Variables

The number of variables examined together is a major consideration in the selection of the appropriate statistical technique. Univariate statistics use only one variable at a time to generalize about a population from a sample. For example, if the researcher wants to examine the average number of cups of Starbucks coffee college students drink during finals, only a single variable is used and univariate statistics is appropriate. If the business researcher is interested in the relationship between the average number of cups of Starbucks coffee college students drink during finals and the number of hours spent studying for finals, two variables are involved and a bivariate statistical technique is required. Often business researchers will need to examine many variables at the same time to represent the real world and fully explain relationships in the data. In such cases, multivariate statistical techniques are required. We examine univariate and bivariate statistics in this chapter and multivariate statistics in a later chapter.

Scale of Measurement

We discussed measurement and scaling in Chapter 9. We use that information here to show which statistical techniques are used with a particular type of scale. Exhibit 13-3 provides an overview of the types of scales used in different situations. Suppose the researcher wants to compare two groups – Starbucks brand coffee drinkers versus Costas coffee drinkers. When we want to examine two groups, such as those who prefer Starbucks versus Costas brand of coffee, the groups are identified with a nominal scale and the mode would be the only appropriate measure of central tendency. That is, we could only compare the number of individuals who say they prefer Costas versus Starbucks. **Nominal data** is a name or label that enables the researcher to place respondents into categories, but you cannot make comparisons like bigger/smaller or faster/slower. A Chi square test could be used to test whether the observed number of Starbucks brand coffee drinkers is what one would expect it to be. For example, if a sample survey showed that 24 % of college students at your university drink Costas brand coffee and you expected it to be 30 % based on a survey of all the college students in the UK, you could use Chi square to determine if the differences were statistically significant.

Ordinal data is the next higher level of data so responses can be rank ordered into a hierarchical pattern like higher/lower or greater than/less than. With ordinal data you can use the median, percentile and Chi square, plus anything you can use with nominal data. For example, if we have ranking data for two factors that are thought to be important in the selection of a coffee house, we would use the median, percentile and Chi square. If the two ranking factors are coffee taste and atmosphere, we could use the Chi square statistic to determine whether customers of Starbucks and

Type of Scale	Measure of Central Tendency	Measure of Dispersion	Statistic
Nominal	Mode	None	Chi square
Ordinal	Median	Percentiles or Quartiles	Chi square
Interval or Ratio	Mean	Standard Deviation	T-Test, ANOVA

EXHIBIT 13-3

Type of Scale and Appropriate Statistic

customers of Costas ranked these factors differently. **Interval** and **ratio data** are the highest level of measurement. The units of measurement are constant so differences in any two adjacent points on a scale are equal and almost any mathematical procedure such as a mean or standard deviation can be calculated with them. Thus, if we have the actual count of the number of cups of coffee the typical customer of Starbucks and Costas drank each time they were in the store we have ratio data and could calculate means and standard deviations. This would enable us to determine if there are differences in the average number of cups consumed using the t-test or ANOVA.

OTHER CONSIDERATIONS IN HYPOTHESIS TESTING

There are two major groups of statistical procedures. The groups are referred to as parametric and nonparametric. The major difference in these two groups of statistics lies in the underlying assumptions about the data. When the data are measured using an interval or ratio scale and the sample size is large, **parametric statistics** are appropriate. It is also assumed the sample data are collected from populations with normal (bell-shaped) distributions. When the assumption of a normal distribution is not possible, the researcher should use **nonparametric statistics**. When data are measured using an ordinal or nominal scale it is generally not appropriate to make the assumption the distribution is normal. Therefore, nonparametric or distribution-free statistics should be used. In this chapter we discuss a nonparametric statistic Chi square and two parametric statistics – the t-test and ANOVA.

While parametric statistical tests assume the data has a normal distribution, most tests are quite robust and when ignored this assumption seldom causes problems. The same is true for the assumption that two or more groups will have the same variance. That is, problems seldom arise when parametric tests are used to compare two groups with different variances (or standard deviations) when the groups are comparable in size.

We previously defined a population as the total of all the elements that share some common set of characteristics. For example, the population could be all the students at your university or the company you work at, it could be all the persons who live in a particular city or country, or it could be all the customers of Samouel's and Gino's restaurants. In contrast, a sample is a small subset or some part of all the individuals in the population. For example, if we wanted to determine the average number of glasses of wine consumed with dinner at Samouel's restaurant, we would not interview all the customers. This would be expensive, take a long time, and likely be impossible because of the difficulty of finding all the customers. Instead, a sample of 100 customers (out of a total of 1,000 customers) might be considered large enough by Phil to provide accurate information about the average number of glasses of wine consumed.

RESEARCH IN ACTION
COUNTY CARS: MAKING BETTER USE OF DRIVERS

County Cars is located in Henley-on-Thames, Oxon, UK. Their business is providing transportation to individuals in private cars. They have 22 drivers working for them and have been in business almost 25 years. Services are provided mostly in the area southwest of London. Most of their customers are travelling to-and-from London and the Heathrow and Gatwick airports. Traffic problems in recent years on the M25, M3 and M4 as well as feeder roads have created significant problems in estimating journey time for customers. For the past two years they have been collecting information on origin of pickups, destination, travel time in towns, travel time outside of towns, travel time on motorways, and total journey time. All the time data are in minutes. They have also added limited comments about weather and time of day for the journey. The owners hope to use the information to better predict journey time.

Would statistical analysis of the data help to answer this question? If yes, what statistical technique would be most helpful, and how might the technique be applied? What other data might be collected to improve their estimates? ∎

SINGLE GROUP HYPOTHESIS TESTING

Testing hypotheses using statistics involves much more than the tabulations included in a frequency distribution or the calculation of measures of central tendency or dispersion. Researchers not only describe data using means or percentages. They provide tests of the likelihood the sample numbers correctly or incorrectly estimate the population characteristics. The simplest types of tests are univariate tests of significance. **Univariate tests** of significance are used to test hypotheses when the researcher wishes to test a proposition about a sample characteristic against a known or given standard. The following are some examples of some propositions:

- The new product will be preferred by 90 % of our current customers.

- The average monthly electric bill in Leeds, England exceeds £30.00.

- The market share for Ahmad Tea in London is at least 30 %.

- The average cost of living in the UK is higher than in France.

- More than 50 % of current Coke Light customers will prefer the new Coke Light that includes a taste of lime.

We can translate these propositions into null hypotheses and test them. In the following paragraphs we provide an example from our restaurant database of a univariate hypothesis test.

Phil Samouel would like to know if his customers think his prices are reasonable. He also would like to know how Gino's customers perceive that restaurant's prices. Survey respondents indicated their perceptions of prices using a seven-point scale on which 1 = "Strongly Disagree" the restaurant has reasonable prices, and 7 = "Strongly Agree". Phil's business consultant has told him the question is an interval scale and previous research has shown the responses are approximately normally distributed.

To examine Phil's question about pricing we first must develop the hypothesis and agree upon the level of significance for rejecting/accepting the hypothesis. Phil thinks customers consider the prices of menu items to be somewhat reasonable. After talking with his consultant, they have agreed that a rating of 5 on a seven-point scale would represent somewhat reasonable prices. Therefore, they would expect the responses to the question on reasonable prices to have a mean of 5.0. The null hypothesis is the sample mean will not be different from 5.0 (the standard for reasonable prices established by Phil and his consultant). The alternative hypothesis is the sample mean of the answers to X_7 – Reasonable Prices, will be different from 5.0.

Recall that researchers often consider <0.05 (5%) as the most risk they want to take in rejecting the null hypothesis. In this case, however, Phil has decided he only needs to be 90% certain the mean is different from 5.0. That is, he is willing to assume a 10% risk in examining the pricing issue. Using this significance level means that if the survey of customers were conducted many times, the probability of incorrectly rejecting the null hypothesis when it is actually true would occur 10 or fewer times out of 100 (0.10).

The null hypothesis that the mean of the perceptions of pricing is not different from 5.0 can be tested using the **one sample t-test**. The results of using this test are shown in Exhibit 13-4. The first table labeled One-Sample Statistics displays the mean and standard deviation for X_{10} – Reasonable Prices. Phil Samouel's customers give him a mean of 4.14 and Gino's 3.97. The respective standard deviations are 0.932 and 0.937. The one-sample test table shows the results of the t-test for the null hypothesis that the mean response to X_{10} – Reasonable Prices is 5.0. The t-test statistic for Samouel's is – 9.225, and the significance level is 0.000. Similarly, the t-test statistic for Gino's is – 10.993, and the significance level is 0.000. This means that the null hypothesis for both restaurants can be rejected and the alternative hypothesis accepted with a high level of confidence. The level of significance of 0.000 means there are no chances in 10,000 that rejecting the null hypothesis would be incorrect. The use of the software SPSS to execute this test is explained in the Data Analysis box.

One-Sample Statistics

X_{25} – Competitor		N	Mean	Std. Deviation
Samouel's	X_{10} – Reasonable Prices	100	4.14	0.932
Gino's	X_{10} – Reasonable Prices	100	3.97	0.937

One-Sample Test

		Test Value = 5.0			
		t	df	Sig. (2-tailed)	Mean Difference
X_{25} – Competitor					
Samouel's	X_{10} – Reasonable Prices	– 9.225	99	0.000	−0.86
Gino's	X_{10} – Reasonable Prices	−10.993	99	0.000	−1.03

EXHIBIT 13-4

One Sample T-Test of Samouel's and Gino's Prices

From a practical standpoint, the results of the univariate hypothesis test indicate that customers from both restaurants felt the prices of the menu items were not very reasonable. This is because in both instances the mean response is significantly below the standard of 5.0 which Phil set as being "reasonable". From Phil's point of view, this means his customers believe his prices are not as reasonable as he thought. Of course, Gino's customers think his prices are not very reasonable either so neither restaurant has a competitive advantage, although perceptions for Phil's restaurant are slightly more favourable than for Gino's.

DATA ANALYSIS

USING SPSS TO CALCULATE A ONE-SAMPLE T-TEST

Since Phil would like to know the answer for both his restaurant and for Gino's, before testing the hypotheses we must split the sample into Samouel's customers and Gino's customers. Recall that this involves going to the Data pull-down menu and doing the following: Data → Split File and then click on Compare groups. Next highlight X_{28} – Competitor and click on the arrow button to move it in the Groups Based On box. Now click OK and you will be back to the SPSS Data Editor screen. All data analysis now will be comparing customers from the two restaurants.

The click-thru sequence to run the one-sample t-test is: ANALYSE → COMPARE MEANS → ONE-SAMPLE T-TEST. Click on X_{10} – Reasonable Prices to highlight it and then on the arrow box to move X_{10} into the Test Variables box. In the box labelled Test Value, enter the number 5.0. This is the number you want to compare the respondents' answers against. When you click on the Options box, note that 95 is the default in the confidence interval box. This is the same as setting the significance level at 0.05. Since Phil has decided to accept more risk we must change this number. The level of risk Phil will accept is 10 % (0.10) so change the 95 in the Confidence Interval box to 90. Then, click on the "Continue" button and "OK" to execute the program. The results are shown in Exhibit 13-4. ■

Phil needs to determine if the problem is real. That is, are his prices really considered not very reasonable? Or is the problem one of customer misperceptions – that is, are his prices perceived to be too high when in fact they are not? Once this is determined, he must develop a plan to improve customer perceptions of the pricing of his menu items. It may involve actually changing prices or it may require changing portion sizes or some other approach. But improvement in pricing perceptions from a mean of 4.14 could become a significant competitive advantage for Samouel's restaurant.

MULTIPLE GROUP HYPOTHESIS TESTING

Business researchers often test hypotheses that one group differs from another group in terms of attitudes, behaviour or some other characteristic. For example, Phil Samouel might like to know if there are any differences in the perceptions of older and younger patrons of his restaurant. If there are differences, he could develop separate marketing strategies to appeal to each segment. Where more than one group is involved, **bivariate statistical tests** must be used. In statistical terminology, the null hypothesis is there are no significant differences between the two groups.

In the following section, we describe three multiple group hypothesis tests. We first show you how to use Chi square to test for differences between groups using nominal data. Then we explain how to use the t-test and ANOVA to test for differences in group means using metric (interval) data.

Cross-Tabulation Using Chi square Analysis (X^2)

One of the simplest methods for describing sets of relationships is cross-tabulation. A **cross-tabulation** is a frequency distribution of responses on two or more sets of variables. For example, a cross-tabulation might compare the number or individuals at the Wimbledon tennis match who say they are UK citizens versus the number who say they are from the European Union. To do a cross-tabulation, we count the responses for each of the groups and compare them. Chi square (X^2) analysis enables us to test whether there are statistical differences between the number of individuals at the tennis match who are from the UK versus outside the UK. Below are examples of questions that could be answered using cross tabulations and testing with Chi square analysis:

- Is brand awareness of Guinness Beer (aware, not aware) related to the geographic area in which individuals live (UK, Europe, Asia, South Africa, and so on)?

- Do males and females differ in their recall of an advertisement?

- Is there a relationship between gender and work type (full-time versus part-time) for Samouel's restaurant employees.

- Does frequency of patronage (very frequent, somewhat frequent and occasional) differ between Samouel's and Gino's restaurants?

- Is usage (heavy, moderate and low) of the Internet related to educational level?

- Does job satisfaction differ between blue collar versus white collar workers?

Business researchers use the Chi square test to determine whether responses observed in a survey follow the expected pattern. For example, Phil Samouel might believe there is no difference in the frequency of dining between male and female customers. Similarly, he may think there is no difference in the number of male and female customers who saw an ad he ran in the *London Times*. Thus, the null hypotheses would be: (1) no difference in frequency of patronage between male and female customers and (2) no difference in ad recall between male and female customers. Hypotheses such as these can be tested using the Chi square statistic. Phil would want to know the answer to these questions because if there are differences he could use this information in developing his business plan.

The **Chi square (X^2) statistic** can be used to test whether the frequencies of two nominally scaled variables are related. Nominal data from questions about job type (professor, physician, manager, and so on), gender, ad recall, or other categorical variables can be examined. The Chi square statistic compares the observed frequencies (sometimes referred to as "actual") of the responses with the expected frequencies. The observed frequencies are the actual cell counts of data from our survey. The expected frequencies are the theoretical frequencies derived from your null hypothesis of no relationship between the two variables. The statistic tests whether or not the observed frequencies "fit" the expected frequencies. In other words, it tests the "**goodness of fit**" for the observed frequency distribution with the expected distribution.

RESEARCH IN ACTION

CAN PEOPLE TELL THE DIFFERENCES IN THE TASTE OF BEER?

We have conducted many blind taste tests with our students. Taste tests provide a good example of how to use Chi square to determine if people are able to identify the taste of brand name beers in a blind taste test. Suppose you have 20 students in your class. You pour Heineken beer in 20 paper cups that have no identification on them. Next you ask your students to taste the beer and tell you whether it is Heineken or Amstel. Since there are an even number of students in the test, if they all guess randomly you would expect the results to be 50 % Heineken and 50 % Amstel. The null hypothesis then is: There is no relationship between the Heineken beer being tested and the brand the students select based on the taste test. Following the taste test you count the number of times each brand is selected and find that 14 of the students said the beer was Amstel and six said it was Heineken. Your expected frequencies were 10 and 10, but your observed frequencies are 14 and 6. There seems to be a relationship that indicates students definitely cannot identify the brand of beer based on a taste test. But to be certain we must use a statistical test like Chi square to determine if the difference in expected and observed frequencies is statistically significant.

When we conduct a Chi square analysis, we set up a contingency table with a number of cells. A **cell** refers to the intersection of a row and a column that represents a specific combination of two variables. For example, a cell in the example in Exhibit 13-5 would be the number of Japanese that prefer Macallan single malt scotch (N = 145) over Laphroaig. Another cell would be the number of British respondents that prefer Laphroaig (N = 270). A 2 × 2 contingency table would have four cells as does our example. A 3 × 3 contingency table would have nine cells. Proper use of Chi square requires that each expected cell frequency have a sample size of at least 5. If this sample size minimum cannot be met, the researcher can either take a larger sample or combine individual response categories so the minimum cell size can be met. The **observed counts** are the actual number of responses from the sample in each cell. The **expected counts** are the number of responses we expect to get in each cell.

How do we determine the expected counts? The expected counts (number) in a cell are calculated by multiplying the cell column total by the cell row total and dividing it by the total sample size. For example, look in the far right column and you will see that 450 Japanese respondents in the sample. Now look at the sample sizes (bottom of table) and there were 475 respondents who prefer Macallan and 575 who prefer the more "peaty tasting" Laphroaig. When you multiply the column total of 575 who prefer Laphroaig (cell column total) by 450 (cell row total) you get 258,750. Divide this number by 1050 and you get 246.43 (number of expected Japanese who would prefer Laphroaig). All of the expected counts are calculated in a similar manner. The Chi square test has not been calculated, but it appears there is a significant difference in the actual versus expected preference for the two brands of single malt

Frequencies Table

Ethnic Heritage	Prefer Macallan	Prefer Laphroaig	Totals
Japanese Count	145	305	450
Expected Count	203.57	246.43	
British Count	330	270	600
Expected Count	271.43	328.57	
Totals	475	575	1,050

EXHIBIT 13-5

Cross Tabulation Table for Macallan versus Laphroaig brand Single Malt Scotch Drinkers

scotch. In short, British respondents prefer Macallan more than expected and Laphroaig less than expected, while Japanese prefer Laphroaig more than expected and Macallan less than expected.

When testing hypotheses, we begin by formulating the null hypothesis and selecting the appropriate level of statistical significance for our research problem. About two weeks before the survey Phil ran an ad for his restaurant in the *London Times*. He wants to see if there is a difference in recall of the ad by males and females. He does not think ad recall will differ between males and females but he would like to know. The null hypothesis is that males and females do not differ in their recall of the ad. We will assume the acceptable level of statistical significance is 0.05.

The observed and expected counts for males and females interviewed in his survey cross-tabulated with ad recall are shown in Exhibit 13-6. Looking at the observed count in the column of males we see that the survey found there were 13 males who did not see the ad. If we compare this to the expected count of 12.2 we see there is little difference between observed and expected. Recall that the expected counts (number) in a cell are calculated by multiplying the cell column total times the cell row total and dividing it by the total sample size. For example, look in the far right column and you will see that 177 individuals in the sample saw the ad. Now look at the sample sizes (bottom of table) and there were 106 males and 94 females. When you multiply 94 females (cell column total) times 177 (cell row total) you get 16,638. Divide this number by 200 and you get 83.2 (number of expected females who saw the ad). All of the expected counts are calculated in a similar manner.

Looking at the results, we see there is little difference in the actual and expected counts for both males and females. Moreover, the Pearson Chi square test in the lower portion of the exhibit shows that indeed there are no statistically significant differences (sig. = 0.719) in the expected versus actual number of males and females who saw the ad. In fact, a very high percentage of both males and females recall having seen the ad. We therefore accept the null hypothesis that there is no difference between the ad recall of females and males.

The Chi square statistic should be estimated only on counts of data. When the data are in percentage form, we must first convert them to absolute counts or numbers. Additionally, we assume the observations are drawn independently. This means one group of respondents does not in

X21 – Who Saw an Ad * X25 – Gender Cross Tabulation

			X22 – Gender		Total
			Male	Female	
X21 – Who Saw an Ad	Did Not See AD	Count	13	10	23
		Expected Count	12.2	10.8	23.0
	Saw AD	Count	93	84	177
		Expected Count	93.8	83.2	177.0
Total		Count	106	94	200
		Expected Count	106.0	94.0	200.0

Chi square Test

	Value	df	Asymp. Sig. (2-sided)
Pearson Chi square	0.129*	1	0.719
N of Valid Cases	200		

*0 cells (0 %) have expected count less than 5. The minimum expected count is 10.81.

EXHIBIT 13-6

Observed and Expected Counts for Gender Cross-Tabulated with Ad Recall

any way influence the other group's responses. That is, in the ad recall example women's responses to the question "Do you recall an ad by Samouel's Greek Cuisine?" in no way influence men's responses to the same question.

Testing Differences in Group Means

One of the most frequently examined questions in business research is whether the means of two groups of respondents on some attitude or behaviour are significantly different. For example, in a sample survey we might examine any of the following questions:

- Do the coffee consumption patterns (measured using the mean number of cups consumed daily) of males and females differ?
- Does the number of hours an individual spends on the Internet each week differ by income level?. . . by gender?. . . by education?
- Do younger workers exhibit higher job satisfaction than do older workers?
- Do multinational firms have a more favourable image than do local family-owned businesses?

When we examine questions like the above, we first develop the null and alternative hypotheses. Then we select the significance level for testing the null hypothesis. Finally, we select the appropriate statistical test and apply it to our sample data. In this section we cover two statistical tests that can be used to examine questions that compare the means of two groups.

Independent and Related Samples   Business researchers often find it useful to compare the means of two groups. When comparing group means two situations are possible. The first situation is when the means are from independent samples. The second situation is when the samples are related. An example of the first situation, independent samples, might be when the researcher interviews a sample of females and males. If the researcher is comparing the average number of Cokes consumed per day by females with the average number of Cokes consumed by males, this is considered an independent samples situation. An example of the second situation, related samples, is when the researcher collects data from a sample of females only and compares the average number of times a week they drink bottled water with the average number of times a week they drink a glass of fruit juice. The following paragraph presents a brief overview of related sample testing. But the remainder of our discussion of hypothesis testing assumes independent samples.

The researcher must examine the information cautiously when confronted with a related-samples problem. While the questions are independent, the respondents are the same so the researcher does not have independent samples. Instead you are dealing with what is referred to as paired samples and you must use a paired samples t-test. The SPSS software has options for both the related-samples and independent-samples t-tests, so chose the appropriate one for each situation.

Comparing Two Means with the t-test   The t-test can be used to test a hypothesis stating that the means for the variables associated with two independent samples or groups will be the same. The use of a t-test requires interval or ratio data, and we assume the sample populations have normal distributions and the variances are equal. The t-test assesses whether the observed differences between two sample means occurred by chance, or if there is a true difference. Although a normal distribution is assumed with the t-test, it is quite robust to departures from normality.

The t-test is appropriate in situations where the sample size is small (n = 30 or less) and the population standard deviation is unknown. The t-test uses the t-distribution, also called the Student's t-distribution, to test hypotheses. The t-distribution is a symmetrical, bell-shaped distribution with a mean of zero and a standard deviation of 1. Other statistical distributions may be used in situations where the sample size (n) is larger than 30. But the t-distribution is used quite often for sample sizes larger than 30 because the distributions are almost identical with larger sample sizes.

To demonstrate the use of a t-test to compare two means, we will examine the level of satisfaction for Phil Samouel's customers and Gino's customers. The null hypothesis is no differences in the level of satisfaction of the customers of the two restaurants. This hypothesis is tested using a t-test and the results are shown in Exhibit 13-7. The independent samples test was used because we are comparing Samouel's customers to Gino's customers. The SPSS instructions to calculate this test are shown in the Data Analysis box.

The top table in Exhibit 13-7 contains the group statistics. The mean satisfaction level for Samouel's customers was considerably lower at 4.78, compared to 5.96 for Gino's customers. The standard deviation for Samouel's was somewhat larger (1.16), however, than for Gino's (0.974). To determine if the mean satisfaction levels are significantly different, we look at the information in the Independent Samples Test table. Information in the column labelled Sig. (2-tailed) shows the means are significantly different (<0.05) for assumptions of either equal or unequal variances. Thus, Samouel's customers are significantly less satisfied than Gino's customers so Phil Samouel definitely needs to develop strategies to improve the satisfaction level of his customers.

Group Statistics

	X_{28} – Competitor	N	Mean	Std. Deviation
X_{17} – Satisfaction	Samouel's	100	4.78	1.16
	Gino's	100	5.96	0.974

Independent Samples Test

		t-test for Equality of Means			
		t	df	Sig. (2-tailed)	Mean Difference
X_{17} – Satisfaction	Equal variances assumed	−7.793	198	0.000	−1.18
	Equal variances not assumed	−7.793	192.232	0.000	−1.18

EXHIBIT 13-7

Testing Differences in Two Means Using the t-test

DATA ANALYSIS

USING SPSS TO TEST THE DIFFERENCES IN TWO MEANS – A COMPARISON OF SAMOUEL'S AND GINO'S CUSTOMERS

To answer this question we can use the SPSS Compare Means program. First make sure you are analysing all 200 cases. To do so, go to the Data pull down menu and click on Split File. If the Analyse all cases is checked click OK and go back to the Data Editor. If Compare Groups is checked then click on Analyse all cases and then on OK to go back to the Data Editor.

The SPSS click-thru sequence is: ANALYSE → COMPARE MEANS → INDEPEN-DENT–SAMPLES–T TEST. When you get to the dialogue box click variable X_{17} – Satisfaction into the Test Variables box and variable X_{28} – Competitor into the Grouping Variable box. Now click on Define Groups and put a 0 for group 1 (Samouel's) and a 1 for group 2 (Gino's) and then Continue. For the Options we will use the defaults so just click on "OK" to execute the program. The results will be the same as in Exhibit 13-7. ■

ANALYSIS OF VARIANCE (ANOVA)

ANOVA is used to assess the statistical differences between the means of two or more groups. For example, the circulation manager of the *Financial Times* conducted a readership survey and found that individuals 39 and younger read the paper an average of 2.5 times a week, individuals 40 to 49 read the paper an average of 3.1 times a week, and individuals 50 and older read the paper an average of 4.7 times a week. The circulation manager wants to know whether these observed differences are statistically significant? Knowing the answer to questions such as this would be quite useful for managers and business researchers, and particularly for the circulation manager of the *Financial Times*. ANOVA can test for statistical differences between the average number of times the *Financial Times* is read by several age groups whereas the t-test could compare at most two means. In our example, the null hypothesis is the average frequency of readership of the three age groups is the same.

The term ANOVA stands for Analysis of Variance. It is a test of differences in means for two or more populations. The null hypothesis is the means are equal. We discuss **one-way ANOVA** in this section. The term "one-way" is used since there is only one independent variable. ANOVA also can examine research problems that involve several independent variables. When several independent variables are included it is called **N-way ANOVA**. The independent variable (or variables) in an ANOVA must be categorical (nonmetric). In ANOVA, we refer to the categorical independent variables as **factors**. Each factor has two or more levels or groups. Each level is referred to as a treatment. For example, if we are examining the preference of a sample of individuals for Coke Light the dependent variable might be a preference measure using a seven-point scale where 7 = Very Strong Preference and 1 = No Preference at All. Likewise, the independent variable (factor) might be consumption measured using heavy, medium and light. Since we have only one independent variable this is a one-way ANOVA. If we added a second independent variable, such as brand loyalty (measured using highly loyal versus not loyal at all) this would be two-way ANOVA.

Differences between the group means are examined with the F-test instead of the t-test when we use ANOVA. To do so, the total variance is partitioned into two forms of variation and they are compared. The first is the **variation within the groups** and the second is the **variation between the groups**. The **F-distribution** is the ratio of these two forms of variance and can be calculated as follows:

$$F = \text{Variance between groups (VB)/Variance Within groups (VW)}$$

When the variance between the groups relative to within the groups is larger, then the F-ratio is larger. Larger F-ratios indicate significant differences between the groups and a high likelihood the null hypothesis will be rejected.

*RESEARCH
IN ACTION*   **WHICH STATISTIC IS APPROPRIATE?**

Ossi and his fellow students are planning which classes they will take next fall and want to know which professors are rated the highest. They obtain information on student evaluations the past year of several professors from a Web site that collects the data. The evaluations were obtained using a 10-point scale of "Strongly Agree" and

"Strongly Disagree" with eight statements about teaching methods. Information also was collected on what classes a particular professor taught and which time of the day. What statistic could be used to answer this question? ■

In our example we want to compare the satisfaction of three groups of restaurant customers, so a t-test cannot be used. ANOVA which uses the F-test, however, can be used with three or more groups as long as the dependent variable is measured either as interval or ratio. Also, the independent variable(s) must be categorical. All of these conditions are met so ANOVA can be used. As with other bivariate tests, the null hypothesis is that all three groups of restaurant customers (groups based on frequency of patronage) will express the same level of satisfaction with the restaurants.

Our research question has two parts. Firstly, we must determine if significant differences in satisfaction exist between any of the three customer groups defined by frequency of patronage. Secondly, if differences are identified we must determine between which groups the differences are statistically significant. We will do this using ANOVA and the Scheffe follow-up test. The results of testing this hypothesis are shown in Exhibit 13-8.

The descriptive statistics table in Exhibit 13-8 shows the number of customers in each of the frequency groups and the mean level of satisfaction by frequency of patronage. Note that in all cases higher frequency of patronage is associated with higher satisfaction. In the "N" column at the right of the table we see that Gino's has many more very frequent and somewhat frequent customers than does Samouel's. Moreover, customer satisfaction for Samouel's restaurant is not as high (4.78) as it is for Gino's (5.96). The task for Phil Samouel, therefore, is to analyse the survey data and develop a strategy to improve customer satisfaction levels, attract new customers, and increase the frequency of dining at his restaurant.

Information in the table labelled "Tests of Between–Subjects Effects" (Exhibit 13-8) reveals that satisfaction levels differ significantly between the groups identified by their frequency of patronage. You determine this by looking under the "Sig." column for variable X_{20} (located in the Source column). Note the level of significance for Samouel's is 0.000 and for Gino's is 0.000, so satisfaction levels for customers of both restaurants vary significantly based on frequency of patronage. The null hypothesis of no differences is therefore rejected.

Unfortunately, ANOVA only enables the researcher to conclude that statistical differences are present somewhere between the group means. It does not identify where the differences are. In our example of satisfaction levels of customers, we could conclude that differences in satisfaction levels based on frequency of patronage are statistically significant, but we would not know if the differences are between very frequent versus somewhat frequent customers, somewhat frequent versus occasional, or occasional versus very frequent. We would only be able to say there are significant differences somewhere between the groups. For this reason, business researchers must use follow-up tests to determine where the differences lie.

ANOVA using Follow-up Tests

Several follow-up tests have been developed to identify the location of significant differences. Many are available in statistical software packages such as SPSS or SAS. All of the follow-up tests involve simultaneous assessment of differences between several means. Discussion of these techniques is well beyond the scope of this book, but the techniques differ in the extent to which they are able to control for the error rate. The SPSS software has 14 tests that assume equal variances and four where

Descriptive Statistics

Dependent Variable: X_{17} – Satisfaction

X_{28} – Competitor	X_{20} – Frequency of Patronage	Mean	N
Samouel's	Occasional Customer	4.04	47
	Somewhat Frequent Customer	4.62	21
	Very Frequent Customer	5.97	32
	Total	4.78	100
Gino's	Occasional Customer	4.78	9
	Somewhat Frequent Customer	5.69	29
	Very Frequent Customer	6.26	62
	Total	5.96	100

Tests of Between-Subjects Effects

Dependent Variable: X_{17} – Satisfaction

X_{28} – Competitor	Source	Type III Sum of Squares	df	Mean Square	F	Sig.
Samouel's	Corrected Model	71.324[a]	2	35.662	55.942	0.000
	Intercept	2137.359	1	2137.359	3352.800	0.000
	X_{20}	71.324	2	35.662	55.942	0.000
	Error	61.836	97	0.637		
	Total	2418.000	100			
	Corrected Total	133.160	99			
Gino's	Corrected Model	20.207[b]	2	10.103	13.309	0.000
	Intercept	1729.763	1	1729.763	2278.680	0.000
	X_{20}	20.207	2	10.103	13.309	0.000
	Error	73.633	97	0.759		
	Total	3646.000	100			
	Corrected Total	93.840	99			

[a] R Squared = 0.536 (Adjusted R Squared = 0.526) (Samouel's)
[b] R Squared = 0.215 (Adjusted R Squared = 0.199) (Gino's)

EXHIBIT 13-8

Analysis of Variance Testing Mean Differences in Satisfaction Levels of Samouel's and Gino's Customers Based on Frequency of Custom

equal variance is not assumed. In our example we will use the Scheffe procedure because it is the most conservative method of assessing significant differences between group means. But the Tukey and Duncan tests are widely utilized in the literature.

The information in the "multiple comparisons" table in Exhibit 13-9 shows which group means are significantly different. The far-right column labeled Sig. shows the level of significance. For both

Multiple Comparisons
Dependent Variable: X_{17} – Satisfaction

Scheffe Test

			Mean Difference (I-J)	Sig.
X_{28} – Competitor Samouel's	(I) X_{20} – Frequency of custom	(J) X_{20} – Frequency of custom		
	Occasional customer	Somewhat Frequent customer	−0.58*	0.026
		Very Frequent customer	−1.93*	0.000
	Somewhat Frequent customer	Occasional customer	0.58*	0.026
		Very Frequent customer	−1.35*	0.000
	Very Frequent customer	Occasional customer	1.93*	0.000
		Somewhat Frequent customer	1.35*	0.000
Gino's	Occasional customer	Somewhat Frequent customer	−0.91*	0.027
		Very Frequent customer	−1.48*	0.000
	Somewhat Frequent customer	Occasional customer	0.91*	0.027
		Very Frequent customer	−0.57*	0.018
	Very Frequent customer	Occasional customer	1.48*	0.000
		Somewhat Frequent customer	0.57*	0.018

*The mean difference is significant at the 0.05 level.

EXHIBIT 13-9

Comparisons of Individual Group Means for Significant Differences

Samouel's and Gino's there are statistically significant differences between all the groups. This means the "Very Frequent" "Somewhat Frequent" and "Occasional" customers differ significantly in their satisfaction levels. If there were any comparisons in which the group means were not significantly different, it would have been shown in the "Sig." column of numbers.

To determine the nature of the differences we look back at the means shown earlier in the descriptive statistics table in Exhibit 13-8. For Samouel's the mean satisfaction level of the "Very Frequent" customers is 5.97, for the "Somewhat Frequent" customer the mean is 4.62, and for the "Occasional" customer it is 4.04. Thus, as would be expected, the more frequent customers are significantly more satisfied. A similar finding is true for Gino's. The mean satisfaction level of the "Very Frequent" customer is 6.26, for the "Somewhat Frequent" customers the mean is 5.69, and for the "Occasional" customers the mean is 4.78. Phil must be concerned that Gino has more frequent customers then he does. A business plan must be devised to increase frequency of patronage as well as other performance indicators.

FACTORIAL DESIGN: TWO-WAY ANOVA

One-way ANOVA designs involve a single nonmetric independent variable and a single metric dependent variable. A **factorial design** examines the effect (if any) of two or more nonmetric independent variables on a single metric dependent variable. With one-way ANOVA the total variance is partitioned into the between-group variance and the within-group variance. But in factorial designs (**two-way ANOVA**), the between-group variance itself is partitioned into: (1) variation due to each of the independent variables (factors); and (2) variation due to the interaction of the two variables – that is, their combined effects on the dependent variable beyond the separate influence of each. Therefore, three null hypotheses are tested simultaneously by a two-way factorial design: (1) the effect of variable one on the dependent variable; (2) the effect of variable two on the dependent variable; and (3) the combined (joint) effect of variables one and two on the dependent variable. The effects of the two independent variables are referred to as **main effects**, and their combined effect is referred to as the **interaction effect**.

Example of Two-Way ANOVA

Phil Samouel has observed that the frequency of patronage of his male and female customers appears to be different. If in fact the patronage frequency is statistically different he would like to better understand why and determine how he could use that information to grow his business. He also would like to know how gender of customers and frequency of patronage are related to satisfaction. The null hypotheses are: (1) no differences in mean satisfaction levels based on frequency of patronage; (2) no differences in mean satisfaction levels based on gender; and (3) no differences in mean satisfaction levels based on the combined effects of frequency of patronage and gender. The metric dependent variable for these hypotheses is X_{17} – Satisfaction and the nonmetric independent variables are X_{20} – Frequency of Patronage and X_{25} – Gender. The results for the tests of the hypotheses are reported in Exhibits 13-10 to 13-12. Instructions on how to use SPSS to execute this test are shown in the data analysis box.

The top table in Exhibit 13-10 labelled "Tests of Between Subjects Effects" shows the results of the two-way ANOVA program. The null hypotheses were that there would be no difference between the mean scores for X_{17} – Satisfaction for customers with different patronage rates (X_{20}), no difference in mean scores on X_{17} – Satisfaction between females and males (X_{25}), and no interaction effect. The purpose of the N-Way ANOVA analysis is first to see if statistically significant differences exist, and if they do between which groups.

Tests of Between-Subjects Effects

Dependent Variable: X17 – Satisfaction

Source	Type III Sum of Squares	df	Mean Square	F	Sig.
Corrected Model	86.828[a]	5	17.366	35.232	0.000
Intercept	1848.007	1	1848.007	3749.330	0.000
X20	39.076	2	19.538	39.639	0.000
X25	12.620	1	12.620	25.604	0.000
X20 * X25	2.377	2	1.189	2.412	0.095
Error	46.332	94	0.493		
Total	2418.000	100			
Corrected Total	133.160	99			

[a]R Squared = 0.652 (Adjusted R Squared = 0.634)

EXHIBIT 13-10

Two-Way ANOVA for Frequency of Patronage and Gender

DATA ANALYSIS

USING SPSS TO EXECUTE A TWO-WAY ANOVA

We must separate Samouel's customers from Gino's for this analysis. To do so we go to the Data pull down menu and then scroll down and click on Select Cases. Next click on "If condition satisfied", and then on "If …". Now highlight variable X_{28} and click the Arrow box to move it into the box on the top right side. Next click below on the equal sign (=) and then zero (0). This tells the program to select for analysis only cases coded 0 for variable X_{28} (i.e., Samouel's customers). Finally click on Continue and then OK. We use this process to select only Samouel's customers for this analysis.

The click through sequence is: ANALYSE → GENERAL LINEAR MODEL → UNIVARIATE. Highlight the dependent variable X_{17} – Satisfaction by clicking on it and move it to the Dependent variable box. Next, highlight X_{20} – Frequency of Patronage and move it into the box labelled "Fixed Factors". Now do the same for variable X_{25} – Gender. Click on the Post Hoc box and highlight X_{20} in the Factor(s) box and then click on the Arrow box to move this variable to the box for Post Hoc Tests. We do not move X_{25} because it has only two groups and not three. Look to the lower left side of the screen and click on Scheffe test and then Continue. Now go to the Options box and click on Descriptive statistics and then Continue. Finally, click on "OK" since we do not need to specify anything else for this test. The results are shown in Exhibit 13-10. ■

To assess the mean differences for each independent variable comparison, an F-ratio is used. As discussed earlier, the approach used in two-way ANOVA compares the variance from the *between* groups grand mean to the variance *within* the groups. In this case, the groups are the three groups of customers who exhibit different patronage rates and the two gender groups. When the F-ratio is large, we are more likely to have larger differences between the means of the various groups examined.

The first main effect we examine is the impact of variable X_{20} – Frequency of Patronage on variable X_{17} – Satisfaction. The F-ratio for X_{20} – Frequency of Patronage for Samouel's customers is 39.639, which is statistically significant at the 0.000 level. From the Descriptive Statistics table in Exhibit 13-11 below we can see that for Samouel's restaurant satisfaction is higher for somewhat frequent (mean = 4.62) and very frequent customers (5.97) than it is for the occasional customer (4.04). Thus, we reject the null hypothesis and conclude satisfaction does vary by frequency of patronage of Samouel's restaurant. Moreover, as would be expected, the more frequent customers are significantly more satisfied than the less frequent customers.

Descriptive Statistics

Dependent Variable: X17 – Satisfaction

X20 – Frequency of Patronage	X25 – Gender	Mean	Std. Deviation	N
Occasional Customer	Male	4.38	0.805	21
	Female	3.77	0.430	26
	Total	**4.04**	0.690	47
Somewhat Frequent Customer	Male	4.89	0.782	9
	Female	4.42	0.793	12
	Total	**4.62**	0.805	21
Very Frequent Customer	Male	6.29	0.464	24
	Female	5.00	1.309	8
	Total	**5.97**	0.933	32
Total	Male	5.31	1.113	54
	Female	4.15	0.868	46
	Total	**4.78**	1.160	100

EXHIBIT 13-11

Means and Standard Deviations for Customer Satisfaction By Gender and Frequency of Patronage

The second main effects comparison was whether there is a difference in satisfaction based on X_{25} – Gender. The F-ratio for gender is 25.604 and statistically significant (0.000) (See Exhibit 13-10). We therefore reject the null hypothesis of no differences and conclude that satisfaction of Samouel's customers differs based on gender. Specifically, for Samouel's Greek Cuisine the females are significantly less satisfied than males (female mean satisfaction levels are consistently lower than those for males).

The third hypothesis was no differences based on the combined effect of frequency of patronage and gender. The interaction between patronage frequency and gender is nonsignificant (0.095), meaning that the difference in satisfaction when both independent variables are considered together is very small. The null hypothesis of no difference is therefore not rejected for the interaction effect.

To better understand the results let's look first at the information in the Multiple Comparisons table shown in Exhibit 13-12. There are significant differences between all of the groups of customers – "Occasional", "Somewhat Frequent" and "Very Frequent". Thus, higher frequency of patronage does indicate a higher level of satisfaction and the significant differences exist for all the group comparisons.

Multiple Comparisons

Dependent Variable: X17 – Satisfaction
Scheffe

(I) X20 – Frequency of Patronage	(J) X20 – Frequency of Patronage	Mean Difference (I-J)	Sig.
Occasional Customer	Somewhat Frequent Customer	−0.58*	0.010
	Very Frequent Customer	−1.93*	0.000
Somewhat Frequent Customer	Occasional Customer	0.58*	0.010
	Very Frequent Customer	−1.35*	0.000
Very Frequent Customer	Occasional Customer	1.93*	0.000
	Somewhat Frequent Customer	1.35*	0.000

*The mean difference is significant at the 0.05 level.

EXHIBIT 13-12

Now that you have learned about ANOVA, see if you can answer the questions in the Research in Action box.

RESEARCH IN ACTION

APPLICATION OF ANOVA TO RESOLVE A QUALITY CONTROL ISSUE

Herb Claxton is Chief Work-Study Analyst for, _____, a large international chemical company. Mr Spiby, production manager of the agricultural division, approached him for help as far too many production runs in the fertilizer plant were failing quality checks performed by analysts in the company's chemical laboratory. He wondered how could this situation could have arisen when there had been no recent changes in procedure at the plant? In 15 years as division production manager he had never experienced this level of rejection.

Mr Spiby was adamant that the fertilizer met the required standards and that the fault lay with the laboratory analysts. But the Chief Chemist, Mr De Leeuw, insisted that the fertilizer runs were being correctly rejected. His analysts were highly qualified and experienced and there was no possibility that they could be at fault.

Herb Claxton, after some thought, recognized there were two key sources of variation that could be at the root of the problem. The sources had to be either the production runs or the analysts. To assist him in finding the problem, he called in his Chief Statistician, Johan du Plessis, to design a study to examine the situation.

Johan recognized this as an analysis of variance (ANOVA) problem. He asked that five samples be taken at random from a production run and that each of the samples be analysed by four analysts chosen at random. Each sample was to be analysed for nitrogen and iron content. Thus, two separate ANOVAs were to be performed – one comparing the five samples and another comparing the analysts.

The results of the ANOVA revealed that the variation between the five samples (rows) was not significant at the 5 % level for both nitrogen and iron content. This revealed that the sample results did not differ significantly. In other words, the analysts did not find real differences between the samples. Further, it was established that the variation between the analysts (columns) was significant at the 1 % level, indicating that the analysts did differ significantly among themselves with respect to their evaluation of the samples. This was the case for both nitrogen and iron content. Thus it was concluded that the analysts were unreliable in their evaluation of the samples.

What are the independent and dependent variables in the ANOVA? What should Herb Claxton report to Mr Spiby? The above formulation is for a simple two-way ANOVA as there is only one observation recorded for each combination of sample and analyst. What is the limitation of such a formulation? ■

MULTIVARIATE ANALYSIS OF VARIANCE (MANOVA)

MANOVA (Multivariate Analysis of Variance) is similar to ANOVA. The difference is that instead of one metric dependent variable the technique can examine two or more. The objective is the same since both techniques assess differences in groups (categorical variables) as they impact metric dependent variables. While ANOVA examines difference in a single metric dependent variable, MANOVA examines group differences across multiple metric dependent variables at the same time. With ANOVA the null hypothesis is the means of the single dependent variable are the same across the groups. In MANOVA the null hypothesis is the means of the multiple dependent variables are the same across the groups.

As an example, our customer survey has three relationship outcome variables – satisfaction, recommend to friend, and likelihood of returning in the future. All of these variables are measured metrically. An appropriate MANOVA would be to examine the relationship between gender (nonmetric) and the three outcome variables (metric). Similarly, another appropriate MANOVA application to our customer survey would be to examine the relationship between frequency of patronage (nonmetric) and the three outcome variables. MANOVA will not be covered in this text.

CONTINUING CASE   SAMOUEL'S GREEK CUISINE

Developing relationships and testing hypotheses

With the surveys completed, edited and entered into a computer file, a decision has to be made regarding the best way to analyse the data to understand the individuals interviewed, and how the information could be used to help Phil and his brother improve the restaurant's operations. The data analysis should be lead by the theory used to guide the design of the studies, as well as by the business experience of Phil and his brother. Phil, his brother, and the consultant have been brainstorming on how to best analyse the data to understand both the customer and employee surveys.

1. Draw several conceptual models to represent relationships that could be tested with the Samouel's restaurant surveys.

2. Which statistical techniques would be appropriate to test the proposed relationships?

3. Give examples of relationships that could be tested with Chi square? ... with ANOVA?

SUMMARY

■ Understand how to represent hypothesized relationships for testing

Conceptual models are an excellent way to display hypothesized relationships between independent and dependent variables visually. The relationships can indicate whether they are positive or negative in direction. Statistical techniques enable us to determine whether the proposed hypotheses can be confirmed by the empirical evidence.

■ Clarify the difference between sample statistics and population parameters

The purpose of inferential statistics is to develop estimates about a population using a sample from that population. A sample is a small subset of all the elements within the population. Sample statistics refers to measures obtained directly from the sample or calculated from the data in the sample. A population parameter is a variable or some sort of measured characteristic of the entire population. Sample statistics are useful in making inferences regarding the population's parameters. Generally, the actual population parameters are unknown since the cost to perform a census of the population is prohibitively high.

■ **Describe how to choose the appropriate statistical technique to test hypotheses**
The choice of a particular technique depends on (1) the number of variables and (2) the scale of measurement. Univariate statistics can assess only a single variable. Bivariate statistics can assess two variables. Multivariate statistics can examine many variables simultaneously, and can handle both multiple dependent and independent variables. The appropriate statistic also varies depending upon whether your data is measured nominally, ordinally, intervally or ratio.

■ **Explain when and how to use the t-test, ANOVA and Chi square to examine hypotheses**
Business researchers frequently want to test the hypothesis that one group differs from another group in terms of attitudes, behaviour or some other characteristic. Where more than one group is involved, bivariate tests must be used. In statistical terminology, the null hypothesis is that there are no significant differences between the two groups. Three bivariate hypothesis tests were discussed in this chapter. The first, Chi square, tests differences between groups using data that are measured on either a nominal and ordinal scale. The t-test and ANOVA are used to test differences in group means when data is measured with either an interval or ratio scale. Moreover, the t-test is appropriate to test difference in only two groups, while ANOVA can test differences in three or more groups. ■

Ethical Dilemma

Dan Henderson, President of a family owned business with a total of seven stores, believes the company needs to create a customer loyalty programme designed to reward customers who spend more than £200 per shopping trip. Therefore, he asks his younger sister to create a programme that can help the company identify and profile its most profitable customers. When the report is completed, the data indicate that the more affluent shoppers who spend more than £200 per shopping trip represent only a small part of the company's overall sales because they only shop 3–4 times a year and tend to buy only lower margin, designer clothing. But the report notes that the most profitable store customers tend to be over 40 years old from average income households and shop at least twice a month spending an average of £100 per trip on everything from cosmetics to housewares to high-margin private label clothing. After reviewing the report, Dan decides he still wants the customer loyalty programme to reward the high-dollar purchase customers justifying the decision by claiming that they are responsible for the store's upscale image that appeals to the regular store customer.

What do you think about Dan's decision?

REVIEW QUESTIONS

1. What is the difference between sample statistics and population parameters?
2. How does the researcher choose the correct statistical test?
3. What is the difference between the t-test, ANOVA and Chi square?
4. Why do we use follow-up tests in ANOVA?
5. What is the difference in one-way and two-way ANOVA?

DISCUSSION AND APPLICATION QUESTIONS

1. Draw a conceptual model of hypothesized relationships for the Samouel's customer database. Identify the hypotheses and indicate whether they are directional or nondirectional.
2. How do you select the appropriate statistical method to test a hypothesis?
3. A business researcher uses two-way ANOVA in a report for a client. The researcher does not check the assumptions of using the technique. Is this a problem?
4. **SPSS Application:** Use the customer survey database and compare the satisfaction, likelihood to recommend and likelihood to return for Samouel's Greek Cuisine and Gino's Italian Ristorante using the t-test. Are they statistically different and, if so, how would you interpret the findings?

INTERNET EXERCISES   www

1. Go to one of the following Web sites. Participate in a survey at one of the sites and prepare a report on what you learned.
   a. www.cc.gatech.edu/gvu/user_surveys
   b. www.survey.net
2. The Federal Reserve Bank of St Louis has a database called FRED (Federal Reserve Economic Data). Go to their Web site http://research.stlouisfed.org/fred/abotfred.html and report what you found. Identify some research questions that can be examined with the statistical techniques covered in this chapter.
3. Want more information on the fundamentals of statistical analysis and definitions of concepts and terms. Go to the Platonic Realms Interactive Mathematics Encyclopedia at www.mathacademy.com/pr/index.asp. Click on the Platonic Realms logo and then on Encyclopedia. Prepare a report summarizing the value of this Web site.

CHAPTER 14
EXAMINING RELATIONSHIPS USING CORRELATION AND REGRESSION

CONTENTS

LEARNING OUTCOMES

- Describe the nature of relationships between variables.
- Explain the concepts of correlation and regression analysis.
- Clarify the difference between bivariate and multiple regression analysis.
- Understand how multicollinearity can influence regression models.
- Describe how to use dummy variables in regression.

INTRODUCTION

Many business questions are concerned with the relationship between two or more variables. Questions such as "Are sales related to advertising?" "Is product quality related to customer loyalty?" "Is educational level associated with the purchase of a particular stock?" or "How much safety training is required to reduce accidents?" can be answered by using statistics to examine relationships between variables. This chapter explains how you can use statistics to examine questions like this. To better illustrate the statistical analysis, we have used the SPSS software. Specific instructions on how to use this software to calculate the results presented in this chapter can be found on this book's Web site at www.wileyeurope.com/college/hair.

TYPES OF RELATIONSHIPS BETWEEN VARIABLES

When variables have a consistent and systematic linkage between them, a relationship is present. Statistics are used to determine whether there is a statistical linkage or association between the variables. If there is a statistical association it is important to understand the relationship is not necessarily causal. That is, one variable cannot be said to cause the other one. Correlation and regression are associative techniques that help us to determine if there is a consistent and systematic relationship between two or more variables. There are four basic concepts we need to understand about relationships between variables: presence, nature of relationships, direction and strength of association. We will describe each of these concepts.

Presence

Presence assesses whether a systematic relationship exists between two or more variables. We rely on the concept of statistical significance to measure whether or not a relationship is present. If statistical significance is found between the variables we say that a relationship is present. That is, we say knowledge about the behaviour of one or more variables enables us to predict the behaviour of another variable. For example, if we found a statistically significant relationship between customer perceptions of the employees of Gino's Ristorante and their satisfaction with the restaurant, we would say a relationship is present and that perceptions of the employees will tell us what the perceptions of satisfaction are likely to be. We previously introduced the concept of a null hypothesis. With associative analysis, the null hypothesis is no association is present between the variables. If we find statistical significance then we reject the null hypothesis and accept the alternative hypothesis that a relationship exists between employee perceptions and satisfaction.

Nature of Relationships

A second important concept is how variables are related to one other. We typically say the relationship between variables is either linear or nonlinear. A **linear relationship** is a "straight-line association" between two or more variables. A **nonlinear relationship**, often referred to as **curvilinear**, is one in which the relationship is best described by a curve instead of a straight line. With a linear relationship the strength and nature of the relationship between the variables remains the same over the range of the variables. But with a nonlinear relationship the strength and nature changes over the range of both variables (for example, Y's relationship with X first gets weaker as X increases, but then gets stronger as the value of X continues to increase).

Linear relationships between variables are much easier to work with than are curvilinear. If we know the value of variable X, we can use the formula for a straight line ($Y = a + bX$) to determine the value of Y. But, when variables have a curvilinear relationship, the formula that best describes that linkage will be much more complex. Curvilinear relationships are beyond the scope of this book and most business researchers work with relationships that they believe are linear. In fact, most of the statistics covered in this book are based on the assumption that a linear relationship is an efficient way to describe the association between the variables being examined.

Direction

If a relationship is present between the variables we also need to know the **direction**. The direction of a relationship can be either positive or negative. In our restaurant example, a positive relationship exists if customers who rate employees favourably also are highly satisfied. Similarly, a negative relationship exists if customers say the portions are small (low rating) but they are still satisfied (high rating). A negative relationship between two variables is denoted with a minus ($-$) sign while a positive relationship has a plus ($+$) sign.

Strength of Association

Depending on the type of relationship being examined we generally categorize the strength of association as slight, small but definite, moderate, high or very strong. The **strength of association** measures the association between two variables. A slight, almost negligible situation is one in which a consistent and systematic relationship is not present between the variables. When a relationship is present, the business researcher must determine the strength of the association. A small association means the variables may have something in common but not much. A moderate or strong association means there is a consistent and systematic relationship and the relationship is much more evident when it is strong.

COVARIATION AND VARIABLE RELATIONSHIPS

Business researchers often want to know whether two or more variables are linked together. Variables are linked together if they exhibit covariation. **Covariation** is when one variable consistently and systematically changes relative to another variable. The correlation coefficient is used to assess this linkage. Large coefficients indicate high covariation and a strong relationship. Small coefficients indicate little covariation and a weak relationship. Thus, a **correlation coefficient** measures the degree of "covariation" between two variables. For example, if we know that purchases over the Internet are related to age, then we want to know the extent to which younger age persons make more purchases on the Internet, and ultimately which kinds of products they purchase most often and why. Thus, when two variables change together on a reliable and consistent basis (that is, covary), that information helps us to make predictions for use in developing sound business strategies.

One of the first issues we need to determine is whether the correlation coefficient is statistically significant. Regardless of its absolute size, a correlation coefficient has no meaning unless it is statistically significant. Most popular software programs tell you if a correlation is statistically significant. Thus, **statistical significance** means you are very sure the results of your statistical analysis are reliable. It doesn't mean the findings are important or that they are useful for decision making. Researcher judgement in light of the research objectives determines whether the findings are important and useful. The SPSS program reports significance as the probability the null hypothesis is supported (Excel uses the label p-value for statistical significance). Typical guidelines say that to be considered statistically significant the probability must be at least <0.05, and in some instances <0.01. This means to reject the null hypothesis there must be fewer than five chances in 100 you will be wrong if you reject the null hypothesis. In some business situations, a level of <0.10 is considered acceptable. But by accepting this probability level the researcher assumes more risk and must decide if the situation warrants the higher level of risk.

Once we have determined that the relationship is statistically significant, we then must decide what strength of association is acceptable. The size of the correlation coefficient is used to quantitatively describe the **strength of the association** between two or more variables. Rules of thumb have been proposed to characterize the strength of the association between variables, based on the absolute size of the correlation coefficient. As Exhibit 14-1 below suggests, correlation coefficients between ±0.91 and ±1.00 are considered "very strong". That is, covariance is definitely shared between the two variables being examined. In contrast, if the correlation coefficient is between ±0.00 and ±0.20, even though the coefficient is greater than zero in the sample, there is a good chance that the null hypothesis won't be rejected (unless you are using a large sample). These levels are only suggestions and other guidelines regarding the strength of the relationship are possible.

Coefficient Range	Strength of Association
±0.91 – ±1.00	Very Strong
±0.71 – ±0.90	High
±0.41 – ±0.70	Moderate
±0.21 – ±0.40	Small but definite relationship
±0.00 – ±0.20	Slight, almost negligible

*Assumes correlation coefficient is statistically significant

EXHIBIT 14-1

RULES OF THUMB ABOUT CORRELATION COEFFICIENT SIZE*

Scatter diagrams are an easy way to display the covariation between two variables visually. A **scatter diagram**, sometimes referred to as a **scattergram**, is a plot of the values of two variables for all the observations in the sample. It is customary to plot the dependent variable on the vertical axis and the independent variable on the horizontal axis. Exhibits 14-2a – c are examples of possible relationships between two variables that might be plotted on a scatter diagram. In Exhibit 14-2a, there is no apparent relationship or association between the variables. That is, there is no predictable or identifiable pattern to the points. Knowing the values of Y or X would not tell you very much (probably nothing at all) about the possible values of the other variable. Exhibit 14-2a suggests there is no consistent and systematic relationship between Y and X, and thus very little or no covariation shared by the two variables. If the amount of covariation shared by these two variables were measured, it would be very close to zero.

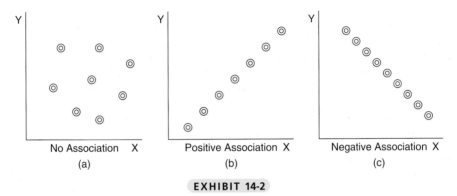

EXHIBIT 14-2

Scatter Diagrams Illustrating Various Relationships

In Exhibit 14-2b, the pattern of the two variables shows a very different picture. There is a distinct pattern to the points on the scatter diagram that is easily described as a straight line. We refer to this relationship as positive, because increases in the value of Y are associated with increases in the value of X. Similarly, if the values of Y decrease, the values of X will decrease as well. If we measured the covariation between the values of Y and X, it would be relatively high. Thus, changes in the value of Y are consistently and systematically related to changes in the value of X.

Exhibit 14-2c shows a similar type of pattern between the values of Y and X, but the direction of the relationship is opposite to that in Exhibit 14-2b. There is a linear pattern, but now when the value of Y increases the values of X decrease. That is, the values of Y and X change in the opposite direction. This type of relationship is described as a negative relationship. There is a large amount of covariation between the two variables because Y and X consistently change together. The difference is they move in the opposite direction from Exhibit 14-2b. Covariation refers to the amount of shared movement between two variables, not the direction of the relationship.

CORRELATION ANALYSIS

Scatter diagrams enable us to demonstrate visually the relationship between two variables and the extent to which they covary. For example, a scatter diagram can tell us that as age increases the average consumption of aspirin increases too, or that on a hot day we consume more water. But even though a visual display of data is very useful, as we learned in Chapter 13 some situations may need a quantitative measure of the covariation between two variables to fully understand the relationship.

The **Pearson correlation** measures the linear association between two metric variables. The number representing the Pearson correlation is referred to as a correlation coefficient. It ranges from -1.00 to $+1.00$, with zero representing absolutely no association between the two metric variables. While -1.00 or $+1.00$ is possible and represents a perfect association between two variables, it very seldom occurs. The larger the correlation coefficient the stronger the linkage or level of association. Correlation coefficients can be either positive or negative, depending upon the direction of the relationship between the variables. If there is a positive correlation coefficient between X and Y, then increases in the value of X are associated with increases in the value of Y, and vice versa.

The correlation coefficient assesses the association between two variables. The null hypothesis states there is no association between two variables and that the correlation coefficient is zero (or very small). For example, we may hypothesize that there is no relationship between preference for McDonald's fries and income levels. If you take measures of the two variables (consumption of McDonald's fries and income) from a sample of the population and calculate the correlation coefficient for that sample to be 0.36, the question is "What is the probability that you would get a correlation coefficient of 0.36 in your sample if the correlation coefficient in the population is actually zero?" That is, if you calculate a large correlation coefficient between two variables in your sample – consumption of McDonald's fries and income (and your sample was properly selected from the population of interest), then the chances the population correlation coefficient is really zero are small. If the correlation coefficient is statistically significant, you can reject the null hypothesis and conclude with some degree of confidence the two variables you are examining share some association in the population. In other words, consumption of McDonald's fries is related to income.

In addition to examining the correlation coefficient, we often square the correlation coefficient to get the **coefficient of determination**, or r^2. The coefficient of determination ranges from 0.00 to 1.0 and represents the amount of variation explained or accounted for in one variable by one or more other variables. If a correlation coefficient is 0.543, then the r^2 would be 0.294, meaning that approximately 29.4% of the variation in one variable is associated with the other variable. As with the correlation coefficient, the larger the coefficient of determination, the stronger the relationship between the variables being examined.

When we use the Pearson correlation coefficient we must make several assumptions about the nature of the data. Firstly, the two variables are assumed to have been measured using interval or ratio-scaled measures (that is, metric). Other types of correlation coefficients can be used if they are nominal or ordinal measures. Later in the chapter we discuss the Spearman correlation coefficient for use with ordinal data. Another assumption of the Pearson correlation coefficient is the relationship we are examining is linear. That is, a straight line is an accurate description of the relationship between the two metric variables.

A third assumption of the Pearson correlation coefficient is the variables you are examining are from a normally distributed population. A normal distribution, also referred to as a bell-shaped curve (see Chapter 12), is a common assumption for many statistical techniques used by business researchers. But it is often difficult to determine whether sample data are normally distributed. Since correlation is considered a reasonably robust statistic when the distribution varies from normal, this assumption frequently is taken for granted.

EXAMPLE OF PEARSON BIVARIATE CORRELATION

Phil Samouel collected information in his employee survey on employee cooperation and teamwork as well as likelihood to search for a job. Since a stable workforce would be good for his restaurant, he wants to use his survey findings to understand better what can be done to retain good employees. One of the options he is considering implementing is a new training programme for employees. He would therefore like to know if the relationship between the perceived cooperation among his employees and likelihood to search for a new job is significant and positive. If there is a relationship he can use this information in developing a training programme to ensure that his employees cooperate more in preparing meals and serving customers.

The null hypothesis is that no relationship exists between perceived cooperation among Samouel's employees and likelihood to search for a new job. Recall from the employee questionnaire described in Chapter 9 that information was collected on Intention to Search for another job (X_{16}) and perceived cooperation among members of a work group (X_4). To test this hypothesis, we must calculate the correlation between these two variables. This has been done and is reported in Exhibit 14-3. The Data Analysis box explains how to execute this correlation.

DATA ANALYSIS
USING SPSS TO CALCULATE A PEARSON BIVARIATE CORRELATION

The SPSS click-through sequence to execute the Pearson bivariate correlation is: ANALYSE → CORRELATE → BIVARIATE, which leads to a dialogue box where you select the variables. Highlight X_{16} and X_4 and move them into the Variables box. We will use the three default options: Pearson correlation, two-tailed test of significance, and flag significant variables. Next go to the Options box and click on Means and Standard Deviations and then Continue. Finally, click "OK" at the top right of the dialogue box to run the programme. The results will be the same as those in Exhibit 14-3. ■

The Correlations table in Exhibit 14–3 shows us how the two variables are related. Stated another way, it tells us if the two variables covary. To interpret the table, look at the column and row where the variables intersect. For example, the far-right column in the table is variable X_{16} – Intention to Search and the number at the top of the column is −0.416**. This indicates the correlation between variable X_4 – Work Group Cooperation and X_{16} – Intention to Search is −0.416, and the significance level is .001 (this number is right below −0.416** and in the row labelled Sig. (two-tailed), which is the t-test that shows the correlation is significant). The numbers in the row labelled N represent the number of respondents used to compute the correlation = the sample size of 63 Samouel's employees.

The results reported in Exhibit 14-3 have confirmed that perceived work group cooperation is significantly correlated with intention to search for another job. This means we can reject the null hypothesis of no relationship between these two variables. Moreover, the correlation is negative and moderately strong so we can conclude that employees who believe there is less work group cooperation exhibit a higher intention to search for another job. To ensure a more stable workforce, Phil needs to implement the employee training he is considering so that he can improve cooperation within employee work groups.

PRACTICAL SIGNIFICANCE OF THE CORRELATION COEFFICIENT

If the correlation coefficient is strong and statistically significant, you can conclude there is a relationship between the variables. In our example, Phil Samouel can be reasonably confident the variables work group cooperation and intention to search are related because the correlation is −0.416 and highly significant (0.001). But if the correlation coefficient is small there are two

Descriptive Statistics

	Mean	Std. Deviation	N
X_4 – Work Group Cooperation	3.51	1.11	63
X_{16} – Intention to Search	4.32	1.86	63

Correlations

		X_4 – Work Group Cooperation	X_{16} – Intention to Search
X_4 – Work Group Cooperation	Pearson Correlation	1.0	−0.416**
	Sig. (two-tailed)	.	0.001
	N	63	63
X_{16} – Intention to Search	Pearson Correlation	−0.416**	1.0
	Sig. (two-tailed)	0.001	.
	N	63	63

**Correlation is significant at the 0.01 level (two-tailed).

EXHIBIT 14-3

Bivariate Correlation between Work Group Cooperation and Intention to Search for Another Job

possibilities. One, either a consistent, systematic relationship does not exist between the variables or, two, the association exists but it is not linear and other types of relationships must be considered.

Even if the correlation coefficient is statistically significant, this does not mean it is practically significant. To determine **practical significance**, we must also ask whether the numbers we calculated are meaningful. In calculating the statistical significance of a correlation coefficient the sample size is a major influence. With large sample sizes it is possible to have a statistically significant correlation coefficient that is really too small to be of any practical use. For example, if the correlation coefficient between work group cooperation and intention to search was 0.20 (significant at 0.05 level), the coefficient of determination would be 0.04. Is this coefficient of determination of practical significance? Is the value of knowing that you have explained 4 % of the variation worth the cost of collecting and analysing the data? It depends upon the research objectives. So, you must always look at both types of significance (statistical and practical) before you develop your conclusions, particularly when examining more complex issues.

MEASUREMENT SCALES AND CORRELATION

Business researchers often find the answers to their questions can only be measured with ordinal or nominal scales. For example, if we wanted to see if gender is related to soft drink consumption we have a problem because gender is a nominal variable. If we used the Pearson correlation coefficient to examine fruit juice consumption of males and females, and assumed the measure has interval or ratio-scale properties, our results would be misleading. For example, using a two-point scale (nonmetric) instead of a five-point scale (metric) substantially reduces the amount of information available and may result in an understatement of the "true" correlation coefficient in the population.

When scales used to collect data are nominal or ordinal (nonmetric) what can the analyst do? One option is to use the Spearman rank-order correlation coefficient rather than the Pearson product-moment correlation. The Spearman correlation coefficient typically results in a lower coefficient, but is considered a more conservative statistic.

EXAMPLE OF SPEARMAN'S RANK ORDER CORRELATION

The survey of restaurant customers collected data on four restaurant selection factors. Customers were asked to rank the following four factors in terms of their importance in selecting a restaurant where they want to dine – food quality, atmosphere, prices and employees. The survey variables were X_{13} to X_{16} and they were measured ordinally. Phil Samouel would like to know whether "food quality" rankings are related to "atmosphere" rankings. An answer to this question will help Phil to know whether to emphasize food quality in his advertising or atmosphere, or both variables. These are ordinal data (ranking) so the Pearson correlation cannot be used. The Spearman rho is the appropriate correlation to calculate. The null hypothesis is there is no difference in the rankings of the two restaurant selection factors. Instructions on how to use SPSS to calculate the Spearman rho are provided in the Data Analysis box.

DATA ANALYSIS

USING SPSS TO CALCULATE SPEARMAN'S RHO CORRELATION

Using the Samouel's customer database, the SPSS click-through sequence is: "ANALYSE → CORRELATE → BIVARIATE". Highlight variables X_{13} and X_{14} and move them to the Variables box. The Pearson correlation is the default along with the two-tailed test of significance and Flag significant correlations. "Unclick" the Pearson Correlation and click on Spearman. Then click on "OK" at the top right of the dialogue box to run the program. The results will be the same as that shown in Exhibit 14-4. ■

Information in the Correlations table in Exhibit 14-4 shows that the correlation between variables X_{13} – Food Quality and X_{14} – Atmosphere is -0.801, and the significance level is 0.000. This demonstrates there is a significant, negative relationship between the two restaurant selection factors. The negative correlation means that customers who rank food quality high in importance as a selection factor will rank atmosphere as significantly less important. The restaurant customers rank food quality as very important much more often than atmosphere, as shown visually in the bar charts in Exhibit 14-5.

Phil now knows that customers rank food quality as relatively more important than atmosphere. But he does not know the rankings of the selection factors in general. Variables X_{13} to X_{16} are ordinal data. Therefore, we cannot compare them by calculating the means. Instead, we must use

Nonparametric Correlations

			X_{13} – Food Quality Ranking	X_{14} – Atmosphere Ranking
Spearman's rho	X_{13} – Food Quality Ranking	Correlation Coefficient	1.000	−0.801**
		Sig. (two-tailed)	.	0.000
		N	200	200
	X_{14} – Atmosphere Ranking	Correlation Coefficient	−0.801**	1.000
		Sig. (two-tailed)	0.000	.
		N	200	200

**Correlation is significant at the. 01 level (2-tailed).

EXHIBIT 14-4

Correlation of Food Quality and Atmosphere Using Spearman's rho

the median to compare the rankings of the four restaurant selection factors. This will enable us to understand the relationships better.

The rankings are shown in Exhibit 14-6. Recall the four selection factors were ranked from 1 to 4, with 4 = most important. Thus, the variable with the largest median is ranked the highest and is the most important, and the variable with the lowest median is the least important. Food quality (X_{13}) is ranked as the most important (median = 4) while X_{15} – Prices is the least important (median = 1). Moreover, note the minimum for variables X_{13} and X_{14} is 2 and for X_{15} and X_{16} is 1. Thus, based on the median rankings customers of these two restaurants are interested in food quality first and atmosphere second. Moreover, by comparing the medians we can see that employees and prices are the least important selection factors. This does not mean they are unimportant and can be ignored by Phil. But that relatively speaking food quality and atmosphere are more important. In developing an action plan to compete with Gino's, Phil needs to focus initially on his food, then on atmosphere and to some extent on his employees (some customers ranked employees most important, as shown by the maximum value of 4).

STATISTICAL TECHNIQUES AND DATA ANALYSIS

Most business problems involve many variables. Managers look at multiple performance dimensions when they evaluate their employees. Consumers evaluate many characteristics of products in deciding which to purchase. Multiple factors influence the stocks a broker recommends. Restaurant customers consider many factors in deciding where to dine. As the world becomes more complex, more factors influence the decisions managers make. Thus, increasingly business researchers must rely on more sophisticated methods of data analysis.

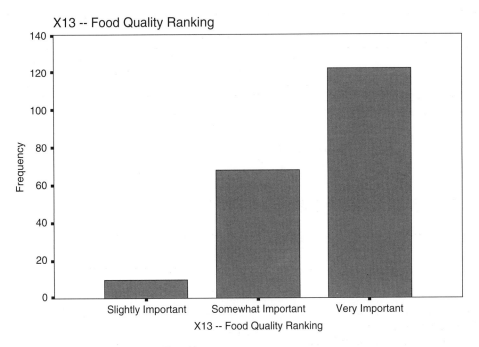

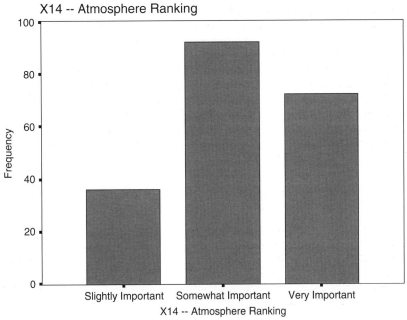

EXHIBIT 14-5

Bar Charts of Rankings for Food Quality and Atmosphere

Statistics

		X$_{13}$ – Food Quality Ranking	X$_{14}$ – Atmosphere Ranking	X$_{15}$ – Prices Ranking	X$_{16}$ – Employees Ranking
N	Valid	200	200	200	200
	Missing	0	0	0	0
Median		4.00	3.00	1.00	2.00
Minimum		2	2	1	1
Maximum		4	4	3	4

EXHIBIT 14-6

Customer Rankings of Restaurant Selection Factors

Our discussion to this point has dealt with univariate and bivariate analysis. **Univariate analysis** involves statistically testing a single variable, while **bivariate analysis** involves two variables. When business problems involve three or more variables they are inherently multidimensional and require the use of multivariate analysis. **Multivariate analysis** involves using statistical methods to analyse multiple variables at the same time. For example, managers trying to better understand their employees might examine job satisfaction, job commitment, work type (part-time versus full-time), shift worked (day or night), age and so on. Similarly, consumers comparing supermarkets might look at the freshness and variety of produce, store location, hours of operation, cleanliness, courtesy and helpfulness of employees, and so forth. Business researchers need multivariate statistical techniques to understand such complex problems fully.

Exhitit 14-7 displays a useful classification of statistical techniques. As you can see at the top, we divide the techniques into dependence and interdependence depending on the number of dependent variables. If there is a single dependent variable a technique is referred to as a dependence method. That is, we have both dependent and independent variables in our analysis. In contrast, when we do not have a dependent variable we refer to the technique as an interdependence method. That is, all variables are analysed together and our goal is to form groups or give meaning to a set of variables or respondents.

Using the classification we can select the appropriate statistical technique. If we have a research problem that involves association or prediction using both dependent and independent variables, we should look at the dependence techniques on the left side of the diagram. The choice of a particular statistical technique depends on whether we have a metric or nonmetric dependent variable. With a nonmetric, ordinally measured dependent we would use the Spearman correlation that we have already discussed. With a nonmetric, nominal dependent we use discriminant analysis or logistic regression. On the other hand, if our dependent variable is metric, we can use correlation, regression, ANOVA or MANOVA. The various statistical techniques are defined in Exhibit 14-8. In Chapter 13 we discussed ANOVA and MANOVA. In this chapter we discuss correlation and regression. The other statistical techniques are beyond the scope of this text but are discussed on the book's Web site at www.wileyeurope.com/college/hair.

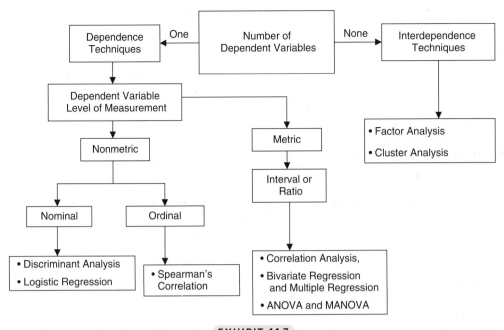

EXHIBIT 14-7

Classification of Statistical Techniques

REGRESSION ANALYSIS

Regression analysis is perhaps the most widely applied data analysis technique for measuring linear relationships between two or more variables. Correlation tells us if a relationship exists between two variables, as well as the overall strength of the relationship. Sometimes, however, these answers do not provide enough information for management to make the proper decision. For example, Phil Samouel may want to examine the relationship between several work environment measures and the commitment of his employees. Exhibit 14-9 shows the three supervision variables (X_3, X_6 and X_{10}) from the employee survey and one of the commitment variables (X_{14} – Effort). If Phil Samouel used bivariate regression he would have to run three regression models, one for each of the three supervision variables. But with multiple regression Phil could run only one regression model. That is, the metric dependent variable would be X_{14} – Effort and the three metric independent variables would be X_3, X_6 and X_{10} (all of these variables measure employee perceptions of supervision at Samouel's Greek restaurant).

Managers would often like to be able to predict, for example, how much impact an advertising campaign will have on sales. The three typical methods to make these predictions are: (1) informed judgment; (2) extrapolation from past behaviour; and (3) regression. Informed judgement and extrapolation both assume that events and behaviours in the past will continue into the future. When these past events change, extrapolation and judgement cannot help the business researcher

ANOVA – ANOVA stands for analysis of variance. It is used to examine statistical differences between the means of two or more groups. The dependent variable is metric and the independent variable(s) is nonmetric. One-way ANOVA has a single nonmetric independent variable and two-way ANOVA can have two or more nonmetric independent variables.

Bivariate Regression – this is a type of regression that has a single metric dependent variable and a single metric independent variable.

Cluster Analysis – This type of analysis enables researchers to place objects (for example, customers, brands, products) into groups so that objects within the groups are similar to each other. At the same time, objects in any particular group are different from objects in all other groups.

Correlation – correlation examines the association between two metric variables. The strength of the association is measured by the correlation coefficient.

Discriminant Analysis – This enables the researcher to predict group membership using two or more metric independent variables. The group membership variable is a nonmetric dependent variable.

Factor Analysis – This technique is used to summarize the information from a large number of variables into a much smaller number of variables or factors. It is used to combine variables whereas cluster analysis is used to identify groups with similar characteristics.

Logistic Regression – this is a special type of regression that can have a nonmetric dependent variable.

Multiple Regression – this type of regression has a single metric dependent variable and several metric independent variables.

MANOVA – same technique as ANOVA but it can examine group differences across two or more metric dependent variables at the same time.

EXHIBIT 14-8

Definitions of Statistical Techniques

predict the future with an acceptable level of accuracy. In such cases, the business researcher needs a technique like regression analysis.

Our initial discussion will focus on bivariate linear regression. **Bivariate regression** analysis is a statistical technique that examines information about the relationship between one independent (predictor) variable and one dependent (criterion) variable and makes predictions. Values of the independent variable are examined and the behaviour of the dependent variable is observed and compared using the formula for a straight line. The formula for linear regression is:

$$Y = a + bX$$

3. My supervisor gives credit and praise for work well done.	Strongly Disagree Strongly Agree 1 2 3 4 5 6 7
6. My supervisor recognizes my potential.	Strongly Disagree Strongly Agree 1 2 3 4 5 6 7
10. My supervisor is friendly and helpful.	Strongly Disagree Strongly Agree 1 2 3 4 5 6 7

14. I am willing to put in a great deal of effort beyond that normally expected to help Samouel's restaurant to be successful.	Strongly Disagree Strongly Agree 1 2 3 4 5 6 7

EXHIBIT 14-9

Selected Variables from the Samouel's Employee Survey

Where

Y = the predicted variable
X = the variable used to predict Y
a = the intercept, or point where the line cuts the y axis when $X = 0$
b = the slope or the change in y for any corresponding change in one unit of X

This is similar to the straight-line relationship we described underlying the correlation coefficient. When the scatter diagram is a straight line that is not horizontal there is a correlation between the two variables. Regression is directly related to correlation and indeed bivariate regression and correlation analysis are the same.

The task of the business researcher is to find the best method to fit a straight line to the data. The **least squares method** is a relatively simple mathematical method of ensuring the straight line that runs through the points on the scatter diagram is positioned so as to be the best possible. To do this, it minimizes the distances from the straight line to all the points on the scatter diagram. It measures these distances by looking at the errors in predicting Y from X. The least squares criterion minimizes the sum of the squared deviations between the actual values and the straight line predicted by the regression.

We must evaluate certain assumptions when we use regression analysis just as with correlation. Firstly, regression analysis assumes the relationship between two variables is linear. If the scatter diagram of the values of both variables looks like the plot in Exhibit 14-2b or 14-2c, this assumption would seem to be a good one. If the plot looks like 14-2a, regression analysis is not the appropriate choice.

Secondly, we refer to the two variables as independent and dependent but this does not mean we can say that one variable causes the behaviour of the other. Regression analysis assesses the magnitude and type of association between two variables and makes predictions, but it is nothing more than a statistical tool. It is often a temptation to apply causation to the results of a regression analysis. But causation must come from theory, which is beyond the field of statistics. Consequently, even though two variables, such as sales and advertising, are logically related, regression analysis does not permit the business researcher to make cause-and-effect conclusions.

The remaining assumptions of simple regression are: (1) the variables are measured using interval or ratio scales and come from a normal population; and (2) the error terms are independent and distributed normally. We will cover these assumptions in more detail when we discuss multiple regression. One point we should make, however, is that nominal and ordinal scales can be included in a regression if they are converted to a dummy variable coding (discussed later in this chapter).

With bivariate regression analysis, we have one independent variable and one dependent variable. But business researchers are often interested in examining the combined influence of several independent variables on one dependent variable. For example, are purchasing patterns on the Internet related not only to age, but also to income, ethnicity, gender, geographic location, education level, and so forth? Similarly, Phil Samouel might want to know whether customer satisfaction with his restaurant is related only to perceptions of the restaurant's food quality (X_1), or is satisfaction also related to perceptions of menu variety (X_9), whether it is a fun place to go (X_8); reasonable prices (X_{10}), and/or any of the other perceptions variables? Multiple regression enables us to measure these relationships without running several separate bivariate regressions. We first look at an example of bivariate or simple regression analysis and then move on to multiple regression.

EXAMPLE OF BIVARIATE REGRESSION

Phil Samouel regularly reads the European Restaurant Association trade publications to better understand the restaurant and trends. He consistently sees studies that report food quality as the most important variable used by customers in selecting and deciding to return to a particular restaurant again. He wants to know if having high quality food will help him to retain customers and grow his business. Bivariate regression analysis can provide information to help answer this question.

Phil's customer survey collected information on satisfaction (X_{17}). This variable was measured as 1 = Not Very Satisfied and 7 = Highly Satisfied. Variable X_1 was a measure of respondents' perceptions of the quality of food (1 = Strongly Disagree, 7 = Strongly Agree). The null hypothesis in this case is there is no relationship between X_{17} – Satisfaction and X_1 – Excellent Food Quality. The alternative hypothesis is that X_{17} and X_1 are significantly related. This hypothesis can be tested using bivariate regression because we have a single metric dependent variable and a single metric independent variable. Instructions on how to run bivariate regression are given in the Data Analysis box.

DATA ANALYSIS
USING SPSS TO CALCULATE A BIVARIATE REGRESSION

(Samouel's and Gino's customers are considered separately)

The SPSS software can help us to test the null hypothesis of no relationship between customer satisfaction and food quality. Since we want to look at the customers from the two restaurants separately, we must first use the Data pull-down menu to split the sample into Samouel's and Gino's customers. To do so, go to the Data pull down menu, click on Compare groups, and then highlight variable X_{28} – Competitor and move it into the box labelled "Groups based on": and then click OK. As noted earlier, we do this because Phil wants to compare his restaurant with Gino's.

To run the bivariate regression, the SPSS click-through sequence is: ANALYSE → REGRESSION → LINEAR: Click on X_{17} – Satisfaction and move it to the Dependent Variable box. Click on X_1 – Excellent Food Quality and move it to the Independent Variables box. Use the default Enter in the box labeled "Method". Click on the "Statistics" button and use the defaults for "Estimates" and "Model fit", then click on "Descriptives". Finally, click "Continue" and "OK" to execute the program. The results will be the same as in Exhibit 14-10. ■

The results for testing our hypothesis using bivariate regression analysis are shown in Exhibit 14-10. Note that we have separated the customer surveys into two groups – customers from Samouel's and customers from Gino's. This enables us to make comparisons between the results for the two restaurants. The Descriptive Statistics table displays the mean of Samouel's and Gino's for both the dependent variable X_{17} (Samouel's = 4.78; Gino's = 5.96) and the independent variable X_1 (Samouel's = 5.24; Gino's = 5.81). In the table labelled Model Summary we see that the r^2 for Samouel's regression model is 0.263 and for Gino's is 0.110. As you recall from our earlier discussion, r^2 shows the amount of variation in one variable that is accounted for by another variable. In this case, customer perceptions of Samouel's food quality account for 26.3% of the total variation in customer satisfaction with the restaurant, while for Gino's it is only 11.0%.

There are several other aspects of bivariate regression you need to know about. These include an understanding of the F-ratio, the regression and residual sums of squares, and the regression coefficient. Exhibit 14-11 contains this information for the bivariate regression of customer satisfaction and food quality. The ANOVA table shows the F-ratio for the regression models. This statistic assesses the statistical significance of the overall regression model. Under the Sum of Squares column, the variance in X_{17} – Customer Satisfaction that is associated with X_1 – Excellent Quality Food is referred to as **explained variance** (Regression Sum of Squares). The remainder of the total variance in X_{17} that is not associated with X_1 is referred to as **unexplained variance** (referred to as Residual Sum of Squares in the table). The **F-ratio** is the result of comparing the amount of explained variance to the unexplained variance. Specifically, if you divide the mean square for the regression (35.001) by the mean square for the residual (1.002) you will get the F-ratio for Samouel's

Descriptive Statistics

X$_{28}$ – Competitor		Mean
Samouel's	X$_{17}$ – Satisfaction	4.78
	X$_1$ – Excellent Food Quality	5.24
Gino's	X$_{17}$ – Satisfaction	5.96
	X$_1$ – Excellent Food Quality	5.81

Model Summary

X$_{28}$ – Competitor	Model	R	R Square
Samouel's	1	0.513[a]	0.263
Gino's	1	0.331[a]	0.110

Predictors: X$_1$ – Excellent Food Quality

EXHIBIT 14-10

Bivariate Regression of Satisfaction and Food Quality

ANOVA

X$_{28}$ – Competitor		Sum of Squares	Mean Square	F	Sig.
Samouel's	**Regression**	35.001	35.001	34.945	0.000
	Residual	98.159	1.002		
	Total	133.160			
Gino's	**Regression**	10.310	10.310	12.095	0.001
	Residual	83.530	0.852		
	Total	93.840			

Predictor Variable: X$_1$ – Excellent Quality Food
Dependent Variable: X$_{17}$ – Satisfaction

EXHIBIT 14-11

Other Aspects of Bivariate Regression

Coefficients						
		Unstandardized Coefficients		Standardized Coefficients	t	Sig.
		B	Std. Error	Beta		
X_{28} – Competitor Samouel's	X_1 – Food Quality	0.459	0.078	0.513	5.911	0.000
Gino's	X_1 – Food Quality	0.284	0.082	0.331	3.478	0.001

Dependent Variable: X_{17} – Satisfaction

EXHIBIT 14-11

continued

of 34.945. The larger the F-ratio, the more variance in the dependent variable is explained by the independent variable. In our bivariate regression example, the F-ratio for Samouel's (34.945) indicates the model is highly significant at the 0.000 level. The relationship for Gino's is relatively less significant (F-ratio = 12.095) but still very strong (0.001).

The Sums of Squares also provides useful information in understanding regression. For Samouel's the Regression Sum of Squares is 35.001 and the Residual Sum of Squares is 98.159. For Gino's the Regression Sum of Squares is 10.310 and the Residual Sum of Squares is 83.530. Examination of the regression, residual and total sums of squares tells us that for both regression models there is a lot of unexplained (residual) variance in the dependent variable. Specifically, to determine the percentage of unexplained variance for a regression model you simply divide the residual variance by the total variance. For Samouel's, you divide 98.159 (residual sum of squares) by 133.160 (total sum of squares) and you find out that 73.7% of the total variance is not explained by this bivariate regression model (98.159/133.160 = 73.7 %). Moreover, if you divide 35.001 (regression sum of squares) by 133.160 (total sum of squares) and you find out that 26.3% of the total variance is explained by this bivariate regression model (35.001/133.160 = 26.3 %). Note that dividing the regression sum of squares by the total sum of squares gives you the r^2 for this regression model (26.3%).

Regression coefficients tell us how much of the variance in the dependent variable is explained by the independent variable. Let's look at the regression coefficient for X_1 for Samouel's restaurant that is shown in the Coefficients table in Exhibit 14-11. The column labelled "Unstandardized Coefficients" reveals the unstandardized regression coefficient for X_1 is 0.459. The column labelled Sig. indicates the statistical significance of the regression coefficient for X_1. The t-test tells us whether the regression coefficient is different enough from zero to be statistically significant. The t statistic is calculated by dividing the regression coefficient by its standard error (labelled Std. error in the Coefficients table). If you divide 0.459 by 0.078, you will get a t-value of 5.911, which is significant at the 0.000 level (Note: any differences in calculating the numbers are due to rounding errors).

The relationship between customer satisfaction and food quality for Samouel's is positive but only somewhat strong. The regression coefficient (b) for X_1 is interpreted as: "for every unit that X_1 increases, X_{17} will increase by 0.459 units". Recall Phil Samouel wanted to know: "Will excellent quality food improve customer satisfaction, and therefore the ability to attract and retain customers?" The answer is "Somewhat." The model was significant at the 0.000 level and the r^2 was 0.263, but is this practically significant? An r^2 of 0.263 suggests Phil should focus on improving his food quality, but continue looking for other areas to improve that also are related to customer satisfaction. He also must be concerned because Gino's food is rated as higher in quality (5.81 versus 5.24) and while not as closely related to satisfaction there is still a significant relationship.

The Coefficients table contains both "Unstandardized Coefficients" (b) and "Standardized Coefficients" (betas). We need not be concerned with standardized coefficients in bivariate regression. But in multiple regression when several independent variables are used the scales measuring the several independent variables may not always be the same (using number of salespersons and advertising expenditures to predict sales). **Standardization** is a method of adjusting for different units of measure across variables. The term "**Beta**" refers to regression coefficients that have been standardized.

MULTIPLE REGRESSION ANALYSIS

Recall that in bivariate regression we used a single independent variable to predict a single dependent variable. With **multiple regression** analysis we enter several independent variables into the same type of regression equation and predict a single dependent variable. A separate regression coefficient then is calculated for each independent variable that describes its individual relationship with the dependent variable. These coefficients enable the researcher to evaluate the relative influence of several independent variables on the dependent variable. Multiple regression is a more realistic model because in the world we live in predictions almost always depend upon multiple factors, not just one.

The relationship between each independent variable and the dependent measure is assumed to be linear as it was with bivariate regression. The task of the researcher is to find the best means of fitting a straight line to the data. The least squares method is a relatively simple mathematical technique that makes sure the straight line will best represent the relationship between the multiple independent variables and the single dependent variable. The logic of least squares is that no straight line can completely represent every dot in a regression scatter diagram. Even if there were a perfect correlation between the variables (and there never is) there will always be some differences between the actual scores (each dot) and the predicted scores using the regression line. In short, any regression line will produce some errors. The least squares method minimizes the errors in predicting the dependent variable from the independent variables. An F-test is then used to compare the variance explained by the regression to the unexplained variance (residual) and the result tells us if the overall relationship is statistically significant.

To understand the relationship between the multiple independent variables and the single dependent variable, we examine the regression coefficients for each independent variable. These coefficients describe the average amount of change in Y (dependent variable) given a unit change in the independent variable (X) you are examining. Additionally, a regression coefficient describes the relationship of each independent variable with the dependent variable. For example, assume the dependent variable is the number of bottles of water consumed in an afternoon. The two independent variables are temperature and distance walked. The regression coefficients for both of these independent variables are likely to be rather large because both are logically related to the number of bottles of water consumed.

Multiple regression is essentially the same as bivariate regression except you are working with more than one independent variable. With the addition of more than one independent variable a couple of new issues must be considered. One issue is whether the independent variables are measured using the same or a different scale. If a different scale is used we cannot make direct comparisons between the regression coefficients to determine the relative importance of each independent variable in predicting the dependent variable. For example, assume we want to predict annual sales revenue of the Mercedes dealership using number of salespeople and advertising expenditures. These two variables are measured using different scale units. Salespeople are measured using the actual number and advertising expenditures are measured in dollars. When several independent variables are measured with different scales, it is not proper to directly compare the regression coefficients to see which independent variable most influences the dependent variable.

Since independent variables often are measured with different scale units, and business researchers typically want to identify which variables are relatively more important, we must have a way to overcome this problem. To do this, we use the standardized regression coefficient, referred to as a beta coefficient. This standardization process adjusts the regression coefficients to account for the different scales of measurement. Beta coefficients range from -1.00 to $+1.00$. When we use beta coefficients in multiple regression we can make direct comparisons between the independent variables to determine which have the most influence on the dependent variable. The larger the absolute value of a standardized beta coefficient the more relative importance it assumes in predicting the dependent variable.

Another issue we must be concerned about is that the several independent variables are statistically independent and uncorrelated with one another. If high correlations exist among the independent variables multicollinearity will definitely be a problem, particularly with stepwise multiple regression. As a researcher you must test for and remove multicollinearity if it is present. One way is to examine the correlation matrix for the independent variables and use only those that have low correlations. Another approach is to use internal checks included in most software programs that will signal multicollinearity is a problem and identify where problems exist.

STATISTICAL VERSUS PRACTICAL SIGNIFICANCE

When we discussed bivariate regression, we used the coefficient of determination (denoted as r^2) to see if the variance in the dependent variable was consistently and systematically related to the independent variable. The same concept applies to multiple regression. The term multiple coefficient of determination indicates we are measuring the ability of the multiple independent variables to predict the single dependent variable. But when we refer to the **multiple coefficient of determination** (with multiple independent variables) we denote it as R^2. Just as in bivariate regression, the multiple coefficient of determination can be interpreted as the proportion of the variability in the dependent variable that can be explained by the several independent variables in the model.

The first step in examining the overall regression model is to see if it is statistically significant. We do this using the F statistic. If the F statistic is significant, it means it is unlikely your sample will produce a large R^2 when the population R^2 is actually zero. To be considered statistically significant, a rule of thumb is there must be <0.05 probability the results are due to chance. Some business situations will accept a lower probability level of perhaps <0.10, but most require a <0.05 level and some expect <0.01.

If the R^2 is statistically significant, we then evaluate the strength of the linear association between the dependent variable and the several independent variables. Multiple R^2, also called the multiple coefficient of determination, is a handy measure of the strength of the overall relationship. If you recall our discussion of r^2 from the section on correlation analysis, the coefficient of determination is a measure of the amount of variation in the dependent variable associated with the variation in the independent variable. In the case of multiple regression analysis, the R^2 shows the amount of variation in the dependent variable associated with all of the independent variables considered together (it also is referred to as a measure of the goodness of fit). Multiple R^2 ranges from 0 to $+1.0$ and represents the amount of the dependent variable "explained" by the independent variables combined. A large multiple R^2 indicates the straight line works well while a small R indicates it does not work well.

The larger the R^2 the more the dependent variable is associated with the independent variables we are using to predict it. For example, if the multiple R^2 between the number of bottles of water consumed in an afternoon (dependent variable), and the independent variables temperature and distance walked is 0.69, that would mean that we can account for, or "explain", 69% of the variation in bottled water consumption by using the variation in temperature and distance walked. A larger R^2 indicates a stronger relationship between the independent variables and the dependent measure. As before, the measure of the strength of the relationship between an individual independent variable and the dependent measure of interest is shown by the standardized regression coefficient (beta) for that variable. Thus, we would use the beta coefficient to tell us whether temperature or distance walked is a better predictor of bottled water consumption.

Just as we did with bivariate regression, it is necessary in multiple regression to test for the statistical significance of the regression coefficients (betas) for each of the independent variables. We again must determine whether sampling error is influencing the regression results. The basic question is still the same: "What is the likelihood we would get a coefficient of this size for our sample if the true regression coefficient in the population were zero?" SPSS and most other statistical software calculate the t-test statistics for each regression coefficient so we can easily answer this question. If any of the regression coefficients is not statistically significant, that particular independent variable is not a good predictor of the dependent variable. In other words, an insignificant beta means the relationship is due to sampling error and not a true relationship in the population. In short, the use of an independent variable that has an insignificant beta is meaningless and should be removed from the regression model. By removing insignificant independent variables and rerunning the regression the result is the simplest model possible.

In summary, to evaluate the results of a multiple regression analysis do the following: (1) assess the statistical significance of the overall regression model using the F statistic; (2) if the F is significant, then evaluate the R^2 to see if it is large enough (see Exhibit 14-1); (3) examine each of the regression coefficients and their t statistics to identify which independent variables have statistically significant coefficients; and (4) rerun the regression with the significant independent variables and look at the beta coefficients to determine the relative influence of each of the independent variables. If you follow these steps you will have answers to the four basic questions about the relationships between your single dependent variable and your multiple independent variables: "Does a relationship exist?" "If there is a relationship, how strong is it?" "Is the relationship positive or negative?" and "If there is a relationship, what is the best way to describe it?"

EXAMPLE OF MULTIPLE REGRESSION

Phil Samouel would like to predict how satisfied his customers are based on their experiences while dining in his restaurant. As part of his customer survey, Phil collected information on customer perceptions regarding various characteristics of his restaurant. The first 12 variables in the database are the perceptions characteristics. They are metric variables and can be used as independent variables in a regression model. The perceptions are measured using a seven-point Likert-type rating scale with 7 = strongly agree (favourable) and 1 = strongly disagree (unfavourable). Variables X_{13} to X_{16} are nonmetric variables because they are ranking data, and it is not appropriate to use them in a regression equation. Variables X_{17}, X_{18} and X_{19} are metric dependent variables measured on a seven-point Likert-type rating scale. These variables measure customers' reactions to their dining experience such as satisfaction and likelihood to return in the future. Variable X_{20} – Frequency of Patronage is nonmetric as are X_{24} – Length of Time a Customer, X_{25} – Gender and X_{28} – Restaurant Competitors = Gino's versus Samouel's customers. Thus, Phil's survey has collected information that could be used to develop a multiple regression predictive model that hopefully will be a much better predictor than his judgement or extrapolation from past information.

Several empirical studies have shown that food quality is the most important factor in selecting a restaurant. These same studies have shown that when restaurant customers mention food quality they are thinking of taste, proper temperature, good seasoning, variety, and so on. Thus, it is clear Phil Samouel will want to know whether in this situation perceptions of his food are related to satisfaction, as well as the other outcome variables like recommend to a friend and return to his restaurant in the future. A multiple regression model can answer these questions. For the initial regression model, we will examine the single dependent metric variable X_{18} – Likely to Return in Future, and the food independent variables X_1 – Excellent Food Quality, X_4 – Excellent Food Taste, and X_9 – Wide Variety of Menu Items. These variables are shown in Exhibit 14-12 as they

1. Excellent Food Quality	Strongly Disagree Strongly Agree 1 2 3 4 5 6 7
4. Excellent Food Taste	Strongly Disagree Strongly Agree 1 2 3 4 5 6 7
9. Wide Variety of Menu Items	Strongly Disagree Strongly Agree 1 2 3 4 5 6 7

18. How likely are you to return to Samouel's restaurant in the future?	Definitely Will Not Return Definitely Will Return 1 2 3 4 5 6 7

EXHIBIT 14-12

Selected Variables from Samouel's Customer Survey

were used in the survey. The null hypothesis would be there is no relationship between X_{18} and X_1, X_4, and X_9. The alternative hypothesis would be X_1, X_4 and X_9 are significantly related to X_{18} – Likely to Return in Future.

The results of this initial multiple regression model are shown in Exhibit 14-13 (see the Data Analysis box for instructions on how to run SPSS for this example). For this example we have divided the sample into two groups – Samouel's customers and Gino's customers, so we can compare them. We show information for each of the multiple regression models. The Descriptive Statistics table shows the means of the variables in the regression analysis. Note the means for Samouel's on the independent variables X_1 – Excellent Food Quality (5.24), X_4 – Excellent Food Taste (5.16) and X_9 – Wide Variety of Menu Items (5.45) are above the mid-point of the seven-point scale (4.0) and therefore represent relatively positive perceptions of these attributes. The dependent variable X_{18} – Return in Future (Samouel's = 4.37) is lower but still slightly above the mid-point. What is of concern to Phil, however, is that Gino's customers are more likely to return to his restaurant in the future (mean = 5.55) and on all three food variables Gino's has relatively more positive perceptions. This is information Phil can use to develop an action plan to improve his restaurant.

Descriptive Statistics

X_{28} – Competitor	Variable	Mean
Samouel's	X_{18} – Return in Future	4.37
	X_1 – Excellent Food Quality	5.24
	X_4 – Excellent Food Taste	5.16
	X_9 – Wide Variety of Menu Items	5.45
Gino's	X_{18} – Return in Future	5.55
	X_1 – Excellent Food Quality	5.81
	X_4 – Excellent Food Taste	5.73
	X_9 – Wide Variety of Menu Items	5.56

Model Summary[b]

X_{28} – Competitor	R	R Square	Adjusted R Square
Samouel's	0.512[a]	0.262	0.239
Gino's	0.482[a]	0.232	0.208

[a]Predictors: (Constant), X_9 – Wide Variety of Menu Items, X_1 – Excellent Food Quality, X_9 – Excellent Food Taste
[b]Dependent Variable: X_{18} –Return in Future

EXHIBIT 14-13

Multiple Regression of Return In Future and Food Independent Variables

Since we will be comparing Samouel's customers' perceptions with those of Gino's, go to the Data pull-down menu to split the sample. Scroll down and click on Split File, then on Compare Groups. Highlight variable X_{28} and move it into the box labelled "Groups based on": and then click OK. Now you can run the regression.

The SPSS click through sequence is ANALYSE $\rightarrow$ REGRESSION $\rightarrow$ LINEAR. Highlight X_{18} and move it to the dependent variables box. Highlight X_1, X_4 and X_9 and move them to the independent variables box. Use the default "Enter" in the Methods box. Click on the Statistics button and use the defaults for "Estimates" and "Model Fit". Next click on "Descriptives" and then Continue. There are several other options you could select at the bottom of this dialogue box but for now we will use the program defaults. Click on "OK" at the top right of the dialogue box to run the regression. The results are the same as in Exhibit 14-13 and 14-14. ■

Information in the Model Summary table in Exhibit 14–13 indicates the R^2 for the regression of Samouel's restaurant is 0.262. This means that 26.2% of the variation in return in future (dependent variable) can be explained from the three independent variables. In general, R^2 always increases as independent variables are added to a multiple regression model. To avoid overestimating the impact of adding an independent variable to the model, some analysts prefer to use the **adjusted R^2** (it recalculates the R^2 based on the number of predictor variables in the model). This makes it easy compare the explanatory power of regression models with different numbers of independent variables. The adjusted R^2 for the model is 0.239, which indicates only a slight overestimate with this model.

The remaining diagnostic information for the multiple regression models is shown in Exhibit 14-14. The regression model for Samouel's is statistically significant (F-ratio = 11.382; probability level = 0.000). The probability level of 0.000 means that the chances are 0.000 that the regression model results are due to random events instead of a true relationship. The Gino's multiple regression model also is significant at a very high level (0.000). Thus, the food independent variables do predict whether a customer is likely to return in the future for both restaurants. We can therefore reject the null hypothesis of no relationship between the variables.

Information provided in the Coefficients table of Exhibit 14-14 tells us which of the independent variables are significant predictors of likely to return. In the significance column, we note that the beta coefficient for Samouel's food quality is significant (0.028). Similarly, with Gino's food quality is the only significant predictor (0.024). Examining the Standardized Coefficients Beta column for Samouel's, we note X_1 – Excellent Food Quality is most closely associated with return in future (Beta = 0.324) and the same situation is true for Gino's (Beta = 0.316). For both regression models Excellent Food Taste approaches significance but does not meet our criteria of <0.05. This is based on the use of a two-tailed test, which is discussed later.

A note of caution is in order regarding the Beta coefficients and their significance. We have concluded that only one independent variable in each regression model is statistically significant based

ANOVA[b]

X$_{28}$ – Competitor		Sum of Squares	df	Mean Square	F	Sig.
Samouel's	Regression	28.155	3	9.385	11.382	0.000[a]
	Residual	79.155	96	0.825		
	Total	107.310	99			
Gino's	Regression	22.019	3	7.340	9.688	0.000[a]
	Residual	72.731	96	0.758		
	Total	94.750	99			

[a] Predictor Variables: X$_9$ – Wide Variety of Menu Items, X$_1$ – Excellent Food Quality, X$_4$ – Excellent Food Taste

[b] Dependent Variable: X$_{18}$ – Return in Future

Coefficients[a]

X$_{28}$ – Competitor		Unstandardized Coefficients		Standardized Coefficients	t	Sig.
		B	Std. Error	Beta		
Samouel's	X$_1$ – Excellent Food Quality	0.260	0.116	0.324	2.236	0.028
	X$_4$ – Excellent Food Taste	0.242	0.137	0.291	1.770	0.080
	X$_9$ – Wide Variety of Menu Items	−0.082	0.123	−0.094	−0.668	0.506
Gino's	X$_1$ – Excellent Food Quality	0.272	0.119	0.316	2.295	0.024
	X$_4$ – Excellent Food Taste	0.241	0.132	0.264	1.823	0.071
	X$_9$ – Wide Variety of Menu Items	−0.053	0.125	−0.065	−0.421	0.675

[a]Dependent Variable: X$_{18}$ – Return in Future

EXHIBIT 14-14

Other Information for Multiple Regression Models

on the reported significance levels. But levels of significance can vary if there is multicollinearity among the independent variables. Similarly, the signs indicating a negative or positive relationship between the independent and dependent variables can be reversed if there is multicollinearity among the independent variables. For this reason, when developing a multiple regression model we always recommend that the simple correlations among the independent and dependent variables be examined closely to ensure the proper interpretation of the findings.

Another concept of importance in interpreting the significance of the regression coefficients is whether a one-tailed or a two-tailed test is used. A **one-tailed test** is used when you can predict the direction of your hypothesized relationship (positive or negative). A **two-tailed test** must be used if you cannot predict the direction of your hypothesized relationship. For example, a one-tailed test would be used to test these null hypotheses: excellent food taste is positively related to return in the future or excellent food quality is positively related to satisfaction. In each case, the hypothesis predicts the direction of the relationship. A two-tailed test would be used to test these hypotheses: There is not a significant relationship between excellent food taste and return in the future or excellent food quality is not related to satisfaction.

The one-tailed probability is exactly half the value of the two-tailed probability. There is some controversy on whether or not it is appropriate to use a one-tailed test. It is safer to use two-tailed tests, but there are situations where a one-tailed test seems more appropriate. For example, we recommend a one-tailed test in examining the relationship between excellent food taste and return in the future for the two restaurants. Since SPSS reports the two tailed test results, and if we divide the level of significance in half (Samouel's Food Taste Sig. $= 0.08/2 = 0.04$), we can then conclude that indeed perceptions of excellent food taste are significantly related to likelihood of returning in the future. Thus, the researcher can choose whether to use one-tailed or two-tailed tests depending upon the research situation.

We interpret regression coefficients somewhat differently with multiple regression than we did with bivariate regression. In bivariate regression we interpret the unstandardized regression coefficient as the amount of change in the dependent variable for every one-unit change in the independent variable. But in multiple regression this interpretation must be modified somewhat. In our example above, if we use the beta coefficient for Samouel's X_1 – Excellent Food Quality we would say the dependent variable would change 0.324 for every one-unit change in food quality, when all other independent variables are held constant. Thus, 0.324 is the estimated increase in likelihood to return in the future associated with a one-unit increase in food quality when food taste and variety of menu items are held constant. Note the signs of the coefficients are interpreted the same as with a correlation coefficient. Thus, with more positive perceptions of food quality there is an increased likelihood to return in the future. This is consistent with the mean value of 5.24 for food quality that indicates Samouel's customers are relatively happy with his food. Similar findings were found for Gino's but it should be noted that Gino's food quality is perceived to be somewhat higher (5.81) than Samouel's.

This means we can reject both null hypotheses that the three food independent variables are not associated with X_{18} – Return in Future for Samouel's and Gino's restaurants. Using the beta coefficient for food quality, for example, we can conclude that every time X_1 increases by 1 unit, X_{18} will increase on average by 0.324 units for Samouel's and 0.316 units for Gino's, assuming the other variables are held constant. If we apply the one-tailed test for food taste it is significant too, but wide variety of menu items is not. Thus, since two of the three variables are significant we can conclude that perceptions of food definitely are a predictor of likelihood to return in future.

Two other problems still remain, however. The first problem is the initial regression model for Samouel's explains only about 26.2 % of the variation in X_{18} (Gino's explains 23.2 %) so we need to consider other independent variables that might help us increase the predictive capability of our regression model, such as the other perceptions variables. Increasing the predictive capability of our regression by adding other independent variables will help Phil Samouel to develop a more effective business plan to compete with Gino. The second problem is Gino's customers are more likely to return in the future (5.55 versus 4.37) to his restaurant so Phil's business plan must address this issue as well.

MULTICOLLINEARITY AND MULTIPLE REGRESSION

In our discussion of multiple regression we have used the term independent variable to refer to any variable being used to predict or explain the value of the dependent variable. This does not mean the independent variables are independent in a statistical sense. Indeed, most independent variables in multiple regression are correlated. **Multicollinearity** in multiple regression analysis refers, therefore, to the correlation among the independent variables.

Multicollinearity can cause a number of problems with regression. For example, the F-test of the overall multiple regression model may indicate a statistically significant relationship. But when we examine the t-tests for the individual coefficients we may find none of them is significant. If this happens it is not possible to determine the individual effect of any particular independent variable on the dependent variable. In addition, in some cases multicollinearity will cause the regression coefficients to have a sign opposite that of the actual relationship (i.e., a negative relationship when in reality the relationship is positive). Thus, with a high degree of multicollinearity we cannot rely on the individual coefficients to interpret the results. Multicollinearity problems do not have an impact on the size of the R^2, or your ability to predict values of the dependent variable. But they certainly can affect the statistical significance of the individual regression coefficients and your ability to use them to explain the relationships.

So how do we know when multicollinearity is too high? A general rule of thumb adopted by statisticians is a correlation coefficient between two independent variables greater than $+/-0.60$ is evidence of potential problems with multicollinearity. Indeed, when there are several independent variables all of which are intercorrelated, multicollinearity can be a problem at levels lower than 0.60. When this situation exists you should remove one or more of the independent variables from the regression model and rerun it, or combine the highly correlated variables into a single composite summated variable.

Statisticians have developed more precise tests than the above rule of thumb to determine whether multicollinearity is high enough to cause problems, but these tests are beyond the scope of this book. They are the tolerance and VIF tests. For more information on these tests see the book's Web site at www.wileyeurope.com/college/hair.

EXAMPLE OF MULTICOLLINEARITY

Phil Samouel certainly needs to know whether multicollinearity is a problem with his regression models. An assessment of multicollinearity is necessary to ensure that he can interpret the relative importance of the individual independent variables in the regression models. Based on conversations with his consultant he wants to examine whether compensation issues are related to the loyalty of his employees. He collected information related to this on his employee survey and we will use that to answer this question. To do so, we will use the single dependent metric variable X_{13} – Loyalty, and the three metric independent variables X_1 – Paid Fairly, X_9 – Pay Reflects Effort and X_{12} – Benefits Reasonable. These variables are shown in Exhibit 14-15 as they appear on the employee questionnaire. The null hypothesis is there is no relationship between X_{13} – Loyalty and the three independent variables. We will test this hypothesis using multiple regression analysis. The instructions on how to use SPSS to examine this relationship are provided in the Data Analysis box.

DATA ANALYSIS

MULTIPLE REGRESSION AND MULTICOLLINEARITY

The SPSS click through sequence is ANALYSE → REGRESSION → LINEAR. Highlight X_{13} and move it to the dependent variables box. Highlight X_1, X_9 and X_{12} and move them to the independent variables box. Use the default "Enter" in the Methods box. Click on the Statistics button and use the defaults for "Estimates" and "Model Fit". Next click on "Descriptives" and then Continue. There are several other options you could select at the bottom of this dialogue box but for now we will use the program defaults. Click on "OK" at the top right of the dialogue box to run the regression. The results are shown in Exhibits 14-16 and 14-17. ∎

1. I am paid fairly for the work I do.	Strongly Disagree Strongly Agree 1 2 3 4 5 6 7
9. My pay reflects the effort I put into doing my work.	Strongly Disagree Strongly Agree 1 2 3 4 5 6 7
12. The benefits I receive are reasonable.	Strongly Disagree Strongly Agree 1 2 3 4 5 6 7

13. I have a sense of loyalty to Samouel's Restaurant.	Strongly Disagree Strongly Agree 1 2 3 4 5 6 7

EXHIBIT 14-15

Compensation and Loyalty Variables from the Samouel's Employee Survey

Model Summary

Model	R	R Square	Adjusted R Square	Std. Error of the Estimate
1	0.499[a]	0.249	0.211	0.859

[a] Predictor Variables: X_{12} – Benefits Reasonable, X_9 – Pay Reflects Effort, X_1 – Paid Fairly

ANOVA[b]

Model		Sum of Squares	df	Mean Square	F	Sig.
1	Regression	14.468	3	4.823	6.536	0.001[a]
	Residual	43.532	59	0.738		
	Total	58.000	62			

[a] Predictor Variables: X_{12} – Benefits Reasonable, X_9 – Pay Reflects Effort, X_1 – Paid Fairly
[b] Dependent Variable: X_{13} – Loyalty

EXHIBIT 14-16

Summary Statistics for Employee Regression Compensation Model

The results from running the multiple regression model are shown in Exhibits 14-16 and 14-17. Information from the Model Summary table indicates the R-Square for the model is 0.249. Looking at the ANOVA table we see that the model is highly significant (0.001). The next question is which of the three independent variables are contributing to the predictive ability of this regression model and how? To determine this we look at the Coefficients table in Exhibit 14-17. Recall the Beta coefficients tell us which independent variables contribute the most to explaining the relationship between the dependent and independent variables. Variables X_1 – Paid Fairly and X_9 – Pay Reflects Effort are statistically significant (<0.05). The third independent variable X_{12} – Reasonable Benefits is not significant in this regression model. Therefore, the coefficients information suggests that only two of the independent variables are statistically significant in this model. But does that mean the other variable is not related to the dependent variable? Not necessarily. Another problem is the sign of the Beta for X_9 – Pay Reflects Effort negative. This is not logical because it suggests that employees who are less favourable about their pay are more loyal. We need to look further to explain these results and understand the regression model.

To understand the multicollinearity issue, let's look at the bivariate correlations between the variables shown in Exhibit 14-17. The top of the table shows the correlations and the bottom half the level of significance. Two of the three compensation variables are significantly correlated with the dependent variable loyalty. With regard to multicollinearity between the independent variables, there definitely are some problems. Variables X_1 and X_{12} are correlated 0.88, X_1 and X_9 are correlated 0.763, and X_9 and X_{12} are correlated 0.877. All three of the correlations are above the

Coefficients[a]

Variables	Unstandardized Coefficients		Std. Error	Standardized Coefficients	t	Sig.
	B			Beta		
X_1 – Paid Fairly	0.739		0.251	0.699	2.945	0.005
X_9 – Pay Reflects Effort	−0.625		0.299	−0.491	−2.090	0.041
X_{12} – Benefits Reasonable	0.110		0.377	0.093	0.292	0.771

[a] Dependent Variable: X_{13} – Loyalty

Bivariate Correlations

		X13 – Loyalty	X1 – Paid Fairly	X9 – Pay Reflects Effort	X12 – Benefits Reasonable
Pearson Correlation	X13 – Loyalty	1.00	0.0407	0.124	0.278
	X1 – Paid Fairly	0.407	1.00	0.763	0.880
	X9 – Pay Reflects Effort	0.124	0.763	1.00	0.877
	X12 – Benefits Reasonable	0.278	0.880	0.877	1.00
Sig. (1-tailed)	X13 – Loyalty	.	0.000	0.166	0.014
	X1 – Paid Fairly	0.000	.	0.000	0.000
	X9 – Pay Reflects Effort	0.166	0.000	.	0.000
	X12 – Benefits Reasonable	0.014	0.000	0.000	.

EXHIBIT 14-17

Coefficients for Employee Regression Model

recommended 0.6. Thus, multicollinearity has influenced this regression model. The information provided on the significance of the Betas (Exhibit 14-17) indicates that variable X_{12} is not related to the dependent variable when in fact it may be related, and variable X_9 has a negative sign for the Beta when in fact the sign is positive based on the bivariate correlations. These findings need to be explored further.

One approach to assessing the problems of multicollinearity in regression is to examine the correlations between the independent variables. If any are too high (>0.60) you could remove one or more of the highly correlated variables from the regression model. But, how do you decide which independent variable to remove? One possibility is to first identify the independent variables that are most closely related to each other (highest correlation). Then keep the independent variable in your regression model that is most highly correlated with the dependent variable. Another approach is to run regression models with all combinations of variables and see which model has the largest R^2. A third possibility is to create new composite summated variables from the independent variables that are highly correlated. Each regression model involves different issues so each situation must be considered in light of the research objectives and constraints.

ADVANCED TOPICS IN MULTIPLE REGRESSION

Multiple regression is a very useful statistical technique in business research. Entire books have been written about the topic so many issues are too advanced for this text. If you wish to learn more take a look at some of the sources cited at the end of this chapter. You could also go to the Web site for this book at www.wileyeurope.com/college/hair where we provide additional material on topics like advanced diagnostics to examine multicollinearity, stepwise regression, dealing with residuals, and so on.

THE ROLE OF DUMMY VARIABLES IN REGRESSION

A dummy independent variable is a variable that has two (or more) distinct levels, which are coded 0 and 1. Dummy coded variables enable us to use independent variables not measured using interval or ratio scales to predict the dependent variable. For example, if you wanted to include the gender of customers of the two restaurants to understand satisfaction with the restaurant, it is obvious your measure for gender only includes two possible categories – male or female. In this case, we could use gender in a regression model by coding males as 0 and females as 1. Similarly, we might have purchasers versus nonpurchasers and include them as an independent variable using a $1 - 0$ coding. This represents a slight but acceptable violation of the assumption of metric scaling for the independent variables.

To use dummy variables we must choose one category of the variable to serve as a reference category and then add as many dummy variables as there are possible values of the variable, minus the reference category. Each category is coded as either 0 or 1. In the example above, if you choose the male category as the reference category, you would have one dummy variable for the female category. That dummy variable would be assigned the value of 1 for females and 0 for males. In the restaurant employee database, X_{19} – Gender is already coded as a dummy variable for gender, using males as the reference category (males are coded 0).

We can also use dummy coding with categorical independent variables that have more than two categories. Let's say you wanted to use an independent variable like occupation and you have physicians, attorneys and professors in your sample. To use dummy variables in your regression, you choose one category as a reference group (physicians), and add two dummy variables for the remaining categories. The variables would be coded as follows, using zero and one:

Category	X_1	X_2
Physician	0	0
Attorney	1	0
Professor	0	1

As you can tell from the list above, when the respondent is a physician, X_1 and X_2 will be zero (the reference category is always coded 0). For attorneys, the regression coefficient for X_1 represents the difference in the dependent variable compared to physicians. The regression coefficient associated with X_2 represents the difference in the dependent variable for professors compared to physicians.

EXAMPLE OF DUMMY VARIABLES

To enable him to prepare a better business plan, Phil wants to know more about his employees and what he can do to increase their productivity and commitment to working at his restaurant. In the employee survey Phil gathered data on the employee work environment, commitment to the restaurant, likelihood of searching for another job, and selected demographic information, such as gender. The gender variable was measured in the survey as shown below.

Gender Coded as a Dummy Variable

19. Your Gender	0	Male
	1	Female

To investigate the relationship between work environment and job commitment, we will use X_{13} – Loyalty as the dependent variable in a regression model, and two of the metric work environment variables used in the preceding multicollinearity example – X_1 – Paid Fairly and X_9 – Pay Reflects Effort. We will delete X_{12} – Benefits Reasonable from this regression model because of the previously identified multicollinearity problems. In addition to the work environment variables, however, Phil wants to determine if the gender of his employees influences their loyalty to the restaurant. Therefore, we also include X_{19} – Gender (coded male = 0 and female = 1) in our regression model.

Results of the multiple regression analysis are shown in Exhibits 14-18 and 14-19. The R^2 for the model is 0.393, as shown in the Model Summary table. Thus, approximately 39.3 % of the total variation in X_{13} can be predicted by X_1 – Paid Fairly, X_9 – Pay Reflects Effort, and X_{19} – Gender. The regression model is highly significant, with a probability level of 0.000, as revealed in the ANOVA table.

The Coefficients table in Exhibit 14-19 reveals that X_{19} – Gender is a significant and strong predictor of X_{13} – Loyalty with a Beta coefficient of 0.605 (probability of 0.000). Paid Fairly (X_1)

Model Summary

R	R Square	Adjusted R Square
0.773	0.597	0.577

[a]Predictor Variables: X_{19} – Gender, X_1 – Paid Fairly and X_9 – Pay Reflects Effort

ANOVA

	Sum of Squares	df	Mean Square	F	Sig.
Regression	34.638	3	11.546	29.159	0.000
Residual	23.362	59	0.396		
Total	58.000	62			

[a]Predictor Variables: X_{19} – Gender, X_1 – Paid Fairly and X_9 – Pay Reflects Effort
[b]Dependent Variable: X_{13} – Loyalty

EXHIBIT 14-18

Regression Model of Samouel's Employees Using Work Environment and Gender as Independent Variables and Loyalty as a Dependent Variable

Coefficients[a]					
	Unstandardized Coefficients		Standardized Coefficients	t	Sig.
	B	Std. Error	Beta		
X_1 – Paid Fairly	0.579	0.138	0.548	4.186	0.000
X_9 – Pay Reflects Effort	−.351	0.166	−0.275	−2.117	0.038
X_{19} – Gender	1.205	0.169	0.605	7.148	0.000

[a]Dependent Variable: X_{13} – Loyalty

EXHIBIT 14-19

Beta Coefficients for Regression Model Using Dummy Variables

is also significant (0.000) and strong, with a Beta coefficient of 0.548, as is Pay Reflects Effort (X_9), with has only a moderately strong Beta coefficient of −0.275, but is still significant (0.038). Thus, "gender" is the best predictor of "loyalty" but the work environment variables also are important in predicting loyalty.

Looking now at the signs (+/−) for the gender Beta note that it is positive (+). This means higher values of the gender variable are associated with higher loyalty. Since females are coded 1 and males 0, this means that females are more loyal than are males. The means shown in Exhibit 14-20 confirm this.

DATA ANALYSIS

USING SPSS TO EXAMINE DUMMY VARIABLES

The SPSS click-through sequence is: ANALYSE → REGRESSION → LINEAR. Click on X_{13} – Loyalty and move it to the Dependent Variables box. Click on X_1, X_9 and X_{19} and move them to the Independent Variables box. The box labelled "Method" has ENTER as the default and we will use it. Click on the "Statistics" button and use the "Estimates" and "Model fit" defaults. Click on "Descriptives" then "Continue" and "OK" to run the regression. The results will be the same as shown in Exhibits 14-18 and 14-19. ■

To explain the results for gender, let's compare male and female employees' responses. The results of this comparison are in Exhibit 14-20. As you can see, females are relatively more favourable (higher mean) on X_1 and less favourable about X_9, but the differences are not statistically significant. Differences are significant only for X_{13} – Loyalty (See ANOVA table). Thus, females are significantly more

Descriptives

	X_{19} – Gender	N	Mean	Std. Deviation
X1 – Paid Fairly	Males	40	4.18	0.903
	Females	23	4.39	0.941
	Total	63	4.25	0.915
X9 – Pay Reflects Effort	Males	40	4.53	0.716
	Females	23	4.48	0.846
	Total	63	4.51	0.759
X13 – Loyalty	Males	40	5.18	0.747
	Females	23	6.52	0.665
	Total	63	5.67	0.967

ANOVA

		Sum of Squares	df	Mean Square	F	Sig.
X1 – Paid Fairly *	Between Groups	0.683	1	0.683	0.813	0.371
X_{19} – Gender	Within Groups	51.253	61	0.840		
	Total	51.937	62			
X9 – Pay Reflects Effort *	Between Groups	0.032	1	0.032	0.054	0.816
X_{19} – Gender	Within Groups	35.714	61	0.585		
	Total	35.746	62			
X13 – Loyalty *	Between Groups	26.486	1	26.486	51.267	0.000
X_{19} – Gender	Within Groups	31.514	61	0.517		
	Total	58.000	62			

EXHIBIT 14-20

Comparison of Male and Female Employees

loyal to Samouel's restaurant than are males. This finding suggests that Phil needs to learn more about male and female employees and why they differ in their feelings about working at Samouel's restaurant. Indeed, he needs to go beyond these variables and look at all aspects of working at the restaurant.

DATA ANALYSIS   USING SPSS TO COMPARE GROUP MEANS

Using SPSS it is simple to compare the responses of male and female employees. The SPSS click through sequence is: ANALYSE → COMPARE MEANS → MEANS. Click on

X_{13} – Loyalty, and X_1 and X_9 and move them to the Dependent List box. Now click on X_{19} – Gender and move it to the Independent List box. Click on the box labelled "Options" and then at the bottom left hand corner of the screen click on <u>A</u>nova and eta. Next click Continue and OK to run the program. The results are the same as in Exhibit 14-20. ∎

SUMMARY

■ **Describe the nature of relationships between variables**

There are four basic concepts we need to understand about relationships between variables: presence, type of relationship, direction and strength of association. We will describe each of these concepts. Presence assesses whether a systematic relationship exists between two or more variables. We rely on the concept of statistical significance to measure whether or not a relationship is present. A second important concept is the type of relationship. We typically say there are two types of relationships – linear and nonlinear. A linear relationship is a "straight-line association" between two or more variables. A nonlinear relationship, often referred to as curvilinear, is one in which the relationship is best described by a curve instead of a straight line. If a relationship is present between the variables we also need to know the direction. The direction of a relationship can be either positive or negative. Finally, when a relationship is present, the business researcher must determine the strength of the association. Depending on the type of relationship being examined we generally categorize the strength of association as slight, small but definite, moderate, high or very strong.

■ **Explain the concepts of correlation and regression analysis**

Correlation analysis calculates the association between two variables. The Pearson correlation measures the linear association between two metric variables. The number representing the Pearson correlation is referred to as a correlation coefficient. It ranges from -1.00 to $+1.00$, with zero representing absolutely no association between the two metric variables. While -1.00 or $+1.00$ are possible and represents a perfect association between two variables, it very seldom occurs. The larger the correlation coefficient the stronger the linkage or level of association. Correlation coefficients can be either positive or negative, depending upon the direction of the relationship between the variables. If there is a positive correlation coefficient between X and Y, then increases in the value of X are associated with increases in the value of Y, and vice versa.

Managers often would like to be able to predict, for example, how much impact an advertising campaign will have on sales. The three typical methods to make these predictions are: (1) informed judgement; (2) extrapolation from past behaviour; and (3) regression. Informed judgement and extrapolation both assume that events and behaviours in the past will continue into the future. When these past events change, extrapolation and judgement cannot help the business researcher predict the future with an acceptable level of accuracy. In such cases, the business researcher needs a technique like regression analysis.

Regression analysis is perhaps the most widely applied data analysis technique for measuring linear relationships between two or more variables. Correlation tells us if a relationship exists between two variables, as well as the overall strength of the relationship. Sometimes, however, these answers do not provide enough information for management to make the proper decision. For example, Phil Samouel may want to examine how both the atmosphere and food variables are related to satisfaction, instead of only one at a time. In such instances we use regression analysis because it enables us to use several independent variables to predict a single dependent variable.

■ **Clarify the difference between bivariate and multiple regression analysis**
Bivariate regression has only two variables – a single metric dependent variable and a single metric independent variable. Multiple regression has a single metric dependent variable and several metric independent variables. With bivariate regression the coefficient of determination is r^2. For multiple regression the multiple coefficient of determination is R^2.

■ **Understand how multicollinearity can influence regression models**
Multicollinearity can cause a number of problems with regression. For example, the F-test of the overall multiple regression model may indicate a statistically significant relationship. But when we examine the t-tests for the individual coefficients we may find none of them is significant. If this happens it is not possible to determine the individual effect of any particular independent variable on the dependent variable. Multicollinearity problems do not have an impact on the size of the R^2, or your ability to predict values of the dependent variable. But they certainly can affect the statistical significance of the individual regression coefficients.

So how do we know when multicollinearity is too high? A general rule of thumb adopted by statisticians is a sample correlation coefficient between two independent variables greater than $+0.60$ or less than -0.60 is evidence of potential problems with multicollinearity. But statisticians have developed more precise tests than the above rule of thumb to determine whether multicollinearity is high enough to cause problems. The tests are referred to as the tolerance and VIF tests. They can be examined using SPSS and other statistical software packages.

■ **Describe how to us dummy variables in regression**
A dummy independent variable is a variable that has two (or more) distinct levels, which are coded 0 and 1. Dummy coded variables enable us to use qualitative independent variables not measured using interval or ratio scales to predict the dependent variable. For example, if you wanted to include the gender of customers of the two restaurants to understand satisfaction with the restaurant, it is obvious that your measure for gender only includes two possible categories – male or female. In this case, we could use gender in a regression model by coding males as 0 and females as 1. Similarly, we might have purchasers versus nonpurchasers and include them as an independent variable using a $1 - 0$ coding. This represents a slight but acceptable violation of the assumption of metric scaling for the independent variables.

To use dummy variables we must choose one category of the variable to serve as a reference category and then add as many dummy variables as there are possible values of the variable, minus the reference category. Each category is coded as either 0 or 1. In the example above, if you choose the male category as the reference category, you would have one dummy variable for the female category. That dummy variable would be assigned the value of 1 for females and 0 for males. We can also use dummy coding with categorical independent variables that have more than two categories. ■

Ethical Dilemma

The national telephone company offers a variety of services. A business research firm is hired to determine the level of customer satisfaction by target audience for their land-based telephone, wireless and Internet services. Terry Brown, the firm's lead researcher, uses Pearson's r to calculate the relationships in the survey data. When checking the results before preparing the first draft of the executive summary, Terry's assistant notices that she includes the outliers in some calculations and not in others. Does this inconsistency affect the validity of the research? What should Terry's assistant do?

REVIEW QUESTIONS

1. What is the value of a correlation coefficient in measuring relationships between variables?

2. What is the difference between the statistical techniques correlation and regression?

3. Explain the relationship between explained and unexplained variance in multiple regression.

DISCUSSION AND THINKING ACTIVITIES

1. Why would the business researcher use multiple regression instead of bivariate regression?

2. Why is it important to understand multicollinearity when using multiple regression?

3. **SPSS Application:** With the customer database, use X_{17} – Satisfaction as the dependent variable and $X_1 - X_{12}$ as independent variables. Split your sample by X_{28} – Competitor and run a multiple regression and determine the predictive capability for all 12 metric independent variables.

4. **SPSS Application:** Do the same as in question 3 but now select the stepwise option. Which independent variables are included in the final regression model? How does the R^2 differ from what you found in question 3.

5. **SPSS Application:** Calculate the median and modal responses for the restaurant selection factors $(X_{13} - X_{16})$. Compare the responses of male and female customers. Are the rankings the same? If not, how do they differ and how would Phil use this information in preparing his business plan.

INTERNET EXERCISES   WWW

1. Use the Google and Yahoo search engines. Type in the key words "multiple regression". Prepare a brief report of what you found and how the search results differed.

2. The Federal Reserve Bank of St. Louis has a database called FRED (Federal Reserve Economic Data). Go to their Web site `http://research.stlouisfed.org/fred/abotfred.html` and report what you found. Review the variables they provide information for and select a variable to be used as a dependent variable in a multiple regression model. Now look at the variables again and select several variables to use as the multiple independent variables to predict the dependent variable you chose. Prepare a brief report summarizing your logic in selecting the variables.

3. Go to the following Web site: `http://www.statpac.com/surveys/statistical-significance.htm`. Prepare a report on the concept of statistical significance. Distinguish between "one-tailed" and a "two-tailed" tests of significance based on the information provided.

4. Go to the following Web site: `www.surveysystem.com/correlation.htm`. Prepare a brief report on the discussion of correlation.

PART V
COMMUNICATING THE RESULTS

Chapter 15
Reporting and Presenting Research

CHAPTER 15
REPORTING AND PRESENTING RESEARCH

CONTENTS

LEARNING OUTCOMES

- Convey the importance of effective communication to research success.
- Describe the elements of a research proposal.
- Provide and overview of effective research reports.
- Summarize effective ways to deliver a research presentation.

INTRODUCTION

Good research is made useful by effectively communicating its purpose, methodology, results and implications. The purpose of research is to answer specific research questions and thereby enable better decision making. Methodology is a detailed account of the research design and the way the project was implemented. The results and implications summarize the major findings and conclusions as they relate to the study's objectives.

Researchers use three formal communication approaches. These include the research proposal, the written research report and the oral presentation. Occasionally, a project may skip one of the steps above; for example, the oral presentation. On other occasions, however, more than one presentation or report may be required. In any case, these three mechanisms provide opportunities to make the project useful. Certainly there have been occasions when the research was correctly executed, but the results were ignored because they were presented poorly. If the research is to be useful in addressing the decision question that initiated it, careful attention must be given to these crucial communication opportunities.

This chapter describes proposals, reports and presentations. The final form and content of these communication tools will vary depending upon the type of project and the extent of involvement required of the researcher. But the examples used here provide a basic framework from which to work. The different elements of each of the three communication tools are explained and illustrated using a project performed for Samouel's restaurant. In so doing, the characteristics of effective communication within each stage are described. Chapter 2 includes the research proposal for Samouel's restaurant. A sample report to Phil Samouel covering the primary research questions identified in the proposal is shown on the Web site at www.wileyeurope.com/college/hair.

WRITTEN AND ORAL COMMUNICATION

A primary role of the researcher is to place the decision maker in the best position to make an informed decision. The report and presentation should clearly highlight the key findings that will affect organizational decision making. Not all decision makers, however, process information in the same way. Therefore, the researcher must consider the level of sophistication of the audience in preparing both written and oral communications.

AUDIENCE SOPHISTICATION

The researcher must present the results as simply as possible without being misleading or seeming mysterious. Consider the following potential audiences: business professors, engineers, scientists, managers for Vodafone and an entrepreneur (former car salesman) wishing to start his/her own car dealership. The researcher would likely use different communication styles for each audience. However, the basic format of the communication devices would not change a great deal between these audiences.

Scientists, engineers and professors would be assumed to be relatively sophisticated. For this audience, the researcher places more emphasis on technical aspects of the research methods results since they are likely to have greater interest in this information and an ability to understand these things. Likewise, a scientist probably is familiar with basic research techniques. But care must be taken to define key business terms that may be unfamiliar to a technical audience. Overall, a slightly higher level of sophistication can be used when communicating with these groups.

For both the managers and the local automobile entrepreneur, the report likely would place less emphasis on technical aspects. Details of any statistical tests, for example, would be placed in a technical appendix. Moreover, any statistical analysis would be reported in a more elementary way. This audience, however, is likely to be much more familiar with basic business terminology.

Remember, decision makers are less likely to act on results they do not understand. Thus, the researcher should gear written and oral communication to the level of the least sophisticated potential user in the audience. This is sometimes referred to as the **least common denominator** principle.

WRITTEN COMMUNICATION

''Just the facts'' is a phrase that implies to get to the important points quickly. ''Just the facts'' is a good orientation for writing business research documents. The writer must remember that the primary purpose of the document is not to entertain or impress someone with literary eloquence. Rather, it is to assist in decision making. The Research in Action Box below provides a manager's view of the typical internal research report.

RESEARCH IN ACTION   MBAS OVERDO IT AGAIN

Managers often struggle to get the most essential information from a research report. Consider the following managerial views:

''First line supervisors are intimidated by the blather and complicated, convoluted, thick reports circulated by the young MBAs on the staff''. What this supervisor didn't know was that the president of the division had virtually confessed the same thing to me on a flight to Los Angeles. He had suggested the reports from some of his own staff people – the ones with the graduate degrees – were a little ''intimidating'' and sent him to the dictionary more than once. Not possessing a business degree himself he felt a little out of his depth and was loath to talk directly to them about the reports and, perhaps, show his ignorance. They (the report authors with MBAs) had fallen prey to the seductive reasoning that ''the boss will be impressed that the authors had really done a lot of homework if they included sophisticated words in their reports and made them look physically impressive'' (Hull, 1995, pp. 8–9).

Research reports would be more useful if they simply addressed the following points:

1. Where are we now? Describe the situation that gave rise to the research.

2. Where are we headed? Stay on course and make sure everything in the report is fulfilling its purpose.

3. How do we propose to get there? Describe the analytical results that help accomplish the report's purpose.

4. How will we know when we have arrived? Make sure the "answers" (or end result) are easy to find and not hidden within the body of the text.

Source: Hull, W. W. (1995). "Writing Reports for Top Management", *Supervision*, 56 (February), 8–13. ■

Guidelines for Technical Writing

Research proposals and reports are typically considered technical writing. The following simple guidelines can greatly improve the writing quality of a technical report.

1. **Front-End Loading.** The writer should realize that the first few pages of the report are the most read pages. Therefore, the researcher should strive to pack the most content possible into the first few pages. Thus, the key findings, implications and recommendations, if requested, should appear in the first pages of the document, usually referred to as an executive summary.

2. **KISS - Keep it Short and Simple.** One of the best guides to technical writing is to be short and to the point. Follow these guides:
   - Shorter sentences are better than longer sentences.
   - Shorter words are better than longer words.
   - Summarize information in tables/charts when possible.
   - Use few prepositions (of, for, to, in, from, and so on).
   - Use as little statistical jargon as possible.

3. **Have Empathy.** Remember readers have varying abilities to understand technical information. Not everyone can gain meaning from technical details within the document. Respect the reader's time by eliminating unnecessary information. Technical details can be included in an appendix where they will not distract the less sophisticated reader.

4. **Goal Orientation.** Remember the document has a clear goal(s). It is designed to accomplish some important purpose for the business. All writing should be framed within the context of providing this information. The reader should be clear, therefore, about how the purpose is accomplished.

5. **Edit, Edit, Edit!** Eliminate paragraphs, sentences and words that are not necessary to complete a thought that helps build a case for the project.

6. **Be Graceful in Ignorance.** Avoid topics for which the report cannot shed any light. Furthermore, any limitations or shortcomings of the study must be spelled out clearly. Not only is this the ethical approach, it is better for the researcher to disclose any problems with the study as opposed to having them discovered later by the decision maker.

7. **Organization.** Clearly organize the paper's sections. Use a lot of headings and subheadings. These aid the reader tremendously. Also, include a listing of charts/figures/tables to assist the reader in finding information within the report with minimal loss of time. The headings and subheadings provide an outline for the table of contents.

RESEARCH PROPOSALS

Research proposals are written during Phase I of the research process. Recall that proposals help ensure effective communication between the researcher and the decision maker. They describe the reasons for the study, including listing and explaining the research questions, a detailed description of the study design and tools to be used (research design), and a summary of the potential results. Finally, the research proposal includes a clear statement of the time schedule and proposed budget for the project.

Chapter 2 contains example proposals. One of the proposals is the result of an interview between a professional business researcher and Phil Samouel, owner of Samouel's Greek Cuisine. The researcher used several of the creative problem-solving techniques to identify and refine the following research questions:

1. Are employees being managed to maximize their productivity as well as commitment to the success of the restaurant?

2. What are the best approaches to attract new customers and to keep and grow existing customers?

The interview process creates a common understanding of the business situation faced by Samouel's. It is very important, however, to commit this understanding to writing. By doing so, it is less likely the research will produce useless results. This is because the decision maker, in this case Phil Samouel, will review and sign the proposal describing the research and its deliverables before the project gets underway. In other words, the proposal documents that the researcher and decision maker are "on the same page". The key sections of the proposal are described in Exhibit 15-1.

Section	Description
Background Information	Describes the relevant business situation and the scope of the study. This includes an overview of related background material and previous research. The scope includes a statement of how the results are to be interpreted. For example, does the decision maker want operating recommendations from the researcher, such as strategies to improve Samouel's restaurant operations, or just a summary of research results. Some decision makers only want the researcher to answer the specific research questions, leaving the overall substantive interpretation to the decision maker.

EXHIBIT 15-1

The Sections and Content of a Research Proposal

Section	Description
Problem Statement and Research Questions	Clearly defines the research problem. Lists and describes research questions to be addressed. If specific hypotheses can be derived, they should be listed and explained briefly.
Research Strategy and Methods	Describes how the study will be conducted. Referring back to the basic research process illustrated in Chapter 2, this section describes the processes listed in Phases II and III. That is, it describes the research design to be used, the variables that must be measured, the data collection approach, data sources (sample), how data will be collected, and the statistical techniques that will be used to analyse the data, thereby testing the research questions.
Final Report Outline	A basic outline of the final report is provided. It lists the key sections of the final report along with a brief description of the expected contents. This is where dummy (or pro-forma) tables can be used to illustrate the type of quantitative results the researcher expects to find.
Budget and Schedule	A breakdown of the expected costs of performing the research project, including the researcher's fee and conditions of billing. It lists a time frame within which the research is to be conducted. This statement also may contain a brief description of the qualifications of the researcher.
Qualifications	Listing of qualifications of project consultants and research firm.

EXHIBIT 15-1

(*continued*)

THE WRITTEN RESEARCH REPORT

The written report is the tangible result of a research project. For ongoing research, reports are often generated automatically through a company's information system. While the content of the reports would be much the same, this chapter focuses on reports written for "one-off"' research projects. The format of all **research reports** is similar. In some ways, they simply build on the research proposal by describing what happened instead of what will happen.

AN OUTLINE OF AN APPLIED BUSINESS RESEARCH REPORT

Recall that business research can be described as either basic or applied. The content and style of the final report will vary slightly depending upon which type of research is being performed. We first describe the outline of an applied business project. This type of report commonly results from projects completed by a business research consultant for a decision maker, like Mr Samouel. Afterwards, we'll discuss how the sections of the report might vary between applied and basic research projects.

Title Page

The **title page** lists the title of the project, the principal decision maker for whom the research is being performed, the date and names, affiliations and contact information of the primary investigator(s). Titles should be kept short but still descriptive of the research performed.

Executive Summary

Beyond any doubt, the **executive summary** is the most read portion of a research report. Remember, business people are busy, so they want the key information summarized in an easy to read and concise format. In fact, many decision makers read only this section. So, it is a stand-alone, very brief overview of the entire report that clearly emphasizes the most important findings. The contents of the executive summary include: (1) a statement of the purpose and key research questions; (2) a brief description of the research design and related details; (3) a summary of statistical results of testing research questions and/or hypotheses; (4) a written interpretation of the findings framed as answers to the research questions; and (5) if requested, a list of practical business implications derived from the research.

Executive summaries should be short. Two pages are acceptable but a one-page executive summary is preferable. It's important that the primary and/or most interesting findings be formatted to attract attention. A good idea here is to list them in a neat, bullet-type fashion. The executive summary also is the opportunity to "sell" the report. It should try to convince the reader that the project accomplished its purpose, and it should entice them to read further into the report.

Table of Contents

A **table of contents** makes the document more useful. It should list the headings and subheadings by page number. The location of all exhibits, tables and/or figures also should be listed. These should be labelled by their titles.

Introduction

The **introduction** is similar to that written for the proposal. It describes the purpose of the study in detail including a list of research questions and hypotheses along with explanations of each. It also includes background material that describes in detail how the study came to be conducted, including a reference back to the original proposal. The introduction prepares the reader for the information to come.

Research Methods

The **research methods** section, as in the proposal, describes the way the study was conducted. It includes a description of the sampling process and sample characteristics, and the procedures used to gather data, including a description of the measures. In addition, this section may sometimes include a summary overview of all variables by presenting basic frequencies and/or descriptive statistics for all variables. This section also may refer to appendices that are included at the end of the document. These appendices usually contain an actual copy of the data collection devices such as a questionnaire and tables containing the frequencies and/or descriptive statistics. This is a good way to provide the user with data that may be interesting but do not specifically address a research question.

Results

In the **results** section, the findings that emerge from the tests addressing the research questions and/or hypotheses are presented. The choice of data analysis techniques is explained and details of the results are presented. Quantitative results are presented in tables and/or charts. Several examples of appropriate tables and charts for specific statistical approaches are shown in this text. Managers generally appreciate results presented graphically. Exhibits 15-2 and 15-3 illustrate the use of two versatile charts to present different types of results.

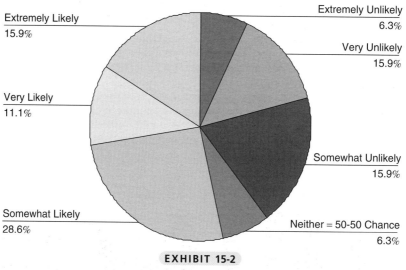

EXHIBIT 15-2

X16 Pie Chart for Intention to Search

The famous pie chart is particularly useful in showing tabulated frequencies for nominal or ordinal variables. This particular pie chart displays the percentage of Samouel's restaurant employees and their likelihood of searching for another job. The size of the slice of pie is proportional to the number (percentage) of employees in each category. In this case, the chart graphically shows the likelihood of searching for another job. From the information provided in the frequency chart we can see a high likelihood of searching. Indeed, 55.6% of employees are at least somewhat likely to search for a new job (28.6 + 11.6 + 16.3 = 15.6%). This is something that needs to be addressed by Phil Samouel in developing a new business plan for his restaurant.

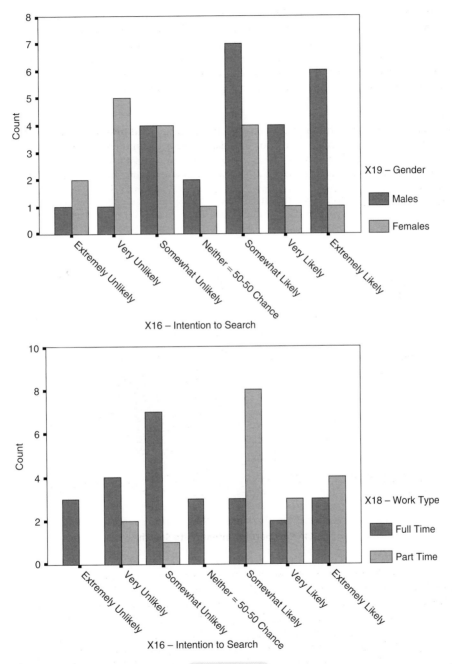

EXHIBIT 15-3

Displaying Report Results Using Bar Charts

X16 – Intention to Search

	Frequency	%	Cumulative %
1 Extremely Unlikely	4	6.3	6.3
2 Very Unlikely	10	15.9	22.2
3 Somewhat Unlikely	10	15.9	38.1
4 Neither = 50–50 Chance	4	6.3	44.4
5 Somewhat Likely	18	28.6	73.0
6 Very Likely	7	11.1	84.1
7 Extremely Likely	10	15.9	100.0
Total	63	100.0	

Exhibit 15-3 shows how bar charts can be used to display cross-tabulation results. The charts compare Intention to Search with Gender and Work Type. In the Likely to Search categories males are much more likely to search as are the part-time employees of Samouel's. This situation clearly deserves attention by Phil Samouel.

Pie and bar charts can be useful in depicting other results. For example, bar charts can be used to depict means or standardized regression weights. Both types of charts are easily constructed using computer software. Virtually all spreadsheet packages have a click-through sequence for creating pie and bar charts, as well as other types of charts. Finally, statistical packages like SAS and SPSS can be used to construct some charts.

Once again the researcher can make use of an appendix. The report itself should be kept as free of clutter as possible. While all statistical analyses should be documented, not all of them need to be reported in the body of the report. Statistical results that cannot be presented in a simple straightforward fashion should be placed in an appendix.

The main emphasis in the results section is to report on the research questions and/or hypotheses. But the researcher may wish to include a section highlighting other results discovered during the study. Some may seem particularly relevant and worthy of highlighting and perhaps suggest ideas for a follow-up study. Such results should be considered exploratory since they do not address a current research question or hypothesis.

Recommendations and Conclusions

This section of the report begins by summarizing the results in everyday language. It is good practice to use bulleted text to highlight key results addressing specific research questions. Any logical implications that emerge from the results also are discussed. If requested, a list of recommendations is provided. Recommendations may include suggestions for further research that builds on the current results. The **recommendations and conclusions** section also contains a discussion of the limitations of the research. No study is perfect. But the decision maker needs to be able to assess the confidence that can be placed in the results in light of a full accounting of the project's weaknesses.

Appendices

The **appendix** contains the questionnaire, descriptive statistics and detailed statistical analyses. Another important component of the appendix is a reference list. A **reference list** provides a complete description of the sources cited in the report. There are several different styles for reference lists. You will notice quite a few reference lists following the chapters in this book.

RESEARCH IN ACTION

REFLECTIONS ON DECISION BASED RESEARCH

Ronald L. Tatham, PhD, Chairman and CEO (retired), Burke Inc.

The key to our mission at Burke, Inc. is embodied in the phrase "**Applying Knowledge – Improving Decisions**". This phrase gains its true meaning when you accept that for every manager in every organization the true job description is: "*to make and implement decisions that increase the value of the organization*".[1] Typical job descriptions enumerate tasks, skills, or areas of management control . . . all of which should be supportive of the real job of "making and implementing decisions". A clear job description starts by describing the nature of the decisions that are to be made by the job holder. For a business researcher the appropriate job description starts with: "*to make and implement research decisions that improve the organization's business decisions*".

Everything in an organization revolves around decision making and at a practical level this requires you to wear two hats: one as a skilled research designer[2] and the second as a consultant. I want to be clear in my meaning when I use the term "consultant". You are using your skills to help other managers think through their issues until they can articulate a decision and the basis on which they would make that decision. Often a manager will say to a researcher, "What I want to know is _____ (you fill in the blank)". The researcher's job is to trace that request back to a decision. What will this person do with the information? What decision is to be made? What are the alternative potential solutions within the decision? On what basis would that decision be made? What knowledge does the manager need to be most comfortable making the decision? If the decision were to be based on this knowledge . . . can it be implemented?[3] As a business researcher, this requires tact and perseverance. Many times the manager requesting research has never thought in terms of a true decision and needs someone to pose alternatives to cause the decision to jell. I assure you (based on over 30 years of dealing with these issues) that when you pursue this line of discussion the request from the manager changes in over 50 % of the instances. A thorough discussion of both the decision and of the necessity of prespecifying how the decision would be made very often change a manager's perspective.

Without a specified decision and a specified basis for making the decision you have unfocused management and unfocused research. You may find yourself in the position of presenting research results only to hear a manager say, "You have given me a lot of good information and I learned a lot about the market." By my definition this is a poor outcome, the criterion for a successful research presentation is very simple. You *always* want to hear the key managers saying "Thanks for a thorough presentation. We now know what decision we are going to make on this issue. Let's move ahead to the next steps to get it done!" ■

AN OUTLINE OF A BASIC RESEARCH REPORT

Basic research is presented in much the same way as applied research. A basic research report has the same sections as an applied report. The Executive Summary is sometimes replaced, however, with an "Abstract". The abstract is shorter than an Executive Summary. Abstracts are 100–150 words and describe the general study purpose and give a hint of the study results.

A **basic research report** usually is more "theoretically" positioned. Therefore, a more thorough presentation of previous topical literature is presented. The hope is that this literature can be used to develop hypotheses, which generally are placed at the end of the literature review. Also, the term "Conceptual Background" is often used to title a special section focusing on how the research is conceptualized. That is, the relationships between the various elements that are being examined are displayed visually in a chart, and the text of the report describes and explains the relationships.

The research methods and results section differ little from an applied report. One exception in the style of reports is based on the intended audience. The primary audience for basic research is other researchers! Therefore, the writer is typically more technical and presents more detail about statistical and/or analytical issues. For example, a basic report usually includes tables with more detailed information while an applied report will rely more on charts. Because the presumption is that the reader of a basic research report is more sophisticated, the casual reader will sometimes find basic research reports esoteric and difficult to read.

The Implications and Conclusions section will be similar to that of the applied report. However, it may focus more on theoretical results. That is, what are the implications for others who may study this same issue? Since it is a basic report, the implications will not pertain to any specific business, but rather to businesses or industries in general. For example, an implication may be that employees should be allowed input into their weekly work schedule. The desired result would be higher employee commitment. A basic research report also may provide more detail on future basic research. These studies are suggested as follow-ups to the present effort. In this way, basic researchers develop a theoretical body of knowledge about important topics.

Finally, the basic research report contains appendices and a reference list. There is less reliance on appendices to present statistical results, however, since much of this material will be included in the body of the report. A typical outline for a basic research report follows:

- Title Page
- Abstract
- Introduction
- Conceptual Background
- Research Methods
- Results
- Implications and Conclusions
- Reference List
- Appendices

Examples of basic business research reports can be found in any of the leading academic journals within each business discipline.

ORAL PRESENTATIONS

Decision makers often require the researcher to make a formal presentation when the report is finished. Researchers should enthusiastically welcome this opportunity. The presentation provides an opportunity to follow up on the report. Thus, the researcher can clarify any material that may be difficult to understand in writing. The report also is interactive. This means members of the audience may and often do ask questions. In answering these questions, the researcher has another chance to communicate important findings. Put simply, the presentation is the best opportunity to "sell" the research and gain the enthusiasm of the decision makers.

CONSIDER THE AUDIENCE

Just as in the written presentation, the researcher should consider the varying abilities of managers to understand the presentation content. It is usually a good idea to try to find out ahead of time which individuals may attend the presentation. Sometimes, the presentation may be delivered only to the decision maker who requested the research. More commonly, however, others will be involved. The decision maker may invite any employee who might be affected by decisions that will be made. This might include superiors and subordinates. In some situations, line personnel or employees with little technical experience may attend. It is not unusual to present before eight to 12 key employees in a boardroom type setting. You should bear in mind that each person may have different concerns. A line manager may be most concerned with how a decision might affect production schedules. An accountant is likely to be interested in the impact on company profits and/or expenses. A manager may be most interested in the effect the decisions will have on his or her subordinates. Communication is enhanced when the presenter can tailor the presentation to the audience.

Audiences almost always ask questions or raise issues during the presentation. In fact, it may be a bad sign if the audience fails to interact with the presenter. Have they fallen asleep? Questions and comments should be encouraged. It is good practice to try to anticipate questions and prepare a response before the presentation. Remember, researchers have an ethical obligation to make sure the research is useful. If the key players involved understand the research it is more likely to be useful.

In preparing an oral presentation, it is a good idea to use your creative skills. Creative tools can be useful in designing effective presentation themes, identifying the assumptions and misconceptions of potential audience members and developing lists of questions that may be asked. Creativity is especially needed in developing a title that is both catchy and informative.

PRESENTATION FORMAT

There are many useful approaches for delivering a business research presentation. Avoid a strictly oral (spoken) presentation. But even more important, do not read the report to the audience. Reading the report almost never makes a positive impact, and gives the appearance of a lack of familiarity with the project. It also may be insulting since the material can be read by the audience. Presenters may use slides, transparencies, videos, flip charts, preprepared posters or even a web-based presentation. Visual aids are helpful to both the presenter and the audience. They cue the audience to important pieces of information as well as helping to hold their attention. Moreover, they also serve as "cue cards" to the presenter by reminding them of the flow of the presentation and making sure important points are not forgotten.

Perhaps the most common presentation format today is the computer-based slide show. Several software packages can be used to construct these shows including Corel's Presentations and Microsoft's Power Point. These software packages are similar and easy to use. They allow the presenter to prepare professional graphical aids including charts such as those discussed above. It is also easy to make last-minute changes to presentations.

PRESENTATION DOS AND DON'TS

The following "top ten" list gives advice for preparing an effective presentation:[4]

1. **Prepare your own slides.** Presentation software is easy to use and anyone who does business research presentations should gain some competency with these important tools. Remember, as the presenter, you'll be blamed for any shortcomings in the visual aids. Do you want to trust this to someone else? Moreover, by preparing your own presentation, you maximize your familiarity with the material.

2. **Create an effective title.** Try to use the title to communicate. You would like it to be short but insightful. This applies to both the overall presentation title and to the titles of the various slides. Suppose a researcher is presenting results about the effectiveness of salaried versus commission-based salespeople on customer satisfaction. The slide could be entitled "Statistical Results" or "Commission Leads to Satisfaction". Which is more effective?

3. **Avoid clutter in your visuals.** Use a simple font such as Ariel or Tahoma. If you want to be a little fancy use bold, italicized and shadowed Tahoma. Titles can be as large as 32–40 points. Lists of texts (bullets) are effective when they are 24–28 points. Avoid fonts smaller than 18 points for any important text. Limit the number of lines of text on any particular slide to six and the number of words to about 30.

4. **Use simple backgrounds that produce high contrasts.** Elaborate backgrounds may be decorative, but they also can be distracting and sometimes inhibit readability. Use either a dark background with light letters or a white background with dark letters.

5. **Vary the slide layouts.** Slides do not always have to have clip art on the right and text on the left. If there is no picture that pairs well with a slide's content, do not use any. Take advantage of the "white space" beside charts to drop in (add by using transition or animation) a meaningful word or phrase.

6. **Arrive early.** Presenters sometimes make presentations in a familiar room with familiar equipment. But more often, presentations are in an unfamiliar location with unfamiliar equipment. Particularly in these situations, arrive early enough to test the presentation. For example, different versions of the same software may not always work exactly the same. Animation or transitions may work differently or not at all. Allow enough time to make any last minute changes to insure the presentation "looks" as it should.

7. **Use the time allowed.** Make good use of the entire time allowed for the presentation. Business people normally allow between 20 and 60 minutes for a presentation. While it varies from person to person, a rule of thumb is that the presentation will last two to three times the number of slides. Plan on using the entire time while still allowing time for questions. Plan ahead for material that can be skipped should the presentation begin to run behind. Stay until all questions are answered.

8. **Use humour when possible.** Cartoons and funny phrases are usually acceptable. They help win the audience over and the break the monotony of what might otherwise be very dry material. The humour should always be in good taste. If there is any doubt over the appropriateness of a particular piece of humour, leave it out.

9. **Invite audience participation.** Ask questions of the audience. For example, if the research involves employee reactions to a new company policy, invite one of the key decision makers to guess at how a typical employee responded to a key question about the policy. This keeps their interest up and helps them become part of the presentation. Remember to always respond favourably to their answers to your questions. The wrong response could demean the audience.

10. **Do sweat the small stuff.** Presenters are part of the research package so they must appear credible and professional. Pay attention to the details including your dress and mannerisms during the presentation. Dress appropriately and remember it is usually better to overdress than underdress. Like it or not, people will base their judgements of you and your work on your appearance. This may not always mean a business suit. If you are making a presentation to decision makers on a retreat in Tahiti, a suit may not make the best impression. However, anything less formal to the same decision makers in a London office building would be very risky. Also, do not use distracting mannerisms and phrases. Try to limit the use of "you know" for example. If this is a concern, have someone else watch you do a presentation and count the number of times you use such phrases. You also may want to videotape yourself to identify distracting mannerisms. Usually, awareness of distractions is the best way to reduce them.

Some researchers are uncomfortable making presentations. Also, junior analysts or entry level researchers seldom are called upon to make presentations. As the researcher advances, however, this changes. The Research in Action box gives advice to those who may be apprehensive about delivering presentations.

RESEARCH IN ACTION

PRESENTATION ANXIETY? HAVE NO FEAR WITH THIS CURE-ALL

Giving an oral research presentation clearly is public speaking. Oral presentations absolutely frighten many people. Speaking about an innocuous topic or giving a classroom presentation is hard enough. A research presentation demonstrates the researcher's professional competence as well as the competence of any colleagues who also were involved in the research. Thus, there is considerable pressure to make a good presentation. If you are afraid, consider this advice:

1. You will make a mistake during the presentation! But, even the best presenter will make mistakes. They are not fatal. Part of the apprehension may go away when you realize that mistakes are inevitable and that reasonable people expect them occasionally.

2. Study your material. One of the best ways to deal with nervousness is to be EXTREMELY familiar with the material. Discussing it becomes second nature at some point. It's as easy as dinnertime conversation. So, make sure you know all the sordid details of the research. Find an audience to discuss the research with ahead of the presentation. Rehearsing the presentation relieves anxiety among some presenters. But, having the confidence that you will be able to make some intelligent comment no matter what occurs is a good way of fighting presentation fear.

3. Practise your presentation out loud. Go in a room by yourself, perhaps stand in front of a mirror, and give your presentation. Try speaking at slower speeds, use pauses and change the tone of your voice to avoid a monotone sound. When you cannot speak out loud, then mentally rehearse the presentation.

4. Take advantage of opportunities to do public speaking. At some point, you'll become quite comfortable standing in front of an audience of faces staring up at you.

5. Laugh. Use humour when (a) it is appropriate and (b) you have confidence that others will laugh with you. If you are unsure, don't use it because a punch line that doesn't deliver will only increase apprehension.

6. Be confident. The reason you are giving a presentation is because you probably know something the audience doesn't. Therefore, you have an advantage. You can tell them something worthwhile. Expect to do a good presentation and you usually will.

Source: Kaye, S. (1998). "It's Showtime! How to Give Effective Presentations", *Supervision*, 60 (March), 8–10. ■

SUMMARY

■ **Convey the importance of effective communication to research success**
Communication is essential to avoid wasting all the effort that went into the research. The research proposal, report and presentation provide the means for the researcher to communicate the purpose, methodology, results and implications of the research. If these are done poorly, it is less likely the research will ever be used to aid decision making. Therefore, these reporting vehicles "sell" the research project. This means they try to convince the users that the information is useful and helpful.

■ **Describe the elements of a research proposal**
The research proposal is used to maximize the chances that the decision maker and researcher will have the same understanding of the research purpose(s) and types of information it will produce prior to beginning the study. Proposals contain an introduction, a list of the research questions, a description of

the research methods, a proposed outline of the final research report, including dummy tables and a description of the time and financial resources required to complete the research project.

■ **Provide an overview of effective research reports**
There are many ways to increase the effectiveness of research reports. Executive summaries precede the body of a research report. They are, in effect, mini reports in themselves. They include the following sections: (1) a statement of the research purpose; (2) a brief description of the research design and implementation; (3) a summary of results derived from testing research questions and/or hypotheses; (4) a written interpretation of the findings framed as answers to the research questions; and (5) if requested, a list of practical business implications derived from the research. Given that this is often the only part of the report read in detail, great attention must be paid to make sure it communicates effectively. In preparing reports, the researcher must be sensitive to the audience. Do not overwhelm readers with technical jargon unless they have an everyday working knowledge of such terms. Finally, research reports are not a work of fiction and should present the facts in a concise way.

■ **Summarize effective ways to deliver a research presentation**
Much like the report, effective communication in an oral presentation is essential. Careful consideration of the expected audience pays off by presenting the most important results and anticipating questions and objections. Ten suggestions are provided for aiding a presentation. Some of the more important ones include the strong suggestion to use visual aids of some type, invite audience participation and to be creative in developing effective presentation titles and content. ■

Ethical Dilemma

Monarch is a consumer products company selling in most EU countries. The company has a long-term relationship with Oxford Data Group, a UK research firm whose growth has been largely tied to Monarch's. When Barbara Newcomb is hired as Monarch's new president to help the company achieve the next level in growth, she schedules a meeting with the president of Oxford Data Group to discuss a recently completed study of their employees. During the meeting Barbara asks to see the original data from the study, including individual employee information, so she can work on improving employee productivity. Monarch is Oxford's largest client and the president doesn't want to risk losing the business by disappointing their new president. How should he respond to the request?

REVIEW QUESTIONS

1. List and briefly describe the three communication mechanisms used by business researchers. Is one mechanism better than the other?

2. List and briefly describe the elements of a research proposal.

3. What is an executive summary? Why is it so important? How long should it be?

4. What is the least common denominator principle and how would it apply when making a presentation to a group of military officers and enlisted people?

5. Explain the role humour in a formal presentation.

DISCUSSION AND THINKING ACTIVITIES

1. Find an academic research report. Just about any article from The Academy of Management, the *Journal of Management*, the *Journal of Marketing*, the *Journal of Business Research* or the *Journal of Retailing*, among others, will do. Read the abstract. Try rewriting it as if it were being presented to a group of line managers none of which has a business or technical college degree.

2. The sample research report available on the Web site (www.wileyeurope.com/college/hair) shows the results of examining only two research questions for the employee study. Develop a list of at least three more employee research questions and tell why they need to be examined. Similarly, the customer survey results examined only three research questions. Develop a list of at least three more customer research questions and tell why they need to be examined.

3. Use data analysis software and examine the research questions you developed in question 2. Prepare a brief report summarizing your findings and recommendations.

4. Using the SPSS customer data set accompanying this book, compute a cross tabulation of the selection factors prices (X_{13}) and employees (X_{14}) by restaurant (X_{28}). In other words, do Gino's and Samouel's customers rate prices and employees as equally important? Present the results graphically using bar charts as shown in the chapter. Prepare the bar charts up using a presentations software package.

5. Prepare a 20-minute presentation for Phil Samouel to present the results shown in the sample research report available on the Web site (www.wileyeurope.com/college/hair). Assume he will be there along with his financial manager, floor manager, chef and a member of the wait staff. Be sure to anticipate questions.

INTERNET EXERCISES   W W W

1. Access the Web site for this text (www.wileyeurope.com/college/hair). Locate the "Presentation for Samouel's". Critique the presentation for possible areas of improvement.

2. Go to the following Web site: http://powerreporting.com/. Browse the Web site and prepare a brief report summarizing how a researcher might use this site.

3. Use the search engine of your choice. Input the key words research reporting. Prepare a brief report summarizing what you found.

NOTES

1. In a nonprofit organization this could mean increasing the value to the beneficiaries of the organization. In a for-profit organization it implies increasing value to all stakeholders.
2. The research designer makes the decisions that create an effective research plan, effective execution, and clear interpretation. These decisions cannot be made optimally without knowing the marketing decision to be made based on the research.
3. We often hear of the segmentation study that the sales force can't actualize because of the difficulty of measuring the segmenting characteristics in the marketplace.
4. Kaye, S. (1999). "It's Showtime! How to Give Effective Presentations". *Supervision*, 60 (March), 8–10. Wareham, J. (2001). "From the Podium", *Across the Board*, 38 (March/April), 67–69.

GLOSSARY

A

Access complications can include: cost implications, lack of familiarity with various parties that provide the data, or because of the way the data are summarized and the conclusions drawn from it are reported.

Aided question is one that provides the respondent with a stimulus that jogs the memory, whereas **unaided questions** do not have a stimulus.

Algorithm a list of steps that are computer commands.

Alternative hypothesis is that there is a difference between the groups being compared. It is the opposite of the null hypothesis.

Analytical phase where the data are analysed.

Applied business research is motivated by an attempt to solve a particular problem faced by a particular organization.

Automatic Interaction Detection (AID) software that considers possible relationships between all pairs of quantified data within a data set.

Average summated score involves calculating the summated score and then dividing it by the number of variables.

Balanced scale is where the number of favourable and unfavourable categories is equal. With an **unbalanced scale** the number of favourable and unfavourable categories is unequal.

Bar charts show the data in the form of bars that can be displayed either horizontally or vertically (the only difference between a bar chart and a histogram is that there is no space between the bars in a histogram).

Basic business research is motivated by a desire to better understand some business related phenomenon as it applies to all of an industry or all of business in general.

Behavioural learning theory provides managers with normative decision rules about issues dealing with the amount and timing of employee compensation.

Branching questions are used to direct respondents to answer the right questions as well as questions in the proper sequence.

Business ethics, as a field of study, addresses the application of moral principles and/or ethical standards to human actions within the exchange process.

Business researchers pursue the "truth" about business phenomena.

Card reader enables an analyst to feed data into a computer using elongated cardboard index cards.

Case studies focus on collecting information about a specific event or activity – often a particular firm or industry.

Categorical scales are nominally-measured opinion scales that have two or more response categories.

Causality means a change in X (the cause) makes a change in Y (the effect) occur!

Causal research tests whether or not one event causes another. Does X cause Y? More precisely, a causal relationship means a change in one event brings about a corresponding change in another event.

Census is when a researcher collects data from all members of a population under investigation.

Classification questions often seek information of a more personal nature, such as age and income.

Closed questions are where the respondent is given the option of choosing from a number of predetermined answers.

Cluster sampling is when the target population is viewed as made up of heterogeneous groups called clusters.

Coding is the process assigning meaningful numerical values that facilitate understanding of your data.

Coding units include words, phrases, themes, items, images, graphics, photographs, and so on.

Coefficient alpha, also referred to as Cronbach's alpha, is a measure of reliability. To obtain coefficient alpha you calculate the average of the coefficients from all possible combinations of split halves.

Comparative analysis involves evaluating the accuracy of secondary data by looking at the same data from multiple sources or by evaluating trends to see if there is any questionable data at a particular point in time.

Concept is a mental abstraction or idea formed by the perception of some phenomena.

Conceptual framework is the section of your literature review that describes the conceptual model being studied.

Conceptualization is the process of developing a conceptual model.

Conceptual model is a diagram that connects variables/constructs based on theory and logic to visually display the hypotheses that will be tested.

Concurrent validity requires some prespecified association to be established between the scores on the construct being validated and the scores on a dependent variable as determined by theory.

Constant sum scale asks respondents to divide a constant sum over several categories to indicate, for example, the relative importance of the attributes.

Construct is when several questions/statements are used in combination to represent a characteristic/concept. It is a higher level of abstraction that represents a latent variable.

Construct validity assesses what the construct (concept) or scale is in fact measuring.

Content analysis obtains data by observing and analysing the content or message of written text.

Content or **face validity** of a scale involves a systematic but subjective assessment of a scale's ability to measure what it is supposed to measure.

Context effect occurs when the position of a question relative to other questions influences the response.

Convenience sample involves selecting sample elements that are most readily available to participate in the study and who can provide the information required.

Convergent validity is the extent to which the construct is positively correlated with other measures of the same or similar constructs.

Cost savings arise because data that have already been collected and compiled into a suitable format present the initial owner with the opportunity to provide it to third parties for considerably less than the original cost.

Criterion validity assesses whether a construct performs as expected relative to other variables identified as meaningful criteria.

Cross-sectional studies are descriptive studies that provide a "snapshot" or description of business elements at a given time.

Cross-tabulation is a frequency distribution of responses on two or more sets of variables.

Customer churn is the annual turnover rate of customers.

Customer commitment – the degree to which customers identify with and are committed to the values of a firm.

Customer share is the proportion of resources a customer spends with one firm in a given competitor set.

Data display goes beyond data reduction by organizing the information in a way that facilitates drawing conclusions.

Data mining electronically mines data warehouses for information that identifies ways to improve organizational performance.

Data reduction involves selecting, simplifying and transforming the data to make them more manageable and understandable.

Data triangulation requires collecting data from several different sources at different times and comparing them.

Data warehouses store and catalogue company information in an electronic format.

Deductive reasoning works from the more general to the more specific and involves descriptive or confirmatory aspects.

Dependent variable is the variable you are trying to understand, explain and/or predict.

Depth, or **in-depth interview,** is an unstructured one-to-one discussion session between a trained interviewer and a respondent.

Descriptive research is designed to obtain data that describes the characteristics of the topic of interest in the research.

Descriptive theory is just that – theory that describes the way things are.

Directional hypothesis is when you use terms like more than, less than, positive or negative in stating the relationship between two groups or two variables.

Discriminant validity is the extent to which the construct does not correlate with other measures that are different from it.

Disproportionately stratified sampling is based on economic or other reasons. The sample size from each stratum is determined independently without considering the size of the stratum relative to the overall sample size. The more important a particular stratum is considered, the higher will be the proportion of the sample elements from the stratum.

Double-barrelled questions include two or more issues and make interpretation difficult, and often impossible.

Drawing conclusions involves deciding what the identified themes and patterns mean and how they help to answer the research questions.

Electronic communication Email and technologies such as video conferencing and Skype are examples.

Elements are objects that make up the population and share a common set of characteristics. Examples include people, supermarkets, churches, hospitals, etc.

Ethics checklist is a list of questions that can be useful in guiding ethical decision making.

Ethnographic researchers prefer to interpret behaviour through observation of actual life experiences.

Ethnography is the qualitative description of human socio-cultural phenomena, based on field observation.

Execution phase is when the researcher actively gathers information from the appropriate sources. The information is then checked for errors, coded and then stored in a way that allows it to be analysed quickly and conveniently.

Exploratory research is used when the researcher has little information or knowledge of the research problem. Exploratory designs are used when the researcher knows little about the problem or opportunity and wants to discover new relationships, patterns, themes, ideas and so on. Thus, it is not intended to test specific research hypotheses.

Extended fieldwork involves collection of data over an extended period of time and is likely to improve both discovery and interpretation.

External peer review is by other research experts, including those both familiar with the research as

well as disinterested parties. It is often used to verify interpretations and conclusions.

External source is when secondary data are obtained from outside the company.

Field-generated data typically come from interviews or focus groups in the field and consist of words and phrases in textual format.

Focus groups are semi-structured interviews that use an exploratory research approach and are considered a type of qualitative research.

Forced choice scale are designed to force respondents to make a choice.

Formulation phase involves defining the substance and process of the research.

Found data are those from existing sources like newspaper articles, speeches, diaries, advertisements, audio and video records, and so forth.

Frequency distributions examine the data one variable at a time and provide counts of the different responses for the various values of the variable.

Funnel approach is when the interviewer moves from general to specific questions.

Geographic Information Systems (GIS) can create, within a few minutes, numerous maps that overlay information from census data inventories on top of satellite photo imagery.

Graphic ratings scale is one that provides measurements on a continuum in the form of a line with anchors that are numbered and named.

Grounded theory is a process involving a set of steps that if carefully executed is thought to "guarantee" that the outcome will be a good theory.

Hermeneutics attempts to understand and explain human behaviour based on an analysis of stories people tell about themselves.

Hypothesis is an unproven supposition or proposition that tentatively explains certain facts or phenomena.

Hypothesis tests are systematic procedures followed to "accept" or "reject" hypotheses about proposed patterns or relationships.

Independent variable is a measurable characteristic that influences or explains the dependent variable.

Inductive reasoning is how effective an individual is in identifying patterns within a large amount of data.

Inferential statistics help us to make judgements or predictions about the population from a sample.

Information-only businesses are those that exchange information or information-related services such as distribution and storage, for some type of fee.

Internal source is when data come from within the company.

Inter-rater reliability means that multiple "raters" will evaluate the same qualitative data point.

Interval scale uses numbers to rate objects or events so that the distances between the numbers are equal.

Interview is where the researcher "speaks" to the respondent directly.

Interviewer-completed methods involve direct contact with the respondents through personal interviews either face-to-face or via telephone.

Interview guide specifies the topics to cover, the questions to be asked, the sequence of questions/topics, and the wording of the questions.

Intranets are Internet-like networks that link computers internally within a single organization.

Issues are the things that if altered will close the gap between the actual and desired states.

Judgement sample, sometimes referred to as a **purposive sample,** involves selecting elements in the sample for a specific purpose.

Kiosk survey is one that uses a self-contained kiosk located in a high traffic area and individuals sign on to obtain information and submit survey information.

Kurtosis is a measure of a distribution's peakedness (or flatness).

Lack of familiarity with the initial motivation and processes followed when gathering the data also represents a potential weakness to using secondary data.

Leading questions imply that a particular answer is correct or lead a respondent to a socially desirable answer.

Literature review typically has two broad objectives. Firstly, it helps to develop and expand your research ideas. Secondly, although you may have some knowledge of your research topic, the literature review ensures you are familiar with recent developments and have a complete understanding of the relevant topics.

Longitudinal analysis involves comparing findings across time to identify trends or seasonal patterns.

Longitudinal studies provide data that describe events over time.

Market responsibility means a concern for making sure that products are produced that consumers actually need and that the prices charged for these products are fair.

Mean is the arithmetic average, and is one of the most commonly used measures of central tendency.

Measures of dispersion describe the tendency for sample responses to depart from the central tendency.

Median is the value that is in the middle of the distribution.

Method triangulation involves conducting similar research using several different methods and comparing the findings, including sometimes using both qualitative and quantitative approaches.

Metric scales often are referred to as quantitative and **nonmetric** as qualitative.

Missing data are blank responses.

Mode is the measure of central tendency that identifies the value that occurs most often in the sample distribution.

Moderator encourages discussion in focus groups and keeps the group "on track", meaning they don't stray too far from the primary topic. A good moderator is a key to a successful focus group.

Multi-item scale consists of a number of closely related individual statements (items or indicators) whose responses are combined into a composite score or summated rating used to measure a concept.

Networking refers to systems of computers that are connected to each other through various servers.

New insights occur when re-examination of secondary data and the conclusions extracted from these data presents a researcher with the opportunity to develop.

Nominal data is a name or label that enables the researcher to place respondents into categories, but you cannot make comparisons like bigger/smaller or faster/slower.

Nondirectional hypotheses postulate a difference or relationship between variables, but do not indicate a direction for the differences or relationship. There is a relationship between two groups or two variables, but we are not able to say whether the relationship is positive or negative.

Nonmetric scales are nominal and ordinal scales that are considered qualitative and sometimes referred to as comparative scales.

Nonprobability sampling is where the inclusion or exclusion of elements in a sample is left to the discretion of the researcher.

Normal distribution describes the expected distribution of sample means as well as many other chance occurrences. Also referred to as a bell-shaped curve.

Normative decision rule explains what someone should do when faced with a situation described by a theory.

Null hypothesis is that there is no difference in the group statistics; for example, there is no difference in the means, medians, and so on, of two or more groups.

Numerical scales have numbers as response options, rather than verbal descriptions.

Observational data are collected by systematically recording observations of people, events or objects.

Observation guides are used to record data that are observed. They indicate what the observer is to look for and provide a place to record the information.

Off-the-shelf data are readily available information compiled and sold by content provision companies.

One-shot research projects are performed to address a single issue at a specific point in time.

Open-ended questions place no constraints on respondents who are free to answer in their own words.

Opening questions are designed to establish rapport with the respondent by gaining their attention and stimulating their interest in the research topic.

Ordinal data are the next higher level of data above nominal. Ordinal responses can be rank ordered into a hierarchical pattern like higher/lower or greater than/less than.

Ordinal scale is a ranking scale. It places objects into a predetermined category that is rank ordered according to some criterion such as preference, age, income group, importance, etc.

Organizational learning can be defined as the internalization of both external and internal information to be used as an input to decision making.

Organizational memory is a formal system aimed at recording all important events in a database.

Outside research consultants are researchers not employed within a firm.

Panel is a fixed sample arranged for the purpose of collecting data.

Parsimony. This means that a simpler solution is better than a complex solution. Parsimonious research means applying the simplest approach that will address the research questions satisfactorily.

Participant feedback is the information provided by research participants that facilitates the researcher's interpretations and insights.

Pattern matching is where the data are used to predict or suggest particular outcomes and the actual results are evaluated to determine if they fit the predicted pattern.

Phenomenology is a qualitative research method that studies human experiences and consciousness.

Pie charts display relative proportions of the responses in a circle format.

Placebo is a false treatment. An example is a medical experiment that tests a drug's effectiveness on, for example, weight loss, but one of the treatments is not the actual drug.

Population is a group of knowledgeable people (see **Universe**).

Population parameters are the characteristics of the population.

Postal surveys are surveys delivered to respondents via regular post, fax and overnight delivery.

Predictive validity assesses the ability of a construct measured at one point in time to predict another criterion at a future point in time.

Probability sampling is where the sampling elements are selected randomly and the probability of being selected is determined ahead of time by the researcher.

Probing is when a researcher delves deeply into a response to identify possibly hidden reasons for a particular behaviour.

Projective interviewing is where the researcher presents the respondent with an ambiguous stimulus and attempts to obtain answers using an indirect questioning method.

Proportionately stratified sampling uses the total of all the elements from each of the strata as a basis of determining the size of the strata.

Proxy is a variable that represents a single component of a larger concept. Taken together several proxies are said to measure a concept. Proxies are also referred to in business research as indicator or manifest variables because they indirectly measure constructs.

Push polls are short phone calls used to spread negative and often false information about a candidate or issue under the guise of a poll.

Qualitative data represent descriptions of things that are made without assigning numbers directly. Qualitative data are generally collected using some type of unstructured interviews or observation.

Qualitative research reliability is the degree of consistency in assignment of similar words, phrases or other kinds of data to the same pattern or theme by different researchers.

Quality research topics are those that address gaps in existing knowledge that currently inhibit informed decision making.

Quantitative data are measurements in which numbers are used directly to represent the characteristics of something. Since they are recorded directly with numbers, they are in a form that easily lends itself to statistical analysis.

Quantitative data collection involves gathering numerical data using structured questionnaires or observation guides to collect primary data from individuals.

Questionnaire is a prepared set of questions (or measures) used by respondents or interviewers to record answers (data).

Quota sampling is similar to stratified random sampling. The objective is for the total sample to have proportional representation of the strata of the target population. Quota sampling differs from stratified sampling in that the selection of elements is done on a convenience basis.

Range is the simplest measure of dispersion. It is the spread of the responses and represents the distance between the largest and smallest values of a sample frequency distribution.

Rank order scale is an ordinal scale that asks respondents to rank a set of objects or characteristics in terms of preference, similarity, importance or similar adjectives.

Rating scales typically involve the use of statements on a questionnaire accompanied by precoded categories, one of which is selected by the respondents to indicate the extent of their agreement or disagreement with a given statement.

Rational decision making is based upon explanation and prediction.

Ratio scale provides the highest level of measurement. A distinguishing characteristic of a ratio scale is that it possesses a unique origin or zero point, which makes it possible to compute ratios of points on the scale.

Relationship is a meaningful link believed to exist between two variables/constructs.

Relationship marketing emphasizes long-term interactions between a business and its stakeholders.

Reliability is when a scale or question consistently measures a concept.

Replicable means that another researcher could produce the same results using the identical procedures employed by the original researcher.

Representative is when the sample findings mirror characteristics of the population, thereby minimizing the error associated with sampling.

Research is a discerning pursuit of the truth.

Research brief is an overview of the sponsor's (company or individual) initial perceptions of the problem or opportunity and may be written or presented orally.

Researcher triangulation involves comparing the methods, analysis and interpretation of different researchers on the same topic.

Research question poses an issue of interest to the researcher and is related to the specific decision faced by the company.

Research questions rephrase research issues into a form that is researchable.

Research topic questions, includes those designed to provide information on the topic being researched.

Respondent fatigue is most often thought of as the fatigue that occurs within the context of single study rather than in terms of the fatigue that occurs when individuals find themselves repeatedly surveyed for similar but varied reasons.

Sample is a relatively small subset of the population.

Sample frame is a comprehensive list of the elements from which the sample is drawn.

Sample statistics are the characteristics computed from the sample.

Sampling interval is the number of population elements between each unit selected when using systematic sampling.

Sampling units are the elements or objects that are available for selection during the sampling process.

Scale is a measurement tool that can be used to measure a question with a predetermined number of outcomes.

Science seeks to explain the world that really is.

Scientific method is the systematic, logical method researchers use to gain accurate knowledge.

Screening questions, sometimes referred to as filtering questions, are another type of opening question.

Secondary data is obtained from research in which the data are not gathered directly and purposefully for the project under consideration.

Self-completion methods include postal surveys, Internet/electronic surveys, drop-off/pick up, and similar approaches when the respondent completes a questionnaire without the help of an interviewer.

Semantic differential scale is an approach to measure attitudes. It has several individual scales combined and uses bipolar endpoints labelled with opposite adjectives and the intermediate points are numbered or have blanks to tic.

Semi-structured interviews are where researchers are free to exercise their own initiative in following up an interviewee's answer to a question.

Simple random sampling is a method of sampling that assigns each element of the target population a known and equal probability of being selected.

Skewness measures the departure from a symmetrical (or balanced) distribution.

Skipping questions direct respondents to the appropriate section of the questionnaire.

Snowball sample, also called a **referral sample**, is one where the initial respondents are typically chosen using probability methods. Then the researcher uses the initial respondents to help identify the other respondents in the target population. This process is continued until the required sample size is reached.

Social responsibilities involve a concern for the way actions affect society or groups of people including employees, customers and the community.

Sorting scales ask respondents to indicate their beliefs or opinions by arranging objects (items) on the basis of perceived similarity or some other attribute.

Split-half reliability. The researcher randomly divides the scale items in half and correlates the two sets of items.

Standard deviation describes the spread or variability of the sample distribution values from the mean, and is perhaps the most valuable index of dispersion.

Stickiness is how much it costs to transfer a given unit of information to an information seeker.

Stratified sampling requires the researcher to partition the sampling frame into relatively homogeneous subgroups that are distinct and nonoverlapping, called strata.

Structured interviews are when the interviewer uses an interview sequence with predetermined set of open-ended questions.

Summated ratings scales attempt to measure attitudes or opinions. Summated scales often use a five-point or seven-point scale to assess the strength of agreement about a group of statements.

Symptoms are signals that some change may be needed to avoid further problems or take advantage of some opportunity.

Systematic sampling is a process that involves randomly selecting an initial starting point on a list, and thereafter every nth element in the sampling frame is selected.

Target population is the complete group of objects or elements relevant to the research project.

Test-retest reliability is obtained through repeated measurement of the same respondent or group of respondents using the same measurement device and under similar conditions.

Theory is a set of systematically related statements, including some law-like generalizations that can be tested empirically.

Theory triangulation is using multiple theories and perspectives to interpret and explain the data.

Translational equivalence means text can be translated from one language to another, then back to the original language with no distortion in meaning.

Triangulate is comparing the findings established from the primary collection method and confirming the validity of the research.

Trust is believing in someone or something and is an overriding issue in business ethics.

Type I error, referred to as alpha (α), occurs when the sample results lead to rejection of the null hypothesis when it is true.

Type II error occurs when, based on the sample results, the null hypothesis is not rejected when it is in fact false.

Universe is a group of knowledgeable people (see **Population**).

Unobtrusive means the respondent is unaware of his/her participation in a research project.

Validity is associated with the term accuracy. A construct measures what it is supposed to measure.

Variables are the observable and measurable characteristics in a conceptual model.

Verification involves checking and re-checking the data to ensure the initial conclusions are realistic, supportable and valid.

Web-hosted Internet surveys maintain anonymity of respondents and increase response rates and are typically created and hosted by an independent research company on their own server (computer).

REFERENCES

Ahmed, M. M., Chung, K. Y. and Eichenseher, J. W. (2003). "Business Students' Perception of Ethics and Moral Judgment: A Cross-Cultural Study", *Journal of Business Ethics*, 43, 89–102.

Allen, N. J. and Meyer, J. P. (1990). "The Measurement and Antecedents of Affective, Continuance and Normative Commitment to the Organisation", *Journal of Occupational Psychology*, 63, 1–18.

Axinn, C. N., Blair, M. E., Heorhiadi, A. and Thach, S. V. (2004). "Comparing Ethical Ideologies Across Cultures", *Journal of Business Ethics*, 54, 103–19.

Babin, B. J. and Attaway, J. P. (2000). "Atmospheric Affect as a Tool for Creating Value and Gaining Share of Customer", *Journal of Business Research*, 49 (August), 91–101.

Badke, W., *Research Strategies*, http://www.acts.twu.ca/lbr/textbook.htm

Banham, C. *A Student's Guide to Research on the WWW*, St Louis University, http://www.slu.edu/departments/english/research/

Baron, R. A. (1977). *Aggression*. New York, Plenun Press.

Begley, S., Foote, D. and Rogers, A. (2001). "Dying for Science", *Newsweek*, 138 (7/30), 36.

Bleicher, J. (1980). *Contemporary Hermeneutics: Hermeneutics as Method, Philosophy and Critique*. London, Routledge & Kegan Paul.

Blumer, H. (1969). *Symbolic Interactionism: Perspective and Method*. Englewood Cliffs, NJ, Prentice Hall.

Brown, B. B. (2003). "Employees' Organisational Commitment and Their Perception of Supervisors' Relations-Oriented and Task-Oriented Leadership Behaviours." Doctoral Dissertation, Virginia Polytechnic Institute and State University.

Brown, K. and Wiel J. (2002). "When Enron Auditors Were on a Tear", *Wall Street Journal*, 239 (3/21), C1.

Bryman, A. and Burgess R. G. (1994). *Analyzing Qualitative Data*. London, Routledge.

Business Week online, 12 January 2004.

Caulkin, S. (2002). "Management: A Mess in Theory, A Mess in Practice", *The Observer*, (13 January), 9.

Chamberlin, E. H. (1939). *The Theory of Monopolistic Competition*. Cambridge, MA, Harvard University Press.

Chebat, J.-C., Chebat, C. G. and Vaillant D. (2001). "Environmental Background Music and In-Store Selling", *Journal of Business Research*, 54 (November), 115–24.

Cohen, J., West, S., Aiken, L. and Cohen, P. (2002). *Applied Multiple Regression/Correlation Analysis for the Behavioral Sciences*, 3rd edn. Hillsdale, NJ, Lawrence Erlbaum Associates.

Cole, B. C. and Smith, D. L. (1995). "Effects of Ethics Instruction on the Ethical Perceptions of College Business Students", *Journal of Education for Business*, 70 (July/August), 351–57.

Cronin, J. and Taylor, S. (1992). "Measuring Service Quality: a Re-examination and Extension", *Journal of Marketing*, 56, (July), 55–68.

Cronin, J. J., Jr., and Morris, M. H. (1989). "Satisfying Customer Expectations: The Effect of Conflict and Repurchase Intentions in Industrial Marketing Channels", *Journal of Academy of Marketing Sciences*, 17, (Winter), 41–49.

Denscombe, M. (1998). *The Good Research Guide for Small Scale Social Research Projects*. Buckingham, Open University Press.

Dey, I. (1993). *Qualitative Data Analysis: A User-Friendly Guide for Social Scientists*. London, Routledge.

Dickson, P. R. (1992). "Toward a General Theory of Competitive Rationality", *Journal of Marketing*, 56 (January), 69–83.

Dyer, W. G. Jr. and Wilkins, A. L. (1991). "Better Stories, Not Better Constructs, to Generate Better Theory: A Rejoinder to Eisenhardt", *Academy of Management Review*, 16(3), 613–19.

Eastern Economist Daily (2000). "Russia Begins Selling Cars in the US", (12 October). Global News Wire.

Evers, K. (2004). "Standards for Ethics in Research", *Codes of Conduct*. Luxembourg, Office for Official Publications of the European Communities.

Farrell, B. J. and Cobin, M. (1996). "A Content Analysis of Codes of Ethics in Australian Enterprises", *Journal of Managerial Psychology*, 11 (1), 37–56.

Ferrell, O. C. and Fraedrich, J. (1997). *Business Ethics*. Boston, MA, Houghton Mifflin.

Fielding, N. G. and Lee, R. M. (1998). *Computer Analysis and Qualitative Research*. London, Sage.

Gibbens, R. (2002). "Toyota Extends One-Price Retailing: Montreal now, Vancouver and Toronto to Follow", *National Post*, (22 January), FP3.

Glantz, W. (2001). "Gorbachev Touts Russian Workers", *Washington Times*, (25 April). B8.

Grace, V. R. (1961). *Amphoras and the Ancient Wine Trade*. Princeton, NJ, American School of Classical Studies at Athens.

Greenbaum, T. L. (1993). *Handbook of Focus Group Research,* New York, Lexington.

Griffin, M., Babin, B. J. and Modianos, D. (2000). "Shopping Values of Russian Consumers: The Impact of Habituation in a Developing Economy", *The Journal of Retailing*, 76 (Spring), 20–53.

Hair, J. F., Black, B. Babin, B., Anderson, R. and Tatham, R. (2006). *Multivariate Data Analysis*, 6th edn. Englewood Cliffs, NJ, Prentice Hall.

Hall, E. (1999). "Broadening the View of Corporate Diversification: an International Perspective", *International Journal of Organizational Analysis*, 7 (January), 25–54.

Hardy, M. A. and Bryman A. E. (2004). *Handbook of Data Analysis*. Newbury Park, CA, Sage.

Holthausen, R. and Larcker D. F. (1995). "Business Unit Innovation and the Structure of Executive Compensation", *Journal of Accounting and Economics*, 19 (May), 279–304.

Hunt, S. (1983). *Marketing Theory: The Philosophy of Marketing Science*. Homewood, IL, Irwin.

Hunt, S. D. and Morgan, R. M. (1996). "The Resource-Advantage Theory of Competition: Dynamis, Path Dependencies, and Evolutionary Dimensions", *Journal of Marketing*, 60 (October), 107–14.

Hunt, S. D. and Morgan, R. M. (1997). "Resource-Advantage Theory: A Snake Swallowing Its Tail or a General Theory of Competition", *Journal of Marketing*, 61 (October), 74–83.

Hunt, W. (1995). "Getting the Word on Deception", *Security Management*, 39 (June), 26–27.

Hunter, P. (2000). "Using Focus Groups In Campaigns: A Caution", *Campaigns and Elections*, 21 (August), 38–41.

Internal Auditor (1997). "EAR Focus Groups Target ISO 14,000", 54 (June), 8.

James, D. (2002). "Skoda is Taken from Trash to Treasure", *Marketing News*, 36 (18 February), 4–5.

James, D. (2002). "This Bulletin Just In: Online Research Technique Proving Invaluable", *Marketing News*, 36 (4 March), 45–46.

Johnson, R. A., and Wichern, D. (2002). *Applied Multivariate Statistical Analysis*, 5th edn. Upper Saddle River, NJ, Prentice-Hall.

Au, K. N. *Business Research Strategy.* http://newarkwww.rutgers.edu/guides/business/busres.htm

Khermouch, G. (2001). "Consumers in the Mist", *Business Week*, 3721 (2/26), 92–93.

Klara, R. (1999). "Fast and Fancy", *Restaurant Business*, 98 (6/1), 19–21.

Lawrence, J. and Berger, P. (1999). "Let's Hold a Focus Group", *Direct Marketing*, 61 (December), 40–44.

Lewin, C. (1948). *Resolving Conflicts and Field Theory in Social Science.* New York, Harper and Row.

Lingard, H. (2001). "The Effect of First Aid Training on Objective Safety Behaviour in Australian Small Business Construction Firms", *Construction Management and Economics*, 19 (October), 611–19.

Lofland, J. and Lofland, L. H. (1995). *Analyzing Social Settings: A Guide to Qualitative Observation and Analysis,* 3rd edn. Belmont, CA, Wadsworth.

Lok, P. and Crawford, J. (1999). "The Relationship Between Commitment and Organisational Culture, Subculture, Leadership Style and Job Satisfaction in Organisational Change and Development", *Leadership and Organisation Development Journal*, 20 (7), 365–74.

Lussier, R. N. (1995). "Flexible Work Arrangement from Policy to Implementation", *Supervision*, 56 (September), 10.

Mathieu, J. E. and Zajac, D. M. (1990). "A Review and Meta-Analysis of the Antecedents, and Consequences of Organizational Commitment", *Psychological Bulletin*, 108 (September), 171–95.

Maynard, M. L. and Taylor, C. R. (1999). "Girlish Images Across Cultures: Analyzing Japanese versus US Seventeen Magazine Ads", *Journal of Advertising*, 28 (Spring), 39–49.

McNath, R. M. (2002). "Smokeless Isn't Smoking", *American Demographics*, 18 (October), 60.

Miles, M. B. and Huberman, A. M. (1984). *Qualitative Data Analysis: A Sourcebook of New Methods*. Newbury Park, CA, Sage Publications.

Miles, M. B. and Huberman, A. M. (1994). *Qualitative Data Analysis,* Newbury Park, CA, Sage.

Morey, N.C. and Luthans, F. (1984). "An Emic Perspective and Ethnoscience Methods for Organizational Research", *Academy of Management Review*, 9(1) (January), 27–36.

Morse, J. M. and Richards, L. (2002). *Read Me First for a User's Guide to Qualitative Methods*. Newbury Park, CA, Sage.

MTI Econews (2000). "GAZ to Open Office in Hungary", (30 March). MTI Hungarian News Agency.

Neter, J., Kutner, M., Wassermann, W. and Nachtsheim, C. (1996). *Applied Linear Regression Models*, 3rd edn. Homewood, IL, Irwin.

Nevett, T. R. and Nevett, L. (1994). "The Origins of Marketing: Evidence from Classical and Early Hellenistic Greece (500-30 BC)", *Research in Marketing*, 6, 3–12.

Nezleck, G. S. and Hidding, G. J. (2001). "An Investigation into the Differences in the Business Practices of Information Industries", *Human Systems Management*, 20(2), 71–82.

Papmehl, A. (2001). "Russia has Emerged as an Enticing Business Market", *CMA Management*, 75 (November), 50–1.

Parasuraman, A., Zeithaml, V. A. and Berry, L. L. (1988). "SERVQUAL: a Multi-item Scale for Measuring Consumer Perceptions of the Service Quality", *Journal of Retailing*, 64(1), 12–40.

Philip, H. V., Petrick, J. A., Quinn, J. F. and Brady, T. J. (1995). "The Impact of Gender and Major on Ethical Perceptions of Business Students: Management Implications for the Accounting Profession", *Journal of Academy of Business Administration*, 1 (Spring), 46–50.

Philip, G. and Hazlett, S. A. (1995). "The Measurement of Service Quality: A New P-C-P Attributes Model". *International Journal of Quality & Reliability Management*, 14(3), 260–86.

Philllips, E. M. and Pugh, D. S. (2000). *How to Get a PhD?* 3rd edn. Buckingham, Maidenhead, Open University Press.

Pitt, L. F., Foreman, S. K. and Bromfield, D. (1995). "Organisational Commitment and Service Delivery: Evidence from an Industrial Setting in the UK", *International Journal of Human Resource Management*, 6 (1), 369–89.

Punj, G. N and Staelin, R. (1983). "A Model of Consumer Information Behavior for New Automobiles", *Journal of Consumer Research*, 9, 366–80.

Ragin, C. C. (1987). *The Comparative Method: Moving Beyond Qualitative and Quantitative Strategies*, Berkeley, University of California Press.

Reichers, A. E. (1985). "A Review and Reconceptualization of Organizational Commitment", *Academy of Management Review*, 10(3), 465–75.

Reichheld, F. F. (2001). "Lead for Loyalty", *Harvard Business Review*, 79 (July/August), 76–84.

Remington, L. (2002). "Arizona Firms Return to More Conservative Dress". *The Tribune*, Mesa, Arizona (8 February).

Roberts, Z. (2001). "UK Businesses Sustain their Highest Labour Turnover Costs", *People Management*, 7 (11 October), 11.

Robin, D. P., Reidenbach, E. R. and Babin, B. J. (1997). "Ethical Judgments", *Psychological Review*, 80, 563–80.

Robin, D. P., Gialourakis, M. F., David, F. and Moritz, T. E. (1989). "A Different Look at Codes of Ethics, *Business Horizons*, 32 (1), 66–73.

Rolph, A. (1991). *Professional Personal Selling*, Englewood Cliffs, NJ, Prentice Hall.

Rose, S. (2006). *Online Consumer Information Search: An Empirical Investigation*, Unpublished DBA, Henley Management College, UK.

Rubin, H. and Rubin, I. (1995). *Qualitative Interviewing: The Art of Hearing Data.* San Diego, Sage Publications.

Sacirbey, O. (2000). "On-Line Grocers Restock Capital", *IPO Reporter*, 24 (29 May), 10.

Sahlman, W. A. (1999). "The New Economy is Stronger than you Think!" *Harvard Business Review*, 77 (November/December), 99–107.

Saporito, B. (1988). "The Tough Cookie at RJR Nabisco", *Fortune*, 118(2), 32–41.

Schmidt, J. B. and Spreng, R. A. (1996). "A Proposed Model of External Consumer Information Search", *Journal of the Academy of Marketing Science*, 24(3), 246–56.

Silverman, D. (1993). *Interpreting Qualitative Data*. London, Sage Publications.

Singh, J. (1995). "Measurement Issues in Cross-National Research", *Journal of International Business*, 26(3), 597–619.

Singhapakdi, A. and Vitell, S. J. (1994). "Ethical Ideologies of Future Marketeers: The Relative Influences of Machiavellianism and Gender", *Journal of Marketing Education*, Spring, 34–42.

Steenkamp, J.-B. and Baumgartner, H. (1998). "Assessing Measurement Invariance in Cross-National Research", *Journal of Consumer Research*, 25 (June), 78–90.

Stern, J. and Stern, M. (2000). "Familiarity Usually Breeds Regular Restaurant Customers", *Nation's Restaurant News*, 34(11/20), 24–26.

Strauss, A. (1987). *Qualitative Analysis for Social Scientists*. Cambridge, Cambridge University Press.

Strauss, A. L. and Corbin, J. (1990). *Basics of Qualitative Research: Grounded Theory Procedures and Techniques*. Newbury Park, CA, Sage.

Swaddling, J. D. and Zobel, M. W. (1996). "Beating the Odds", *Marketing Management*, 4 (Spring/Winter), 20–34.

Teresko, J. (1997). "Research Renaissance", *Industry Week*, 246 (6/9), 139–50.

Von Hippel, E. (1998). "Economics of Product Development by Users: the Impact of 'Sticky' Local Information", *Management Science*, 44(5), 629–44.

Walsh, M. (1999). "Focus Groups Set a New Agenda", *Bulletin with Newsweek*, 117 (2/9), 7.

Woodside, A. G., and Wilson, E. J. (1995). "Applying Long Interview in Direct Marketing Research", *Journal of Direct Marketing Research*, 9(1), 37–65.

Zeithaml, V., Berry, L. and Parasuraman, A. (1996). "The Behavioral Consequences of Service Quality". *Journal of Marketing*, 60(2), 31.

INDEX